Praise for *The Art of Agile Development*

"Jim Shore and Shane Warden expertly explain the practices and benefits of Extreme Programming. They offer advice from their real-world experiences in leading teams. They answer questions about the practices and show contraindications—ways that a practice may be misapplied. They offer alternatives you can try if there are impediments to applying a practice, such as the lack of an on-site customer.

"The explanations do not stop with just the practices. Discussion of people-related issues, such as strategies for creating trust and team cohesiveness, rounds out the book."

—Ken Pugh, author of the Jolt-Award-winning book, *Prefactoring*

"I will leave a copy of this book with every team I visit."

—Brian Marick, Exampler Consulting

The Art of Agile Development

Other resources from O'Reilly

The Art of Agile Development

James Shore and Shane Warden

O'REILLY®

Beijing · Cambridge · Farnham · Köln · Paris · Sebastopol · Taipei · Tokyo

The Art of Agile Development
by James Shore and Shane Warden

Copyright © 2008 O'Reilly Media, Inc., Inc. All rights reserved.
Printed in the United States of America.

Published by O'Reilly Media, Inc., 1005 Gravenstein Highway North, Sebastopol, CA 95472

O'Reilly books may be purchased for educational, business, or sales promotional use. Online editions are also available for most titles (*http://safari.oreilly.com*). For more information, contact our corporate/institutional sales department: (800) 998-9938 or *corporate@oreilly.com*.

Editor: Mary O'Brien	**Indexer:** Joe Wizda
Copy Editor: Sarah Schneider	**Cover Designer:** Karen Montgomery
Production Editor: Sarah Schneider	**Interior Designer:** David Futato
Proofreader: Sada Preisch	**Illustrator:** Robert Romano

Printing History:

    October 2007:   First Edition.

This book uses RepKover™, a durable and flexible lay-flat binding.

ISBN-10: 0-596-52767-5
ISBN-13: 978-0-596-52767-9

[C]

To our families.

Table of Contents

Part I. Getting Started

Part II. Practicing XP

Part III. Mastering Agility

Preface

Q: How do you get to Carnegie Hall?

A: Practice, man, practice!

We want to help you master the art of agile development.

Agile development, like any approach to team-based software development, is a fundamentally *human* art, one subject to the vagaries of individuals and their interactions. To master agile development, you must learn to evaluate myriad possibilities, moment to moment, and intuitively pick the best course of action.

How can you possibly learn such a difficult skill? Practice!

First and foremost, this book is a detailed description of *one* way to practice agile development: Extreme Programming (XP). It's a practical guide that, if followed mindfully, will allow you to successfully bring agile development in the form of XP to your team—or will help you decide that it's not a good choice in your situation.

Our second purpose is to help you master the art of agile development. Mastering agility means going beyond our cookbook of practices. Agile development is too context-sensitive for one approach to be entirely appropriate, and too nuanced for any book to teach you how to master it. Mastery comes from within: from experience and from an intuitive understanding of ripples caused by the pebble of a choice.

We can't teach you how your choices will ripple throughout your organization. We don't try. *You* must provide the nuance and understanding. This is the only way to master the art. Follow the practices. Watch what happens. Think about why they worked... or didn't work. Then do them again. What was the same? What was different? Why? Then do it again. And again.

At first, you may struggle to understand how to do each practice. They may look easy on paper, but putting some practices into action may be difficult. Keep practicing until they're easy.

As XP gets easier, you will discover that some of our rules don't work for you. In the beginning, you won't be able to tell if the problem is in our rules or in the way you're following them. Keep practicing until you're certain. When you are, break the rules. Modify our guidance to work better for your specific situation.

Parts I and II of this book contain our approach to XP. Part I helps you get started with Extreme Programming; Part II provides detailed guidance for each of XP's practices. Parts I and II should keep you occupied for many months.

When you're ready to break the rules, turn to Part III. A word of warning: there is nothing in Part III that will help you practice XP. Instead, it's full of ideas that will help you understand XP and agile development more deeply.

One day you'll discover that rules no longer hold any interest for you. After all, XP and agile development aren't about following rules. "It's about simplicity and feedback, communication and trust," you'll think. "It's about delivering value—and having the courage to do the right thing at the right time." You'll evaluate myriad possibilities, moment to moment, and intuitively pick the best course of action.

When you do, pass this book on to someone else, dog-eared and ragged though it may be, so that they too can master the art of agile development.

For the Pragmatists

What if you don't want to master a so-called art? What if you just want to develop good software?

Don't worry—this book is for you, too. Parts I and II are just what you need. We took our years of experience with agile development and Extreme Programming and distilled them into a single, clearly defined, comprehensive approach.

This approach allows us to use plain, straightforward language without caveats or digressions. We get to include a lot of practical tips. We candidly describe when our approach won't work and what alternatives to consider when it doesn't.

There's a downside to discussing just one approach: no single methodology is appropriate for everyone. Our advice may not be appropriate for your team or situation. Be sure to read Chapter 4 before putting our advice into practice.

You may be able to adopt part of XP even if you can't adopt all of it. The "Contraindications" section of each practice in Part II describes when a practice is inappropriate. If this applies to your situation, the "Alternatives" section will help you decide what to do instead.

Don't go too far and automatically assume that a particular practice won't work for you. Some of the ideas in this book are counterintuitive or just don't sound like fun. Most of them work best in concert with the others. If you can, try the practices as written for a few months, gain some real-world experience on how they work in your environment, and *then* change them.

We've been putting these ideas into practice for years. In the right environment, they really work. Agile development has been more fun, and more successful, than any other approach to team software development we've tried. Come join the ride.

Who Should Read This Book

This book is for anyone who is, will be, or wants to be part of an agile team. That includes programmers, of course, but it also includes domain experts, testers, projects managers, architects, designers, and business analysts. Agile teams are cross-functional; this book reflects that fact.

If you're a leader or you're interested in bringing agile development to your team or organization, you should read the whole book from cover to cover. Part I introduces agile concepts and describes how to adopt XP. Part II describes each of XP's practices in detail. Part III goes beyond XP, looking at the principles that allow you to create your own agile method by customizing XP to your particular situation.

If you just want to learn enough to do your job, you can focus primarily on Part II. Start with Chapter 3 in Part I to get an overview, then read through the practices in Part II that apply to your work. Each practice starts with a description of the audience it applies to, such as "Programmers," "Customers," or "Testers."

If you're merely curious about agile development, start by reading Part I. Again, Chapter 3 provides a good introduction. Afterwards, take a look at the practices in Part II. Start with the ones that look most interesting; you can read them in any order.

About the Études

Have you ever heard a musician playing scales? That's an étude (if a boring one). An étude teaches mastery through precise and careful repetition. Eventually, the étude is abandoned, but the skills remain.

Extreme Programming is our étude for software development. We hope that practicing Extreme Programming week after week will help you master agile development. Eventually, you'll change your practices, but the underlying principles will remain.

Besides the overarching étude of Extreme Programming, we've included a *mini-étude* for each major theme of agile development. Beginning agile teams can use the études to refine their practice of agile development. As you gain experience, look deeper; use the études to help connect Part II's detailed practices to Part III's general principles.

NOTE

These études are also useful for teams not currently practicing XP.

Either way, the études require thought to be effective. Each étude provides information, but it doesn't tell you how to act on that information. Think about it. What did you learn from the étude? What was frustrating or exciting? How does that information affect your work? What will you do about it? Without attention and reflection—that is, mindfulness—the études are just games.

NOTE

It's no coincidence that you need mindfulness to master the art of agile development as well. You have to think about more than XP's practices for it to be effective.

Like musical études, our mini-études work best when you repeat them. We've designed them to take half an hour, so you can (and should) practice them every day for a week or more. Unlike musical études, these agile exercises work best when you include your whole team. The more you all understand about the process and where everyone fits in, the better you will work together.

To start, you need a quiet work area capable of holding everyone in your team comfortably. There should be a whiteboard or wall where you can hang or post index cards between meetings. There must also be sufficient space to break into groups of two or three people and to talk softly without disturbing other groups.

We've found it valuable to use a timer, whether a stopwatch or a kitchen timer, to keep the session moving. Each étude has a few parts of 5 to 10 minutes. Although that time will seem to flow quickly on your first day, respect the time limits. You'll perform the étude again tomorrow, so it's OK if you don't finish everything.

Choose one member of your team to facilitate the étude by watching the time (perhaps calling out "one minute remaining" when appropriate) and promoting discussion. Again, the first session may be hard, but a good facilitator can encourage everyone to continue.

At the end of each étude, we recommend spending a few minutes debriefing. What did you learn? Are there questions and ideas you can follow up on during your regular work? If you've been trying this exercise for more than a week, are you still getting valuable results?

If you're new to XP and agile development, we strongly recommend that you perform each étude while you study the related chapter as a team. Besides exploring one particular theme in agile development, each étude can illuminate an aspect of how your team works together on your agile project.

About Pronouns

We speak in first-person singular rather than first-person plural in the rest of this book. (We say "I," not "we.") We include a lot of personal anecdotes and experiences, and the singular form works better as a result. However, this book is unquestionably the result of a partnership between two authors and our use of the word "I" is merely a convenience.

Using Code Examples

This book is here to help you get your job done. In general, you may use the code in this book in your programs and documentation. You do not need to contact us for permission unless you're reproducing a significant portion of the code. For example, writing a program that uses several chunks of code from this book does not require permission. Selling or distributing a CD-ROM of examples from O'Reilly books does require permission. Answering a question by citing this book and quoting example code does not require permission. Incorporating a significant amount of example code from this book into your product's documentation does require permission.

We appreciate, but do not require, attribution. An attribution usually includes the title, author, publisher, and ISBN. For example: *The Art of Agile Development* by James Shore and Shane Warden. Copyright 2008 O'Reilly Media, Inc., 978-0-596-52767-9."

If you feel your use of code examples falls outside fair use or the permission given above, feel free to contact us at *permissions@oreilly.com*.

Safari® Enabled

When you see a Safari® Enabled icon on the cover of your favorite technology book, that means the book is available online through the O'Reilly Network Safari Bookshelf.

Safari offers a solution that's better than e-books. It's a virtual library that lets you easily search thousands of top tech books, cut and paste code samples, download chapters, and find quick answers when you need the most accurate, current information. Try it for free at *http://safari.oreilly.com*.

How to Contact Us

Please address comments and questions concerning this book to the publisher:

O'Reilly Media, Inc.
1005 Gravenstein Highway North
Sebastopol, CA 95472
800-998-9938 (in the United States or Canada)
707-829-0515 (international or local)
707 829-0104 (fax)

We have a web page for this book, where we list errata, examples, and any additional information. You can access this page at:

http://www.oreilly.com/catalog/9780596527679

To comment or ask technical questions about this book, send email to:

bookquestions@oreilly.com

For more information about our books, conferences, Resource Centers, and the O'Reilly Network, see our web site at:

http://www.oreilly.com

Acknowledgments

We owe a debt of gratitude to Elisabeth Hendrickson for her contribution of the "Exploratory Testing" section. Her expertise and writing skill made the material sparkle. For more of Elisabeth's writing, visit *http://www.testobsessed.com/*.

We stole good ideas wherever we could find them. Kent Beck, Ron Jeffries, and Ward Cunningham each had a hand in the ideas that led to XP, and we stole liberally from those. In addition to XP itself, Kent Beck introduced us to the idea of XP practices as études. Ward Cunningham introduced us to the notion of technical debt, a concept we use heavily. Brian Marick's series of essays, "Agile Testing Directions,"[*] influenced our thoughts on agile testing and the role of testers on agile teams.

James had the opportunity to work with Joshua Kerievsky on an *Industrial XP* (*IXP*)[†] project for half a year. He learned a lot from that project; the Vision practice in particular was inspired by IXP's Project Chartering practice. David Schwartz and Amy Schwab of True North pgs, Inc.,[‡] provided the specific vision format that we use, as well as the term *project community*. Their *Mastering Projects* workshop is excellent; take it when you have the opportunity.

Thank you to our editor, Mary Treseler O'Brien, for providing vision (where necessary), trust (where appropriate), and deadlines (where frightening). This book would not be what it is without you gently nudging us in directions different from our original ideas.

Thanks also to our army of reviewers, who provided over one thousand comments and suggestions on our mailing list. In particular, thanks to Adrian Howard, Adrian Sutton, Ann Barcomb, Andy Lester,

---

[*] *http://www.testing.com/cgi-bin/blog/2004/05/26*

[†] *http://www.industrialxp.org/*

[‡] *http://www.projectcommunity.com/*

Anthony Williams, Bas Vodde, Bill Caputo, Bob Corrick, Brad Appleton, Chris Wheeler, Clarke Ching, Daði Ingólfsson, Diana Larsen, Erik Petersen, George Dinwiddie, Ilja Preuß, Jason Yip, Jeff Olfert, Jeffery Palermo, Jonathan Clarke, Keith Ray, Kevin Rutherford, Kim Gräsman, Lisa Crispin, Mark Waite, Nicholas Evans, Philippe Antras, Randy Coulman, Robert Schmitt, Ron Jeffries, Shane Duan, Tim Haughton, and Tony Byrne for their extensive comments. Special thanks to Brian Marick, Ken Pugh, and Mark Streibeck for their comments on the completed draft.

James Shore

Every work builds on what came before. I was fortunate to have not just one, but many giants to stand on. Without the inspired work of Kent Beck, Alistair Cockburn, Ward Cunningham, Tom DeMarco, Martin Fowler, Ron Jeffries, Timothy Lister, Steve McConnell, and Gerald Weinberg, I wouldn't have anything close to the understanding of software development I have today. It's thanks to their example that this book exists. In particular, thanks to Alistair Cockburn for generously inviting me to his roundtable and introducing me to the agile community.

If giants enabled me to contribute to this book, then Kim Eaves and the Denali team brought the stepladder. Without their enthusiastic support, I never would have been able to try that crazy XP thing. Thanks also to Rob Myers for his ever-friendly consideration of my rants.

I also gratefully acknowledge my coauthor and friend, Shane Warden. This project morphed from a little 100-page second edition into a 400-page monster. You didn't complain once. Thanks for putting up with me. (And hey! Nice book.)

Finally, thank you, Neeru, my loving and patient wife. I used to think authors thanking their families was cliché. Now I understand. I couldn't have finished this book without your support.

Shane Warden

Thanks to Jim for arguing with me while writing the first version of this book (it's better for it) and for convincing me that the second edition was worth doing.

Thanks to Allison and Andrew for the tools we used to write this book.

Thanks to my family for supporting me (and not grumbling too much while I sat upstairs and wrote very slowly), and to my friends for dragging me out of my house once in a while.

Thanks also to the other contributors to Parrot and Perl 6 for being unwitting collaborators, examples, and victims of some of the ideas in this book. The work we do continually amazes me.

PART I

Getting Started

CHAPTER 1

Why Agile?

Agile development is popular. All the cool kids are doing it: Google, Yahoo, Symantec, Microsoft, and the list goes on.[*] I know of one company that has already changed its name to Agili-something in order to ride the bandwagon. (They called me in to pitch their "agile process," which, upon further inspection, was nothing more than outsourced offshore development, done in a different country than usual.) I fully expect the big consulting companies to start offering Certified Agile Processes and Certified Agile Consultants—for astronomical fees, of course—any day now.

Please don't get sucked into that mess.

In 1986, [Brooks] famously predicted that there were no silver bullets: that by 1996, no single technology or management technique would offer a tenfold increase in productivity, reliability, or simplicity. None did.

Agile development isn't a silver bullet, either.

In fact, I don't recommend adopting agile development solely to increase productivity. Its benefits— even the ability to release software more frequently—come from working *differently*, not from working *faster*. Although anecdotal evidence indicates that agile teams have above-average productivity,[†] that shouldn't be your primary motivation. Your team will need time to learn agile development. While they learn—and it will take a quarter or two—they'll go slower, not faster. In addition, emphasizing productivity might encourage your team to take shortcuts and to be less rigorous in their work, which could actually *harm* productivity.

Agile development may be the cool thing to do right now, but that's no reason to use it. When you consider using agile development, only one question matters.

Will agile development help us be more successful?

[*] Source: various experience reports at the Extreme Programming and Agile conferences.

[†] See, for example, [Van Schooenderwoert], [Mah], and [Anderson 2006].

When you can answer that question, you'll know whether agile development is right for you.

Understanding Success

The traditional idea of *success* is delivery on time, on budget, and according to specification. [Standish] provides some classic definitions:

Successful
"Completed on time, on budget, with all features and functions as originally specified."

Challenged
"Completed and operational but over budget, over the time estimate, [with] fewer features and functions than originally specified."

Impaired
"Cancelled at some point during the development cycle."

> Despite their popularity, there's something wrong with these definitions.

Despite their popularity, there's something wrong with these definitions. A project can be successful even if it never makes a dime. It can be challenged even if it delivers millions of dollars in revenue.

CIO Magazine commented on this oddity:

> Projects that were found to meet all of the traditional criteria for success—time, budget and specifications—may still be failures in the end because they fail to appeal to the intended users or because they ultimately fail to add much value to the business.
>
> ... Similarly, projects considered failures according to traditional IT metrics may wind up being successes because despite cost, time or specification problems, the system is loved by its target audience or provides unexpected value. For example, at a financial services company, a new system... was six months late and cost more than twice the original estimate (final cost was $5.7 million). But the project ultimately created a more adaptive organization (after 13 months) and was judged to be a great success—the company had a $33 million reduction in write-off accounts, and the reduced time-to-value and increased capacity resulted in a 50 percent increase in the number of concurrent collection strategy tests in production.[*]

Beyond Deadlines

There has to be more to success than meeting deadlines... but what?

When I was a kid, I was happy just to play around. I loved the challenge of programming. When I got a program to work, it was a major victory. Back then, even a program that didn't work was a success of some sort, as long as I had fun writing it. My definition of success centered on *personal rewards*.

As I gained experience, my software became more complicated and I often lost track of how it worked. I had to abandon some programs before they were finished. I began to believe that maintainability was the key to success—an idea that was confirmed as I entered the workforce and began working with teams of other programmers. I prided myself on producing elegant, maintainable code. Success meant *technical excellence*.

---

[*] R. Ryan Nelson, "Applied Insight—Tracks in the Snow," *CIO Magazine, http://www.cio.com/archive/090106/applied.html.*

Figure 1-1. Types of success

Despite good code, some projects flopped. Even impeccably executed projects could elicit yawns from users. I came to realize that my project teams were part of a larger ecosystem involving dozens, hundreds, or even thousands of people. My projects needed to satisfy those people ... particularly the ones signing my paycheck. In fact, for the people funding the work, the value of the software had to exceed its cost. Success meant *delivering value* to the organization.

These definitions aren't incompatible. All three types of success are important (see Figure 1-1). Without personal success, you'll have trouble motivating yourself and employees. Without technical success, your source code will eventually collapse under its own weight. Without organizational success, your team may find that they're no longer wanted in the company.

The Importance of Organizational Success

Organizational success is often neglected by software teams in favor of the more easily achieved technical and personal successes. Rest assured, however, that even if *you're* not taking responsibility for organizational success, the broader organization is judging your team at this level. Senior management and executives aren't likely to care if your software is elegant, maintainable, or even beloved by its users; they care about results. That's their return on investment in your project. If you don't achieve this sort of success, they'll take steps to ensure that you do.

Unfortunately, senior managers don't usually have the time or perspective to apply a nuanced solution to each project. They wield swords, not scalpels. They rightly expect their project teams to take care of fine details.

When managers are unhappy with your team's results, the swords come out. Costs are the most obvious target. There are two easy ways to cut them: set aggressive deadlines to reduce development time, or ship the work to a country with a lower cost of labor. Or both.

These are clumsy techniques. Aggressive deadlines end up increasing schedules rather than reducing them [McConnell 1999, p. 220], and offshoring has hidden costs [Overby].

Do aggressive deadlines and the threat of offshoring sound familiar? If so, it's time for your team to take back responsibility for its success: not just for personal or technical success, but for organizational success as well.

WHAT DO ORGANIZATIONS VALUE?

Although some projects' value comes directly from sales, there's more to organizational value than revenue. Projects provide value in many ways, and you can't always measure that value in dollars and cents.

Aside from revenue and cost savings, sources of value include:[*]

- Competitive differentiation
- Brand projection
- Enhanced customer loyalty
- Satisfying regulatory requirements
- Original research
- Strategic information

Enter Agility

Will agile development help you be more successful? It might. Agile development focuses on achieving personal, technical, *and* organizational successes. If you're having trouble with any of these areas, agile development might help.

Organizational Success

Agile methods achieve organizational successes by focusing on delivering value and decreasing costs. This directly translates to increased return on investment. Agile methods also set expectations early in the project, so if your project won't be an organizational success, you'll find out early enough to cancel it before your organization has spent much money.

Specifically, agile teams increase value by including business experts and by focusing development efforts on the core value that the project provides for the organization. Agile projects release their most valuable features first and release new versions frequently, which dramatically increases value. When business needs change or when new information is discovered, agile teams change direction to match. In fact, an experienced agile team will actually *seek out* unexpected opportunities to improve its plans.

Agile teams decrease costs as well. They do this partly by technical excellence; the best agile projects generate only a few bugs per month. They also eliminate waste by cancelling bad projects early and replacing expensive development practices with simpler ones. Agile teams communicate quickly and accurately, and they make progress even when key individuals are unavailable. They regularly review their process and continually improve their code, making the software easier to maintain and enhance over time.

[*] Based partly on [Denne & Cleland-Huang].

Technical Success

Extreme Programming, the agile method I focus on in this book, is particularly adept at achieving technical successes. XP programmers work together, which helps them keep track of the nitpicky details necessary for great work and ensures that at least two people review every piece of code. Programmers continuously integrate their code, which enables the team to release the software whenever it makes business sense. The whole team focuses on finishing each feature completely before starting the next, which prevents unexpected delays before release and allows the team to change direction at will.

In addition to the structure of development, Extreme Programming includes advanced technical practices that lead to technical excellence. The most well-known practice is test-driven development, which helps programmers write code that does exactly what they think it will. XP teams also create simple, ever-evolving designs that are easy to modify when plans change.

Personal Success

Personal success is, well, personal. Agile development may not satisfy all of your requirements for personal success. However, once you get used to it, you'll probably find a lot to like about it, no matter who you are:

Executives and senior management
>They will appreciate the team's focus on providing a solid return on investment and the software's longevity.

Users, stakeholders, domain experts, and product managers
>They will appreciate their ability to influence the direction of software development, the team's focus on delivering useful and valuable software, and increased delivery frequency.

Project and product managers
>They will appreciate their ability to change direction as business needs change, the team's ability to make and meet commitments, and improved stakeholder satifaction.

Developers
>They will appreciate their improved quality of life resulting from increased technical quality, greater influence over estimates and schedules, and team autonomy.

Testers
>They will appreciate their integration as first-class members of the team, their ability to influence quality at all stages of the project, and more challenging, less repetitious work.

Working on agile teams has provided some of the most enjoyable moments in my career. Imagine the camaraderie of a team that works together to identify and deliver products of lasting value, with each team member enthusiastically contributing to a smooth-running whole. Imagine how it feels to take responsibility for your area of expertise, whether technical, business, or management, with the rest of the team trusting your professional judgment and ability. Imagine how pleasant it is to address the frustrations of your project and to see quality improve over time.

Agile development changes the game. Developing and delivering software in a new way will take a lot of work and thought. Yet if you do it consistently and rigorously, you'll experience amazing things: you'll ship truly valuable software on a regular basis. You'll demonstrate progress on a weekly basis. You'll have the most fun you've ever had in software development.

Ready? Let's go.

CHAPTER 2

How to Be Agile

What does it mean to "be agile"?

The answer is more complicated than you might think. Agile development isn't a specific process you can follow. No team practices *the* Agile method. There's no such thing.

Agile development is a philosophy. It's a way of thinking about software development. The canonical description of this way of thinking is the Agile Manifesto, a collection of 4 values (Figure 2-1) and 12 principles (Figure 2-2).

To "be agile," you need to put the agile values and principles into practice.

Agile Methods

A *method*, or *process*, is a way of working. Whenever you do something, you're following a process. Some processes are written, as when assembling a piece of furniture; others are ad hoc and informal, as when I clean my house.

Agile methods are processes that support the agile philosophy. Examples include Extreme Programming and Scrum.

Agile methods consist of individual elements called *practices*. Practices include using version control, setting coding standards, and giving weekly demos to your stakeholders. Most of these practices have been around for years. Agile methods combine them in unique ways, accentuating those parts that support the agile philosophy, discarding the rest, and mixing in a few new ideas. The result is a lean, powerful, self-reinforcing package.

Manifesto for Agile Software Development

We are uncovering better ways of developing software by doing it and helping others do it. Through this work we have come to value:

- Individuals and interactions over processes and tools
- Working software over comprehensive documentation
- Customer collaboration over contract negotiation
- Responding to change over following a plan

That is, while there is value in the items on the right, we value the items on the left more.

Kent Beck	James Grenning	Robert C. Martin
Mike Beedle	Jim Highsmith	Steve Mellor
Arie van Bennekum	Andrew Hunt	Ken Schwaber
Alistair Cockburn	Ron Jeffries	Jeff Sutherland
Ward Cunningham	Jon Kern	Dave Thomas
Martin Fowler	Brian Marick	

© 2001, the above authors
This declaration may be freely copied in any form,
but only in its entirety through this notice.

Figure 2-1. Agile values

Don't Make Your Own Method

Just as established agile methods combine existing practices, you might want to create your own agile method by mixing together practices from various agile methods. At first glance, this doesn't seem too hard. There are scores of good agile practices to choose from.

However, creating a brand-new agile method is a bad idea if you've never used agile development before. Just as there's more to programming than writing code, there's more to agile development than the practices. The practices are an expression of underlying agile principles. (For more on agile principles, see Part III.) Unless you understand those principles intimately—that is, unless you've already mastered the art of agile development—you're probably not going to choose the right practices. Agile practices often perform double- and triple-duty, solving multiple software development problems simultaneously and supporting each other in clever and surprising ways.

Principles behind the Agile Manifesto

We follow these principles:

Our highest priority is to satisfy the customer through early and continuous delivery of valuable software.

Welcome changing requirements, even late in development. Agile processes harness change for the customer's competitive advantage.

Deliver working software frequently, from a couple of weeks to a couple of months, with a preference to the shorter timescale.

Business people and developers must work together daily throughout the project.

Build projects around motivated individuals. Give them the environment and support they need, and trust them to get the job done.

The most efficient and effective method of conveying information to and within a development team is face-to-face conversation.

Working software is the primary measure of progress.

Agile processes promote sustainable development. The sponsors, developers, and users should be able to maintain a constant pace indefinitely.

Continuous attention to technical excellence and good design enhances agility.

Simplicity, the art of maximizing the amount of work not done, is essential.

The best architectures, requirements, and designs emerge from self-organizing teams.

At regular intervals, the team reflects on how to become more effective, then tunes and adjusts its behavior accordingly.

Figure 2-2. Agile principles

Every project and situation is unique, of course, so it's a good idea to have an agile method that's customized to your situation. Rather than making an agile method from scratch, start with an existing, proven method and iteratively refine it. Apply it to your situation, note where it works and doesn't, make an educated guess about how to improve, and repeat. That's what experts do.

The Road to Mastery

The core thesis of this book is that mastering the art of agile development requires real-world experience using a specific, well-defined agile method. I've chosen Extreme Programming for this purpose. It has several advantages:

- Of all the agile methods I know, XP is the most complete. It places a strong emphasis on technical practices in addition to the more common teamwork and structural practices.
- XP has undergone intense scrutiny. There are thousands of pages of explanations, experience reports, and critiques out there. Its capabilities and limitations are very well understood.
- I have a lot of experience with XP, which allows me to share insights and practical tips that will help you apply XP more easily.

To master the art of agile development—or simply to use XP to be more successful—follow these steps:

1. Decide why you want to use agile development. Will it make your team and organization more successful? How? (For ideas, see "Enter Agility" in Chapter 1.)

> Teams new to XP often underapply its practices.

2. Determine whether this book's approach will work for your team. (See "Is XP Right for Us?" in Chapter 4.)

3. Adopt as many of XP's practices as you can. (See Chapter 4.) XP's practices are self-reinforcing, so it works best when you use all of them together.

4. Follow the XP practices rigorously and consistently. (See Part II.) If a practice doesn't work, try following the book approach *more* closely. Teams new to XP often underapply its practices. Expect to take two or three months to start feeling comfortable with the practices and another two to six months for them to become second nature.

5. As you become confident that you are practicing XP correctly—again, give it several months—start experimenting with changes that *aren't* "by the book." (See Part III.) Each time you make a change, observe what happens and make further improvements.

Find a Mentor

As you adapt XP to your situation, you're likely to run into problems and challenges. I provide solutions for a wide variety of common problems, but you're still likely to encounter situations that I don't cover. For these situations, you need a *mentor*: an outside expert who has mastered the art of agile development.

> **NOTE**
> If you can get an expert to coach your team directly, that's even better. However, even master coaches benefit from an outside perspective when they encounter problems.

The hardest part of finding a mentor is finding someone with enough experience in agile development. Sources to try include:

- Other groups practicing XP in your organization
- Other companies practicing XP in your area
- A local XP/Agile user group
- XP/Agile consultants
- The XP mailing list: *extremeprogramming@yahoogroups.com*

I can't predict every problem you'll encounter, but I can help you see when things are going wrong. Throughout this book, I've scattered advice such as: "If you can't demonstrate progress weekly, it's a clear sign that your project is in trouble. Slow down for a week and figure out what's going wrong. Ask your mentor for help."

When I tell you to ask your mentor for help, I mean that the correct solution depends on the details of your situation. Your mentor can help you troubleshoot the problem and offer situation-specific advice.

CHAPTER 3

Understanding XP

"Welcome to the team, Pat," said Kim, smiling at the recent graduate. "Let me show you around. As I said during the interview, we're an XP shop. You may find that things are a little different here than you learned in school."

"I'm eager to get started," said Pat. "I took a software engineering course in school, and they taught us about the software development lifecycle. That made a lot of sense. There was a bit about XP, but it sounded like it was mostly about working in pairs and writing tests first. Is that right?"

"Not exactly," said Kim. "We do use pair programming, and we do write tests first, but there's much more to XP than that. Why don't you ask me some questions? I'll explain how XP is different than what you learned."

Pat thought for a moment. "Well, one thing I know from my course is that all development methods use the software development lifecycle: analysis, design, coding, and testing [see Figure 3-1]. Which phase are you in right now? Analysis? Design? Or is it coding or testing?"

"Yes!" Kim grinned. She couldn't help a bit of showmanship.

"I don't understand. Which is it?"

"All of them. We're working on analysis, design, coding, *and* testing. Simultaneously. Oh, and we deploy the software every week, too."

Pat looked confused. Was she pulling his leg?

Kim laughed. "You'll see! Let me show you around.

"This is our team room. As you can see, we all sit together in one big workspace. This helps us collaborate more effectively."

Kim led Pat over to a big whiteboard where a man stood frowning at dozens of index cards. "Brian, I'd like you to meet Pat, our new programmer. Brian is our product manager. What are you working on right now?"

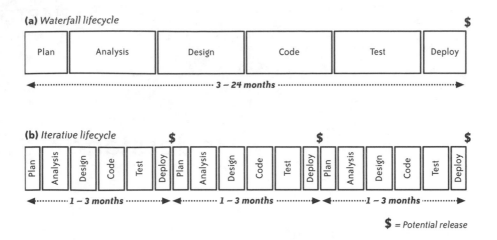

Figure 3-1. Traditional lifecycles

"I'm trying to figure out how we should modify our release plan based on the feedback from the user meeting last week. Our users love what we've done so far, but they also have some really good suggestions. I'm trying to decide if their suggestions are worth postponing the feature we were planning to start next week. Our success has made us visible throughout the company, so requests are starting to flood in. I need to figure out how to keep us on track without alienating too many people."

"Sounds tough," Kim said. "So, would you say that you're working on requirements, then?"

"I'm working on making our stakeholders happy," Brian shrugged, turning back to the whiteboard.

"Don't mind him," Kim whispered to Pat as they walked away. "He's under a lot of pressure right now. This whole project was his idea. It's already saved the company two and a half million dollars, but now there's some political stuff going on. Luckily, we programmers don't have to worry about that. Brian and Rachel take care of it—Rachel's our project manager."

"Wait... I thought Brian was the project manager?"

"No, Brian is the *product* manager. He's in charge of deciding what we build, with the help of stakeholders and other team members, of course. Rachel is the *project* manager—she helps things run smoothly. She helps management understand what we're doing and gets us what we need, like when she convinced Facilities to tear down the cubicle walls and give us this nice open workspace.

"Let me introduce you to some more members of the team," Kim continued, leading Pat over to two people sitting at a workstation. "This is Mary and Jeff. Mary is a mechanical engineer. She normally works in manufacturing, but we asked her to join us as an on-site customer for this project so she can help us understand the issues they face on the floor. Jeff is one of our testers. He's particularly good at finding holes in requirements. Guys, this is Pat, our new programmer."

Pat nodded hello. "I think I recognize what you're doing. That looks like a requirements document."

"Sort of," Jeff replied. "These are our customer tests for this iteration. They help us know if the software's doing what it's supposed to."

"Customer tests?" Pat asked.

Mary spoke up. "They're really examples. This particular set focuses on placement of inventory in the warehouse. We want the most frequently used inventory to be the easiest to access, but there are other concerns as well. We're putting in examples of different selections of inventory and how they should be stored."

"You can see how things are progressing," Jeff continued. "Here, I'll test these examples." He pressed a button on the keyboard, and a copy of the document popped up on the screen. Some sections of the document were green. Others were red.

"You can see that the early examples are green—that means the programmers have those working. These later ones are red because they cover special cases that the programmers haven't coded yet. And this one here is brand-new. Mary realized there were some edge cases we hadn't properly considered. You can see that some of these cases are actually OK—they're green—but some of them need more work. We're about to tell the programmers about them."

"Actually, you can go ahead and do that, Jeff," said Mary, as they heard a muffled curse from the area of the whiteboard. "It sounds like Brian could use my help with the release plan. Nice to meet you, Pat."

"Come on," said Jeff. "Kim and I will introduce you to the other programmers."

"Sure," said Pat. "But first—this document you were working on. Is it a requirements document or a test document?"

"Both," Jeff said, with a twinkle in his eye. "And neither. It's a way to make sure that we get the hard stuff right. Does it really matter what we call it?"

"You seem pretty casual about this," Pat said. "I did an internship last year and nobody at that company could even *think* about coding until the requirements and design plans were signed off. And here you are, adding features and revising your requirements right in the middle of coding!"

"It's just crazy enough to work," said Jeff.

"In other words," Kim added, "we used to have formal process gates and signoffs, too. We used to spend days arguing in meetings about the smallest details in our documents. Now, we focus on doing the right things right, not on what documents we've signed off. It takes a lot less work. Because we work on everything together, from requirements to delivery, we make fewer mistakes and can figure out problems much more easily."

"Things were different for me," Jeff added. "I haven't been here as long as Kim. In my last company, we didn't have any structure at all. People just did what they felt was right. That worked OK when we were starting out, but after a few years we started having terrible problems with quality. We were always under the gun to meet deadlines, and we were constantly running into surprises that prevented us from releasing on time. Here, although we're still able to do what we think is right, there's enough structure for everyone to understand what's going on and make constant progress."

"It's made our life easier," Kim said enthusiastically. "We get a lot more done..."

"...*and* it's higher quality," Jeff finished. "You've got to watch out for Kim—she'll never stop raving about how great it is to work together." He grinned. "She's right, you know. It is. Now let's go tell the other programmers about the new examples Mary and I added."

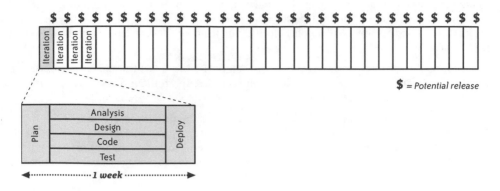

Figure 3-2. XP lifecycle

The XP Lifecycle

One of the most astonishing premises of XP is that you can eliminate requirements, design, and testing phases as well as the formal documents that go with them.

This premise is so far off from the way we typically learn to develop software that many people dismiss it as a delusional fantasy. "These XP folks obviously don't know what they're talking about," they say. "Just last month I was on a project that failed due to inadequate requirements and design. We need *more* requirements, design, and testing, not *less*!"

That's true. Software projects *do* need more requirements, design, and testing—which is why XP teams work on these activities every day. Yes, every day.

You see, XP emphasizes face-to-face collaboration. This is so effective in eliminating communication delays and misunderstandings that the team no longer needs distinct phases. This allows them to work on all activities every day—with *simultaneous phases*—as shown in Figure 3-2.

Using simultanous phases, an XP team produces deployable software every week. In each iteration, the team analyzes, designs, codes, tests, and deploys a subset of features.

Although this approach doesn't necessarily mean that the team is more productive,[*] it does mean that the team gets feedback much more frequently. As a result, the team can easily connect successes and failures to their underlying causes. The amount of unproven work is very small, which allows the team to correct some mistakes on the fly, as when coding reveals a design flaw, or when a customer review reveals that a user interface layout is confusing or ugly.

The tight feedback loop also allows XP teams to refine their plans quickly. It's much easier for a customer to refine a feature idea if she can request it and start to explore a working prototype within a few days. The same principle applies for tests, design, and team policy. Any information you learn in one phase can change the way you think about the rest of the software. If you find a design defect during coding or testing, you can use that knowledge as you continue to analyze requirements and design the system in subsequent iterations.

---

[*] Productivity is notoriously difficult to study. I'm not aware of any formal research on XP productivity, although anecdotal evidence indicates that agile teams are more productive than traditional teams.

How It Works

XP teams perform nearly every software development activity simultaneously. Analysis, design, coding, testing, and even deployment occur with rapid frequency.

That's a lot to do simultaneously. XP does it by working in *iterations*: week-long increments of work. Every week, the team does a bit of release planning, a bit of design, a bit of coding, a bit of testing, and so forth. They work on *stories*: very small features, or parts of features, that have customer value. Every week, the team commits to delivering four to ten stories. Throughout the week, they work on all phases of development for each story. At the end of the week, they deploy their software for internal review. (In some cases, they deploy it to actual customers.)

The following sections show how traditional phase-based activities correspond to an XP iteration.

Planning

Every XP team includes several business experts—the *on-site customers*—who are responsible for making business decisions. The on-site customers point the project in the right direction by clarifying the project vision, creating stories, constructing a release plan, and managing risks. Programmers provide estimates and suggestions, which are blended with customer priorities in a process called *the planning game*. Together, the team strives to create small, frequent releases that maximize value.

The planning effort is most intense during the first few weeks of the project. During the remainder of the project, customers continue to review and improve the vision and the release plan to account for new opportunities and unexpected events.

In addition to the overall release plan, the team creates a detailed plan for the upcoming week at the beginning of each iteration. The team touches base every day in a brief stand-up meeting, and its informative workspace keeps everyone informed about the project status.

Analysis

Rather than using an upfront analysis phase to define requirements, on-site customers sit with the team full-time. On-site customers may or may not be real customers depending on the type of project, but they are the people best qualified to determine what the software should do.

On-site customers are responsible for figuring out the requirements for the software. To do so, they use their own knowledge as customers combined with traditional requirements-gathering techniques. When programmers need information, they simply ask. Customers are responsible for organizing their work so they are ready when programmers ask for information. They figure out the general requirements for a story before the programmers estimate it and the detailed requirements before the programmers implement it.

Some requirements are tricky or difficult to understand. Customers formalize these requirements, with the assistance of testers, by creating *customer tests*: detailed, automatically checked examples. Customers and testers create the customer tests for a story around the same time that programmers implement the story. To assist in communication, programmers use a ubiquitous language in their design and code.

The user interface (UI) look and feel doesn't benefit from automated customer tests. For the UI, customers work with the team to create sketches of the application screens. In some cases, customers work alongside programmers as they use a UI builder to create a screen. Some teams include an interaction designer who's responsible for the application's UI.

Design and Coding

XP uses incremental design and architecture to continuously create and improve the design in small steps. This work is driven by *test-driven development* (*TDD*), an activity that inextricably weaves together testing, coding, design, and architecture. To support this process, programmers work in pairs, which increases the amount of brainpower brought to bear on each task and ensures that one person in each pair always has time to think about larger design issues.

Programmers are also responsible for managing their development environment. They use a version control system for configuration management and maintain their own automated build. Programmers integrate their code every few hours and ensure that every integration is technically capable of deployment.

To support this effort, programmers also maintain coding standards and share ownership of the code. The team shares a joint aesthetic for the code, and everyone is expected to fix problems in the code regardless of who wrote it.

Testing

XP includes a sophisticated suite of testing practices. Each member of the team—programmers, customers, and testers—makes his own contribution to software quality. Well-functioning XP teams produce only a handful of bugs per month in completed work.

Programmers provide the first line of defense with test-driven development. TDD produces automated unit and integration tests. In some cases, programmers may also create end-to-end tests. These tests help ensure that the software does what the programmers intended.

Likewise, customer tests help ensure that the programmers' intent matches customers' expectations. Customers review work in progress to ensure that the UI works the way they expect. They also produce examples for programmers to automate that provide examples of tricky business rules.

Finally, testers help the team understand whether their efforts are in fact producing high-quality code. They use exploratory testing to look for surprises and gaps in the software. When the testers find a bug, the team conducts root-cause analysis and considers how to improve their process to prevent similar bugs from occuring in the future. Testers also explore the software's nonfunctional characteristics, such as performance and stability. Customers then use this information to decide whether to create additional stories.

The team *doesn't* perform any manual regression testing. TDD and customer testing leads to a sophisticated suite of automated regression tests. When bugs are found, programmers create automated tests to show that the bugs have been resolved. This suite is sufficient to prevent regressions. Every time programmers integrate (once every few hours), they run the entire suite of regression tests to check if anything has broken.

The team also supports their quality efforts through pair programming, energized work, and iteration slack. These practices enhance the brainpower that each team member has available for creating high-quality software.

Deployment

XP teams keep their software ready to deploy at the end of any iteration. They deploy the software to internal stakeholders every week in preparation for the weekly iteration demo. Deployment to real customers is scheduled according to business needs.

As long as the team is active, it maintains the software it has released. Depending on the organization, the team may also support its own software (a batman is helpful in this case; see "Iteration Planning" in Chapter 8). In other cases, a separate support team may take over. Similarly, when the project ends, the team may hand off maintenance duties to another team. In this case, the team creates documentation and provides training as necessary during its last few weeks.

XP PRACTICES BY PHASE

The following table shows how XP's practices correspond to traditional phases. Remember that XP uses iterations rather than phases; teams perform every one of these activities each week. Most are performed every day.

Table 3-1. XP Practices by Phase

XP Practices	Planning	Analysis	Design & Coding	Testing	Deployment
Thinking					
Pair Programming			✓	✓	
Energized Work	✓	✓	✓	✓	✓
Informative Workspace	✓				
Root-Cause Analysis	✓			✓	
Retrospectives	✓			✓	
Collaborating					
Trust	✓	✓	✓	✓	✓
Sit Together	✓	✓	✓	✓	
Real Customer Involvement		✓			
Ubiquitous Language		✓			
Stand-Up Meetings	✓				
Coding Standards			✓		
Iteration Demo					✓
Reporting	✓	✓	✓	✓	✓
Releasing					
"Done Done"			✓		✓
No Bugs			✓	✓	
Version Control			✓		
Ten-Minute Build			✓		✓
Continuous Integration			✓		✓
CollectiveCode Ownership			✓		
Documentation					✓
Planning					

XP Practices	Planning	Analysis	Design & Coding	Testing	Deployment
Vision	✓	✓			
Release Planning	✓	✓			
The Planning Game	✓	✓			
Risk Management	✓				
Iteration Planning	✓		✓		
Slack	✓		✓		
Stories	✓	✓			
Estimating	✓				
Developing					
Incremental Requirements		✓	✓		
Customer Tests		✓		✓	
Test-Driven Development			✓	✓	
Refactoring			✓		
Simple Design			✓		
Incremental Design and Architecture			✓		
Spike Solutions			✓		
Performance Optimization			✓		
Exploratory Testing				✓	

Our Story Continues

"Hey, guys, I'd like you to meet Pat, our new programmer," Kim announced. She, Jeff, and Pat had walked over to a series of large tables. Index cards and pencils were scattered around the tables, and whiteboards covered the walls. Six programmers were working in pairs at three of the workstations.

"Hi, Pat," the team chorused. Kim introduced everyone.

"Welcome aboard," said Justin, one of the programmers. He stood up and grabbed a rubber chicken from a nearby desk. "Kevin and I are going to integrate our changes now," he announced to the rest of the group. A few people nodded abstractly, already intent on their work.

"Mary and I just made some changes to the customer tests," said Jeff. "Who's working on the warehouse story?"

"That's us," said Justin. "What's up?"

"We added some examples to cover some new edge cases. I think they're pretty straightforward, but if you have any questions, let us know."

"Will do," Justin replied. "We were about to finish off the last of the business logic for that story anyway. We'll take a look at it as soon as we've checked in."

"Thanks!" Jeff went off to meet Mary and Brian at the planning board.

"Before you start on your next task, Justin, do you have a few minutes?" Kim asked.

Justin glanced at his pairing partner, Kevin, who was listening in. He gave Justin a thumbs up.

"Sure. We're just waiting for the build's tests to finish, anyway."

"Great," Kim said. "I'm helping Pat get oriented, and he wanted to know which phase of development we're working on. Can you explain what you've been doing?"

Justin flashed Pat a knowing look. "She's on the 'simultaneous phases' kick, huh? I'm sorry." He laughed. "Just kidding, Kim! It *is* pretty different.

"I'm sure Kim is dying to hear me say this: yes, we're doing testing, design, coding, and integration all at once. We deploy every week—because we do internal development, we actually deploy to production—but deployment happens automatically. The real deployment work happens when we update our deployment scripts, which we do as needed throughout the week."

"Right now Kevin and I are integrating, which is something everybody does every few hours. Before that, we were using test-driven development and refactoring to test, code, and design simultaneously." Justin pointed to another pair at a workstation. "Jerry and Suri are doing a in-depth review of a story we finished yesterday. Suri is our other tester—she's very good at exploratory testing." He looked at the third pair, who were talking intensely and sketching on the whiteboard. "And it looks like Mark and Allison over there are working on a larger design problem. We use incremental design and architecture, so we're constantly looking for ways to improve our design."

Allison looked up. "Actually, I think this is something the whole group should see. Can we get everyone's attention for a moment?"

"Sure," said Jerry, pushing away from his desk. He glanced at his partner, who nodded. "We needed a break anyway."

As Allison started sketching on the whiteboard, Pat thought about what he'd seen. Brian was working on planning. Jeff and Mary were working on requirements and tests—no, examples. Kevin and Justin were integrating, and had been testing, designing, and coding a few minutes earlier. Mark and Allison were designing. And Jerry and Suri were doing more testing.

Except that it wasn't quite that simple. Everything seemed fluid; people kept changing what they were working on. Jeff and Mary had gone backward, from requirements to planning, and all the programmers had jumped from integration and testing to design. He frowned. How was he going to keep track of it all?

"Don't worry," said Kim quietly. She had noticed his discomfort. "It's not as confusing as it seems. Jeff has it right: don't worry about what to call what we're doing. We're all doing the same thing—getting stuff done. We work together to make it happen, and we jump back and forth between all the normal development activities as the situation dictates. If you focus on what we're *delivering* rather than trying to figure out what phase of development we're in, it will all make sense."

Pat shook his head. "How do you know what you have to do, though? It looks like chaos."

Kim pointed at a whiteboard filled with index cards. "There's our plan for this week. Green are finished and white are remaining. It's Monday morning and we release on Wednesday, so we have about half a week to go. You tell me; what's our progress?"

Pat looked at the board. About half the cards had a green circle around them. "About halfway through?" he guessed.

Kim beamed. "Perfect! We keep those cards up-to-date. Just keep that in mind for the first week or two and you'll do fine!"

A LITTLE LIE

I've pretended that the only way to do XP is the way I've described it in this book. Actually, that's not really true. The essence of XP isn't its practices, but its approach to software development. [Beck 2004] describes XP as including a philosophy of software development, a body of practices, a set of complementary principles, and a community. Every experienced XP team will have its own way of practicing XP. As you master the art of agile development, you will, too.

In Parts I and II of this book, I'm going to perpetuate the little lie that there's just one way to do XP. It's a lot easier to learn XP that way. As you learn, keep in mind that no practice is set in stone. You're always free to experiment with changes. See "The Road to Mastery" in Chapter 2 and then turn to Part III for guidance.

There are a few differences between my approach to XP and what you'll find in other XP books. Most of the differences are minor stylistic issues, but I've also made a few important changes to XP's planning and acceptance testing practices. I made these changes to address common problems I observed when working with XP teams. Like XP itself, these changes are the result of several years of iterative refinement.

One of the problems I've noticed with XP teams is that the on-site customers often have difficulty with release planning. XP gives them the freedom to change their mind at will, and they do—too much. They slip into *agile thrashing*, which means they overreact to every opportunity, changing direction every time something new comes up. As a result, the team never finishes anything valuable and has trouble showing progress.

To help prevent this problem, I've added the Vision practice and gone into more detail about appropriate release planning. I've also added the Risk Management practice to help teams understand how to make reliable long-term commitments.

I've also noticed that teams struggle with XP's automated acceptance tests. Although they are intended to "allow the customer to know when the system works and tell the programmers what needs to be done" [Jeffries et al.], I've found that they're often too limited to truly fulfill this role. In fact, some customers worry that, by defining acceptance tests, they'll be stuck with software that passes the letter of the tests but fails to fulfill the spirit of their expectations. Worse, most teams implement these tests as system-level tests that take a lot of work to create and maintain. They run slowly and lead to build and integration problems. In short, I've found that automated acceptance tests cost more than they're worth.

In this book, I've replaced automated acceptance tests with customer reviews, customer testing, and exploratory testing. Customer reviews involve customers throughout the development process, allowing them to communicate the spirit as well as the letter of their needs. Customer testing is a variant of automated acceptance testing that focuses on small, targeted tests rather than system-level tests. Its purpose is to communicate complicated business rules rather than confirming that a story has been completed properly. Exploratory testing provides an after-the-fact check on the team's practices. When the team is working well, they should produce nearly zero bugs. Exploratory testing helps the team have confidence that this is true.

Despite these changes, I've only added three brand-new practices in this book (Table 3-2). None of these practices are my invention; I adapted them from other methods and have proven them in real-world projects.

Table 3-2. Practices new to XP

New practice	Reason
Vision	Focuses efforts and helps counteract common "agile thrashing" problem
Risk Management	Improves team's ability to make and meet commitments; reduces costs
Exploratory Testing	Improves quality and helps integrate testers

However, there are several practices that mature XP teams practice intuitively, but aren't explicitly listed as practices in other XP books. I've added those as well (Table 3-3).

Table 3-3. Clarifying practices

Clarifying practice
Retrospectives
Trust
Ubiquitous Language
Stand-Up Meetings
Iteration Demo
Reporting
"Done Done"
No Bugs
Version Control
Documentation
Customer Testing
Spike Solutions
Performance Optimization

There are a few practices in standard XP that I've rarely seen in use and don't practice myself (Table 3-4). I've removed them from this book.

Table 3-4. Practices not in this book

Removed practice	Reason
Metaphor	Replaced with Ubiquitous Language
Shrinking Teams	No personal experience; not essential
Negotiated Scope Contract	Minimal personal experience; not essential
Pay-Per-Use	No personal experience; not essential

Table 3-5 below shows how the practices in this book correspond to Beck's XP practices. I've also included a column for Scrum, another popular agile method.

Key: *n/a*: This practice is not part of the method, although some teams may add it. *implied*: Although this idea isn't a practice in the method, its presence is assumed or described in another way.

Table 3-5. Practices cross-reference

This Book	2nd Edition XP[a]	1st Edition XP[b]	Scrum[c]
Thinking			
Pair Programming	Pair Programming	Pair Programming	*n/a*
Energized Work	Energized Work	40-Hour Week	*implied*
Informative Workspace	Informative Workspace	*implied*	*implied*
Root-Cause Analysis	Root-Cause Analysis	*implied*	*implied*
Retrospectives	*implied*	*implied*	*implied*
Collaborating			
Trust	*implied*	*implied*	*implied*
(in Trust)	Team Continuity	*n/a*	*implied*
Sit Together	Sit Together	*implied*	Open Working Environment
implied	Whole Team	On-Site Customer	Scrum Team
Real Customer Involvmenet	Real Customer Involvement	*implied*	*implied*
Ubiquitous Language	*implied*	(replaces Metaphor)	*n/a*
Stand-Up Meetings	*implied*	*implied*	Daily Scrum
Coding Standards	*implied*	Coding Standards	*n/a*
Iteration Demo	*implied*	*implied*	Sprint Review
Reporting	*implied*	*implied*	*implied*
Releasing			
"Done Done"	*implied*	*implied*	*implied*
No Bugs	*implied*	*implied*	*n/a*
Version Control	*implied*	*implied*	*n/a*
(in Version Control)	Single Code Base	*implied*	*n/a*
Ten-Minute Build	Ten-Minute Build	*implied*	*n/a*
Continuous Integration	Continuous Integration	Continuous Integration	*n/a*
Collective Code Ownership	Shared Code	Collective Ownership *n/a*	
Documentation	*implied*	*implied*	*implied*
Planning			
Vison	*n/a*	*n/a*	*implied*
Release Planning	Quarterly Cycle	Small Releases	Product Backlog
(in Release Planning)	Incremental Deployment	*implied*	*implied*
(in Release Planning)	Daily Deployment	*implied*	*n/a*
The Planning Game	*implied*	The Planning Game	*implied*
Risk Management	*n/a*	*n/a*	*n/a*
Iteration Planning	Weekly Cycle	*implied*	Sprints

This Book	2nd Edition XP[a]	1st Edition XP[b]	Scrum[c]
Slack	Slack	*implied*	*implied*
Stories	Stories	*implied*	Backlog Items
Estimating	*implied*	*implied*	Estimating
Developing			
Incremental Requirements	*implied*	*implied*	*implied*
Customer Tests	*implied*	Testing	*n/a*
Test-Driven Development	Test-First Programming	Testing	*n/a*
Refactoring	*implied*	Refactoring	*n/a*
Simple Design	Incremental Design	Simple Design	*n/a*
Incremental Design and Architecture	Incremental Design	Simple Design	*n/a*
Spike Solutions	*implied*	*implied*	*n/a*
Performance Optimization	*implied*	*implied*	*n/a*
Exploratory Testing	*n/a*	*n/a*	*n/a*
(Not in This Book)			
n/a	Shrinking Teams	*n/a*	*n/a*
n/a	Negotiated Scope Contract	*implied*	*n/a*
n/a	Pay-Per-Use	*n/a*	*n/a*
implied	*implied*	*implied*	Scrum Master
implied	*implied*	*implied*	Product Owner
n/a	*n/a*	*n/a*	Abnormal Sprint Termination
n/a	*n/a*	*n/a*	Sprint Goal

[a] [Beck 2004]
[b] [Beck 1999]
[c] [Schwaber & Beedle]

The XP Team

Working solo on your own project—"scratching your own itch"—can be a lot of fun. There are no questions about which features to work on, how things ought to work, if the software works correctly, or whether stakeholders are happy. All the answers are right there in one brain.

Team software development is different. The same information is spread out among many members of the team. Different people know:

- How to design and program the software (programmers, designers, and architects)
- Why the software is important (product manager)

- The rules the software should follow (domain experts)
- How the software should behave (interaction designers)
- How the user interface should look (graphic designers)
- Where defects are likely to hide (testers)
- How to interact with the rest of the company (project manager)
- Where to improve work habits (coach)

All of this knowledge is necessary for success. XP acknowledges this reality by creating *cross-functional teams* composed of diverse people who can fulfill all the team's roles.

The Whole Team

XP teams sit together in an open workspace. At the beginning of each iteration, the team meets for a series of activities: an iteration demo, a retrospective, and iteration planning. These typically take two to four hours in total. The team also meets for daily stand-up meetings, which usually take five to ten minutes each.

Other than these scheduled activities, everyone on the team plans his own work. That doesn't mean everybody works independently; they just aren't on an explicit schedule. Team members work out the details of each meeting when they need to. Sometimes it's as informal as somebody standing up and announcing across the shared workspace that he would like to discuss an issue. This *self-organization* is a hallmark of agile teams.

On-Site Customers

On-site customers—often just called *customers*—are responsible for defining the software the team builds. The rest of the team can and should contribute suggestions and ideas, but the customers are ultimately responsible for determining what stakeholders find valuable.

Customers' most important activity is release planning. This is a multifaceted activity. Customers need to evangelize the project's vision; identify features and stories; determine how to group features into small, frequent releases; manage risks; and create an achievable plan by coordinating with programmers and playing the planning game.

On-site customers may or may not be real customers, depending on the type of project. Regardless, customers are responsible for refining their plans by soliciting feedback from real customers and other stakeholders. One of the venues for this feedback is the weekly iteration demo, which customers lead.

In addition to planning, customers are responsible for providing programmers with requirements details upon request. XP uses requirements documents only as memory aids for customers. Customers themselves act as living requirements documents, researching information in time for programmer use and providing it as needed. Customers also help communicate requirements by creating mock-ups, reviewing work in progress, and creating detailed customer tests that clarify complex business rules. The entire team must sit together for this communication to take place effectively.

Typically, product managers, domain experts, interaction designers, and business analysts play the role of the on-site customer. One of the most difficult aspects of creating a cross-functional team is finding people qualified and willing to be on-site customers. Don't neglect this role; it's essential to increasing the value of the product you deliver. A great team will produce technically excellent software without on-site customers, but to truly succeed, your software must also bring value to its investors. This requires the perspective of on-site customers.

[Coffin] describes an experience with two nearly identical teams, one that did not have on-site customers and one that did. The team with no on-site customers took fifteen months to produce a product with mediocre value.

> The total cost of the project exceeded initial expectations and the application under delivered on the user's functional expectations for the system... real business value was not delivered until the second and third [releases] and even then the new system was not perceived as valuable by its users because it required them to change while providing no significant benefit.

A team composed of many of the same developers, at the same company, using the same process, later produced a product with compelling value in less than three months.

> The first production release was ready after 9 weeks of development... it surpassed scheduling and functional expectations, while still coming in on-budget.... In the first two months of live production usage over 25,000 citations were entered using the new system. The application development team continued to deliver new releases to production approximately every six weeks thereafter. Every release was an exciting opportunity for the team of developers and users to provide value to the company and to improve the user's ability to accomplish their jobs.

One of the primary reasons for this success was customer involvement.

> Many of the shortcomings of the [first] system stemmed from a breakdown in the collaborative atmosphere that was initially established. Had users been more involved throughout the project, the end result would have been a system that much more closely aligned with their actual needs. They would have had a greater sense of ownership and communication between the various groups would have been less tense.
>
> ...
>
> The success of the [second] system caused many people in the organization to take note and embrace the lessons learned in this project... other projects teams restructured their physical arrangements into a shared project room as the [second] team had done.

Customer involvement makes a huge difference in product success. Make an extra effort to include customers. One way to do so is to move to their offices rather than asking them to move to your office. Make sure the customers agree and that there's adequate space available.

If the customers won't move to the team, move the team to the customers.

WHY SO MANY CUSTOMERS?

Two customers for every three programmers seems like a lot, doesn't it? Initially I started with a much smaller ratio, but I often observed customers struggling to keep up with the programmers. Eventually I arrived at the two-to-three ratio after trying different ratios on several successful teams. I also asked other XP coaches about their experiences. The consensus was that the two-to-three ratio was about right.

Most of those projects involved complex problem domains, so if your software is fairly straightforward, you may be able to have fewer customers. Keep in mind that customers have a lot of work to do. They need to figure out what provides the most value, set the appropriate priorities for the work, identify all the details that programmers will ask about, and fit in time for customer reviews and testing. They need to do all this while staying one step ahead of the programmers, who are right behind them, crunching through stories like freight trains. It's a big job. Don't underestimate it.

The product manager (aka product owner)

The product manager has only one job on an XP project, but it's a doozy. That job is to *maintain* and *promote* the product vision. In practice, this means documenting the vision, sharing it with stakeholders, incorporating feedback, generating features and stories, setting priorities for release planning, providing direction for the team's on-site customers, reviewing work in progress, leading iteration demos, involving real customers, and dealing with organizational politics.

> **NOTE**
> In addition to maintaining and promoting the product vision, product managers are also often responsible for ensuring a successful deployment of the product to market. That may mean advertising and promotion, setting up training, and so forth. These ordinary product management responsibilities are out of the scope of this book.

The best product managers have deep understandings of their markets, whether the market is one organization (as with custom software) or many (as with commercial software). Good product managers have an intuitive understanding of what the software will provide and why it's *the most important thing* their project teams can do with their time.

A great product manager also has a rare combination of skills. In addition to vision, she must have the authority to make difficult trade-off decisions about what goes into the product and what stays out. She must have the political savvy to align diverse stakeholder interests, consolidate them into the product vision, and effectively say "no" to wishes that can't be accommodated.

Product managers of this caliber often have a lot of demands on their time. You may have trouble getting enough attention. Persevere. Theirs is one of the most crucial roles on the team. Enlist the help of your project manager and remind people that software development is very expensive. If the software isn't valuable enough to warrant the time of a good product manager—a product manager who could mean the difference between success and failure—perhaps it isn't worth developing in the first place.

Make sure your product manager is committed to the project full-time. Once a team is running smoothly, the product manager might start cutting back on his participation. Although domain experts and other on-site customers can fill in for the product manager for a time, the project is likely to start drifting off-course unless the product manager participates in every iteration. [Rooney] experienced that problem, with regrettable results:

> We weren't sure what our priorities were. We weren't exactly sure what to work on next. We pulled stories from the overall list, but there was precious little from the Customer [product manager] in terms of what we should be working on. This went on for a few months.

> Then, we found out that the Gold Owner [executive sponsor] was pissed—really pissed. We hadn't been working on what this person thought we should.

In a predictable environment, and by delegating to a solid set of on-site customers, a product manager might be able to spend most of his time on other things, but he should still participate in every retrospective, every iteration demo, and most release planning sessions.

Some companies have a committee play the role of product manager, but I advise against this approach. The team needs a consistent vision to follow, and I've found that committees have trouble creating consistent, compelling visions. When I've seen committees succeed, it's been because one committee member acted as *de facto* product manager. I recommend that you explicitly find a product manager. Her role may be nothing more than consolidating the ideas of the committee into a single vision, and that's likely to keep her hands full. Be sure to choose a product manager with plenty of political acumen in this case.

Domain experts (aka subject matter experts)

Most software operates in a particular industry, such as finance, that has its own specialized rules for doing business. To succeed in that industry, the software must implement those rules faithfully and exactly. These rules are *domain rules*, and knowledge of these rules is *domain knowledge*.

Most programmers have gaps in their domain knowledge, even if they've worked in an industry for years. In many cases, the industry itself doesn't clearly define all its rules. The basics may be clear, but there are nitpicky details where domain rules are implicit or even contradictory.

The team's domain experts are responsible for figuring out these details and having the answers at their fingertips. *Domain experts*, also known as *subject matter experts*, are experts in their field. Examples include financial analysts and PhD chemists.

Domain experts spend most of their time with the team, figuring out the details of upcoming stories and standing ready to answer questions when programmers ask. For complex rules, they create customer tests (often with the help of testers) to help convey nuances.

NOTE

On small teams, product managers often double as domain experts.

Interaction designers

The user interface is the public face of the product. For many users, the UI *is* the product. They judge the product's quality solely on their perception of the UI.

Interaction designers help define the product UI. Their job focuses on understanding users, their needs, and how they will interact with the product. They perform such tasks as interviewing users, creating user personas, reviewing paper prototypes with users, and observing usage of actual software.

You may not have a professional interaction designer on staff. Some companies fill this role with a graphic designer, the product manager, or a programmer.

Interaction designers divide their time between working with the team and working with users. They contribute to release planning by advising the team on user needs and priorities. During each iteration, they help the team create mock-ups of UI elements for that iteration's stories. As each story approaches completion, they review the look and feel of the UI and confirm that it works as expected.

The fast, iterative, feedback-oriented nature of XP development leads to a different environment than interaction designers may be used to. Rather than spending time researching users and defining behaviors before development begins, interaction designers must iteratively refine their models concurrently with iterative refinement of the program itself.

Although interaction design is different in XP than in other methods, it is not necessarily diminished. XP produces working software every week, which provides a rich grist for the interaction designer's mill. Designers have the opportunity to take real software to users, observe their usage patterns, and use that feedback to effect changes as soon as one week later.

Business analysts

On nonagile teams, business analysts typically act as liaisons between the customers and developers, by clarifying and refining customer needs into a functional requirements specification.

On an XP team, business analysts augment a team that already contains a product manager and domain experts. The analyst continues to clarify and refine customer needs, but the analyst does so in support of the other on-site customers, not as a replacement for them. Analysts help customers think of details they might otherwise forget and help programmers express technical trade-offs in business terms.

Programmers

A great product vision requires solid execution. The bulk of the XP team consists of software developers in a variety of specialties. Each of these developers contributes directly to creating working code. To emphasize this, XP calls all developers *programmers*.

If the customers' job is to maximize the value of the product, then the programmers' job is to minimize its cost. Programmers are responsible for finding the most effective way of delivering the stories in the plan. To this end, programmers provide effort estimates, suggest alternatives, and help customers create an achievable plan by playing the planning game.

Programmers spend most of their time pair programming. Using test-driven development, they write tests, implement code, refactor, and incrementally design and architect the application. They pay careful attention to design quality, and they're keenly aware of technical debt (for an explanation of technical debt, see "XP Concepts" later in this chapter) and its impact on development time and future maintenance costs.

Programmers also ensure that the customers may choose to release the software at the end of any iteration. With the help of the whole team, the programmers strive to produce no bugs in completed software. They maintain a ten-minute build that can build a complete release package at any time. They use version control and practice continuous integration, keeping all but the last few hours' work integrated and passing its tests.

This work is a joint effort of all the programmers. At the beginning of the project, the programmers establish coding standards that allow them to collectively share responsibility for the code. Programmers have the right and the responsibility to fix any problem they see, no matter which part of the application it touches.

Programmers rely on customers for information about the software to be built. Rather than guessing when they have a question, they ask one of the on-site customers. To enable these conversations, programmers build their software to use a ubiquitous language. They assist in customer testing by automating the customers' examples.

Finally, programmers help ensure the long-term maintainability of the product by providing documentation at appropriate times.

Designers and architects

Everybody codes on an XP team, and everybody designs. Test-driven development combines design, tests, and coding into a single, ongoing activity.

Expert designers and architects are still necessary. They contribute by guiding the team's incremental design and architecture efforts and by helping team members see ways of simplifying complex designs. They act as peers—that is, as programmers—rather than teachers, guiding rather than dictating.

Technical specialists

In addition to the obvious titles (programmer, developer, software engineer), the XP "programmer" role includes other software development roles. The programmers could include a database designer, a security expert, or a network architect. XP programmers are generalizing specialists. Although each person has his own area of expertise, everybody is expected to work on any part of the system that needs attention. (See "Collective Code Ownership" in Chapter 7 for more.)

Testers

Testers help XP teams produce quality results from the beginning. Testers apply their critical thinking skills to help customers consider all possibilities when envisioning the product. They help customers identify holes in the requirements and assist in customer testing.[*]

NOTE

Include enough testers for them to stay one step ahead of the programmers. As a rule of thumb, start with one tester for every four programmers.

Testers also act as technical investigators for the team. They use exploratory testing to help the team identify whether it is successfully preventing bugs from reaching finished code. Testers also provide information about the software's nonfunctional characteristics, such as performance, scalability, and stability, by using both exploratory testing and long-running automated tests.

However, testers *don't* exhaustively test the software for bugs. Rather than relying on testers to find bugs for programmers to fix, the team should produce nearly bug-free code on their own. When testers find bugs, they help the rest of the team figure out what went wrong so that the team as a whole can prevent those kinds of bugs from occurring in the future.

These responsibilities require creative thinking, flexibility, and experience defining test plans. Because XP automates repetitive testing rather than performing manual regression testing, testers who are used to self-directed work are the best fit.

Some XP teams don't include dedicated testers. If you don't have testers on your team, programmers and customers should share this role.

WHY SO FEW TESTERS?

As with the customer ratio, I arrived at the one-to-four tester-to-programmer ratio through trial and error. In fact, that ratio may be a little high. Successful teams I've worked with have had ratios as low as one tester for every six programmers, and some XP teams have no testers at all.

Manual script-based testing, particularly regression testing, is extremely labor-intensive and requires high tester-to-programmer ratios. XP doesn't use this sort of testing. Furthermore, programmers create most of the automated tests (during test-driven development), which further reduces the need for testers.

If you're working with existing code and have to do a lot of manual regression testing, your tester-to-programmer ratio will probably be higher than I've suggested here.

Coaches

XP teams *self-organize*, which means each member of the team figures out how he can best help the team move forward at any given moment. XP teams eschew traditional management roles.

---

[*] This discussion of tester responsibilities is part of my variant of XP (see the sidebar "A Little Lie," earlier in this chapter). Classic XP doesn't include testers as a distinct role.

Instead, XP leaders lead by example, helping the team reach its potential rather than creating jobs and assigning tasks. To emphasize this difference, XP leaders are called *coaches*. Over time, as the team gains experience and self-organizes, explicit leadership becomes less necessary and leadership roles dynamically switch from person to person as situations dictate.

A coach's work is subtle; it enables the team to succeed. Coaches help the team start their process by arranging for a shared workspace and making sure that the team includes the right people. They help set up conditions for energized work, and they assist the team in creating an informative workspace.

One of the most important things the coaches can do is to help the team interact with the rest of the organization. They help the team generate organizational trust and goodwill, and they often take responsibility for any reporting needed.

Coaches also help the team members maintain their self-discipline, helping them remain in control of challenging practices such as risk management, test-driven development, slack, and incremental design and architecture.

> **NOTE**
> The coach differs from your mentor (see "Find a Mentor" in Chapter 2). Your mentor is someone outside the team who you can turn to for advice.

The programmer-coach

Every team needs a programmer-coach to help the other programmers with XP's technical practices. Programmer-coaches are often senior developers and may have titles such as "technical lead" or "architect." They can even be functional managers. While some programmer-coaches make good all-around coaches, others require the assistance of a project manager.

Programmer-coaches also act as normal programmers and participate fully in software development.

The project manager

Project managers help the team work with the rest of the organization. They are usually good at coaching nonprogramming practices. Some functional managers fit into this role as well. However, most project managers lack the technical expertise to coach XP's programming practices, which necessitates the assistance of a programmer-coach.

Project managers may also double as customers.

> **NOTE**
> Include a programmer-coach and consider including a project manager.

Other Team Members

The preceding roles are a few of the most common team roles, but this list is by no means comprehensive. The absence of a role does not mean the expertise is inappropriate for an XP team; an XP team should include exactly the expertise necessary to complete the project successfully and cost-effectively. For example, one team I worked with included a technical writer and an ISO 9001 analyst.

The Project Community

Projects don't live in a vaccuum; every team has an ecosystem surrounding it. This ecosystem extends beyond the team to the *project community*, which includes everyone who affects or is affected by the project.[*] Keep this community in mind as you begin your XP project, as everybody within it can have an impact on your success.

Two members of your project community that you may forget to consider are your organization's Human Resources and Facilities departments. Human Resources often handles performance reviews and compensation. Their mechanisms may not be compatible with XP's team-based effort (see "Trust" in Chapter 6). Similarly, in order to use XP, you'll need the help of Facilities to create an open workspace (see "Sit Together" in Chapter 6).

Stakeholders

Stakeholders form a large subset of your project community. Not only are they affected by your project, they have an active interest in its success. Stakeholders may include end users, purchasers, managers, and executives. Although they don't participate in day-to-day development, do invite them to attend each iteration demo. The on-site customers—particularly the product manager—are responsible for understanding the needs of your stakeholders, deciding which needs are most important, and knowing how to best meet those needs.

The executive sponsor

The executive sponsor is particularly important: he holds the purse strings for your project. Take extra care to identify your executive sponsor and understand what he wants from your project. He's your ultimate customer. Be sure to provide him with regular demos and confirm that the project is proceeding according to his expectations.

XP PRACTICES BY ROLE

The following table shows the practices you should learn to practice XP. You can always learn more, of course! In particular, if you're in a leadership role (or would like to be), you should study all the practices.

Table 3-6. XP Practices by Role

XP Practices	On-Site Customers	Programmers	Testers	Coaches
Thinking				
Pair Programming		✓		
Energized Work	•	•	•	✓
Informative Workspace	•	•	•	✓
Root-Cause Analysis	•	•	•	✓

• = You will be involved with this practice. Studying it will be helpful, but not necessary.

✓ = You should study this practice carefully.

---

[*] Thanks to David Schmaltz and Amy Schwartz of True North pgs, Inc., for this term.

XP Practices	On-Site Customers	Programmers	Testers	Coaches
Retrospectives	•	•	•	✓
Collaborating				
Trust	•	•	•	✓
Sit Together	•	•	•	✓
Real Customer Involvement	•			✓
Ubiquitous Language		✓		
Stand-Up Meetings	•	•	•	✓
Coding Standards		•		✓
Iteration Demo	✓	✓	•	•
Reporting	•	•	•	✓
Releasing				
"Done Done"	✓	✓	✓	✓
No Bugs	•	✓	✓	✓
Version Control	•	✓	•	
Ten-Minute Build		✓		
Continuous Integration		✓		
Collective Code Ownership		✓		
Documentation	•	•		✓
Planning				
Vision	✓			✓
Release Planning	✓			✓
The Planning Game	•	•		✓
Risk Management	•	•	•	✓
Iteration Planning	•	✓		✓
Slack		•		✓
Stories	•	•	•	✓
Estimating		✓		
Developing				
Incremental Requirements	✓		✓	✓
Customer Tests	✓	✓	✓	
Test-Driven Development		✓	•	
Refactoring		✓		
Simple Design		✓		

• = You will be involved with this practice. Studying it will be helpful, but not necessary.

✓ = You should study this practice carefully.

XP Practices	On-Site Customers	Programmers	Testers	Coaches
Incremental Design and Architecture		✓		
Spike Solutions		✓		
Performance Optimization	•	✓		
Exploratory Testing			✓	

• = You will be involved with this practice. Studying it will be helpful, but not necessary.

✓ = You should study this practice carefully.

Filling Roles

The exact structure of your team isn't that important as long as it has all the knowledge it needs. The makeup of your team will probably depend more on your organization's traditions than on anything else.

In other words, if project managers and testers are typical for your organization, include them. If they're not, you don't necessarily need to hire them. You don't have to have one person for each role—some people can fill multiple roles. Just keep in mind that someone has to perform those duties even if no one has a specific job title saying so.

At a minimum, however, I prefer to see one person clearly designated as "product manager" (who may do other customer-y things) and one person clearly defined as "programmer-coach" (who also does programmer-y things).

The other roles may blend together. Product managers are usually domain experts and can often fill the project manager's shoes, too. One of the customers may be able to play the role of interaction designer, possibly with the help of a UI programmer. On the programming side, many programmers are generalists and understand a variety of technologies. In the absence of testers, both programmers and customers should pick up the slack.

Team Size

The guidelines in this book assume teams with 4 to 10 programmers (5 to 20 total team members). For new teams, four to six programmers is a good starting point.

Applying the staffing guidelines to a team of 6 programmers produces a team that also includes 4 customers, 1 tester, and a project manager, for a total team size of 12 people. Twelve people turns out to be a natural limit for team collaboration.

XP teams can be as small as one experienced programmer and one product manager, but full XP might be overkill for such a small team. The smallest team I would use with full XP consists of five people: four programmers (one acting as coach)and one product manager (who also acts as project manager, domain expert, and tester). A team of this size might find that the product manager is overburdened; if so, the programmers will have to pitch in. Adding a domain expert or tester will help.

On the other end of the spectrum, starting with 10 programmers produces a 20-person team that includes 6 customers, 3 testers, and a project manager. You can create even larger XP teams, but they require special practices that are out of the scope of this book.

Before you scale your team to more than 12 people, however, remember that large teams incur extra communication and process overhead, and thus reduce individual productivity. The combined overhead might even reduce overall

> Prefer *better* to *bigger*.

productivity. If possible, hire more experienced, more productive team members rather than scaling to a large team.

A 20-person team is advanced XP. Avoid creating a team of this size until your organization has had extended success with a smaller team. If you're working with a team of this size, continuous review, adjustment, and an experienced coach are critical.

Full-Time Team Members

All the team members should sit with the team full-time and give the project their complete attention. This particularly applies to customers, who are often surprised by the level of involvement XP requires of them.

Some organizations like to assign people to multiple projects simultaneously. This *fractional assignment* is particularly common in *matrix-managed organization*s. (If team members have two managers, one for their project and one for their function, you are probably in a matrixed organization.)

If your company practices fractional assignment, I have some good news. You can instantly improve productivity by reassigning people to only one project at a time. Fractional assignment is dreadfully counterproductive: fractional workers don't bond with their teams, they often aren't

> Fractional assignment is dreadfully counterproductive.

around to hear conversations and answer questions, and they must task switch, which incurs a significant hidden penalty. "[T]he minimum penalty is 15 percent... Fragmented knowledge workers may look busy, but a lot of their busyness is just thrashing" [DeMarco 2002, p. 19–20].

NOTE

If your team deals with a lot of ad hoc requests, you may benefit from using a batman, discussed in "Iteration Planning" in Chapter 8.

That's not to say everyone needs to work with the team for the entire duration of the project. You can bring someone in to consult on a problem temporarily. However, while she works with the team, she should be fully engaged and available.

XP Concepts

As with any specialized field, XP has its own vocabulary. This vocabulary distills several important concepts into snappy descriptions. Any serious discussion of XP (and of agile in general) uses this vocabulary. Some of the most common ideas follow.

Refactoring

There are multiple ways of expressing the same concept in source code. Some are better than others. *Refactoring* is the process of changing the structure of code—rephrasing it— without changing its meaning or behavior. It's used to improve code quality, to fight off software's unavoidable entropy, and to ease adding new features.

Ally
Refactoring (p. 303)

Technical Debt

Imagine a customer rushing down the hallway to your desk. "It's a bug!" she cries, out of breath. "We have to fix it now." You can think of two solutions: the right way and the fast way. You just *know* she'll watch over your shoulder until you fix it. So you choose the fast way, ignoring the little itchy feeling that you're making the code a bit messier.

Technical debt is the total amount of less-than-perfect design and implementation decisions in your project. This includes quick and dirty hacks intended just to get something working *right now!* and design decisions that may no longer apply due to business changes. Technical debt can even come from development practices such as an unwieldy build process or incomplete test coverage. It lurks in gigantic methods filled with commented-out code and "TODO: not sure why this works" comments. These dark corners of poor formatting, unintelligible control flow, and insufficient testing breed bugs like mad.

The bill for this debt often comes in the form of higher maintenance costs. There may not be a single lump sum to pay, but simple tasks that ought to take minutes may stretch into hours or afternoons. You might not even notice it except for a looming sense of dread when you read a new bug report and suspect it's in *that* part of the code.

Left unchecked, technical debt grows to overwhelm software projects. Software costs millions of dollars to develop, and even small projects cost hundreds of thousands. It's foolish to throw away that investment and rewrite the software, but it happens all the time. Why? Unchecked technical debt makes the software more expensive to modify than to reimplement. What a waste.

XP takes a fanatical approach to technical debt. The key to managing it is to be constantly vigilant. Avoid shortcuts, use simple design, refactor relentlessly... in short, apply XP's development practices (see Chapter 9).

Timeboxing

Some activities invariably stretch to fill the available time. There's always a bit more polish you can put on a program or a bit more design you can discuss in a meeting. Yet at some point you need to make a decision. At some point you've identified as many options as you ever will.

Recognizing the point at which you have enough information is not easy. If you use *timeboxing,* you set aside a specific block of time for your research or discussion and stop when your time is up, regardless of your progress.

This is both difficult and valuable. It's difficult to stop working on a problem when the solution may be seconds away. However, recognizing when you've made as much progress as possible is an important time-management skill. Timeboxing meetings, for example, can reduce wasted discussion.

The Last Responsible Moment

XP views a potential change as an opportunity to exploit; it's the chance to learn something significant. This is why XP teams delay commitment until the *last responsible moment.*[*]

Note that the phrase is the last *responsible* moment, not the last *possible* moment. As [Poppendieck & Poppendieck] says, make decisions at "the moment at which failing to make a decision eliminates an important alternative. If commitments are delayed beyond the last responsible moment, then decisions are made by default, which is generally not a good approach to making decisions."

By delaying decisions until this crucial point, you increase the accuracy of your decisions, decrease your workload, and decrease the impact of changes. Why? A delay gives you time to increase the amount of information you have when you make a decision, which increases the likelihood it is a correct decision. That, in turn, decreases your workload by reducing the amount of rework that results from incorrect decisions. Changes are easier because they are less likely to invalidate decisions or incur additional rework.

See "Release Planning" in Chapter 8 for an example of applying this concept.

Stories

Stories represent self-contained, individual elements of the project. They tend to correspond to individual features and typically represent one or two days of work.

Stories are customer-centric, describing the results in terms of business results. They're not implementation details, nor are they full requirements specifications. They are traditionally just an index card's worth of information used for scheduling purposes. See "Stories" in Chapter 8 for more information.

Iterations

An *iteration* is the full cycle of design-code-verify-release practiced by XP teams. It's a timebox that is usually one to three weeks long. (I recommend one week iterations for new teams; see "Iteration Planning" in Chapter 8) Each iteration begins with the customer selecting which stories the team will implement during the iteration, and it ends with the team producing software that the customer can install and use.

The beginning of each iteration represents a point at which the customer can change the direction of the project. Smaller iterations allow more frequent adjustment. Fixed-size iterations provide a well-timed rhythm of development.

Though it may seem that small and frequent iterations contain a lot of planning overhead, the amount of planning tends to be proportional to the length of the iteration.

See "Iteration Planning" for more details about XP iterations.

---

[*] The Lean Construction Institute coined the term "last responsible moment." [Poppendieck & Poppendieck] popularized it in relation to software development.

Velocity

In well-designed systems, programmer estimates of effort tend to be *consistent* but not *accurate*. Programmers also experience interruptions that prevent effort estimates from corresponding to calendar time. *Velocity* is a simple way of mapping estimates to the calendar. It's the total of the estimates for the stories finished in an iteration.

In general, the team should be able to achieve the same velocity in every iteration. This allows the team to make iteration commitments and predict release dates. The units measured are deliberately vague; velocity is a technique for converting effort estimates to calendar time and has no relation to productivity. See "Velocity" in Chapter 8 for more information.

Theory of Constraints

[Goldratt 1992]'s *Theory of Constraints* says, in part, that every system has a single constraint that determines the overall throughput of the system. This book assumes that programmers are the constraint on your team. Regardless of how much work testers and customers do, many software teams can only complete their projects as quickly as the programmers can program them. If the rest of the team outpaces the programmers, the work piles up, falls out of date and needs reworking, and slows the programmers further.

Therefore, the programmers set the pace, and their estimates are used for planning. As long as the programmers are the constraint, the customers and testers will have more slack in their schedules, and they'll have enough time to get their work done before the programmers need it.

Although this book assumes that programmers are the constraint, they may not be. Legacy projects in particular sometimes have a constraint of testing, not programming. The responsibility for estimates and velocity always goes to the constraint: in this case, the testers. Programmers have less to do than testers and manage their workload so that they are finished by the time testers are ready to test a story.

What should the nonconstraints do in their spare time? Help eliminate the constraint. If testers are the constraint, programmers might introduce and improve automated tests.

Mindfulness

Agility—the ability to respond effectively to change—requires that everyone pay attention to the process and practices of development. This is *mindfulness*.

Sometimes pending changes can be subtle. You may realize your technical debt is starting to grow when adding a new feature becomes more difficult this week than last week. You may notice the amount and tone of feedback you receive from your customers change.

XP offers plenty of opportunities to collect feedback from the code, from your coworkers, and from every activity you perform. Take advantage of these. Pay attention. See what changes and what doesn't, and discuss the results frequently.

CHAPTER 4

Adopting XP

"I can see how XP would work for IT projects, but product development is different." —*a product development team*

"I can see how XP would work for product development, but IT projects are different." —*an in-house IT development team*

Before adopting XP, you need to decide whether it's appropriate for your situation. Often, people's default reaction to hearing about XP is to say, "Well, *of course* that works for other teams, but it couldn't possibly work for us."

Question that assumption. I've helped a wide variety of teams adopt XP: 20-person teams and 1-person teams; huge corporations and small startups; shrinkwrap, in-house, and outsourced software vendors; proprietary and open source developers. Through these experiences, I've learned that software teams are more similar than they are different. XP's applicability has far more to do with your organization and the people involved than with the type of project you're working on.

> XP's applicability is based on organizations and people, not types of projects.

Is XP Right for Us?

You can adopt XP in many different conditions, although the practices you use will vary depending on your situation. The practices in this book were chosen to give you the greatest chance of success. That leads to some prerequisites and recommendations about your team's environment. You don't have meet these criteria exactly, but it's worth trying to change your environment so that you do. This will give you the best chance of succeeding. As Martin Fowler said:[*]

---

[*] *http://martinfowler.com/bliki/EnterpriseRails.html.*

In this sense I see a startling parallel between DHH [David Heinemeier Hansson, creator of Ruby on Rails] and Kent Beck. For either of them, if you present them with a constrained world, they'll look at constraints we take for granted, consider them to be unessential, and create a world without them. I don't have that quality, I tend to try to work within the constraints gradually pushing at them, while they just stick some intellectual dynamite under them and move on. That's why they can create things like Extreme Programming and Rails which really give the industry a jolt.

In other words, if your organization puts a barrier between your work and success, don't just put up with it—find a way to remove it. It's your best path to success.

Similarly, if you want to practice XP, do everything you can to meet the following prerequisites and recommendations. This is a lot more effective than working around limitations.

Prerequisite #1: Management Support

It's very difficult to use XP in the face of opposition from management. Active support is best. To practice XP as described in this book, you will need the following:

- A common workspace with pairing stations. (See "Sit Together" in Chapter 6.)
- Team members solely allocated to the XP project. (See "The XP Team" in Chapter 3.)
- A product manager, on-site customers, and integrated testers. (Also discussed in "The XP Team" in Chapter 3.)

You will often need management's help to get the previous three items. In addition, the more management provides the following things, the better:

- Team authority over the entire development process, including builds, database schema, and version control
- Compensation and review practices that are compatible with team-based effort
- Acceptance of new ways of demonstrating progress and showing results (see "Reporting" in Chapter 6)
- Patience with lowered productivity while the team learns

If management isn't supportive...

If you want management to support your adoption of XP, they need to believe in its benefits. Think about what the decision-makers care about. What does an organizational success mean to your management? What does a *personal* success mean? How will adopting XP help them achieve those successes? What are the risks of trying XP, how will you mitigate those risks, and what makes XP worth the risks? Talk in terms of your managers' ideas of success, not your own success.

If you have a trusted manager you can turn to, ask for her help and advice. If not, talk to your mentor (see "Find a Mentor" in Chapter 2). *Fearless Change: Patterns for Introducing New Ideas* [Manns & Rising] is another good resource.

If management refuses your overtures, then XP probably isn't appropriate for your team. You may be able to demonstrate XP's value incrementally by adopting some standalone practices (see "Extremities: Applying Bits and Pieces of XP," later in this chapter).

Prerequisite #2: Team Agreement

Just as important as management support is the team's agreement to use XP. If team members don't want to use XP, it's not likely to work. XP assumes good faith on the part of team members—there's no way to force the process on somebody who's resisting it.

If people resist...

It's never a good idea to force someone to practice XP against his will. In the best case, he'll find some way to leave the team, quitting if necessary. In the worst case, he'll remain on the team and silently sabotage your efforts.

Reluctant skeptics are OK. If somebody says, "I don't want to practice XP, but I see that the rest of you do, so I'll give it a fair chance for a few months," that's fine. She may end up liking it. If not, after a few months have gone by, you'll have a better idea of what you can do to meet the whole team's needs.

> **NOTE**
> One way to help people agree to try XP is to promise to revisit the decision on a specific date. (Allow two or three months if you can.) At that point, if the team doesn't want to continue using XP, stop.

If only one or two people refuse to use XP, and they're interested in working on another project, let them transfer so the rest of the team can use XP. If no such project is available, or if a significant portion of the team is against using XP, don't use it.

Prerequisite #3: A Colocated Team

XP relies on fast, high-bandwidth communication for many of its practices. In order to achieve that communication, your team members needs to sit together in the same room.

If your team isn't colocated...

Colocation makes a big difference in team effectiveness. Don't assume that your team can't sit together; be sure that bringing the team together is your first option.

That said, it's OK if one or two noncentral team members are off-site some of the time. You'll be surprised, though, at how much more difficult it is to interact with them. (Actually, they're no more difficult to interact with than before; it's the rest of the team that's improved.) Talk with your mentor (see "Find a Mentor" in Chapter 2) about how to best deal with the problem.

If a lot of people are off-site, if a central figure is often absent, or if your team is split across multiple locations, you need help beyond this book. You *can* use XP or another agile method with a distributed team, but it's a complicated problem that's outside the scope of our discussion. Ask your mentor for help, and see "Sit Together" in Chapter 6 for more ideas.

Prerequisite #4: On-Site Customers

On-site customers are critical to the success of an XP team. They, led by the product manager, determine which features the team will develop. In other words, their decisions determine the value of the software.

> The on-site customers' decisions determine the value of the software.

Of all the on-site customers, the product manager is likely the most important. She makes the final determination of value. A good product manager will choose features that provide value to your organization. A poor product manager will dither time away on inconsequential features.

Domain experts, and possibly interaction designers, are also important. They take the place of an upfront requirements phase, sitting with the team to plan upcoming features and answering questions about what the software needs to do.

If your product manager is too busy to be on-site...

If you have an experienced product manager who makes high-level decisions about features and priorities, but who isn't available to sit with the team full-time, you may be able to ask a business analyst or one of the other on-site customers to act as a *proxy*. The proxy's job is to act in the product manager's stead to make decisions about details while following the actual product manager's high-level decisions.

This can work well if your proxy has the authority to act in place of the product manager. If the proxy is unable to answer questions on his own and needs to confirm every decision with the real product manager, he will introduce too many delays for this book's approach to XP to work well.

If your product manager is inexperienced...

This may be OK as long as she has a more experienced colleague she turns to for advice.

If you can't get a product manager at all...

Although good product managers are in high demand, the absence of a product manager is a big danger sign. The right person for the job may not have the title of "product manager" (see "Real Customer Involvement" in Chapter 6), but XP requires that somebody with business expertise take responsibility for determining and prioritizing features.

Remind your organization of the cost of development (presumably, hundreds of thousands of dollars) and the value the software will bring to them (hopefully, millions of dollars). That value hinges on the participation of a good product manager. Is that really something they want to scrimp on?

If you can't find a product manager, someone from the development team can play the part. However, this may be a dangerous approach because this person is unlikely to have the business expertise necessary to deliver an organizational success. If you can't get a product manager, talk with your mentor about how to compensate.

If you can't get other on-site customers...

Because XP doesn't have an upfront requirements phase, the work of figuring out requirements happens concurrently with software development. This compresses the overall schedule, and it means that at least one person—usually several—needs to work on requirements full-time.

Unless you have a small team, this work is probably more than a product manager can handle alone. Typically, the product manager delegates the details to a set of domain experts. In applications that involve a sophisticated user interface, an interaction designer may be involved as well. This allows the product manager to focus on coordinating with stakeholders and resolving questions of value and priorities.

Some business analysts may be domain experts. Be careful of using business analysts that aren't already experts in the domain; although they can relay information from true experts, this process invariably introduces misunderstandings and delays.

As long as somebody is playing the on-site customer role, you can use XP. However, the less expertise your on-site customers have, the more risk there is to the value of your software.

Prerequisite #5: The Right Team Size

I wrote this book for teams as large as 20 people and as small as 1 person. For teams new to XP, however, I recommend 4 to 6 programmers and no more than 12 people on the team (see "The XP Team" in Chapter 3). I also recommend having an even number of programmers so that everyone can pair program (see "Pair Programming" in Chapter 5). If you have ongoing support needs, add one more programmer for a total of five or seven so that the team can have a batman (see "Iteration Planning" in Chapter 8).

Teams with fewer than four programmers are less likely to have the intellectual diversity they need. They'll also have trouble using pair programming, an important support mechanism in XP. Large teams face coordination challenges. Although experienced teams can handle those challenges smoothly, a new XP team will struggle.

If you don't have even pairs...

The easiest solution to this problem is to add or drop one programmer so you have even pairs. If you can't do that, the XP practices are still appropriate for you, but try to find useful nonproduction code work for the programmer who isn't pairing. This will help the team consistently apply XP's technical practices and will improve code quality.

If your team is larger than seven programmers...

The coordination challenges of a large team can make learning XP more difficult. Consider hiring an experienced XP coach to lead the team through the transition. You may also benefit from hiring another experienced XP programmer to assist the coach in mentoring the team.

If your team is larger than 10 programmers, you need guidance that's outside the scope of this book. Hire a coach with experience in scaling XP to large teams.

If your team is smaller than four programmers...

Most of the XP practices are still appropriate for you, but you probably won't be able to pair program much. In this situation, it's best if your team members are conscientious programmers who are passionate about producing high-quality code. That passion will help them apply XP's technical practices with discipline.

You may also have trouble getting on-site customers to sit with you full-time. Instead, sit close to them so you can get their attention when you need it.

If you have many developers working solo...

Some organizations—particularly IT organizations—have a lot of small projects rather than one big project. They structure their work to assign one programmer to each project.

Although this approach has the advantage of connecting programmers directly with projects, it has several disadvantages. It's high-risk: every project is the responsibility of one programmer, so that any programmer who leaves orphans a project. Her replacement may have to learn it from first principles.

Code quality can also be a challenge. Projects don't benefit from peer review, so the code is often idiosyncratic. *Stovepipe systems,* in which each programmer solves the same problem in different ways, appear. Junior programmers, lacking the guidance of their more senior peers, create convoluted, kludgey systems and have few opportunities to learn better approaches. Senior programmers, not realizing the inexperience of their more junior peers, create overly sophisticated code that others have trouble understanding.

You may be able to combine four to seven of these programmers into a single XP team that works on one project at a time, which allows it to complete projects more quickly (see "Release Planning" in Chapter 8). By working together, senior developers have the opportunity to mentor junior developers, and the team can eliminate stovepipe systems.

Combining your programmers into a single team has some drawbacks. The biggest is likely to be a perceived lack of responsiveness. Although projects will be finished more quickly, customers will no longer have a dedicated programmer to talk to about the status of their projects. The team will only work on one project at a time, so other customers may feel they are being ignored.

To resolve these problems, consider dedicating one programmer to deal with customer requests and minor changes (see "Iteration Planning" in Chapter 8). You'll also need an influential, unbiased business person to play the product manager role, addressing conflicts between customers and making prioritization decisions.

Prerequisite #6: Use All the Practices

You may be tempted to ignore or remove some XP practices, particularly ones that make team members uncomfortable. Be careful of this. XP is designed to have very little waste. Nearly every practice directly contributes to the production of valuable software.

For example, pair programming supports collective code ownership, which is necessary for refactoring. Refactoring allows incremental design and architecture. Incremental design and architecture enables customer-driven planning and frequent releases, which are the key to XP's ability to increase value and deliver successful software.

XP doesn't require perfection—it's OK if you accidentally misapply a practice from time to time—but it rarely works well if you arbitrarily remove pieces.

If practices don't fit...

You may think that some XP practices aren't appropriate for your organization. That may be true, but it's possible you just feel uncomfortable or unfamiliar with a practice. Are you sure the practice won't work, or do you just not want to do it? XP will work much better if you give all the practices a fair chance rather than picking and choosing the ones you like.

If you're sure a practice won't work, you need to replace it. For example, in order to achieve the benefits of collective code ownership without pair programming, you must provide another way for people to share knowledge about the codebase. (You'll also have to find ways to replace the other benefits of pairing.)

Replacing practices requires continuous refinement and an in-depth understanding of XP. Ask your mentor for help (see "Find a Mentor" in Chapter 2) and consider hiring an experienced XP coach.

Recommendation #1: A Brand-New Codebase

Easily changed code is vital to XP. If your code is cumbersome to change, you'll have difficulty with XP's technical practices, and that difficulty will spill over into XP's planning practices.

XP teams put a lot of effort into keeping their code clean and easy to change. If you have a brand-new codebase, this is easy to do. If you have to work with existing code, you can still practice XP, but it will be more difficult. Even well-maintained code is unlikely to have the simple design and suite of automated unit tests that XP requires (and produces). New XP teams often experience an epiphany between the second and fourth months. "This is the best code I've ever worked with!" they say, and start to see the power of XP.

To understand and appreciate XP's technical practices fully, you need to experience the practices meshing together to give you complete confidence in your code, tests, and build. You need to feel the delight of making big improvements with small changes. You're unlikely to have that experience when working with existing code. If you can, leave preexisting code to experienced XP teams.

If you have preexisting code...

You *can* dig your way out of this hole. See "Applying XP to an Existing Project," later in this chapter.

Recommendation #2: Strong Design Skills

Simple, easily changed design is XP's core enabler. This means at least one person on the team—preferably a natural leader—needs to have strong design skills.

It's hard to tell if somebody has strong design skills unless you have strong design skills yourself. One clue to look for is an understanding and appreciation of domain-driven design. It requires a crucial shift in thinking—from imperative procedural design to declarative object-oriented design—that programmers with poor design skills can have difficulty grasping.

If no one has strong design skills...

Even lacking a person with strong design skills, you'll probably do as well with XP as you would with any method—perhaps better, because XP includes specific technology practices and advice. However, that doesn't mean you'll be successful. Take it slow and steady, and seek out as much experienced help as you can get.

Meanwhile, start learning! [Evans]' *Domain-Driven Design* is a good place to start, as is [Fowler 2002a]'s *Patterns of Enterprise Application Architecture*. Consider taking a course or hiring somebody to join the team as a mentor. Be careful, though—strong design skills, while essential, are surprisingly rare. Ask someone with good design skills to help you vet your choice.

Recommendation #3: A Language That's Easy to Refactor

XP relies on refactoring to continuously improve existing designs, so any language that makes refactoring difficult will make XP difficult. Of the currently popular languages, object-oriented and dynamic languages with garbage collection are the easiest to refactor. C and C++, for example, are more difficult to refactor.

If your language is hard to refactor...

You can still use XP, but it's a good idea to include someone on your team who has experience with refactoring in your language, if you can.

Recommendation #4: An Experienced Programmer-Coach

Some people are natural leaders. They're decisive, but appreciate others' views; competent, but respectful of others' abilities. Team members respect and trust them. You can recognize a leader by her influence—regardless of her title, people turn to a leader for advice.

> **NOTE**
> Leadership is independent of title or position. You can identify leaders by their followers, not by their desire to give orders. To identify the real leaders on your team, look for the people that team members *want* to follow.

XP relies on *self-organizing teams*. This kind of team doesn't have a predefined hierarchy; instead, the team decides for itself who is in charge of what. These roles are usually informal. In fact, in a mature XP team, there is no one leader. Team members seamlessly defer leadership responsibilities from one person to the next, moment to moment, depending on the task at hand and the expertise of those involved.

When your team first forms, though, it won't work together so easily. Somebody will need to help the team remember to follow the XP practices consistently and rigorously. This is particularly important for programmers, who have the most difficult practices to learn.

In other words, your team needs a coach. The best coaches are natural leaders—people who remind others to do the right thing by virtue of who they are rather than the orders they give. Your coach also needs to be an experienced programmer so she can help the team with XP's technical practices.

If you have no obvious coach...

Explain the situation to the team and ask them to choose a coach by consensus. In other words, ask them to pick one person that they can all agree would be a good coach.

> **NOTE**
> In consensus decisions, everyone has a veto. A quick way to perform a consensus vote is to ask everyone to hold their thumbs out. Thumbs up means "I agree." Thumbs sideways means "I'll go with the team's decision." Thumbs down means "I disagree and want to explain why."

If you can't pick a coach by consensus, your team may be too fractured to use XP. If there's someone you can hire that the team would trust, that may help. Be sure to tell whoever you hire that you weren't able to reach consensus on this issue—an experienced XP coach will see it as a danger sign and should speak to team members before accepting.

If your leaders are inexperienced...

Good leaders aren't always experienced developers, but a good coach should look for subtle cues that indicate upcoming problems, which does require experience. An experienced developer is your best coach.

If your leaders are inexperienced, you may want to try *pair coaching*. Pick one person who's a good leader and one person who has a lot of experience. Make sure they get along well. Ask the two coaches to work together to help the team remember to practice XP consistently and rigorously.

If you're assigned a poor coach...

Your organization may assign somebody to be coach who isn't a good leader. In this case, if the assigned coach recognizes the problem, pair coaching may work for you.

If the assigned coach doesn't recognize the problem and he's damaging the team's ability to function, discuss the situation with your mentor or a manager you trust. This is a delicate situation that requires context-specific advice.

Recommendation #5: A Friendly and Cohesive Team

XP requires that everybody work together to meet team goals. There's no provision for someone to work in isolation, so it's best if team members enjoy working together.

If your team doesn't get along...

XP requires people to work together. Combined with the pressure of weekly deliveries, this can help team members learn to trust and respect each other. However, it's possible for a team to implode from the pressure. Try including a team member who is level-headed and has a calming influence.

If team members won't even attempt to work together, don't use XP. If there's just one person whose behavior encourages other people's bad behavior, you might be able to solve the problem by moving him to a different team.

Go!

Are you ready to adopt XP? Great! Your first step is to arrange for your open workspace (see "Sit Together" in Chapter 6). Start solving this problem now. It will probably take longer than you expect.

Next, find an appropriate project for the team to work on. Look for a project that's valuable, but be wary of projects that will be under intense scrutiny. You need room to make mistakes as you learn.

At the same time, figure out who will be on your team. "The XP Team" in Chapter 3 provides some
suggestions for team structure. Talk with your project's executive sponsor and other stakeholders about
who to include as your on-site customers. (See "Real Customer Involvement" in Chapter 6 for ideas.)
Be sure your team members want to try XP.

As you're forming your team, consider hiring an experienced XP coach to work with the team full-time.
Although a coach isn't necessary—I learned XP by reading about it and trying it—a good coach *will*
make things go more smoothly.

EXTREME SHOPPING

As your project start date draws near, you'll need supplies for the team's open workspace. The following is a
good shopping list.

Equipment:

- Pairing stations (see "Pair Programming" in Chapter 5).
- A dedicated build machine (see "Continuous Integration" in Chapter 7).
- Noise-dampening partitions to define your team's workspace and prevent noise pollution (see "Sit
  Together" in Chapter 6).
- Plenty of wall-mounted whiteboards for discussions and charts (see "Informative Workspace" in
  Chapter 5). Ferrous (magnetic) whiteboards are best because you can stick index cards to them with
  magnets.
- Two big magnetic whiteboards for your release and iteration plans. I like using a two-sided, six-foot
  magnetic whiteboard on wheels—it allows me to move the plan into a meeting room. Some teams prefer
  corkboards, but I think they make it too hard to slide cards around.
- A large plastic perpetual calendar (three months or more) for marking important dates and planned
  absences (see "Informative Workspace" in Chapter 5).
- A plush toy to act as your integration token (see "Continuous Integration" in Chapter 7).
- Miscellaneous toys and conversation pieces to inspire discussion and interaction among team members.
- Any other equipment you normally use.

Software:

- A unit-testing tool such as the xUnit family (see "Test-Driven Development" in Chapter 9).
- An automated build tool such as the Ant family (see "Ten-Minute Build" in Chapter 7).
- Any other software you normally use.

Supplies:

- Index cards—start with 5,000 of white and 2,000 of each color you want. Be sure to choose colors that all members of your team can distinguish (7 to 10 percent of men have a degree of color blindness).
- Pencils for index cards. (Don't use pens; you'll need to make changes from time to time.)
- Food (see "Energized Work" in Chapter 5 and "Trust" in Chapter 6).
- Flip charts and something sticky but nonmarking (such as blue painters tape or poster tack) for hanging charts (see "Informative Workspace" in Chapter 5).
- Dry-erase markers for whiteboards, water-based flip-chart markers for flip charts,* and wet-erase markers for the perpetual calendar. (Be sure the markers are easily distinguishable!)
- Magnets for sticking papers to whiteboards. Office supply stores sell thin, flexible magnets that work well. Make sure they're powerful enough to hold an index card or two to the board.
- Any other supplies you normally use.

The Challenge of Change

It's a fact of life: change makes people uncomfortable. XP is probably a big change for your team. If you previously used a rigid, document-centric process, XP will seem loose and informal. If you previously had no process, XP will seem strict and disciplined. Either way, expect team members and stakeholders to be uncomfortable. This discomfort can extend into the larger organization.

Discomfort and a feeling of chaos is normal for any team undergoing change, but that doesn't make it less challenging. Expect the chaotic feeling to continue for at least two months. Give yourselves four to nine months to feel truly comfortable with your new process. If you're adopting XP incrementally, it will take longer.

To survive the transformation, you need to know *why* you are making this change. What benefits does it provide to the organization? To the team? Most importantly, what benefits does it provide to each individual? As you struggle with the chaos of change, remember these benefits.

A supportive work environment is also important. Team members are likely to experience defense reactions to the lack of familiar structure. Expect mood swings and erratic behavior. Some team members may lash out or refuse to cooperate. Acknowledge the discomfort people are experiencing, and help team members find constructive outlets for their frustration.

> **NOTE**
> The Satir Change Model is one way of understanding teams' reactions to change. [Smith] has a good article on the Satir model at *http://www.stevenmsmith.com/my-articles/article/the-satir-change-model.html* that includes tips for helping team members through each stage.

---

* Avoid permanent markers; they bleed through the paper and damage your whiteboard if you use the wrong pen by mistake.

Your stakeholders may be uncomfortable with your team's new approach to planning and reporting progress. Managers and executives may see the team's initial chaos as a sign that XP won't work. To help everyone feel more comfortable, consider giving them this pledge:

Our pledge to users, management, and other stakeholders.

We promise to:

- Make steady progress
- Finish the features that you consider most valuable first
- Show you working software that reflects our progess every week, on *(day of week)* at *(time)* in *(location)*
- Be honest and open with you about our successes, challenges, and what we can reasonably provide

In return, we ask you to be patient with changes in our productivity and understanding of our mistakes as we learn this new way of working over the next two quarters.

Final Preparation

Before starting XP, it's a good idea to discuss *working agreements*—that is, which practices your team will follow and how your practice of XP will differ from what I describe in this book. (I recommend following the book as closely as you can until you've had several months of experience.) Discuss your roles and what you expect from each other. It's best to hold these conversations as collaborative team discussions. Try to avoid assigning roles or giving people orders.

In the final weeks before starting your new XP project, review the practices in Part II. Try some of the practices in your current work and consider taking courses on the practices that seem challenging.

When you've finished these preparations, if you have a *greenfield project*—meaning your team is creating a new codebase from scratch—you're ready to go. Review the practices in Part II one more time, take a deep breath, and start your first iteration.

"Wait!" you may say. "Isn't there a way we can ease into this?"

Well... yes. You can follow the incremental approach that legacy projects use, but if you have a greenfield project, it's actually easier and faster to adopt all the practices at once. It's the chaos and uncertainty of change that makes adopting XP difficult, not the practices themselves. If you adopt XP incrementally, every new practice will disrupt the equilibrium you'll be fighting to achieve. You'll actually *extend* the period of chaos and uncertainty, making the transition all the more difficult. In my experience, teams that adopt XP incrementally make substantial improvements, but it's the teams that adopt it all at once that really excel.

Be bold. You have the right people, the right workplace, and the will to succeed. Do it!

SECOND ADOPTER SYNDROME

I've noticed a suprising trend among companies that adopt XP: the first team is often very successful, inspiring the organization to use XP on more projects, but then this second wave of XP projects struggles.

I call this *second adopter syndrome*. My theory is that the first XP project gets all the support it needs: eager participants, organizational patience, outside help, and a valuable but noncritical project.

Then, thinking that employees now understand XP, the organization provides little support for the second wave of projects. They staff the teams with people who don't want to use XP, provide no outside help, and impose more schedule pressure.

To avoid second adopter syndrome, remember that success on one team doesn't automatically guarantee success on another team. Every team needs support when it adopts XP for the first time.

Applying XP to a Brand-New Project (Recommended)

When starting a brand-new XP project, expect the first three or four weeks to be pretty chaotic as everyone gets up to speed. During the first month, on-site customers will be working out the release plan, programmers will be establishing their technical infrastructure, and everyone will be learning how to work together.

Some people think the best way to overcome this chaos is to take a week or two at the beginning of the project to work on planning and technical infrastructure before starting the first iteration. Although there's some merit to this idea, an XP team should plan and build technical infrastructure incrementally and continuously throughout the project as needed. Starting with a real iteration on the first day helps establish this good habit.

> Plan and build infrastructure incrementally throughout the entire project.

Your very first activity is to plan your first iteration. Normally, this involves selecting stories from the release plan, but you won't have a release plan yet. Instead, think of one feature that will definitely be part of your first release. Brainstorm a few must-have stories for that feature. These first few stories should sketch out a "vertical stripe" (see Figure 8-3) of your application. If the application involves user interaction, create a story to display the initial screen or web page. If it includes reporting, create a story for a bare-bones report. If it requires installation, create a story for a bare-bones installer.

Ally
Release Planning (p. 206)

Don't expect much from these initial stories. The programmers' estimates for them will be fairly high because they need to establish some technical infrastructure. As a result, the stories should do very little. The report might display headers and footers, but no line items. The installer might just be a *.zip* file. The initial screen might have nothing more than your logo on it.

These basic stories will give you ideas for more stories that will add missing details. Brainstorm 10 to 20 in the first planning session and have the programmers estimate them. These should keep the programmers busy for several iterations. Try to choose stories that the programmers already understand well; this will reduce the amount of time customers need to spend answering programmer questions so they can focus on creating the release plan.

Ally
Estimating (p. 260)

Iteration planning is a little more difficult during the first iteration because you haven't established a velocity yet. Just make your best guess about what your velocity might be. (Some teams add up the available programmer-hours and divide by π.) During the iteration, work on just one or two stories at a time and check your progress every day. This will help you deliver completed stories even if your initial plan is wildly inaccurate.

Ally
Iteration Planning (p. 233)

After you've finished planning, programmers should start establishing their technical infrastructure. Set up an integration machine, create your version control repository, and so forth. (I recommend creating engineering tasks for these items during iteration planning. See "Iteration Planning" in Chapter 8 for more about the role of engineering tasks in iteration planning.) Once that's set up, start working on your stories.

During the first iteration, it's a good idea to have all the programmers work on the first few stories as a group. Set up a projector so the whole team navigates while one person drives. (See "Pair Programming" in Chapter 5 for an explanation of driving and navigating.) Sometimes individual programmers (or pairs) peel off to take care of some necessary issue, such as installing a version control system or setting up the programmers' workstations, but for the most part you should work as a team. This reduces the chaos that occurs when multiple people work on a tiny project and allows you to jointly establish initial conventions, such as project structure, filenames and namespaces, and basic design choices.

After the first few days, the fundamentals should be well-established and the project should be large enough for people to work on separate parts without unduly interfering with each other. At this point, you can break into pairs and work normally. It's also a good time to schedule your first coding standards discussion. For that first meeting, you can usually just document what you agreed on while working as a group.

Ally
Coding Standards (p. 133)

While the programmers are working on stories, customers and testers should work on the vision and release plan. First, work with stakeholders to create the product vision. You probably already have an idea what the vision for the project is; now formalize it. Finalizing the vision can take a few weeks, so while that's in progress, brainstorm the stories for your first feature. Start thinking about other features you want to include, and pick a date for your first release. Decide on your planning horizons as well. (See "Release Planning" in Chapter 8 for more about planning horizons.)

Allies
Vision (p. 201)
Release Planning (p. 206)

Each subsequent iteration will be a little easier to plan. The programmers' estimates will stabilize and your velocity will become predictable. You'll be able to estimate the scope of your next release and fill out your planning horizons. The feeling of chaos will subside as the team works in a steady, predictable rhythm.

Applying XP to an Existing Project

Greenfield projects can adopt all the XP practices at once. You'll experience some bumps along the way, but you'll typically have things figured out in four to nine months.

If you're working with an existing codebase that has no tests, particularly one that's been around for a year or more—in other words, if you have a *legacy project*—you can achieve the same results, but it will take more time. In this case, adopt XP incrementally.

NOTE

In this discussion, I assume you have a project burdened with a lot of technical debt and a high bug rate. If your situation isn't that bad, this process is still appropriate, if much easier.

The big decision

Other than change itself, the biggest challenge in applying XP to an existing project is not writing tests, refactoring, or cleaning up your bug database. The biggest challenge is setting aside enough time to pay down technical debt.

If you have a typical legacy project, your current velocity is a polite fiction based on shortcuts. In other words, you incur new technical debt in order to meet your deadlines. To improve productivity and reduce bug production, not only do you need to stop incurring new technical debt, you need to set aside extra slack (see "Slack" in Chapter 8) for paying down the existing debt. This double hit will cause your velocity to go down. It might go down a lot.

Fortunately, as your technical debt decreases, your velocity will rise again. Eventually it will surpass your current velocity. This can take a while. Depending on the amount of technical debt you have and how much slack you set aside for paying it down, expect your velocity to remain low for at least a quarter, probably more.

> **NOTE**
> The more slack you provide for paying down technical debt, the lower your velocity will be, but the less time it will take for your velocity to rise again. Think of velocity as *cash flow*: the more principal you pay on your debt, the less cash you have each week, but the more quickly you can stop paying interest.

Setting aside slack is a painful decision. However, if you don't stop accumulating technical debt, your velocity will continue to decrease and your defect production rate will increase. Eventually, the cost of development will exceed the value of even simple changes. Your organization will either shelve the product or rewrite it at great expense.

Product managers, avoid this fate by acting decisively now. This is your best option for turning a debt-ridden legacy project into a long-term asset.

> **NOTE**
> You can also rewrite the project from scratch or stop for several weeks to do nothing but pay down technical debt. Although these approaches take less effort than incremental debt paydown, they're risky. These efforts often take much longer than expected, and you lose feedback from stakeholders as well as the opportunity to take advantage of new business opportunities in the meantime.

Bring order to chaos

The first thing you need to do is bring structure to your project. Many legacy projects have a chaotic approach to planning, even if they started out well.

Start by introducing XP's structural practices. Move the team, including customers and testers, into a shared workspace, start pair-programming, conduct iteration planning and retrospectives, and so forth. Apply:

- All the "Thinking" practices (Chapter 5)
- All the "Collaborating" practices (Chapter 6)
- All the "Planning" practices (Chapter 8)
- Version control, collective code ownership, and "done done" (described in Chapter 7), and customer reviews (see "Incremental Requirements" in Chapter 9)

Two-, three-, or even four-week iterations may be best for you. Start with two-week iterations. In particularly challenging environments, you may have trouble making your stories both small and customer-valued (see "Stories" in Chapter 8). Consider increasing your iteration length, but talk to your mentor (see "Find a Mentor" in Chapter 2) before doing so.

> **NOTE**
> At this point, your method is very similar to the Scrum method. You may find Scrum courses and reading material useful.

Other than working more closely together, the biggest changes will be to planning. Take your existing project plan and convert each line item into a story card. If the stories aren't customer-centric, that's OK for now; once the team is used to working in iterations, the customers and the project manager should start revising the stories to make them more customer-centric.

When you are comfortable with the structural practices, begin introducing technical practices.

Pay down technical debt

The biggest problem facing legacy projects is usually excessive technical debt. You need to stop the bleeding by preventing more technical debt from occurring. First, create a ten-minute build. Follow up with continuous integration. Introduce test-driven development.

Meanwhile, reduce existing technical debt by introducing extra slack into your iterations (see "Slack" in Chapter 8). Use it to pay down technical debt as described in "How to Introduce Slack," also in Chapter 8. At first, your clean-up efforts will seem fruitless, but over time, you'll see greater and greater benefits to quality and productivity. As your code quality improves, introduce the remaining practices in Chapter 7 and Chapter 9.

These first steps will allow you to steadily pay down technical debt while continuing to make progress on new stories. As the bug rate for new code drops, you can start organizing your bug backlog.

Organize your backlog

If your team is like most teams, your bug database is full of to-dos, questions, feature requests, and genuine defects. Customers and testers, go through the database and eliminate duplicates and unimportant issues. Close feature requests by turning them into stories or rejecting them. Find another way to address to-dos and questions. When you're done, the only items remaining should be genuine defects.

> **NOTE**
> If users expect to ask questions through your bug database, consider leaving the questions in the database. You risk alienating your users by requiring them to use a different forum.[*]

Depending on the size of your bug database, you may not be able to do this work in a single session. Chip away at it every iteration, just as the programmers do with technical debt.

---

[*] Thanks to Erik Petersen for this insight.

If your bug database is in use by stakeholders, support personnel, or other people outside the team, find a way to keep new entries clean. You may be able to institute new policies for using the database, but your best approach is probably to review, clean up, and categorize new entries every day.

Fix important bugs

Either way, as your bug database becomes a reliable bug repository, make a *fix* or *don't fix* decision for each bug. You should probably involve the product manager at some level and you may need the programmers to estimate the cost of fixing some of the bugs.

Close or defer all the bugs that you decide not to fix in this release. You can revisit them when you plan the next release. At this point, all that remains in the database is bugs that you will fix. Turn these bugs into stories, have the programmers estimate any that remain unestimated, and put them in the release plan.

NOTE

If you have a lot of bugs, consider spreading bug fixes throughout your plan. Although normally it's better to fix bugs immediately, spreading out the bugs will allow you to deliver feature enhancements in each iteration, which may be better for stakeholder relations.

Over the remainder of the release, fix the bugs and work on preventing their causes as described in "No Bugs" in Chapter 7. Continue to pay down technical debt and start applying a bit of root-cause analysis as well.

Move testers forward

When you start this process, your testers will probably spend their time testing each release prior to delivery. A large part of their workload is likely to be manual regression testing. The programmers' focus on test-driven development will slowly create an automated regression suite and reduce the pressure on the testers.

As time passes, productivity improves, and as programmers have less need to pay down technical debt, use your iteration slack to automate the remaining manual regression tests. You may need to create end-to-end tests at first. Over time, refactor the end-to-end tests into more focused unit and integration tests.

Ally

Slack (p. 246)

With the regression testing burden eliminated and the team producing few new bugs, the testers will have time available for other work. Take advantage of this opportunity to finish integrating the testers into the team. Move them forward in the process so that, rather than testing *after* a development phase, they help the team produce higher quality code from the beginning. Have them work with customers to find holes in requirements (see "Customer Tests" in Chapter 9) and begin conducting exploratory testing (see "Exploratory Testing" in Chapter 9).

Emerge from the darkness

This process will allow you to reduce technical debt, increase code quality, and remove defects. As you do, productivity will increase. At first, your progress will be imperceptible. Depending on the amount of technical debt you face, it could take many months to get to the ideal of nearly zero new bugs each month. It will take months more to finish your regression test suite, eliminate the need for a separate pre-release testing phase, and integrate your testers.

As long as each iteration has less debt than the previous, however, you *will* get there. It will take time and hard work, but it will be well worth it. After the first few months, you should start seeing progress in the form of more reliable estimates and more enjoyable programming.

NOTE

If you don't see progress within two months, there may be something wrong. Talk to your mentor (see "Find a Mentor" in Chapter 2) for advice.

Applying XP in a Phased-Based Organization

XP assumes that you use iterations, not phases, which makes using XP in a phase-based environment difficult. If your organization uses a phase-based approach to development, you may be able to use the XP development practices (see Chapter 7 and Chapter 9) even if you can't use the other practices.

Your organization may want to try XP within your existing phase-based structure. Your best course of action is to convince your organization to let you try XP's simultaneous phases. If that doesn't work, you may be able to shoehorn XP into a phase-based structure. It's difficult and the exact approach depends on your organization. The following suggestions are a starting point; talk to your mentor for more specific advice.

Mandatory planning phase

Your organization may have a planning phase or planning gate that expects you to deliver a detailed plan. If you can, allocate a month for the planning phase and use it to run four actual iterations. (You may be able to combine the planning phase and analysis phase to get more time.) Use the approach described in "Release Planning" in Chapter 8 to create your release plan during those first iterations. You'll end up with a good plan and you will have finished some actual software, too.

If you can't use this approach, whatever approach your organization currently uses for planning will be fine, although it probably won't be as accurate as conducting actual iterations.

Mandatory analysis phase

If your organization conducts an upfront analysis phase, you may receive a requirements document as a *fait accompli*. In this case, decompose the requirements document into stories. One starting point is to create a story out of each sentence including the words "must," "shall," or "should."

Ally
Stories (p. 253)

If instead you need to create your own requirements document, XP doesn't have much to add. Use traditional requirements-gathering techniques in this situation, perhaps using iterations and requirements-gathering stories for structure.

Requirements documents aren't a replacement for a good product manager or on-site customers. Without those people, you will have difficulty filling in missing details in the requirements documents. You will also have more trouble making good schedule/scope trade-offs.

> Requirements documents can't replace on-site customers.

Mandatory design phase

XP assumes the use of incremental design and architecture that is intimately tied to programming with test-driven development. An upfront design phase has little to add to this approach.

Allies

Incremental Design and Architecture (p. 321)
Simple Design (p. 314)

If you can, conduct actual XP iterations during the design phase and work on the first stories in your release plan. Use the time to create an initial design and architecture incrementally. Document the results in your design document.

XP focuses on improving and adapting the design throughout the project. Simple design is central to doing so. Dedicated design phases often lead to complex designs, so minimize the amount of time you spend on upfront design if you can.

Mandatory coding phase

XP fits well into the coding phase. Break your coding phase into one-week iterations and conduct XP as normal.

Mandatory testing phase

XP performs a lot of testing every iteration. A phase-based organization that considers XP to be the coding phase and expects a long testing phase might schedule too little time for coding and too much time for testing. However, testing is an important part of XP and should remain integrated.

Mandatory deployment phase

With a good build, you should be ready to deploy at the end of any iteration. You can schedule XP's wrap-up activities for the deployment phase.

Ally

Ten-Minute Build (p. 177)

Extremities: Applying Bits and Pieces of XP

What if your team doesn't meet this book's conditions for using XP? What then?

Although you won't be able to use all the XP practices in this book, you may be able to add some practices to your existing method. Several practices are easy to adopt and are likely to make an immediate difference:

Iterations

If you struggle with frequent interruptions, try adopting day-long iterations (see "Iteration Planning" in Chapter 8). Use the planning game (see "The Planning Game [219]" in Chapter 8) and the team's measured velocity (discussed in "Estimating" in Chapter 8) to conduct a joint planning session at the beginning of each day, then defer all interruptions until the next planning meeting, which will be less than a day away. Be sure to have programmers estimate their own tasks.

If you aren't interrupted frequently, but still feel a sense of chaos in your planning, try using weekly iterations (see "Iterations" in Chapter 3). In this case, you may also benefit from daily stand-up meetings (see "Stand-Up Meetings" in Chapter 6) and weekly iteration demos (see "Iteration Demo" in Chapter 6). As time goes on, consider using index cards for planning and a big chart to show upcoming work, as described in "Release Planning" in Chapter 8.

Retrospectives

Frequent retrospectives (see "Retrospectives" in Chapter 5) are an excellent way for your team to adapt and improve its process. If your team has the authority to make any improvements to its process, try scheduling weekly or biweekly retrospectives.

Ten-minute build

A fast, automated build will make a big difference to your quality of life, and it will open up opportunities for other improvements as well. See "Ten-Minute Build" in Chapter 7 for more.

Continuous integration

Continuous integration not only decreases integration problems, it also drives improvements to your build and tests. See "Continuous Integration" in Chapter 7 for more.

Test-driven development

Although test-driven development (see "Test-Driven Development" in Chapter 9) isn't as easy to adopt as the other practices, it's very powerful. Test-driven development is the basis for reducing bugs, increasing development speed, improving your ability to refactor, and decreasing technical debt. It can take some time to master, so be patient.

Other practices

Other XP practices might help, so review Part II. Many of the practices there require the support of other practices, so be sure to read each practice's "Contraindications" section carefully before trying it.

Assess Your Agility

Suppose you've been using XP for a few months. How can you tell if you're doing it properly? The ultimate measure is the success of your project, but you may wish to review and assess your approach to XP as well.

To help you do this, I've created a quiz that focuses on five important aspects of agile development. It explores results rather than specific practices, so you can score well even after customizing XP to your situation. If you aren't using XP at all, you can also use this quiz to assess your current approach.

This quiz assesses typical sources of risk. Your goal should be to achieve the maximum score in each category—which is well within the grasp of experienced XP teams. Any score less than the maximum indicates risk, and an opportunity for improvement.

To take the quiz, answer the following questions and enter your scores on a photocopy of the blank radar diagram (Figure 4-2). Don't give partial credit for any question, and if you aren't sure of the answer, give yourself zero points. The result should look something like Figure 4-1. The score of the *lowest* spoke identifies your risk, as follows:

- 75 points or less: immediate improvement required (red)
- 75 to 96 points: improvement necessary (yellow)
- 97, 98, or 99: improvement possible (green)
- 100: no further improvement needed

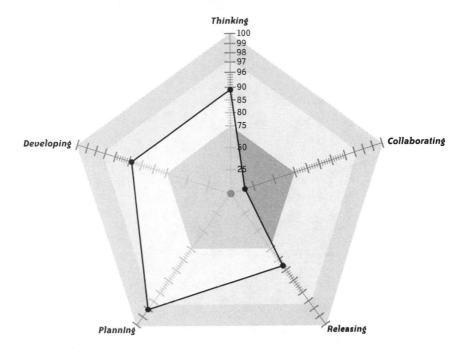

Figure 4-1. Example assessment

NOTE

The point values for each answer come from an algorithm that ensures correct risk assessment of the *total* score.* This leads to some odd variations in scores. Don't read too much into the disparities between the values of individual questions.

To see the XP solution for each of these questions, cross-reference the sections listed under "XP Practices" in Tables 4-1 through 4-5.

Self-Assessment Quiz

Table 4-1. Thinking

Question	Yes	No	XP Practices
Do programmers critique all production code with at least one other programmer?	5	0	Pair Programming

---

* Each question has a red, yellow, or green risk level. A zero score on any question leads to a total score no better than the corresponding color. Questions with scores between 25 and 75 are "red" questions, questions with scores between 3 and 22 are "yellow" questions, and questions with scores of 1 or 2 are "green" questions. Changing the risk level of one question requires reweighting the remainder: all red questions must total 75 points, all yellow questions must total 22 points, and all green questions must total 2 points. To preserve proper scoring, there may be no more than three red questions and seven yellow questions.

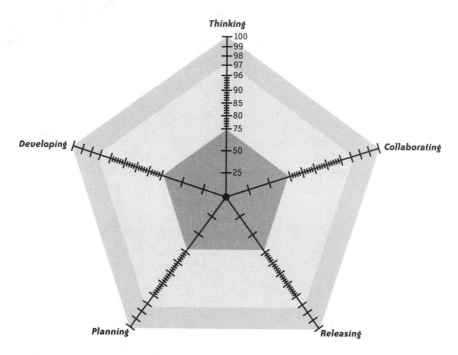

Figure 4-2. Self-assessment chart

Question	Yes	No	XP Practices
Do all team members consistently, thoughtfully, and rigorously apply all the practices that the team has agreed to use?	75	0	Pair Programming; Root-Cause Analysis; Retrospectives
Are team members generally focused and engaged at work?	5	0	Energized Work
Are nearly all team members aware of their progress toward meeting team goals?	4	0	Informative Workspace
Do any problems recur more than once per quarter?	0	5	Root-Cause Analysis; Retrospectives
Does the team improve its process in some way at least once per month?	5	0	Retrospectives

Table 4-2. Collaborating

Question	Yes	No	XP Practices
Do programmers ever make guesses rather than getting answers to questions?	0	75	The XP Team
Are programmers usually able to start getting information (as opposed to sending a request and waiting for a response) as soon as they discover their need for it?	4	0	Sit Together
Do team members generally communicate without confusion?	4	0	Sit Together; Ubiquitous Language
Do nearly all team members trust each other?	4	0	The XP Team; Sit Together
Do team members generally know what other team members are working on?	1	0	Stand-Up Meetings

Question	Yes	No	XP Practices
Does the team demonstrate its progress to stakeholders at least once per month?	4	0	Iteration Demo; Reporting
Does the team provide a working installation of its software for stakeholders to try at least once per month?	1	0	Iteration Demo
Are all important stakeholders currently happy with the team's progress?	3	0	Reporting; Iteration Demo; Real Customer Involvement
Do all important stakeholders currently trust the team's ability to deliver?	3	0	Trust; Reporting

Table 4-3. Releasing

Question	Yes	No	XP Practices
Can any programmer on the team currently build and test the software, and get an unambiguous success/fail result, using a single command?	25	0	Ten-Minute Build
Can any programmer on the team currently build a tested, deployable release using a single command?	5	0	Ten-Minute Build
Do all team members use version control for all project-related artifacts that aren't automatically generated?	25	0	Version Control
Can any programmer build and test the software on any development workstation with nothing but a clean check-out from version control?	25	0	Version Control
When a programmer gets the latest code, is he nearly always confident that it will build successfully and pass all its tests?	5	0	Continuous Integration
Do all programmers integrate their work with the main body of code at least once per day?	4	0	Continuous Integration
Does the integration build currently complete in fewer than 10 minutes?	4	0	Ten-Minute Build
Do nearly all programmers share a joint aesthetic for the code?	1	0	Coding Standards
Do programmers usually improve the code when they see opportunities, regardless of who originally wrote it?	4	0	Collective Code Ownership; Refactoring
Are fewer than five bugs per month discovered in the team's finished work?	1	0	No Bugs

Table 4-4. Planning

Question	Yes	No	XP Practices
Do nearly all team members *understand* what they are building, why they're building it, and what stakeholders consider success?	25	0	Vision
Do all important stakeholders *agree* on what the team is building, why, and what the stakeholders jointly consider success?	25	0	Vision
Does the team have a plan for achieving success?	4	0	Release Planning
Does the team regularly seek out new information and use it to improve its plan for success?	2	0	Release Planning
Does the team's plan incorporate the expertise of business people as well as programmers, and do nearly all involved agree the plan is achievable?	3	0	The Planning Game
Are nearly all the line items in the team's plan customer-centric, results-oriented, and order-independent?	4	0	Stories

Question	Yes	No	XP Practices
Does the team compare its progress to the plan at predefined, timeboxed intervals, no longer than one month apart, and revise its plan accordingly?	4	0	Iterations
Does the team make delivery commitments prior to each timeboxed interval, then nearly always deliver on those commitments?	4	0	Iterations; "Done Done"; Slack; Estimating
After a line item in the plan is marked "complete," do team members later perform unexpected additional work, such as bug fixes or release polish, to finish it?	0	25	"Done Done"
Does the team nearly always deliver on its release commitments?	3	0	Risk Management

Table 4-5. Developing

Question	Yes	No	XP Practices
Are programmers nearly always confident that the code they've written recently does what they intended it to?	25	0	Test-Driven Development
Are all programmers comfortable making changes to the code?	25	0	Test-Driven Development
Do programmers have more than one debug session per week that exceeds 10 minutes?	0	3	Test-Driven Development
Do all programmers agree that the code is at least slightly better each week than it was the week before?	25	0	Refactoring; Incremental Design and Architecture
Does the team deliver customer-valued stories every iteration?	3	0	Iterations; Incremental Design and Architecture
Do unexpected design changes require difficult or costly changes to existing code?	0	3	Simple Design
Do programmers use working code to give them information about technical problems?	1	0	Spike Solutions
Do any programmers optimize code without conducting performance tests first?	0	3	Performance Optimization
Do programmers ever spend more than an hour optimizing code without customers' approval?	0	3	Performance Optimization
Are on-site customers rarely surprised by the behavior of the software at the end of an iteration?	4	0	Incremental Requirements
Is there more than one bug per month in the business logic of completed stories?	0	3	Customer Tests
Are any team members unsure about the quality of the software the team is producing?	0	1	Exploratory Testing; Iteration Demo; Real Customer Involvement

PART II

Practicing XP

Thinking

What's wrong with this sentence?

What we really need is more keyboards cranking out code.

That's a quote from a manager I once worked with. In a way, he was right: you will never give your customer what she wants without typing on a keyboard.

But that wasn't our problem. I later realized our progress had a single bottleneck: the availability of our staging environment. More keyboards wouldn't have helped, even if we had more programmers sitting at them. If we had realized this sooner, we would have been much more productive.

Sometimes the biggest gains in productivity come from stopping to think about *what* you're doing, *why* you're doing it, and *whether* it's a good idea. The best developers don't just find something that works and use it; they also question why it works, try to understand it, and then improve it.

XP doesn't require experts. It *does* require a habit of mindfulness. This chapter contains five practices to help mindful developers excel:

- *Pair programming* doubles the brainpower available during coding, and gives one person in each pair the opportunity to think about strategic, long-term issues.
- *Energized work* acknowledges that developers do their best, most productive work when they're energized and motivated.
- An *informative workspace* gives the whole team more opportunities to notice what's working well and what isn't.
- *Root-cause analysis* is a useful tool for identifying the underlying causes of your problems.
- *Retrospectives* provide a way to analyze and improve the entire development process.

"THINKING" MINI-ÉTUDE

The purpose of this étude is to practice mindfulness. If you're new to agile development, you may use it to help you understand the XP practices, even if you're not currently using XP. If you're an experienced agile practitioner, review Chapter 11 and use this étude to consider how you can go beyond the practices in this book.

Conduct this étude for a timeboxed half-hour every day for as long as it is useful. Expect to feel rushed by the deadline at first. If the étude becomes stale, discuss how you can change it to make it interesting again.

You will need multiple copies of this book (if you don't have enough copies on hand, you can make photocopies of specific practices for the purpose of this exercise), paper, and writing implements.

Step 1. Start by forming pairs. Try for heterogeneous pairs—have a programmer work with a customer, a customer work with a tester, and so forth, rather than pairing by job description. Work with a new partner every day.

Step 2. (Timebox this step to 15 minutes.) Within your pair, pick one practice from Part II of this book and discuss one of the following sets of questions. Pick a practice that neither of you have discussed before, even if you didn't get to lead a discussion yesterday. Timebox your discussion to fifteen minutes. It's OK not to finish the section, particularly if you haven't read it before. You'll have the chance to read it again.

If you aren't using the practice:

- What about the practice would be easy to do? What would be hard? What sounds ridiculous or silly?
- How does it differ from your previous experiences?
- What would have to be true in order for you to use the practice exactly as written?

If you are using the practice:

- What aspects of the practice do you do differently than the book says? (Observations only—no reasons.)
- If you were to follow the practice exactly as written, what would happen?
- What one experimental change could you try that would give you new insight about the practice? (Experiments to prove that the practice is inappropriate are OK.)

Step 3. (Timebox this step to 15 minutes.) Choose three pairs to lead discussions of their answers. Try to pick pairs so that, over time, everyone gets to lead equally. Timebox each presentation to five minutes.

Pair Programming

Audience
Programmers, Whole Team

We help each other succeed.

Do you want somebody to watch over your shoulder all day?
Do you want to waste half your time sitting in sullen silence watching somebody else code?

Of course not. Nobody does—especially not people who pair program.

Pair programming is one of the first things people notice about XP. Two people working at the same keyboard? It's weird. It's also extremely powerful and, once you get used to it, tons of fun. Most programmers I know who tried pairing for a month find that they prefer it to programming alone.

Why Pair?

This chapter is called *Thinking*, yet I included pair programming as the first practice. That's because pair programming is all about increasing your brainpower.

When you pair, one person codes—the *driver*. The other person is the *navigator*, whose job is to think. As navigator, sometimes you think about what the driver is typing. (Don't rush to point out missing semicolons, though. That's annoying.) Sometimes you think about what tasks to work on next and sometimes you think about how your work best fits into the overall design.

This arrangement leaves the driver free to work on the tactical challenges of creating rigorous, syntactically correct code without worrying about the big picture, and it gives the navigator the opportunity to consider strategic issues without being distracted by the details of coding. Together, the driver and navigator create higher-quality work more quickly than either could produce on their own.*

Pairing also reinforces good programming habits. XP's reliance on continuous testing and design refinement takes a lot of self-discipline. When pairing, you'll have positive peer pressure to perform these difficult but crucial tasks. You'll spread coding knowledge and tips throughout the team.

You'll also spend more time in *flow*—that highly productive state in which you're totally focused on the code. It's a different kind of flow than normal because you're working with a partner, but it's far more resilient to interruptions. To start with, you'll discover that your office mates are far less likely to interrupt you when you're working with someone. When they do, one person will handle the interruption while the other continues his train of thought. Further, you'll find yourself paying more attention to the conversation with your programming partner than to surrounding noise; it fades into the background.

If that isn't enough, pairing really is a lot of fun. The added brainpower will help you get past roadblocks more easily. For the most part, you'll be collaborating with smart, like-minded people. Plus, if your wrists get sore from typing, you can hand off the keyboard to your partner and continue to be productive.

---

* One study found that pairing takes about 15 percent more effort than one individual working alone, but produces results more quickly and with 15 percent fewer defects [Cockburn & Williams]. Every team is different, so take these results with a grain of salt.

How to Pair

I recommend pair programming on all production code. Many teams who pair frequently, but not exclusively, discover that they find more defects in solo code. A good rule of thumb is to pair on anything that you need to maintain, which includes tests and the build script.

When you start working on a task, ask another programmer to work with you. If another programmer asks for help, make yourself available. Never assign partners: pairs are fluid, forming naturally and shifting throughout the day. Over time, pair with everyone on the team. This will improve team cohesion and spread design skills and knowledge throughout the team.

When you need a fresh perspective, switch partners. I usually switch when I'm feeling frustrated or stuck. Have one person stay on the task and bring the new partner up to speed. Often, even explaining the problem to someone new will help you resolve it.

> Get a fresh perspective by switching partners.

It's a good idea to switch partners several times per day even if you don't feel stuck. This will help keep everyone informed and moving quickly. I switch whenever I finish a task. If I'm working on a big task, I switch within four hours.

When you sit down to pair together, make sure you're physically comfortable. Position your chairs side by side, allowing for each other's personal space, and make sure the monitor is clearly visible. When you're driving, place the keyboard directly in front of you. Keep an eye out for this one—for some reason, people pairing tend to contort themselves to reach the keyboard and mouse rather than moving them closer.

Paired programmers produce code through conversation. As you drive or navigate, think out loud. Take small, frequent design steps—test-driven development works best—and talk about your assumptions, short-term goals, general direction, and any relevant history of the feature or project. If you're confused about something, ask questions. The discussion may enlighten your partner as much as it does you.

Ally
Test-Driven Development (p. 285)

> **NOTE**
> When a pair *goes dark*—talks less, lowers their voices, or doesn't switch off with other pairs—it's often a sign of technical difficulty.

Expect to feel tired at the end of the day. Pairs typically feel that they have worked harder and accomplished more together than when working alone. Practice energized work to maintain your ability to pair every day.

Ally
Energized Work (p. 79)

Driving and Navigating

When you start pairing, expect to feel clumsy and fumble-fingered as you drive. You may feel that your navigator sees ideas and problems much more quickly than you do. She does—navigators have more time to think than drivers do.

> Pairing will feel natural in time.

The situation will be reversed when you navigate. Pairing will feel natural in time.

When navigating, expect to feel like you want to step in and take the keyboard away from your partner. Relax; your driver will often communicate an idea with both words and code. He'll make typos and little mistakes—give him time to correct them himself. Use your extra brainpower to think about the greater picture. What other tests do you need to write? How does this code fit into the rest of the system? Is there duplication you need to remove? Can the code be more clear? Can the overall design be better?

As navigator, help your driver be more productive. Think about what's going to happen next and be prepared with suggestions. When I'm navigating, I like to keep an index card in front of me. Rather than interrupting the driver when I think of an issue, I write my ideas on the index card and wait for a break in the action to bring them up. At the end of the pairing session, I tear up the card and throw it away.

Similarly, when a question arises, take a moment to look up the answer while the driver continues to work. Some teams keep spare laptops on hand for this purpose. If you need more than a few minutes, research the solution together. Sometimes the best way to do this is to split up, pursue parallel lines of inquiry, and come back together to share what you have learned. Spike solutions are a particularly powerful approach.

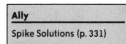

Ally
Spike Solutions (p. 331)

As you pair, switch roles frequently—at least every half hour, and possibly every few minutes. If you're navigating and find yourself telling the driver which keys to press, ask for the keyboard. If you're driving and need a break, pass the keyboard off to your navigator.

PAIRING TIPS

- Pair on everything you'll need to maintain.
- Allow pairs to form fluidly rather than assigning partners.
- Switch partners when you need a fresh perspective.
- Avoid pairing with the same person for more than a day at a time.
- Sit comfortably, side by side.
- Produce code through conversation. Collaborate, don't critique.
- Switch driver and navigator roles frequently.

Pairing Stations

To enjoy pair programming, good pairing stations are essential. You need plenty of room for both people to sit side by side. Typical cubicles, with a workstation located in a corner, won't work. They're uncomfortable and require one person to sit behind another, adding psychological as well as physical barriers to peer collaboration.

You don't need fancy furniture to make a good pairing station; the best ones I've seen are just simple folding tables found at any good office supply store. They should be six feet long, so that two people can sit comfortably side by side, and at least four feet deep. Each table needs a high-powered development workstation. I like to plug in two keyboards and mice so each person can have a set.

Splurge on large monitors so that both people can see clearly. Some teams mirror the display onto two monitors, which makes things a little easier to see, but you may find yourself pointing to the wrong monitor. Others prefer to spread one desktop across two monitors.

NOTE

For ideas about where to put the pairing stations, see "Sit Together" in Chapter 6.

Challenges

Pairing can be uncomfortable at first, as it may require you to collaborate more than you're used to. These feelings are natural and typically go away after a month or two, but you have to face some challenges.

Comfort

It bears repeating: pairing is no fun if you're uncomfortable. When you sit down to pair, adjust your position and equipment so you can sit comfortably. Clear debris off the desk and make sure there's room for your legs, feet, and knees.

Some people (like me) need a lot of personal space. Others like to get up close and personal. When you start to pair, discuss your personal space needs and ask about your partner's.

Similarly, while it goes without saying that personal hygiene is critical, remember that strong flavors such as coffee, garlic, onions, and spicy foods can lead to foul breath. Decide as a team, *before* any issues come up, how to notify people of challenging personal habits respectfully.

Mismatched Skills

Pairing is a collaboration between peers, but sometimes a senior developer will pair with a junior developer. Rather than treating these occasions as student/teacher situations, restore the peer balance by creating opportunities for both participants to learn. For example, if you know you'll be pairing with a junior developer, you can ask him to research a topic that no one else knows, such as the inner workings of a library that the team depends on. Give everyone a chance to be an expert.

Communication style

New drivers sometimes have difficulty involving their partners; they can take over the keyboard and shut down communication. To practice communicating and switching roles while pairing, consider *ping-pong pairing*. In this exercise, one person writes a test. The other person makes it pass and writes a new test. Then the first person makes it pass and repeats the process by writing another test.

> **Ally**
>
> Test-Driven Development (p. 285)

The flip side of too little communication is too much communication—or rather, too much blunt communication. Frank criticism of code and design is valuable, but it may be difficult to appreciate at first. Different people have different thresholds, so pay attention to how your partner receives your comments. Try transforming declarations (such as "This method is too long") into questions or suggestions ("Could we make this method shorter?" or "Should we extract this code block into a new method?"). Adopt an attitude of collaborative problem solving.

Tools and keybindings

Even if you don't fall victim to the endless vi versus emacs editor war, you may find your coworkers' tool preferences annoying. Try to standardize on a particular toolset. Some teams even create a standard image and check it into version control. When you discuss coding standards, discuss these issues as well.

Ally

Coding Standards (p. 133)

Questions

Isn't it wasteful to have two people do the work of one?

In pair programming, two people aren't really doing the work of one. Although only one keyboard is in use, there's more to programming than that. As Ward Cunningham said, "If you don't think carefully, you might think that programming is just typing statements in a programming language."[*] In pair programming, one person is programming and the other is thinking ahead, anticipating problems, and strategizing.

If you're looking for hard data, [Williams] has a chapter on pairing research. Keep in mind that the number of variables in software development make it notoriously difficult to conduct large-scale controlled studies. Sometimes the best way to know whether something will work for your team is just to try it.

How can I convince my team or organization to try pair programming?

Ask permission to try it as an experiment. Set aside a month in which everyone pairs on all production code. Be sure to keep going for the entire month, as pair programming may be difficult and uncomfortable for the first few weeks.

Don't just ask permission of management; be sure your fellow team members are interested in trying pairing as well. The only programmers I know who tried pairing for a month and didn't like it are the ones who were forced to do it against their will.

Do we really have to pair program all the time?

This is a decision that your whole team should make together. Before you decide, try pairing on all production code (everything you need to maintain) for a month. You may enjoy it more than you expect.

Regardless of your rule, you will still produce code that you don't need to maintain. (Spike solutions are one example.) These may benefit from individual study.

Some production tasks are so repetitive that they don't require the extra brainpower a pair provides. Before abandoning pairing, however, consider why your design requires so much repetition. It could be an indication of a design flaw. Use the navigator's extra time to think about design improvements and consider discussing it with your whole team.

> If you're bored while pairing, consider how you can make your design less repetitive.

Ally

Simple Design (p. 314)

How can I concentrate with someone talking to me?

When you navigate, you shouldn't have too much trouble staying several steps ahead

---

[*] *http://en.wikiquote.org/wiki/Ward_Cunningham*

of your driver. If you do have trouble, ask your driver to think out loud so you can understand her thought process.

As driver, you may sometimes find that you're having trouble concentrating. Let your navigator know—she may have a suggestion that will help you get through the roadblock. At other times, you may just need a few moments of silence to think through the problem.

If you find yourself in this situation a lot, you may be taking steps that are too large. Use test-driven development and take very small steps. Rely on your navigator to keep track of what you still need to do (tell him if you have an idea; he'll write it down) and focus only on the few lines of code needed to make the next test pass.

> If you have trouble concentrating, try taking smaller steps.

If you are working with a technology you don't completely understand, consider taking a few minutes to work on a spike solution. You and your partner can work on this together or separately.

Allies

Test-Driven Development (p. 285)

Spike Solutions (p. 331)

What if we have an odd number of programmers?

A programmer flying solo can do productive tasks that don't involve production code. She can research new technologies, or learn more about a technology the team is using. She can pair with a customer or tester to review recent changes, polish the application, or do exploratory testing. She can be the team's batman (see "Iteration Planning" in Chapter 8).

Alternatively, a solo programmer may wish to spend some time reviewing the overall design—either to improve his own understanding, or to come up with ideas for improving problem areas. If a large refactoring is partially complete, the team may wish to authorize a conscientious programmer to finish those refactorings.

If your team is on the smaller side, you may run out of useful solo tasks. In this case, consider relaxing the "no production code" rule or bringing in another programmer.

There are only two (or three) of us. Should we still pair all the time?

Even a saint will get on your nerves if you have to pair with him day-in, day-out. Use your own judgment about when to pair and when you need time to yourself. If you feel fine but your partner is getting cranky, don't escalate; just say *you're* tired and need a break.

I pair programmed with the same person for three months straight during a two-person project. I think it helped that we had a large office and a big desk; it gave us room to move around. We also kept a mini-fridge stocked with goodies.

Even with these comforts, I had my cranky moments. Perhaps the most important factor was that my partner was a very laid-back, easy-going person who put up with my occasional bad mood.

We get engrossed in our work and forget to switch pairs. How can we encourage more frequent pair switching?

One approach is to remember that you can switch when you feel stuck or frustrated. In fact, that is a perfect time to switch partners and get a fresh perspective.

Some teams use kitchen timers to switch partners at strictly defined intervals. [Belshee] reports interesting results from switching every 90 minutes. While this could be a great way to get in the habit of switching pairs, make sure everybody is willing to try it.

How can we pair remotely?

You can use a phone headset and a desktop sharing tool such as VNC or NetMeeting to pair remotely. I have heard of teams who use individual workstations with shared screen sessions and VoIP applications.

When I tried this, I found it to be a poor substitute for pairing in person. XP teams usually sit together, so remote pairing isn't often necessary.

Results

When you pair program well, you find yourself focusing intently on the code and on your work with your partner. You experience fewer interruptions and distractions. When interrupted, one person deals with the problem while the other continues working. Afterward, you slide back into the flow of work immediately. At the end of the day, you feel tired yet satisfied. You enjoy the intense focus and the camaraderie of working with your teammates.

The team as a whole enjoys higher quality code. Technical debt decreases. Knowledge travels quickly through the team, raising everyone's level of competence and helping to integrate new team members quickly.

Contraindications

Pairing requires a comfortable work environment (see "Sit Together" in Chapter 6 for design options). Most offices and cubicles just aren't set up that way. If your workspace doesn't allow programmers to sit side by side comfortably, either change the workspace or don't pair program.

Similarly, if your team doesn't sit together, pairing may not work for you. Although you can pair remotely, it's not as good as in-person.

Programmer resistance may be another reason to avoid pairing. Pairing is a big change to programmers' work styles and you may encounter resistance. I usually work around this by asking people to try it for a month or two before making a final decision. If they still resist, you're probably better off avoiding pairing rather than forcing anyone to pair against his will.

Alternatives

Pairing is a very powerful tool. It reduces defects, improves design quality, shares knowledge amongst team members, supports self-discipline, and reduces distractions, all without sacrificing productivity. If you cannot pair program, you need alternatives.

Formal code inspections can reduce defects, improve quality, and support self-discipline. However, my experience is that programmers have trouble including inspections in their schedules, even when they're in favor of them. Pairing is easier to do consistently, and it provides feedback much more quickly than scheduled inspections. If you're going to use inspections in place of pairing, add some sort of support mechanism to help them take place.

Inspections alone are unlikely to share knowledge as thoroughly as collective code ownership requires. If you cannot pair program, consider avoiding collective ownership, at least at first.

If you'd still like to have collective code ownership, you need an alternative mechanism for sharing knowledge about the state of the codebase. I've formed regular study groups in which programmers meet daily for a timeboxed half-hour to review and discuss the design.

I'm not aware of any other tool that helps reduce distractions as well as pair programming does. However, I find that I succumb to more frequent distractions when I'm tired. In the absence of pairing, put more emphasis on energized work.

Ally
Energized Work (p. 79)

Further Reading

Pair Programming Illuminated [Williams] discusses pair programming in depth.

"The Costs and Benefits of Pair Programming" [Cockburn & Williams] reports on Laurie Williams' initial study of pair programming.

"Promiscuous Pairing and Beginner's Mind: Embrace Inexperience" [Belshee] is an intriguing look at the benefits of switching pairs at strict intervals.

"Adventures in Promiscuous Pairing: Seeking Beginner's Mind" [Lacey] explores the costs and challenges of promiscuous pairing. It's a must-read if you plan to try Belshee's approach.

Peer Reviews in Software: A Practical Guide [Wiegers 2001] discusses formal inspections and peer reviews.

Energized Work

Audience
Coaches, Whole Team

We work at a pace that allows us to do our best, most productive work indefinitely.

I enjoy programming. I enjoy solving problems, writing good code, watching tests pass, and especially removing code while refactoring. I program in my spare time and sometimes even think about work in the shower.

In other words, I love my work. Yet put me on a team with unclear goals, little collective responsibility, and infighting, and I'll wake up dreading going into work. I'll put in my hours at the office, but I'll be tempted to spend my mornings reading email and my afternoons picking at code while surfing through marginally related technical web sites.

We've all been in this situation. Because we're professionals, we strive to produce quality work even when we feel demoralized. Still, consider the times of greatest productivity in your career. Do you notice a big difference when you wake up and feel blessed to go into work? Isn't it much more satisfying to leave on time at the end of the day, knowing that you accomplished something solid and useful?

XP's practice of *energized work* recognizes that, although professionals can do good work under difficult circumstances, they do their best, most productive work when they're energized and motivated.

How to Be Energized

One of the simplest ways to be energized is to take care of yourself. Go home on time every day. Spend time with family and friends and engage in activities that take your mind off of work. Eat healthy foods, exercise, and get plenty of sleep.

> Go home on time.

While you're busy with these other things, your brain will turn over the events of the day. You'll often have new insights in the morning.

If quality time off is the yin of energized work, focused work is the yang. While at work, give it your full attention. Turn off interruptions such as email and instant messaging. Silence your phones. Ask your project manager to shield you from unnecessary meetings and organizational politics.

When the yin and yang mesh perfectly, you'll wake up in the morning well-rested and eager to start your day. At the end of the day, you'll be tired—though not exhausted—and satisfied with the work you've done.

This isn't easy. Energized work requires a supportive workplace and home life. It's also a personal choice; there's no way to force someone to be energized. However, you can remove roadblocks.

Supporting Energized Work

One of my favorite techniques as a coach is to remind people to go home on time. Tired people make mistakes and take shortcuts. The resulting errors can end up costing more than the work is worth. This is particularly true when someone is sick; in addition to doing poor work, she could infect other people.

> Stay home when you're sick. You risk getting other people sick, too.

Pair programming is another way to encourage energized work. It encourages focus like no other practice I know. After a full day of pairing, you'll be tired but satisfied. It's particularly useful when you're not at your best: pairing with someone who's alert can help you stay focused.

Ally

Pair Programming (p. 71)

It may sound silly, but having healthy food available in the workplace is another good way to support energized work. Breakfast really is the most important meal of the day. Mid-afternoon lows are also common. Cereal, milk, vegetables, and energy snacks are a good choice. Donuts and junk food, while popular, contribute to the mid-afternoon crash.

The nature of the work also makes a difference. [McConnell 1996] reports that software developers are motivated to do good, intellectually challenging work. Not every project can feed the poor or solve NP-complete problems, but a clear, compelling statement of why the product is important can go a long way. Creating and communicating this vision is the product manager's responsibility.

Ally

Vision (p. 201)

An achievable goal goes hand-in-hand with a compelling vision. Nothing destroys morale faster than being held accountable for an unachievable goal. The planning game addresses this issue by combining customer value with developer estimates to create achievable plans.

Ally

The Planning Game (p. 219)

Speaking of plans, every organization has some amount of politics. Sometimes, politics lead to healthy negotiation and compromising. Other times, they lead to unreasonable demands and blaming. The project manager should deal with these politics, letting the team know what's important and shielding them from what isn't.

The project manager can also help team members do fulfilling work by pushing back unnecessary meetings and conference calls. Providing an informative workspace and appropriate reporting can eliminate the need for status meetings. In an environment with a lot of external distractions, consider setting aside core hours each day—maybe just an hour or two to start—during which everyone agrees not to interrupt the team.

Allies

Informative Workspace (p. 83)

Reporting (p. 144)

Finally, jelled teams have a lot of energy. They're a lot of fun, too. You can recognize a jelled team by how much its members enjoy spending time together. They go to lunch together, share in-jokes, and may even socialize outside of work. As with energized work, you can't force jelling, but you can encourage it; many of XP's practices do so. The classic work on this subject, [DeMarco & Lister 1999]'s *Peopleware*, is well worth reading.

Taking Breaks

When you make more mistakes than progress, it's time to take a break. If you're like me, that's the hardest time to stop. I feel like the solution is just around the corner—even if it's been just around the corner for the last 45 minutes—and I don't want to stop until I find it. That's why it's helpful for

> Stop when you're making more mistakes than progress.

someone else to remind me to stop. After a break or a good night's sleep, I usually see my mistake right away.

Sometimes a snack or walk around the building is good enough. For programmers, switching pairs can help. If it's already the end of the day, though, going home is a good idea.

You can usually tell when somebody needs a break. Angry concentration, cursing at the computer, and abrupt movements are all signs. In a highly collaborative environment, *going dark*—not talking—can also be a sign that someone needs a break. When I notice a pair of programmers whispering to each other, I ask how long it's been since their last passing test. I often get a sheepish reply, and that's when I remind them to take a break.

Suggesting a break requires a certain amount of delicacy. If someone respects you as a leader, then you might be able to just tell him to stop working. Otherwise, get him away from the problem for a minute so he can clear his head. Try asking him to help you for a moment, or to take a short walk with you to discuss some issue you're facing.

Questions

What if I'm not ready to check in my code and it's time to go home?

If you're practicing test-driven development and continuous integration, your code should be ready to check in every few minutes. If you're struggling with a problem and can't check in, go home anyway. Often the answer will be obvious in the morning.

Allies

Test-Driven Development (p. 285)

Continuous Integration (p. 183)

Some teams revert (delete) code that doesn't pass all its tests at the end of the day. This sounds harsh, but it's a good idea: if you can't easily check in, you've gone far off track. You'll do better work in the morning. If you're practicing continuous integration well, the loss of code will be minimal and you'll still have learned from the experience.

I work in a startup and 40 hours just isn't enough. Can I work longer hours?

A startup environment often has a lot of excitement and camaraderie. This leads to more energy and might mean that you can work long hours and still focus. On the other hand, startups sometimes confuse long work hours with dedication to the cause. Be careful not to let dedication override your good judgment about when you're too tired to make useful contributions.

> If you dread going to work in the morning, you aren't energized.

We have an important deadline and there's no way to make it without putting our heads down and pushing through. Do we set aside energized work for now?

A sprint to the finish line might boost your energy. There's nothing quite like a late-night codefest when the team brings in pizza, everybody works hard, all cylinders fire, and the work comes together at the last moment. A great sprint can help the team jell, giving it a sense of accomplishment in the face of adversity. However...

Sprinting to the finish line is one thing; sprinting for miles is another. Extended overtime will not solve your schedule problems. In fact, it has serious negative consequences. DeMarco calls extended overtime "an important productivity-reduction technique," leading to reduced quality, personnel burnout, increased turnover of staff, and ineffective use of time during normal hours [DeMarco 2002, p. 64].

> Extended overtime will not solve your schedule problems.

If you work overtime one week (whatever "overtime" means in your situation), don't work overtime again the next week. If I see a team sprinting more than once or twice per quarter, I look for deeper problems.

Results

When your team is energized, there's a sense of excitement and camaraderie. As a group, you pay attention to detail and look for opportunities to improve your work habits. You make consistent progress every week and feel able to maintain that progress indefinitely. You value health over short-term progress and feel productive and successful.

Contraindications

Energized work is not an excuse to goof off. Generate trust by putting in a fair day's work.

Some organizations may make energized work difficult. If your organization uses the number of hours worked as a yardstick to judge dedication, you may be better off sacrificing energized work and working long hours. The choice between quality of life and career advancement is a personal one that only you and your family can make.

Alternatives

If your organization makes energized work difficult, mistakes are more likely. Pair programming can help tired programmers stay focused and catch each other's errors. Additional testing may be necessary to find the extra defects. If you can, add additional contingency time to your release plan for fixing them.

> **Ally**
> Pair Programming (p. 71)

The extreme form of this sort of organization is the *death march* organization, which requires (or "strongly encourages") employees to work extensive overtime week after week. Sadly, "Death march projects are the norm, not the exception" [Yourdon, p. ix].

To add insult to injury, [DeMarco & Lister 2003, p. 161] weighs in: "In our experience, the one common characteristic among death-march projects is low expected value. They are projects aimed at putting out products of monumental insignificance. The only real justification for the death march is that with value so minuscule, doing the project at normal cost would clearly result in costs that are greater than benefits... if the project is so essential, why can't the company spend the time and money to do it properly?"

Further Reading

Peopleware [DeMarco & Lister 1999] is a classic work on programmer motivation and productivity. It should be at the top of every software development manager's reading list.

Rapid Development [McConnell 1996] has a chapter called "Motivation" with a nice chart comparing programmer motivations to the motivations of managers and the general population.

Slack [DeMarco 2002] looks at the effects of extended overtime and overscheduling.

Death March [Yourdon] describes how to survive a "death march" project.

Informative Workspace

We are tuned in to the status of our project.

Your workspace is the cockpit of your development effort. Just as a pilot surrounds himself with information necessary to fly a plane, arrange your workspace with information necessary to steer your project: create an informative workspace.

An *informative workspace* broadcasts information into the room. When people take a break, they will sometimes wander over and stare at the information surrounding them. Sometimes, that brief zone-out will result in an aha moment of discovery.

An informative workspace also allows people to sense the state of the project just by walking into the room. It conveys status information without interrupting team members and helps improve stakeholder trust.

Subtle Cues

The essence of an informative workspace is *information*. One simple source of information is the feel of the room. A healthy project is energized. There's a buzz in the air—not tension, but activity. People converse, work together, and make the occasional joke. It's not rushed or hurried, but it's clearly productive. When a pair needs help, other pairs notice, lend their assistance, then return to their tasks. When a pair completes something well, everyone celebrates for a moment.

> Simply poking your head into a project room should give you information about the project.

An unhealthy project is quiet and tense. Team members don't talk much, if at all. It feels drab and bleak. People live by the clock, punching in and punching out—or worse, watching to see who is the first one to dare to leave.

Besides the feel of the room, other cues communicate useful information quickly and subconsciously. If the build token is away from the integration machine, it's not safe to check out the code right now. By mid-iteration, unless about half the cards on the iteration plan are done, the team is going faster or slower than anticipated.

An informative workspace also provides ways for people to communicate. This usually means plenty of whiteboards around the walls and stacks of index cards. A collaborative design sketch on a whiteboard can often communicate an idea far more quickly and effectively than a half-hour PowerPoint presentation. Index cards are great for Class-Responsibility Collaboration (CRC) design sessions, retrospectives, and planning with user stories.

> You can never have too many whiteboards.

> NOTE
>
> Whiteboard design sessions labelled "Do Not Erase" for more than a few days may indicate a problem. Any programmer on the team should be able to re-create the design from memory, perhaps with a bit of help from reviewing the source code. If permanent design diagrams are indispensible, you may benefit from simplifying your design and sharing code ownership.

Big Visible Charts

An essential aspect of an informative workspace is the *big visible chart*. The goal of a big visible chart is to display information so simply and unambiguously that it communicates even from across the room.

The iteration and release planning boards are ubiquitous examples of such a chart. You'll see variants of these planning boards in every XP project. For examples, see the release planning board shown in Figure 8-4 and the iteration planning board shown in Figure 8-9.

Another useful status chart is a team calendar, which shows important dates, iteration numbers, and when team members will be out of the office (along with contact information, if appropriate). A large plastic perpetual calendar, available at most office supply stores, works well here.

Hand-Drawn Charts

Avoid the reflexive temptation to computerize your charts. The benefits of the informative workspace stem from the information being constantly visible from everywhere in the room. It's difficult and expensive for computerized charts to meet that criterion; you'd have to install plasma screens or projectors everywhere.

Don't rush to computerize.

Even if you can afford big screens everywhere, you will constantly change the types of charts you display. This is easier with flip charts and whiteboards than with computers, as creating or modifying a chart is as simple as drawing with pen and paper. Don't let a spreadsheet or project management software constrain what you can track.

Process Improvement Charts

One type of big visible chart measures specific issues that the team wants to improve. Often, the issues come up during a retrospective. Unlike the planning boards or team calendar, which stay posted, post these charts only as long as necessary.

Ally
Retrospectives (p. 91)

Create process improvement charts as a team decision, and maintain them as a team responsibility. When you agree to create a chart, agree to keep it up-to-date. For some charts, this means taking 30 seconds to mark the board when the status changes. Each team member should update his own status. Some charts involve collecting some information at the end of the day. For these, collectively choose someone to update the chart.

There are many possible types of process improvement charts; they take forms as diverse as the types of problems that teams experience. The principle behind all of them is the same: they appeal to our innate desire for improvement. If you show progress toward a mutual goal, people will usually try to improve their status.

> **NOTE**
> I try to create charts in which a line going up or a box filled in indicates improvement. It's a small way to improve clarity. Don't knock yourself out trying to follow this guideline, though: it's more important to get back to work than to twist your measurements to make a line go up rather than down.

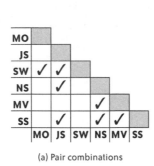

(a) Pair combinations

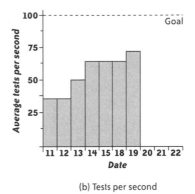

(b) Tests per second

Figure 5-1. Sample process improvement charts

Consider the problems you're facing and what kind of chart, if any, would help. As an example, XP teams have successfully used charts to help improve:

- Amount of pairing, by tracking the percentage of time spent pairing versus the percentage of time spent flying solo
- Pair switching, by tracking how many of the possible pairing combinations actually paired during each iteration (see Figure 5-1)
- Build performance, by tracking the number of tests executed per second
- Support responsiveness, by tracking the age of the oldest support request (an early chart, which tracked the *number* of outstanding requests, resulted in hard requests being ignored)
- Needless interruptions, by tracking the number of hours spent on nonstory work each iteration

Try not to go overboard with your process improvement charts. If you post too many, they'll lose their effectiveness. My maximum is three to five charts. That's not to say that your only decorations should be a handful of charts. Team memorabilia, toys, and works in progress are also welcome. Just make sure the important charts stand out.

Gaming

Although having too many process improvement charts can reduce their impact, a bigger problem occurs when the team has too *much* interest in a chart, that is, in improving a number on a chart. They often start gaming the process. *Gaming* occurs when people try to improve a number at the expense of overall progress.

For example, if programmers focus too much on improving the number of tests in the system, they might be reluctant to remove out-of-date tests, making maintenance more difficult, or they might add unnecessary or redundant tests. They may not even realize they're doing so.

To alleviate this problem, use process improvement charts with discretion. Discuss new charts as a team. Carefully tie charts to the results you want to see. Review their use often and take them down after an iteration or two. By that time, a chart has either done its job or it isn't going to help.

Above all, never use workspace charts in performance evaluations. Don't report them outside the team. People who feel judged according to their performance on a chart are much more likely to engage in gaming. See "Reporting" in Chapter 6 for ideas about what to report instead.

> Never use workspace charts in a performance evaluation.

Questions

We need to share status with people who can't or won't visit the team workspace regularly. How do we do that without computerized charts?

A digital camera can effectively capture a whiteboard or other chart. You can even point a webcam at a chart and webcast it. Get creative.

Remember, though, that most information in the team workspace is for the team's use only. Reporting team progress outside of the team is a separate issue.

Ally

Reporting (p. 144)

Our charts are constantly out of date. How can I get team members to keep them up-to-date?

The first question to ask is, "Did the team really agree to this chart?" An informative workspace is for the team's benefit, so if team members aren't keeping a chart up-to-date, they may not think that it's beneficial. It's possible that the team is passively-aggressively ignoring the chart rather than telling you that they don't want it.

I find that when no one updates the charts, it's because I'm being too controlling about them. Dialing back the amount of involvement I have with the charts is often enough to get the team to step in. Sometimes that means putting up with not-quite-perfect charts or sloppy handwriting, but it pays off.

> If people won't take responsibility, perhaps you're being too controlling.

If all else fails, discuss the issue during the retrospective or a stand-up meeting. Share your frustration, and ask for the team's help in resolving the issue. Prepare to abandon some favorite charts if the team doesn't need them.

Results

When you have an informative workspace, you have up-to-the-minute information about all the important issues your team is facing. You know exactly how far you've come and how far you have to go in your current plan, you know whether the team is progressing well or having difficulty, and you know how well you're solving problems.

Contraindications

If your team doesn't sit together in a shared workspace, you probably won't be able to create an effective informative workspace.

Alternatives

If your team doesn't sit together, but has adjacent cubicles or offices, you might be able to achieve some of the benefits of an informative workspace by posting information in the halls or a common area. Teams that are more widely distributed may use electronic tools supplemented with daily stand-up meetings.

Ally
Stand-Up Meetings (p. 129)

A traditional alternative is the weekly status meeting, but I find these dreary wastes of time that delay and confuse important information.

Further Reading

Agile Software Development [Cockburn] has an interesting section called "Convection Currents of Information" that describes information as heat and big visible charts as "information radiators."

Root-Cause Analysis

We prevent mistakes by fixing our process.

Audience
Whole Team

When I hear about a serious mistake on my project, my natural reaction is to get angry or frustrated. I want to blame someone for screwing up.

Unfortunately, this response ignores the reality of Murphy's Law. If something can go wrong, it will. People are, well, people. Everybody makes mistakes. I certainly do. Aggressively laying blame might cause people to hide their mistakes, or to try to pin them on others, but this dysfunctional behavior won't actually *prevent* mistakes.

Instead of getting angry, I try to remember Norm Kerth's Prime Directive: everybody is doing the best job they can given their abilities and knowledge (see "Retrospectives" later in this chapter for the full text of the Prime Directive). Rather than blaming people, I blame the process. What is it about the way we work that allowed this mistake to happen? How can we change the way we work so that it's harder for something to go wrong?

This is *root-cause analysis*.

How to Find the Root Cause

A classic approach to root-cause analysis is to ask "why" five times. Here's a real-world example.

Problem: When we start working on a new task, we spend a lot of time getting the code into a working state.

Why? Because the build is often broken in source control.

Why? Because people check in code without running their tests.

It's easy to stop here and say, "Aha! We found the problem. People need to run their tests before checking in." That *is* a correct answer, as running tests before check-in is part of continuous integration. But it's also already part of the process. People know they should run the tests, they just aren't doing it. Dig deeper.

Why don't they run tests before checking in? Because sometimes the tests take longer to run than people have available.

Why do the tests take so long? Because tests spend a lot of time in database setup and teardown.

Why? Because our design makes it difficult to test business logic without touching the database.

Asking "why" five times reveals a much more interesting answer than "people aren't running tests." It helps you move away from blaming team members and toward identifying an underlying, fixable problem. In this example, the solution is clear, if not easy: the design needs improvement.

How to Fix the Root Cause

Root-cause analysis is a technique you can use for every problem you encounter, from the trivial to the significant. You can ask yourself "why" at any time. You can even fix some problems just by improving your own work habits.

More often, however, fixing root causes requires other people to cooperate. If your team has control over the root cause, gather the team members, share your thoughts, and ask for their help in solving the problem. A retrospective might be a good time for this.

Ally

Retrospectives (p. 91)

If the root cause is outside the team's control entirely, then solving the problem may be difficult or impossible. For example, if your problem is "not enough pairing" and you identify the root cause as "we need more comfortable desks," your team may need the help of Facilities to fix it.

In this case, solving the problem is a matter of coordinating with the larger organization. Your project manager should be able to help. In the meantime, consider alternate solutions that *are* within your control.

When Not to Fix the Root Cause

When you first start applying root-cause analysis, you'll find many more problems than you can address simultaneously. Work on a few at a time. I like to chip away at the biggest problem while simultaneously picking off low-hanging fruit.

Over time, work will go more smoothly. Mistakes will become less severe and less frequent. Eventually —it can take months or years—mistakes will be notably rare.

At this point, you may face the temptation to over-apply root-cause analysis. Beware of thinking that you can prevent all possible mistakes. Fixing a root cause may add overhead to the process. Before changing the process, ask yourself whether the problem is common enough to warrant the overhead.

> A mistake-proof process is neither achievable nor desirable.

Questions

Who should participate in root-cause analysis?

I usually conduct root-cause analysis in the privacy of my own thoughts, then share my conclusions and reasoning with others. Include whomever is necessary to fix the root cause.

When should we conduct root-cause analysis?

You can use root-cause analysis any time you notice a problem—when you find a bug, when you notice a mistake, as you're navigating, and in retrospectives. It need only take a few seconds. Keep your brain turned on and use root-cause analysis all the time.

We know what our problems are. Why do we need to bother with root-cause analysis?

If you already understand the underlying causes of your problems, and you're making progress on fixing them, then you have already conducted root-cause analysis. However, it's easy to get stuck on a particular solution. Asking "why" five times may give you new insight.

How do we avoid blaming individuals?

If your root cause points to an individual, ask "why" again. Why did that person do what she did? How was it possible for her to make that mistake? Keep digging until you learn how to prevent that mistake in the future.

Keep in mind that lectures and punitive approaches are usually ineffective. It's better to make it difficult for people to make mistakes than to expect them always to do the right thing.

Results

When root-cause analysis is an instinctive reaction, your team values fixing problems rather than placing blame. Your first reaction to a problem is to ask how it could have possibly happened. Rather than feeling threatened by problems and trying to hide them, you raise them publicly and work to solve them.

Contraindications

The primary danger of root-cause analysis is that, ultimately, every problem has a cause outside of your control.

Don't use this as an excuse not to take action. If a root cause is beyond your control, work with someone (such as your project manager) who has experience coordinating with other groups. In the meantime, solve the intermediate problems. Focus on what *is* in your control.

Although few organizations actively discourage root-cause analysis, you may find that it is socially unacceptable. If your efforts are called "disruptive" or a "waste of time," you may be better off avoiding root-cause analysis.

Alternatives

You can always perform root-cause analysis in the privacy of your thoughts. You'll probably find that a lot of causes are beyond your control. Try to channel your frustration into energy for fixing processes that you can influence.

Retrospectives

We continually improve our work habits.

No process is perfect. Your team is unique, as are the situations you encounter, and they change all the time. You must continually update your process to match your changing situations. *Retrospectives* are a great tool for doing so.

Types of Retrospectives

The most common retrospective, the *iteration retrospective*, occurs at the end of every iteration.

In addition to iteration retrospectives, you can also conduct longer, more intensive retrospectives at crucial milestones. These *release retrospectives*, *project retrospectives*, and *surprise retrospectives* (conducted when an unexpected event changes your situation) give you a chance to reflect more deeply on your experiences and condense key lessons to share with the rest of the organization.

These other retrospectives are out of the scope of this book. They work best when conducted by neutral third parties, so consider bringing in an experienced retrospective facilitator. Larger organizations may have such facilitators on staff (start by asking the HR department), or you can bring in an outside consultant. If you'd like to conduct them yourself, [Derby & Larsen] and [Kerth] are great resources.

How to Conduct an Iteration Retrospective

Anybody can facilitate an iteration retrospective if the team gets along well. An experienced, neutral facilitator is best to start with. When the retrospectives run smoothly, give other people a chance to try.

Everyone on the team should participate in each retrospective. In order to give participants a chance to speak their minds openly, non–team members should not attend.

I timebox my retrospectives to exactly one hour. Your first few retrospectives will probably run long. Give it an extra half-hour, but don't be shy about politely wrapping up and moving to the next step. The whole team will get better with practice, and the next retrospective is only a week away.

I keep the following schedule in mind as I conduct a retrospective. Don't try to match the schedule exactly; let events follow their natural pace:

1. Norm Kerth's Prime Directive
2. Brainstorming (30 minutes)
3. Mute Mapping (10 minutes)
4. Retrospective objective (20 minutes)

After you've acclimated to this format, change it. The retrospective is a great venue for trying new ideas. [Derby & Larsen] is full of ideas for iteration retrospectives.

Retrospectives are a powerful tool that can actually be damaging when conducted poorly. The process I describe here skips some important safety exercises for the sake of brevity. Pay particular attention to the contraindications before trying this practice.

Step 1: The Prime Directive

In his essay, "The Effective Post-Fire Critique," New York City Fire Department Chief Frank Montagna writes:

> Firefighters, as all humans, make mistakes. When firefighters make a mistake on the job, however, it can be life-threatening to themselves, to their coworkers, and to the public they serve. Nonetheless, firefighters will continue to make mistakes and on occasion will repeat a mistake.

Everyone makes mistakes, even when lives are on the line. The retrospective is an opportunity to learn and improve. The team should never use the retrospective to place blame or attack individuals.

> Never use a retrospective to place blame or attack individuals.

As facilitator, it's your job to nip destructive behavior in the bud. To this end, I start each retrospective by repeating Norm Kerth's *Prime Directive*. I write it at the top of the whiteboard:

> Regardless of what we discover today, we understand and truly believe that everyone did the best job they could, given what they knew at the time, their skills and abilities, the resources available, and the situation at hand.

I ask each attendee in turn if he agrees to the Prime Directive and wait for a verbal "yes." If not, I ask if he can set aside his skepticism just for this one meeting. If an attendee still won't agree, I won't conduct the retrospective.

NOTE

If someone speaks once during a retrospective, she is more likely to speak again. By waiting for *verbal* agreement, you encourage more participation.

Step 2: Brainstorming

If everyone agrees to the Prime Directive, hand out index cards and pencils, then write the following headings on the whiteboard:

- Enjoyable
- Frustrating
- Puzzling
- Same
- More
- Less

Ask the group to reflect on the events of the iteration and brainstorm ideas that fall into these categories. Think of events that were enjoyable, frustrating, and puzzling, and consider what you'd like to see increase, decrease, and remain the same. Write each idea on a separate index card. As facilitator, you can write down your ideas, too—just be careful not to dominate the discussion.

People can come up with as many ideas as they like. Five to 10 each is typical. There's no need to have an idea in each category, or to limit the ideas in a category. Any topic is fair game, from the banal ("more cookies") to the taboo ("frustrating: impossible deadline"). If people are reluctant to say what they really think, try reading the cards anonymously.

Ask people to read out their cards as they finish each one, then hand them in. Stick the cards up on the board under their headings. If you don't have a ferrous whiteboard, use sticky notes instead of index cards.

If people have trouble getting started, describe what happened during the iteration. ("Wednesday, we had our planning session....") This approach takes longer, but it might be a good way to jump-start things when you first start doing retrospectives.

As people read their cards, others will come up with new ideas. The conversation will feed on itself. Don't worry if two people suggest the same idea—just put them all up on the board. Expect several dozen cards, at least.

As the conversation winds down, check the time. If you have plenty of extra time, let the silences stretch out. Someone will often say something that he has held back, and this may start a new round of ideas. If you're running out of time, however, take advantage of the pause to move on to the next stage.

Step 3: Mute Mapping

Mute mapping is a variant of affinity mapping in which no one speaks. It's a great way to categorize a lot of ideas quickly.

You need plenty of space for this. Invite everyone to stand up, go over to the whiteboard, and slide cards around. There are three rules:

1. Put related cards close together.
2. Put unrelated cards far apart.
3. No talking.

If two people disagree on where to place a card, they have to work out a compromise without talking.

This exercise should take about 10 minutes, depending on the size of the team. As before, when activity dies down, check the time and either wait for more ideas or move on.

Once mute mapping is complete, there should be clear groups of cards on the whiteboard. Ask everyone to sit down, then take a marker and draw a circle around each group. Don't try to identify the groups yet; just draw the circles. If you have a couple of outlier cards, draw circles around those, too. Each circle represents a category. You can have as many as you need.

Once you have circled the categories, read a sampling of cards from each circle and ask the team to name the category. Don't try to come up with a perfect name, and don't move cards between categories. (There's always next time.) Help the group move quickly through this step. The names aren't that important, and trying for perfection can easily drag this step out.

Finally, after you have circled and named all the categories, vote on which categories should be improved during the next iteration. I like to hand out little magnetic dots to represent votes; stickers also work well. Give each person five votes. Participants can put all their votes on one category if they wish, or spread their votes amongst several categories.

Step 4: Retrospective Objective

After the voting ends, one category should be the clear winner. If not, don't spend too much time; flip a coin or something.

Discard the cards from the other categories. If someone wants to take a card to work on individually, that's fine, but not necessary. Remember, you'll do another retrospective next week. Important issues will recur.

NOTE
Frustrated that your favorite category lost? Wait a month or two. If it's important, it will win eventually.

Now that the team has picked a category to focus on, it's time to come up with options for improving it. This is a good time to apply your root-cause analysis skills. Read the cards in the category again, then brainstorm some ideas. Half a dozen should suffice.

Ally
Root-Cause Analysis (p. 88)

Don't be too detailed when coming up with ideas for improvement. A general direction is good enough. For example, if "pairing" is the issue, then "switching pairs more often" could be one suggestion, "ping-pong pairing" could be another, and "switching at specific times" could be a third.

When you have several ideas, ask the group which one they think is best. If there isn't a clear consensus, vote.

This final vote is your *retrospective objective*. Pick just one—it will help you focus. The retrospective objective is the goal that the whole team will work toward during the next iteration. Figure out how to keep track of the objective and who should work out the details.

After the Retrospective

The retrospective serves two purposes: sharing ideas gives the team a chance to grow closer, and coming up with a specific solution gives the team a chance to improve.

The thing I dislike about iteration retrospectives is that they often don't lead to specific changes. It's easy to leave the retrospective and think, "Well, that's done until next week." If you're like me, the ensuing lack of action can be a little frustrating.

To avoid this frustration, make sure someone is responsible for following through on the retrospective objective. It's not that person's job to push or own the objective—that's for the whole team—but it is his job to remind people when appropriate.

To encourage follow-through, make the retrospective objective part of the iteration. For general behavior changes, such as "switch pairs more often," consider adding a big visible chart to your informative workspace. For specific actions, such as "improve database abstraction layer," create task cards and put them in your iteration plan.

Allies

Informative Workspace (p. 83)
Iteration Planning (p. 233)

Questions

What if management isn't committed to making things better?

Although some ideas may require the assistance of others, if those people can't or won't help, refocus your ideas to what you can do. The retrospective is an opportunity for you to decide, as a team, how to improve your own process, not the processes of others.

Your project manager may be able to help convey your needs to management and other groups.

Despite my best efforts as facilitator, our retrospectives always degenerate into blaming and arguing. What can I do?

This is a tough situation, and there may not be anything you can do. If there are just one or two people who like to place blame, try talking to them alone beforehand. Describe what you see happening and your concern that it's disrupting the retrospective. Rather than adopting a parental attitude, ask for their help in solving the problem and be open to their concerns.

If a few people constantly argue with each other, talk to them together. Explain that you're concerned their arguing is making other people uncomfortable. Again, ask for their help.

If the problem is widespread across the group, the same approach—talking about it—applies. This time, hold the discussion as part of the retrospective, or even in place of it. Share what you've observed, and ask the group for their observations and ideas about how to solve the problem. Be careful: this discussion is only helpful if the group can hold it without further arguing.

If all else fails, you may need to stop holding retrospectives for a while. Consider bringing an organizational development (OD) expert to facilitate your next retrospective.

We come up with good retrospective objectives, but then nothing happens. What are we doing wrong?

Your ideas may be too big. Remember, you only have one week, and you have to do your other work, too. Try making plans that are smaller scale—perhaps a few hours of work—and follow up every day.

Another possibility is that you don't have enough slack in your schedule. When you have a completely full workload, nonessential tasks such as improving your work habits go undone. (The sad irony is that improving your work habits will give you more time.)

Ally

Slack (p. 246)

Finally, it's possible that the team doesn't feel like they truly have a voice in the retrospective. Take an honest look at the way you conduct it. Are you leading the team by the nose rather than facilitating? Consider having someone else facilitate the next retrospective.

Some people won't speak up in the retrospective. How can I encourage them to participate?

It's possible they're just shy. It's not necessary for everyone to participate all the time. Waiting for a verbal response to the Prime Directive can help break the ice.

On the other hand, they may have something they want to say but don't feel safe doing it. [Derby & Larsen] have some good suggestions about how to incorporate safety exercises into the retrospective. You can also try talking with them individually outside of the retrospective.

One group of people (such as testers) always gets outvoted in the retrospective. How can we meet their needs, too?

Over time, every major issue will get its fair share of attention. Give the retrospectives a few months before deciding that a particular group is disenfranchised. One team in my experience had a few testers that felt their issue was being ignored. A month later, after the team had addressed another issue, the testers' concern was on the top of everyone's list.

If time doesn't solve the problem—and be patient to start—you can use weighted dot voting, in which some people get more dot votes than others. If you can do this without recrimination, it may be a good way to level the playing field.

Another option is for one group to pick a different retrospective objective to focus on in addition to the general retrospective objective.

Our retrospectives always take too long. How can we go faster?

It's OK to be decisive about wrapping things up and moving on. There's always next week. If the group is taking a long time brainstorming ideas or mute mapping, you might say something like, "OK, we're running out of time. Take two minutes to write down your final thoughts (or make final changes) and then we'll move on."

That said, I prefer to let a retrospective go long and take its natural course during the first month or so. This will allow people to get used to the flow of the retrospective without stressing too much about timelines.

The retrospective takes so much time. Can we do it less often?

It depends on how much your process needs improvement. An established team may not need as many iteration retrospectives as a new team. I would continue to conduct retrospectives at least every other week.

If you feel that your retrospective isn't accomplishing much, perhaps the real problem is that you need a change of pace. Try a different approach. [Derby & Larsen] has many ideas to try.

Results

When your team conducts retrospectives well, your ability to develop and deliver software steadily improves. The whole team grows closer and more cohesive, and each group has more respect for the issues other groups face. You are honest and open about your successes and failures and are more comfortable with change.

Contraindications

The biggest danger in a retrospective is that it will become a venue for acrimony rather than for constructive problem solving. A skilled facilitator can help prevent this, but you probably don't have such a facilitator on hand. Be very cautious about conducting retrospectives if some team members tend to lash out, attack, or blame others.

The retrospective recipe described here assumes that your team gets along fairly well. If your team doesn't get along well enough to use this recipe, refer to [Derby & Larsen] for more options and consider bringing in an outside facilitator.

If only one or two team members are disruptive, and attempts to work the problem through with them are ineffective, you may be better off removing them from the team. Their antisocial influence probably extends beyond the retrospective, hurting teamwork and productivity.

Alternatives

There are many ways to conduct retrospectives. See [Derby & Larsen] for ideas.

I'm not aware of any other techniques that allow you to improve your process and team cohesiveness as well as retrospectives do. Some organizations define organization-wide processes. Others assign responsibility for the process to a project manager, technical lead, or architect. Although these approaches might lead to a good initial process, they don't usually lead to continuous process improvement, and neither approach fosters team cohesiveness.

Further Reading

Project Retrospectives [Kerth] is the definitive resource for project retrospectives.

Agile Retrospectives [Derby & Larsen] picks up where [Kerth] leaves off, discussing techniques for conducting all sorts of agile retrospectives.

"The Effective Post-Fire Critique" [Montagna] is a fascinating look at how a life-and-death profession approaches retrospectives.

CHAPTER 6

Collaborating

Sometimes I like to imagine software development as a pulsing web of light, with blips of information flowing along lines from far-flung points. The information races toward the development team, which is a brilliant, complex tangle of lines, then funnels into a glowing core of software too bright to look at.

I'm a little weird that way.

There's truth to the idea, though. Software development is all about information. The more effectively your programmers can access and understand the information they need, the more effective they will be at creating software. The better information customers and managers have, the better they can manage the schedule and provide feedback to the programmers.

Communication in the real world is a lot messier than it is in my image. There are no glowing lines to sterilely transport information from one brain to another. Instead, people have to work together. They have to ask questions, discuss ideas, and even disagree.

This chapter contains eight practices to help your team and its stakeholders collaborate efficiently and effectively:

- *Trust* is essential for the team to thrive.
- *Sitting together* leads to fast, accurate communication.
- *Real customer involvement* helps the team understand what to build.
- A *ubiquitous language* helps team members understand each other.
- *Stand-up meetings* keep team members informed.
- *Coding standards* provide a template for seamlessly joining the team's work together.
- *Iteration demos* keep the team's efforts aligned with stakeholder goals.
- *Reporting* helps reassure the organization that the team is working well.

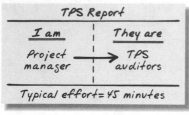
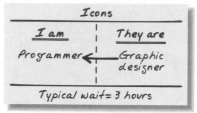

(a) Providing information   (b) Requesting information

Figure 6-1. Sample cards

"COLLABORATING" MINI-ÉTUDE

The purpose of this étude is to explore the flow of information in your project. If you're new to agile development, you may use it to help you understand how collaboration occurs in your project, even if you're not currently using XP. If you're an experienced agile practitioner, review Chapter 12 and use this étude to help you modify your process to remove communication bottlenecks.

Conduct this étude for a timeboxed half-hour every day for as long as it is useful. Expect to feel rushed by the deadline at first. If the étude becomes stale, discuss how you can change it to make it interesting again.

You will need white, red, yellow, and green index cards; an empty table or magnetic whiteboard for your information flow map; and writing implements for everyone.

Step 1. Start by forming pairs. Try for heterogeneous pairs—have a programmer work with a customer, a customer work with a tester, and so forth, rather than pairing by job description. Work with a new partner every day.

Step 2. (Timebox this step to 10 minutes.) Within your pair, discuss the kinds of information that you need in order to do your job, or that other people need from you in order to do their job. Choose one example that you have personally observed or experienced. If you can't think of anything new, pick an existing card and skip to Step 3.

Information usually flows in both directions. For example, during a customer review, a developer may ask a customer if the software behaves correctly. Alternatively, a customer may ask a developer to show her what the software does. Choose just one direction.

Reflect on all the times you remember needing or providing this information. How long did it take? For information you needed, think of the *calendar time* needed from the moment you realized you needed the information to the moment you received it. For information you provided, think of the *total effort* that you and other team members spent preparing and providing the information.

Next, think of the *typical* time required for this piece of information. If the typical time required is less than 10 minutes, take a *green* index card. If it's less than a day, take a *yellow* index card. If it's a day or longer, take a *red* index card. Write down the type of information involved, the group that you get it from (or give it to), the role you play, and the time required, as shown in Figure 6-1.

Step 3. (Timebox this step to 10 minutes.) Within your pair, discuss things that your team can do to *reduce* or *eliminate* the time required to get or provide this information. Pick one and write it on a *white* card.

Step 4. (Timebox this step to 10 minutes.) As a team, discuss all the cards generated by all the pairs. Consider these questions:

- Where are the bottlenecks in receiving information?
- Which latencies are most painful in your current process?
- Which flow is most important to optimize in your next iteration?
- What is the root cause of those latencies?
- What will you do next iteration to improve information flow?

After everyone has had a chance to share their cards, add them to the table. Place colored cards on the table so that the cards visually show information flow. For example, if an interaction designer gets information about usage from real customers and gives it to the development team, those two cards would be placed side by side. Place white cards underneath colored cards.

———————————————————————

Trust

We work together effectively and without fear.

When a group of people comes together to work as a team, they go through a series of group dynamics known as "Forming, Storming, Norming, and Performing" [Tuckman]. It takes the team some time to get through each of these stages. They make progress, fall back, bicker, and get along. Over time—often months—and with adequate support and a bit of luck, they get to know each other and work well together. The team jells. Productivity shoots up. They do really amazing work.

What does it take to achieve this level of productivity? The team must take joint responsibility for their work. Team members need to think of the rest of the team as "us," not "them." If a team member notices something that needs doing, she takes responsibility for it, even if it's not her specialty: she does it, finds someone to help her do it, or recruits someone else to take care of it.

Conversely, team members must rely on each other for help. When one member of a team encounters a question that she cannot answer, she doesn't hesitate to ask someone who does know the answer. Sometimes these quick questions turn into longer pairing sessions.

Trust is essential for the team to perform this well. You need to trust that taking time to help others won't make you look unproductive. You need to trust that you'll be treated with respect when you ask for help or disagree with someone.

The organization needs to trust the team, too. XP is strange and different at first. It doesn't provide the normal indicators of progress that managers are accustomed to seeing. It takes trust to believe that the team will deliver a success.

Trust doesn't magically appear—you have to work at it. Here are some strategies for generating trust in your XP team.

Team Strategy #1: Customer-Programmer Empathy

Many organizations I've worked with have struggled with an "us versus them" attitude between customers and programmers. Customers often feel that programmers don't care enough about their needs and deadlines, some of which, if missed, could cost them their jobs. Programmers often feel forced into commitments they can't meet, hurting their health and relationships.

Sometimes the acrimony is so intense that the groups actually start doing what the others fear: programmers react by inflating estimates and focusing on technical toys at the expense of necessary features; customers react by ignoring programmer estimates and applying schedule pressure. This sometimes happens even when there's no overt face-to-face hostility.

This is a difficult situation with no easy answer. Such badly broken trust takes a long time to heal. Because neither group can force the other to bridge the gap, you have to focus on changing your own attitude.

I find that the biggest missing component in this situation is empathy for the other group's position. Programmers, remember that customers have corporate masters that demand results. Bonuses, career advancement, and even job security depend on successful delivery, and the demands aren't always reasonable. Customers must deliver results anyway.

Customers, remember that ignoring or overriding programmers' professional recommendations about timelines often leads to serious personal consequences for programmers. "Death march teams are the norm, not the exception... [These teams] are often found working 13- to 14-hour days, six days a week... In ["ugly" death march projects], it's not uncommon to see one or two of the project team members collapse from exhaustion, suffer ulcers or a nervous breakdown, or experience a divorce." [Yourdon, p. ix, p. 4, p. 61] The commonality of these experiences among programmers leads to apathy and cynicism about schedules and commitments.

Sitting together is the most effective way I know to build empathy. Each group gets to see that the others are working just as hard. Retrospectives also help, if your team can avoid placing blame. Programmers can help by being respectful of customer goals, and customers can help by being respectful of programmer estimates and technical recommendations. All of this is easier with energized work.

Allies
Sit Together (p. 112)
Retrospectives (p. 91)
Energized Work (p. 79)

Team Strategy #2: Programmer-Tester Empathy

I've also seen "us versus them" attitudes between programmers and testers, although it isn't quite as prevalent as customer-programmer discord. When it occurs, programmers tend not to show respect for the testers' abilities, and testers see their mission as shooting down the programmers' work.

As with customer-programmer discord, empathy and respect are the keys to better relations. Programmers, remember that testing takes skill and careful work, just as programming does. Take advantage of testers' abilities to find mistakes you would never consider, and thank them for helping prevent embarrassing problems from reaching stakeholders and users. Testers, focus on the team's joint goal: releasing a great product. When you find a mistake, it's not an occasion for celebration or gloating. Remember, too, that everybody makes mistakes, and mistakes aren't a sign of incompetence or laziness.

Team Strategy #3: Eat Together

Another good way to improve team cohesiveness is to eat together. Something about sharing meals breaks down barriers and fosters team cohesiveness. Try providing a free meal once per week. If you have the meal brought into the office, set a table and serve the food family-style to prevent

> A good way to improve team cohesiveness is to eat together.

people from taking the food back to their desks. If you go to a restaurant, ask for a single long table rather than separate tables.

Team Strategy #4: Team Continuity

After a project ends, the team typically breaks up. All the wonderful trust and cohesiveness that the team has formed is lost. The next project starts with a brand-new team, and they have to struggle through the four phases of team formation all over again.

You can avoid this waste by keeping productive teams together. Most organizations think of people as the basic "resource" in the company. Instead, think of the *team* as the resource. Rather than assigning people to projects, assign a team to a project. Have people join teams and stick together for multiple projects.

Some teams will be more effective than others. Take advantage of this by using the most effective teams as a training ground for other teams. Rotate junior members into those teams so they can learn from the best, and rotate experienced team members out to lead teams of their own. If you do this gradually, the team culture and trust will remain intact.

> **NOTE**
> Team continuity is an advanced practice—not because it's hard to do, but because it challenges normal organizational structures. While team continuity is valuable, you don't need to do it to be successful.

Impressions

I know somebody who worked in a company with two project teams. One used XP, met its commitments, and delivered regularly. The team next door struggled: it fell behind schedule and didn't have any working software to show. Yet when the company downsized, it let the XP team members go rather than the other team!

Why? When management looked in on the struggling team, they saw programmers working hard, long hours with their heads down and UML diagrams papering the walls. When they looked in on the XP team, they saw people talking, laughing, and going home at five with nothing but rough sketches and charts on the whiteboards.

Like it or not, our projects don't exist in a vaccuum. XP can seem strange and different to an organization that hasn't seen it before. "Are they really working?" outsiders wonder. "It's noisy and confusing. I don't want to work that way. If it succeeds, will they force me to do it, too?"

Ironically, the more successful XP is, the more these worries grow. Alistair Cockburn calls them *organizational antibodies*.[*] If left unchecked, organizational antibodies will overcome and dismantle an otherwise successful XP team.

No matter how effective you are at meeting your technical commitments, you're in trouble without the good will of your stakeholders. Yes, meeting schedules and technical expectations helps, but the nontechnical, interpersonal skills—soft skills—your team practices may be just as important to building trust in your team.

Does this sound unfair or illogical? Surely your ability to deliver high-quality software is all that really matters.

It is unfair and illogical. It's also the way people think—even programmers. If your stakeholders don't trust you, they won't participate in your team, which hurts your ability to deliver valuable software. They might even campaign against you.

Don't wait for them to realize how your work can help them. Show them.

Organizational Strategy #1: Show Some Hustle

> "Things may come to those who wait, but only the things left by those who hustle." —Abraham Lincoln[†]

Several years ago, I hired a small local moving company to move my belongings from one apartment to another. When the movers arrived, I was surprised to see them *hustle*—they moved quickly from the

---

[*] Via personal communication.

[†] Thanks to George Dinwiddie for this quote.

van to the apartment and back. This was particularly unexpected because I was paying them by the hour. There was no advantage for them to move so quickly.

Those movers impressed me. I felt that they were dedicated to meeting my needs and respecting my pocketbook. If I still lived in that city and needed to move again, I would hire them in an instant. They earned my goodwill—and my trust.

In the case of a software team, *hustle* is energized, productive work. It's the sense that the team is putting in a fair day's work for a fair day's pay. Energized work, an informative workspace, appropriate reporting, and iteration demos all help convey this feeling of productivity.

> **Allies**
> Energized Work (p. 79)
> Informative Workspace (p. 83)
> Reporting (p. 144)
> Iteration Demo (p. 138)

Organizational Strategy #2: Deliver on Commitments

If your stakeholders have worked with software teams before, they probably have plenty of war wounds from slipped schedules, unfixed defects, and wasted money. In addition, they probably don't know much about software development. That puts them in the uncomfortable position of relying on your work, having had poor results before, and being unable to tell if your work is any better.

Meanwhile, your team consumes thousands of dollars every week in salary and support. How do stakeholders know that you're spending their money wisely? How do they know that the team is even competent?

Stakeholders may not know how to evaluate your process, but they can evaluate results. Two kinds of results speak particularly clearly to them: working software and delivering on commitments.

Fortunately, XP teams demonstrate both of these results every week. You make a commitment to deliver working software when you build your iteration and release plans. You demonstrate that you've met the iteration commitment in the iteration demo, exactly one week later, and you demonstrate that you've met the release commitment on your predefined release date.

> **Allies**
> Iteration Planning (p. 233)
> Release Planning (p. 206)
> Iteration Demo (p. 138)
> Risk Management (p. 224)

This week-in, week-out delivery builds stakeholder trust like nothing I've ever seen. It's extremely powerful. All you have to do is create a plan that you can achieve... and then achieve it.

Organizational Strategy #3: Manage Problems

Did I say, "All you have to do?" Silly me. It's not that easy.

First, you need to plan well (see Chapter 8). Second, as the poet said, "The best laid schemes o' mice an' men / Gang aft a-gley."[*]

In other words, some iterations don't sail smoothly into port on the last day. What do you do when your best laid plans gang a-gley?

Actually, that's your chance to shine. Anyone can look good when life goes according to plan. Your true character shows when you deal with unexpected problems.

---

[*] "To a Mouse," by renowned Scottish poet Robert Burns. The poem starts, "Wee, sleekit, cow'rin, tim'rous beastie, / O, what a panic's in thy breastie!" This reminds me of how I felt when I was asked to integrate a project after a year of unintegrated development.

The first thing to do is to limit your exposure to problems. Work on the hardest, most uncertain tasks early in the iteration. You'll find problems sooner, and you'll have more time to fix them.

When you encounter a problem, start by letting the whole team know about it. Bring it up by the next stand-up meeting at the very latest. This gives the entire team a chance to help solve the problem.

If the setback is relatively small, you might be able to absorb it into the iteration by using some of your iteration slack. Options for absorbing the problem include reducing noncritical refactorings, postponing a nonessential meeting, or even (as a team decision) cancelling research time. I personally volunteer to work an hour or so longer each day until we have resolved the problem—or the iteration ends, whichever comes first—as long as my family commitments permit.

Ally
Slack (p. 246)

Some problems are too big to absorb no matter how much slack you have. If this is the case, get together as a whole team as soon as possible and replan. You may need to remove an entire story or you might be able to reduce the scope of some stories. (For more about what to do when things go wrong, see "Iteration Planning" in Chapter 8.)

When you've identified a problem, let the stakeholders know about it. They'll appreciate your professionalism even if they don't like the problem. I usually wait until the iteration demo to explain problems that we solved on our own, but bring bigger problems to stakeholders' attentions right away. The product manager is probably the best person to decide who to talk to and when.

> The bigger the problem, the sooner you should disclose it.

The sooner your stakeholders know about a problem (and believe me, they'll find out eventually), the more time *they* have to work around it. I include an analysis of the possible solutions as well as their technical costs. It can take a lot of courage to have this discussion—but addressing a problem successfully can build trust like nothing else.

Be careful, though. It's easy to focus too much on meeting your commitments in such a way that actually damages trust. Suppose you need a few more hours in an iteration to finish a particularly valuable story. A little bit of overtime is fine. Sprinting with a burst of more overtime can even be good for team morale and cohesiveness under the right conditions (see "Energized Work" in Chapter 5). *Relying* on overtime to meet overcommitment saps the team's energy and reduces your ability to absorb problems. Ironically, it leads to more missed commitments; you implicitly promise your stakeholders more than you can deliver for the price they expect to pay in time and resources.

If you find yourself using a lot of overtime, something is wrong. Most iterations shouldn't have problems. When a problem does occur, you should usually be able to solve it by using slack, not overtime. I look for systemic problems if I see a team exceeding 10 percent overtime in more than one iteration per quarter.

> Reliance on overtime indicates a systemic problem.

Organizational Strategy #4: Respect Customer Goals

When XP teams first form, it usually takes individual members a while to think of themselves as part of a single team. In the beginning, programmers, testers, and customers often see themselves as separate groups.

New on-site customers are often particularly skittish. Being part of a development team feels awkward; they'd rather work in their normal offices with their normal colleagues. Those colleagues are often influential members of the company. If the customers are unhappy, those feelings transmit directly back to stakeholders.

When starting a new XP project, programmers should make an extra effort to welcome the customers. One particularly effective way to do so is to treat customer goals with respect. This may even mean suppressing, for a time, cynical programmer jokes about schedules and suits.

Being respectful goes both ways, and customers should also suppress their natural tendencies to complain about schedules and argue with estimates. I'm emphasizing the programmer's role here because it plays such a big part in stakeholder perceptions.

Another way for programmers to take customer goals seriously is to come up with creative alternatives for meeting those goals. If customers want something that may take a long time or involves tremendous technical risks, suggest alternate approaches to reach the same underlying goal for less cost. If there's a more impressive way of meeting a goal that customers haven't considered, by all means mention it—especially if it's not too hard.

As programmers and customers have these conversations, barriers will be broken and trust will develop. As stakeholders see that, their trust in the team will blossom as well.

You can also build trust directly with stakeholders. Consider this: the next time a stakeholder stops you in the hallway with a request, what would happen if you immediately and cheerfully took him to a stack of index cards, helped him write the story, and then brought them both to the attention of the product manager for scheduling?

This might be a 10-minute interruption for you, but imagine how the stakeholder would feel. You responded to his concern, helped him express it, and took immediate steps to get it into the plan.

That's worth infinitely more to him than firing an email into a black hole of your request tracking system.

Organizational Strategy #5: Promote the Team

You can also promote the team more directly. One team posted pictures and charts on the outer wall of the workspace that showed what they were working on and how it was progressing. Another invited anyone and everyone in the company to attend its iteration demos.

Being open about what you're doing will also help people appreciate your team. Other people in the company are likely to be curious, and a little wary, about your strange new approach to software development. That curiosity can easily turn to resentment if the team seems insular or stuck-up.

You can be open in many ways. Consider holding brown-bag lunch sessions describing the process, public code-fests in which you demonstrate your code and XP technical practices, or an "XP open-house day" in which you invite people to see what you're doing and even participate for a little while. If you like flair, you can even wear buttons or hats around the office that say "Ask me about XP."

Organizational Strategy #6: Be Honest

In your enthusiasm to demonstrate progress, be careful not to step over the line. Borderline behavior includes glossing over known defects in an iteration demo, taking credit for stories that are not 100 percent complete, and extending the iteration for a few days in order to finish everything in the plan.

These are minor frauds, yes. You may even think that "fraud" is too strong a word—but all of these behaviors give stakeholders the impression that you've done more than you actually have.

There's a practical reason not to do these things: stakeholders will expect you to complete the remaining features just as quickly, when in fact you haven't even finished the first set. You'll build up a backlog of work that looks done but isn't. At some point, you'll have to finish that backlog, and the resulting schedule slip will produce confusion, disappointment, and even anger.

Even scrupulously honest teams can run into this problem. In a desire to look good, teams sometimes sign up for more stories than they can implement well. They get the work done, but they take shortcuts and don't do enough design and refactoring. The design suffers, defects creep in, and the team finds itself suddenly going much slower while struggling to improve code quality.

> Only sign up for as many stories as the team can reliably complete.

Similarly, don't yield to the temptation to count stories that aren't "done done". If a story isn't completely finished, it doesn't count toward your velocity. Don't even take partial credit for the story. There's an old programming joke: the first 90 percent takes 90 percent of the time... and the last 10 percent takes 90 percent of the time. Until the story is totally done, it's impossible to say for certain how much is left.

Ally
"Done Done" (p. 156)

THE CHALLENGE OF TRUTH-TELLING

The most challenging project I've ever coached had a tight deadline. (Don't they all?) Our end-customer was a critical customer: a large institution that represented the majority of our income. If we didn't satisfy them, we risked losing a huge chunk of vital business.

Knowing what was at stake, I made a reliable release plan our top priority. Six weeks later, we had not only implemented the first six weeks of stories, we also had a reliable estimate of our velocity and a complete estimated list of remaining stories.

It showed us coming in late—very late. We needed to deliver in seven months. According to the release plan, we would deliver in thirteen.

The project manager and I took the release plan to our director. Things went downhill. He forbade us from sharing the news with the end-customer. Instead, he ordered us to make the original deadline work any way we could.

We knew that we couldn't make the deadline work. We didn't have enough time to add staff; it would take too long for them to become familiar with the codebase. We couldn't cut scope because we wouldn't admit the problem to our customer.

Our jobs were on the line and we tried to make it work. We ignored Brooks' Law,[*] hired a bunch of programmers, and did everything we could to ramp them up quickly without distracting the productive members of the team. Despite our best efforts, we shipped defect-ridden software six months late—within a few weeks of our original prediction. We lost the customer.

We might have lost the customer even if we had told them the truth. It's impossible to say. My experience, however, is that customers, stakeholders, and executives appreciate being made part of the solution. When you demonstrate progress on a weekly basis, you establish credibility and trust. With that credibility and trust in place, stakeholders have a greater interest in working with you to balance trade-offs and achieve their goals.

---

[*] "[A]dding manpower to a late software project makes it later" [Brooks, p. 25].

I won't involve myself in hiding information again. Schedules can't keep secrets; there are no miraculous turnarounds; the true ship date comes out eventually.

Instead, I go out of my way to present the most accurate picture I can. If a defect must be fixed in this release, I schedule the fix before new features. If our velocity is lower than I want, I nonetheless report delivery dates based on our actual velocity. That's reality, and only by being honest about reality can I effectively manage the consequences.

Questions

Our team seems to be stuck in the "Storming" stage of team development. How can we advance?

Give it time. Teams don't always progress through the stages of development in an orderly manner. One day, everything may seem rosy; the next, calamitous. Storming is necessary for the team to progress: members need to learn how to disagree with each other. You can help by letting people know that disagreement is normal and acceptable. Find ways to make it safe to disagree.

If the team seems like it hasn't made any progress in a month or two, ask for help. Talk to your mentor (see "Find a Mentor" in Chapter 2) or an organizational development expert. (Your HR department might have somebody on staff. You can also hire an OD consultant.) If there's somebody on the team who is particularly disruptive, consider whether the team would be better off if he moved to a different project.

Isn't it more important that we be good rather than look good?

Both are important. Do great work and make sure your organization knows it.

I thought overtime didn't solve schedule problems. Why did you recommend overtime?

Overtime *won't* solve your schedule problems, especially systemic ones, but it might help if you have a small hiccup to resolve. The key point to remember is that, while overtime can help solve small problems, it mustn't be the first or only tool in your kit.

Why bring big problems to stakeholders' attentions before smaller, already-solved problems? That seems backward.

Problems tend to grow over time. The sooner you disclose a problem, the more time you have to solve it. It reduces panic, too: early in the project, people are less stressed about deadlines and have more mental energy for problems.

You said programmers should keep jokes about the schedule to themselves. Isn't this just the same as telling programmers to shut up and meet the schedule, no matter how ridiculous?

Certainly not. Everybody on the team should speak up and tell the truth when they see a problem. However, there's a big difference between discussing a real problem and simply being cynical.

Many programmers have cynical tendencies. That's OK, but be aware that customers' careers are often on the line. They may not be able to tell the difference between a real joke and a complaint disguised as a joke. An inappropriate joke can set their adrenaline pumping just as easily as a real problem can.

Venting is counterproductive when there's a better way to address the root of the problem.

What if we've committed to finishing a story and then discover that we can't possibly finish it this iteration?

Mistakes happen; it's inevitable. Perhaps programmers underestimated the technical challenge of a story. Perhaps customers neglected to mention an important aspect of the story. Either way, finding the problem early and reworking the plan is your best solution. If you can't, admit your mistake and make a better plan for the next iteration. (See "Iteration Planning" in Chapter 8 for more about changing your plans when something goes wrong.)

Like overtime, reworking the plan shouldn't happen too often. I look for underlying systemic problems if it happens more than once per quarter.

Results

When you have a team that works well together, you cooperate to meet your goals and solve your problems. You collectively decide priorities and collaboratively allocate tasks. The atmosphere in the team room is busy but relaxed, and you genuinely enjoy working with your teammates.

When you establish trust within your organization and with your stakeholders, you demonstrate the value of the project and your team. You acknowledge mistakes, challenges, and problems, and you find solutions instead of trying to hide them until they blow up. You seek solutions instead of blame.

Contraindications

Compensation practices can make teamwork difficult. An XP team produces results through group effort. If your organization relies on individual task assignment for personnel evaluation, teamwork may suffer. Similarly, ranking on a curve—in which at least one team member must be marked unsatisfactory, regardless of performance—has a destructive effect on team cohesion. These practices can transform your team into a group of competing individuals, which will hurt your ability to practice XP.

Even without harmful compensation practices, team members may not trust each other. This is a problem, but it isn't necessarily debilitating. Team members that must deliver software weekly in pursuit of a common goal will learn to trust each other... or implode from the pressure. Unfortunately, I can't tell you which outcome will happen to your team.

If the team doesn't sit together, it's much harder for good teamwork to occur, and if team members also don't trust each other, it's unlikely that trust will ever develop. Be careful of using XP if the team doesn't sit together.

> **Ally**
> Sit Together (p. 112)

Alternatives

Trust is vital for agile projects—perhaps for any project. I'm not sure it's possible to work on an agile project without it.

Further Reading

The Wisdom of Teams [Katzenbach & Smith], which organizational development consultant Diana Larsen describes as "the best book about teams extant."

"Developmental Sequences in Small Groups" [Tuckman] introduces the team development sequence of "Forming, Storming, Norming, and Performing."

The Trusted Advisor [Maister et al.] is a good resource for generating organizational trust.

The Power of a Positive No [Ury] describes how to say no respectfully when it's necessary while preserving important relationships. Diana Larsen desribes this ability as "probably more important than any amount of negotiating skill in building trust."

Sit Together

We communicate rapidly and accurately.

Audience
Whole Team, Coaches

If you've tried to conduct a team meeting via speakerphone, you know how much of a difference face-to-face conversations make. Compared to an in-person discussion, teleconferences are slow and stutter-filled, with uncomfortable gaps in the conversation and people talking over each other.

What you may not have realized is how much this affects your work.

Imagine you're a programmer on a nonagile team and you need to clarify something in your requirements document in order to finish an algorithm. You fire off an email to your domain expert, Mary, then take a break to stretch your legs and get some coffee.

When you get back, Mary still hasn't responded, so you check out a few technical blogs you've been meaning to read. Half an hour later, your inbox chimes. Mary has responded.

Uh-oh... it looks like Mary misunderstood your message and answered the wrong question. You send another query, but you really can't afford to wait any longer. You take your best guess at the answer—after all, you've been working at this company for a long time, and you know most of the answers—and get back to work.

A day later, after exchanging a few more emails, you've hashed out the correct answer with Mary. It wasn't exactly what you thought, but you were pretty close. You go back and fix your code. While you're in there, you realize there's an edge case nobody's handled yet.

You could bug Mary for the answer, but this is a very obscure case. It's probably never going to happen in the field. Besides, Mary's very busy, and you promised you'd have this feature done yesterday. (In fact, you *were* done yesterday, except for all these nitpicky little details.) You put in the most likely answer and move on.

Accommodating Poor Communication

As the distance between people grows, the effectiveness of their communication decreases. Misunderstandings occur and delays creep in. People start guessing to avoid the hassle of waiting for answers. Mistakes appear.

To combat this problem, most development methods attempt to reduce the need for direct communication. It's a sensible response. If questions lead to delays and errors, reduce the need to ask questions!

The primary tools teams use to reduce reliance on direct communication are development phases and work-in-progress documents. For example, in the requirements phase, business analysts talk to customers and then produce a requirements document. Later, if a programmer has a question, he doesn't need to talk to an expert; he can simply look up the answer in the document.

It's a sensible idea, but it has flaws. The authors of the documents need to anticipate which questions will come up and write clearly enough to avoid misinterpretations. This is hard to do well. In practice, it's impossible to anticipate all possible questions. Also, adding up-front documentation phases stretches out the development process.

A Better Way

In XP, the whole team—including experts in business, design, programming, and testing—sits together in a open workspace. When you have a question, you need only turn your head and ask. You get an instant response, and if something isn't clear, you can discuss it at the whiteboard.

Consider the previous story from this new perspective. You're a programmer and you need some information from your domain expert, Mary, in order to code an algorithm.

This time, rather than sending an email, you turn your head. "Mary, can you clarify something for me?"

Mary says, "Sure. What do you need?"

You explain the problem, and Mary gives her answer. "No, no," you reply. "That's a different problem. Here, let me show you on the whiteboard."

A few minutes later, you've hashed out the issue and you're back to coding again. Whoops! There's an edge case you hadn't considered. "Wait a second, Mary," you say. "There's something we didn't consider. What about…."

After some more discussion, the answer is clear. You're a little surprised: Mary's answer was completely different than you expected. It's good that you talked it over. Now, back to work! The code is due today, and it took 20 whole minutes to figure out this nitpicky little issue.

Exploiting Great Communication

Sitting together eliminates the waste caused by waiting for an answer, which dramatically improves productivity. In a field study of six colocated teams, [Teasley et al.] found that sitting together doubled productivity and cut time to market to almost one-third of the company baseline.

Those results are worth repeating: the teams delivered software in *one-third* their normal time. After the pilot study, 11 more teams achieved the same result. This success led the company to invest heavily in open workspaces, by building a new facility in the U.S. that supports 112 such teams and making plans for similar sites in Europe.

How can sitting together yield such impressive results? Communication.

Although programming is the emblematic activity of software development, *communication* is the real key to software success. As [Teasley et al.] report, "Past studies have indicated that less than 30 percent of a programmer's time is spent on traditional programming tasks and less than 20 percent of the time is spent on coding. The rest of the time is spent on meetings, problem resolution with the team, resolving issues with customers, product testing, etc."

My experience is that programmers on XP teams spend a far greater percentage of their time programming. I attribute that to the increased communication effectiveness of sitting together. Rather than sitting in hour-long meetings, conversations last only as long as needed and involve only the people necessary.

Teams that sit together not only get rapid answers to their questions, they experience what [Cockburn] calls *osmotic communication*. Have you ever been talking with someone in a crowded room and then heard your name out of the blue? Even though you were focusing on your conversation, your brain was paying attention to all the other conversations in the room. When it heard your name, it replayed the sounds into your conscious mind. You not only hear your name, you hear a bit of the conversation around it, too, in a phenomenon known as the *cocktail party effect.**

Imagine a team that sits together. Team members are concentrating on their work and talking quietly with their partners. Then somebody mentions something about managing database connections, and another programmer perks up. "Oh, Tom and I refactored the database connection pool last week. You don't need to manage the connections manually anymore." When team members are comfortable speaking up like this, it happens often (at least once per day) and saves time and money every time.

There's another hidden benefit to sitting together: it helps teams jell and breaks down us-versus-them attitudes between groups. In contrast, distance seems to encourage adversarial relationships and blaming "those people." Whenever I see this (for example, between programmers and testers), I suggest that they sit together. This helps the groups interact socially and gain respect for each other professionally.

> When I see an adversarial relationship between separate groups in a team, I suggest that they sit together.

Secrets of Sitting Together

To get the most out of sitting together, be sure you have a complete team (see "The XP Team" in Chapter 3). It's important that people be physically present to answer questions. If someone must be absent often—product managers tend to fall into this category—make sure that someone else on the team can answer the same questions. A domain expert is often a good backup for a traveling product manager.

Similarly, sit close enough to each other that you can have a quick discussion without getting up from your desk or shouting. This will also help encourage osmotic communication, which relies on team members overhearing conversations.

Available instant help doesn't do any good if you don't ask for it. Many organizations discourage interruptions, but I encourage them on my XP teams. There's no sense in banging your head against a wall when the person with the answer is right across the room. To support this attitude, many teams have a rule: "We must always help when asked."

> Ask for help when you're stuck.

Interruptions disrupt flow and ruin productivity, so this rule may sound foolish. It takes a programmer 15 minutes or more to get back into flow after an interruption [DeMarco & Lister 1999].

Fortunately, with pair programming, flow works differently. The delay doesn't seem to occur. One programmer answers the question and the other keeps thinking about the problem at hand. When the interruption is over, a quick "Where were we?" gets work moving again.

Ally
Pair Programming (p. 71)

Pairing helps in a few other ways, too. Osmotic communication depends on a buzz of conversation in the room. If people aren't pairing, there's less talking. Pairing also makes it easier for programmers to ignore irrelevant background conversations.

---

* The best layman's description of the cocktail party effect I've seen is on Wikipedia: *http://en.wikipedia.org/wiki/Cocktail_party_effect*.

Making Room

Sitting together is one of those things that's easy to say and hard to do. It's not that the act itself is difficult—the real problem is finding space.

NOTE
Start arranging for a shared workspace *now*.

A team that sits in adjacent cubicles can convert them into an adequate shared workspace, but even with cubicles, it takes time and money to hire people to rearrange the walls.

When I say "time," I mean weeks or even months.

In a smaller company, you might be able to take matters (and screwdrivers) into your own hands. In a larger company, you could run afoul of Facilities if you do that. That may be a worthwhile cost, but talk to your project manager first. She should have some insight on the best way to get a shared workspace.

While you're waiting for construction on your dream workspace to finish, a big conference room is a good alternative. One team I worked with set up shop in the company boardroom for six weeks while they waited for their workspace to be ready.

Designing Your Workspace

Your team will produce a buzz of conversation in its workspace. Because they'll be working together, this buzz won't be too distracting for team members. For people outside the team, however, it can be very distracting. Make sure there's good sound insulation between your team and the rest of the organization.

Within the workspace, group people according to the conversations they most need to overhear. Programmers should all sit next to each other because they collaborate moment-to-moment. Testers should be nearby so programmers can overhear them talk about issues. Domain experts and interaction designers don't need to be quite so close, but should be close enough to answer questions without shouting.

The product manager and project manager are most likely to have conversations that would distract the team. They should sit close enough to be part of the buzz but not so close that their conversations are distracting.

An open workspace doesn't leave much room for privacy, and pair programming stations aren't very personal. This loss of individuality can make people uncomfortable. Be sure that everyone has a space they can call their own. You also need an additional enclosed room with a door, or cubes away from the open workspace, so people can have privacy for personal phone calls and individual meetings.

> Leave room for individuality in your workspace.

As you design your workspace, be sure to include plenty of whiteboards and wall space for an informative workspace. Try to have at least 24 linear feet of whiteboard space, magnetic if possible. You can never have too many whiteboards.

> **Ally**
> Informative Workspace (p. 83)

Some teams include a projector in their workspace. This is a great idea, as it allows the team to collaborate on a problem without moving to a conference room.

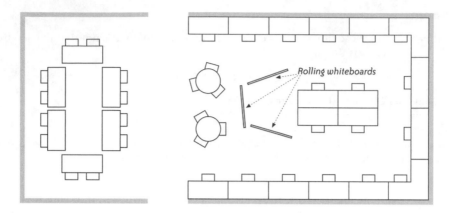

Figure 6-2. A sample workspace

Finally, the center of an XP workspace is typically a set of pairing stations. I like to have the stations facing each other so people can see each other easily. A hollow triangle, square, or oval setup works well. Provide a few more pairing stations than there are programming pairs. This allows testers and customers to pair as well (either with each other or with programmers), and it provides programmers with space to work solo when they need to.

NOTE

For information on building a good pairing station, see "Pair Programming" in Chapter 6.

Sample Workspaces

The sample workspace in Figure 6-2 was designed for a team of 13. They had six programmers, six pairing stations, and a series of cubbies for personal effects. Nonprogrammers worked close to the pairing stations so they could be part of the conversation even when they weren't pairing. Programmers' cubbies were at the far end because they typically sat at the pairing stations. For privacy, people adjourned to the far end of the workspace or went to one of the small conference rooms down the hall.

In addition to the pairing stations, everybody had a laptop for personal work and email. The pairing stations all used a group login so any team member could work at them.

Before creating this workspace, the team had been sitting in cubicles in the same part of the office. To create the workspace, they reconfigured the inner walls.

This workspace was good, but not perfect. It didn't have nearly enough wall space for charts and whiteboards and nonprogrammers didn't have enough desk space. On the plus side, there was plenty of room to accommodate people at the pairing stations, which meant that customers paired with programmers frequently, and there were also extra cubbies for bringing people into the team temporarily.

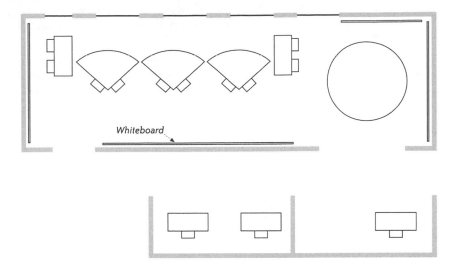

Figure 6-3. A small workspace

A small workspace

The small workspace in Figure 6-3 was created by an up-and-coming startup when they moved into new offices. They were still pretty small so they couldn't create a fancy workspace. They had a team of seven: six programmers and a product manager.

This team arranged its five pairing stations along a long wall. They had a table on the side for meetings, and charts and whiteboards on dividers surrounded them. The programmers had a pod of half-cubicles on the other side for personal effects, and there were small conference rooms close by for privacy.

This was a great workspace with one serious problem: the product manager wasn't in earshot and didn't participate in team discussion. The team couldn't get ready answers to its questions and often struggled with requirements.

Adopting an Open Workspace

Some team members may resist moving to an open workspace. Common concerns include loss of individuality and privacy, implied reduction in status from losing a private office, and managers not recognizing individual contributions. Team members may also mention worries about distractions and noise, but I find that this is usually a cover for one of the other concerns.

As with pair programming, most people come to enjoy the benefits that sitting together provides, but it can take a few months. In [Teasley et al.]'s study, team members initially preferred cubicles to the open workspace, but by the end of the study, they preferred the open workspace.

However, forcing people to sit together in hopes that they'll come to like it is a bad idea. When I've forced team members to do so, they've invariably found a way to leave the team, even if it meant quitting the company. Instead, talk with the team about their concerns and the trade-offs of moving to an

> Don't force people to sit together against their will.

open workspace. Discuss how team members will be evaluated in the new system and what provisions for privacy you can make. You may be able to address some concerns by providing a shared workspace in addition to existing offices and cubicles.

If a large portion of the team is against the open workspace, sitting together is probably not a good choice. If you only have one or two adamant objectors and the rest of the team wants to sit together, you may wish to sit together anyway and allow the objectors to move to a different team.

Questions

How can I concentrate with all that background noise?

A team that's working together in a shared workspace produces a busy hum of activity. This can be distracting at first, but most people get used to it in time.

For programmers, pair programming is an excellent way to focus your attention away from the background noise. You won't notice it if you're pairing. Nonprogrammers can work in pairs, too.

Ally
Pair Programming (p. 71)

If you work alone and find the background noise distracting, put on headphones, wear earplugs, or sit further away from the team for a time. You'll miss out on osmotic communication, but at least you'll be able to concentrate.

Sometimes, the team gets a little noisy and rambunctious. It's OK to ask for quiet—the sound in the team room should be a *hum*, not a full-throated chorus. Some teams have a bell for team members to ring when they want the team to be more quiet.

> Pairing makes background conversations fade away.

When one person is interrupted, the whole team stops what they're doing to listen. What can we do to prevent people from being distracted so easily?

Especially in the beginning of the project, it's possible that the whole team really does need to hear these conversations. As time goes on, team members will learn which conversations they can comfortably ignore.

If this is a continuing problem, try stepping a little further away from the pairing stations when a conversation lasts more than a few minutes. Interested team members can join the conversation, and the rest of the team can continue working.

What if I need privacy for phone calls?

Some people, particularly customers and project managers, need to take a lot of calls as they work. Either situate them further away from the rest of the team or arrange for an enclosed office with a door. Keep the door open as often as possible to allow information to flow smoothly.

Results

When your team sits together, communication is much more effective. You stop guessing at answers and ask more questions. You overhear other people's conversations and contribute answers you may not expect. Team members spontaneously form cross-functional groups to solve problems. There's a sense of camaraderie and mutual respect.

Contraindications

The hardest part about sitting together is finding room for the open workspace. Cubicles, even adjacent cubicles, won't provide the benefits that an open workspace does. Start working on this problem now as it can take months to resolve.

Don't force the team to sit together against their will. Adamant objectors will find a way to leave the team, and possibly the company.

Be careful about sitting together if programmers don't pair program. Solitary programming requires a quiet workspace. *Pair* programming, on the other hand, enables programmers to ignore the noise.

Alternatives

Sitting together is one of the most powerful practices in XP. It's important for communication and team dynamics. Sitting apart tends to fray fragile relationships, particularly between different functional groups, and puts your team at a disadvantage. If your team is in a single location, you're better off figuring out how to sit together.

If you have a multisite team, consider turning each site into its own team. For example, if programmers are in one site and customers are in another, the programmers may engage some business analysts to act as proxy customers. In this scenario, the customers and development team should still work together, face-to-face, for several weeks at the beginning of each release.

> Multisite teams are difficult and expensive.

If you have multiple teams of programmers, consider separating their responsibilities so that each works on entirely different codebases. [Evans] has an excellent discussion of the options for doing so.

You *can* practice XP with a single multisite team, but it requires a lot of travel. [Yap] has a good experience report describing how her team made this work 24 hours a day across 3 time zones. She focused on maximizing communication by regularly flying team members to a single location for several weeks at a time. They also conducted daily phone calls between locations.

If your whole team cannot sit together and you still wish to practice XP, talk to your mentor (see "Find a Mentor" in Chapter 2) about your options and hire experienced XP coaches for each site.

> If you can't sit together, talk to your mentor about your options.

Further Reading

Agile Software Development [Cockburn] has an excellent chapter on communication. Chapter 3, "Communicating, Cooperating Teams," discusses information radiators, communication quality, and many other concepts related to sitting together.

If you can't sit together, "Follow the Sun: Distributed Extreme Programming Development" [Yap] is an interesting experience report describing a single XP team divided into three locations, each eight hours apart.

Similarly, *Domain-Driven Design* [Evans] has an excellent discussion of coordinating multiple development teams in Chapter 14, "Maintaining Model Integrity." While the book's focus is object-oriented domain models, this chapter is applicable to many design paradigms.

Real Customer Involvement

Audience
Coaches, Customers

We understand the goals and frustrations of our customers and end-users.

An XP team I worked with included a chemist whose previous job involved the software that the team was working to replace. She was an invaluable resource, full of insight about what did and didn't work with the old product. We were lucky to have her as one of our on-site customers—thanks to her, we created a more valuable product.

In an XP team, on-site customers are responsible for choosing and prioritizing features. The value of the project is in their hands. This is a big responsibility—as an on-site customer, how do you know which features to choose?

Some of that knowledge comes from your expertise in the problem domain and with previous versions of the software. You can't think of everything, though. Your daily involvement with the project, although crucial, includes the risk of *tunnel vision*—you can get so caught up in the daily details of the project that you lose track of your real customers' interests.

To widen your perspective, you need to involve real customers. The best approach to doing so depends on who you're building your software for.

Personal Development

In *personal development,* the development team is its own customer. They're developing the software for their own use. As a result, there's no need to involve external customers—the team *is* the real customer.

NOTE

I include this type of development primarily for completeness. Most personal development is for small, throwaway applications that don't involve a full-blown XP team.

In-House Custom Development

In-house custom development occurs when your organization asks your team to build something for the organization's own use. This is classic IT development. It may include writing software to streamline operations, automation for the company's factories, or producing reports for accounting.

In this environment, the team has multiple customers to serve: the executive sponsor who *pays for* the software and the end-users who *use* the software. Their goals may not be in alignment. In the worst case, you may have a committee of sponsors and multiple user groups to satisfy.

Despite this challenge, in-house custom development makes it easy to involve real customers because they're easily accessible. The best approach is to bring your customers onto the team—to turn your *real* customers into *on-site* customers.

To do so, recruit your executive sponsor or one of his trusted lieutenants to be your product manager. He will make decisions about priorities, reflecting the desire of the executive sponsor to create software that provides value to the organization.

Also recruit some end-users of the software to act as domain experts. As with the chemist mentioned in the introduction, they will provide valuable information about how real people use the software. They will reflect the end-users' desire to use software that makes their jobs better.

NOTE

If your software has multiple sponsors or user groups, use the ideas in "Vertical-Market Software," later in this chapter.

To avoid tunnel vision, the product manager and other on-site customers should solicit feedback from their colleagues by demonstrating some of the builds created for the iteration demo and discussing their plans for the future.

Ally
Iteration Demo (p. 138)

Outsourced Custom Development

Outsourced custom development is similar to in-house development, but you may not have the connections that an in-house team does. As a result, you may not be able to recruit real customers to act as the team's on-site customers.

Still, you should try. One way to recruit real customers is to move your team to your customer's offices rather than asking them to join you at yours.

If you can't bring real customers onto the team, make an extra effort to involve them. Meet in person with your real customers for the first week or two of the project so you can discuss the project vision and initial release plan. If you're located near each other, meet again for each iteration demo, retrospective, and planning session.

Allies
Vision (p. 201)
Release Planning (p. 206)

If you're far enough apart that regular visits aren't feasible, stay in touch via instant messaging and phone conferences. Try to meet face-to-face at least once per month to discuss plans. If you are so far apart that monthly meetings aren't feasible, meet at least once per release.

Vertical-Market Software

Unlike custom development, *vertical-market software* is developed for many organizations. Like custom development, however, it's built for a particular industry and it's often customized for each customer.

Because vertical-market software has multiple customers, each with customized needs, you have to be careful about giving real customers too much control over the direction of the product. You could end up making a product that, while fitting your on-site customer's needs perfectly, alienates your remaining customers.

> Be careful about giving real customers too much control over vertical-market software.

Instead, your organization should appoint a product manager who understands the needs of your real customers impeccably. His job—and it's a tough one—is to take into account all your real customers' needs and combine them into a single, compelling vision.

Allies
Vision (p. 201)
Iteration Demo (p. 138)

Rather than involving real customers as members of the team, create opportunities to solicit their feedback. Some companies create a *customer review board* filled with their most important customers. They share their release plans with these customers and—on a rotating basis—provide installable iteration demo releases for customers to try.

Depending on your relationship with your customers, you may be able to ask your customers to donate real end-users to join the team as on-site domain experts. Alternatively, as with the chemist in the introduction, you may wish to hire previous end-users to be your domain experts.

In addition to the close relationship with your customer review board, you may also solicit feedback through trade shows and other traditional sources.

Horizontal-Market Software

Horizontal-market software is the visible tip of the software development iceberg: software that's intended to be used across a wide range of industries. The rows of shrinkwrapped software boxes at your local electronics store are a good example of horizontal-market software. So are many web sites.

As with vertical-market software, it's probably better to set limits on the control that real customers have over the direction of horizontal-market software. Horizontal-market software needs to appeal to a wide audience, and real customers aren't likely to have that perspective. Again, an in-house product manager who creates a compelling vision based on all customers' needs is a better choice.

As a horizontal-market developer, your organization may not have the close ties with customers that vertical-market developers do. Thus, a customer review board may not be a good option for you. Instead, find other ways to involve customers: focus groups, user experience testing, community previews, beta releases, and so forth.

NOTE

Web-based software, with its invisible deployment, offers a powerful option for involving real customers. You can roll out minimalist features, mark them "beta," and watch customer reactions. Another option, reportedly used by Amazon, is to deploy changes to a small percentage of visitors and observe how their usage patterns change.

Questions

Who should we use as on-site customers when we can't include real customers on the team?

You organization should supply a product manager and domain experts. See "The XP Team" in Chapter 3.

We're creating a web site for our marketing department. What kind of development is that?

At first glance, this may seem like custom development, but because the actual audience for the web site is the outside world, it's closer to vertical-market or horizontal-market development. The product manager should come from the marketing department, if possible, but you should also solicit the input of people who will be visiting the site.

Results

When you include real customers, you improve your knowledge about how they use the software in practice. You have a better understanding of their goals and frustrations, and you use that knowledge to revise what you produce. You increase your chances of delivering a truly useful and thus successful product.

Contraindications

One danger of involving real customers is that they won't necessarily reflect the needs of *all* your customers. Be careful that they don't steer you toward creating software that's only useful for them. Your project should remain based on a compelling vision. Customer desires inform the vision and may even change it, but ultimately the product manager holds final responsibility for product direction.

Ally

Vision (p. 201)

End-users often think in terms of improving their existing way of working, rather than in terms of finding completely new ways of working. This is another reason why end-users should be *involved* but not *in control*. If innovation is important to your project, give innovative thinkers—such as a visionary product manager or interaction designer—a prominent role on your team.

Alternatives

Real customer involvement is helpful but not crucial. Sometimes the best software comes from people who have a strong vision and pursue it vigorously. The resulting software tends to be either completely new or a strong rethinking of existing products.

In the absence of real customer involvement, be sure to have a visionary product manager. It's best if this person understands the domain well, but you can also hire domain experts to join the team.

Still, feedback from real customers is always informative, even if you choose to ignore it. It's especially useful when you've deployed software to them; their reaction to working software gives you valuable information about how likely you are to reach the greatest levels of success.

Ubiquitous Language

We understand each other.

Audience
Programmers

Try describing the business logic in your current system to a nonprogrammer domain expert. Are you able to explain how the system works in terms the domain expert understands? Can you avoid programmer jargon, such as the names of design patterns or coding styles? Is your domain expert able to identify potential problems in your business logic?

If not, you need a ubiquitous language.

The Domain Expertise Conundrum

One of the challenges of professional software development is that programmers aren't necessarily experts in the areas for which they write software. For example, I've helped write software that controls factory robots, directs complex financial transactions, and analyzes data from scientific instruments. When I started on these projects, I knew nothing about those things.

It's a conundrum. The people who are experts in the problem domain—the *domain experts*—are rarely qualified to write software. The people who are qualified to write software—the programmers—don't always understand the problem domain.

> **NOTE**
> Hiring programmers with expertise in a particular domain will reduce this problem, but it won't eliminate it. In addition, given the choice between a great programmer with no domain experience and a poor programmer with lots of domain experience, I would choose the better programmer.

Overcoming this challenge is, fundamentally, an issue of communication. Domain experts communicate their expertise to programmers, who in turn encode that knowledge in software. The challenge is communicating that information *clearly* and *accurately*.

Two Languages

Imagine for a moment that you're driving to a job interview. You forgot your map, so you're getting directions from a friend on your cell phone (hands free, of course!).

"I just passed a gas station on the right," you say. "That was a major intersection."

"Wait..." says your friend, as he puzzles over a map. "What street are you on? Which direction are you going?"

"I can't tell!" you yelp, slamming on the brakes as a bright yellow sports car cuts you off. "Uh... sorry. It's a pretty twisty road—does that help? Wait... I just passed Hanover."

"Hanover *Street* or Hanover *Loop*?" asks your friend.

The problem in this scenario is that you and your friend are speaking two different languages. You're talking about what you see on the road and your friend is talking about what he sees on his map. You need to translate between the two, and that adds delay and error. You'll get to your job interview eventually, but you'll probably miss a few turns along the way and you might not get there on time.

A similar problem occurs between programmers and domain experts. Programmers program in the language of technology: classes, methods, algorithms, and databases. Domain experts talk in the language of their domain: financial models, chip fabrication plants, and the like.

You *could* try to translate between the two languages, but it will add delays and errors. You'd produce some software eventually, but you'd probably introduce some bugs along the way. Instead, pick just one language for the whole team to use—a *ubiquitous language*.

How to Speak the Same Language

Programmers should speak the language of their domain experts, not the other way around.

Imagine you're creating a piece of software for typesetting musical scores. The publishing house you're working for provides an XML description of the music, and you need to render it properly. This is a difficult task, filled with seemingly minor stylistic choices that are vitally important to your customers.

In this situation, you *could* focus on XML elements, parents, children, and attributes. You could talk about device contexts, bitmaps, and glyphs. If you did, your conversation might sound something like this:

> Programmer: "We were wondering how we should render this clef element. For example, if the element's first child is G and the second child is 2, but the octave-change element is -1, which glyph should we use? Is it a treble clef?"

> Domain expert: *(Thinking, "I have no idea what these guys are talking about. But if I admit it, they'll respond with something even more confusing. I'd better fake it.")* "Um... sure, G, that's treble. Good work."

Instead, focus on domain terms rather than technical terms.

> Programmer: "We were wondering how we should print this G clef. It's on the second line of the staff but one octave lower. Is that a treble clef?"

> Domain expert: *(Thinking, "An easy one. Good.")* "That's often used for tenor parts in choral music. It's a treble clef, yes, but because it's an octave lower we use two symbols rather than one. Here, I'll show you an example."

The domain expert's answer is different in the second example because he understands the question. The conversation in the first example would have led to a bug.

Ubiquitous Language in Code

As a programmer, you might have trouble speaking the language of your domain experts. When you're working on a tough problem, it's difficult to make the mental translation from the language of code to the language of the domain.

A better approach is to design your code to use the language of the domain. You can name your classes, methods, and variables *anything*. Why not use the terms that your domain experts use?

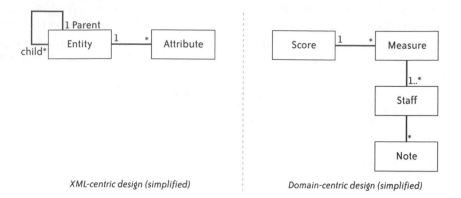

XML-centric design (simplified)   Domain-centric design (simplified)

Figure 6-4. XML and domain-centric design

This is more than learning the domain to write the software; this is reflecting *in code* how the users of the software *think* and *speak* about their work. By encoding your understanding of the domain, you refine your knowledge and—due to code's uncompromising need for precision—expose gaps in your knowledge that would otherwise result in bugs.

> Reflect how the users think and speak about their work.

To continue the example, a program to typeset a musical score based on XML input *could* be designed around XML concepts. A better approach, though, would be to design it around domain concepts, as shown in Figure 6-4.

One powerful way to design your application to speak the language of the domain is to create a *domain model*. This process deserves its own book; [Evans] and [Wirfs-Brock & McKean] are two worthy examples.

> **NOTE**
> The process of creating a domain-centric design is *domain-driven design* or *domain modelling*. Some people consider it synonymous with *object-oriented design*. In this case, domain-centric design is sometimes called *"true" object-oriented design* in order to contrast it with object-oriented designs that don't emphasize domain concepts.

Refining the Ubiquitous Language

The ubiquitous language informs programmers, but the programmers' need for rigorous formalization also informs the rest of the team. I often see situations in which programmers ask a question—inspired by a coding problem—that in turn causes domain experts to question some of their assumptions.

Your ubiquitous language, therefore, is a living language. It's only as good as its ability to reflect reality. As you learn new things, improve the language as well. There are three caveats about doing this, however.

First, ensure that the whole team—especially the domain experts—understands and agrees with the changes you're proposing. This will probably require a conversation to resolve any conflicts. Embrace that!

Second, check that the changes clarify your understanding of the business requirements. It may seem clearer to make a change, but the language must still reflect what the users need to accomplish with the software. Keep out programmer jargon—you can help domain experts refine their understanding of complicated corner cases, but don't replace their language with your own.

Third, update the design of the software with the change. The model and the ubiquitous language must always stay in sync. A change to the language implies a change to the model. Yes, this does mean that you should refactor the code when your understanding of the domain changes. Delaying these changes introduces an insidious type of technical debt: a mismatch between your design and reality, which will lead to ugly kludges and bugs.

Questions

Should we avoid the use of technical terms altogether? Our business domain doesn't mention anything about GUI widgets or a database.

It's OK to use technical language in areas that are unrelated to the domain. For example, it's probably best to call a database connection a "connection" and a button a "button." However, you should typically encapsulate these technical details behind a domain-centric face.

Results

When you share a common language between customers and programmers, you reduce the risk of miscommunication. When you use this common language within the design and implementation of the software, you produce code that's easier to understand and modify.

When the whole team uses the ubiquitous language while sitting together, everyone can overhear domain discussions, especially during pairing sessions. Team members overhear domain and implementation discussions and join in the conversation to resolve questions and expose hidden assumptions.

Contraindications

If you don't have any domain experts sitting with your team, you may have trouble understanding the domain experts' thought process deeply enough to have a ubiquitous language. Attempting a ubiquitous language is even more important in this situation, though, as it will allow you to communicate more effectively with domain experts when you do have the opportunity to speak with them.

Allies

Real Customer Involvement (p. 120)

Sit Together (p. 112)

On the other hand, some problems are so technical they don't involve non-programmer domain knowledge at all. Compilers and web servers are examples of this category. If you're building this sort of software, the language of technology *is* the language of the domain. You'll still have a ubiquitous language, but that language will be technical.

Some teams have no experience creating domain-centric designs. If this is true of your team, proceed with caution. Domain-centric designs require a shift in thinking that can be difficult. See "Further Reading" at the end of this section to get started, and consider hiring a programmer with experience in this area to help you learn.

Alternatives

It's always a good idea to speak the language of your domain experts. However, avoiding a domain-centric design *can* lead to simpler designs in small, technology-centric projects involving trivial business rules. Be careful, though: this design approach leads to defects and complex, unmaintainable designs in larger projects. See [Fowler 2002a] for further discussion of this trade-off.

> **NOTE**
> Even small XP projects typically involve four programmers working for several months, so most XP projects are big enough to need a domain-centric design. Talk to your mentor (see "Find a Mentor" in Chapter 2) before deciding to use another approach.

Further Reading

Domain-Driven Design [Evans] is an excellent and thorough discussion of how to create a domain-centric design.

Object Design [Wirfs-Brock & McKean] discusses roles, responsibilities, and behaviors in the context of modelling applications.

Patterns of Enterprise Application Architecture [Fowler 2002a] has a good discussion of the trade-offs between domain models and other architectural approaches.

Stand-Up Meetings

We know what our teammates are doing.

Audience
Whole Team

I have a special antipathy for status meetings. You know—a manager reads a list of tasks and asks about each one in turn. They seem to go on forever, although my part in them is typically only five minutes. I learn something new in perhaps 10 of the other minutes. The remaining 45 minutes are pure waste.

There's a good reason that organizations hold status meetings: people need to know what's going on. XP projects have a more effective mechanism: informative workspaces and the daily stand-up meeting.

Ally
Informative Workspace (p. 83)

How to Hold a Daily Stand-Up Meeting

A *stand-up meeting* is very simple. At a pre-set time every day, the whole team stands in a circle. One at a time, each person briefly describes new information that the team should know.

> **NOTE**
> I prefer to stand in an empty area of the team room rather than around a table—it feels a little more friendly that way. If you have room near the planning boards, that's a particularly good spot for the stand-up.

Some teams use a formal variant of the stand-up called the *Daily Scrum* [Schwaber & Beedle]. It comes from an agile process also called Scrum. In the Daily Scrum, participants specifically answer three questions:

1. What did I do yesterday?
2. What will I do today?
3. What problems are preventing me from making progress?

I prefer a more informal approach, but both styles are valid. Try both and use whichever approach works best for you.

One problem with stand-up meetings is that they interrupt the day. This is a particular problem for morning stand-ups; because team members know the meeting will interrupt their work, they sometimes wait for the stand-up to end before starting to work. If people arrive at different times, early arrivals sometimes just waste time until the stand-up starts. You can reduce this problem by moving the stand-up to later in the day, such as just before lunch.

> Don't wait for the stand-up to start your day.

Be Brief

The purpose of a stand-up meeting is to give everybody a rough idea of where the team is. It's not to give a complete inventory of everything happening in the project. The primary virtue of the stand-up meeting is *brevity*. That's why we stand: our tired feet remind us to keep the meeting short.

Each person usually only needs to say a few sentences about her status. Thirty seconds per person is usually enough. More detailed discussions should take place in smaller meetings with only the people involved. Here are some examples:

> Thirty seconds per person is usually enough.

A programmer:

> Yesterday, Bob and I refactored the database pooling logic. Check it out—we made some nice simplifications to the way you connect to the database. I'm open today, and I'd enjoy doing something GUI-related.

The product manager:

> As you know, I've been away at the trade show for the last week, getting some great feedback on the user interface and where we're going with the product. We need to make a few changes to the release plan; I'll be working with the other customers today to work out the details. I can give a lunch-and-learn in a day or two if you want to know more. [Several team members express enthusiasm.]

A domain expert:

> After you guys [nodding to the programmers] asked us about that financial rule yesterday, I talked it over with Chris and there was more to it than we originally thought. I have some updates to our customer tests that I'd like to go over with somebody.

A programmer responds:

> I've been working in that area; I can pair with you any time today.

If the stand-up lasts longer than 10 minutes—15 at the very most—it's taking too long. If people typically speak for 30 seconds each, then a team of 10 should be able to have a 5-minute stand-up meeting on most days.

Brevity is a tough art to master. To practice, try writing your statement on an index card in advance, then read from the card during the stand-up.

Another approach is to timebox the stand-up. Set a timer for 5 or 10 minutes, depending on the size of the team. When the timer goes off, the meeting is over, even if there are some people who haven't spoken yet. At first, you'll find that the meeting is cut off prematurely, but the feedback should help people learn to speak more briefly after a week or two.

If you're tactful, you can also interrupt extended reports or conversations and ask that people hold the discussion in a smaller group after the stand-up.

Questions

Can people outside the team attend the stand-up?

Yes; I ask that outsiders stand outside the circle and not speak unless they have something brief and relevant to add.

Some people, due to their position or personality, disrupt the smooth flow of the stand-up. If they're not members of the team, I prefer to use other mechanisms to keep them up-to-date, such as the informative workspace, reports, and iteration demos. The product manager or project manager are probably the best people to manage this relationship.

Allies

Informative Workspace (p. 83)

Reporting (p. 144)

Iteration Demo (p. 138)

Participants are being too brief. What should we do?

If they rush to finish quickly, participants might devolve into no-content statements like "same as yesterday" or "nothing new." If this happens a lot, gently remind participants to go into a bit more detail.

> Combine brevity with an unhurried calm.

People are always late to the stand-up. Can we treat them to parking-lot therapy?

I've been tempted to introduce Mr. Laggard to Mr. Baseball Bat myself. Keep in mind that this is illegal in most countries and tough on team cohesiveness.

Instead, the most effective way I know of combatting this problem is to start and end meetings on time even if people are absent.

We don't sit together. Can we still have stand-up meetings?

Yes; you can either convene in a common location, or you can use speakerphones and a teleconference. If you can possibly stand together, do—stand-up meetings by teleconference are a lot less effective. I find that people tend to ramble.

You can improve a teleconference stand-up by investing in good phone equipment, reminding people to stand up even when they're off-site, and being diligent about taking conversations offline.

Results

When you conduct daily stand-up meetings, the whole team is aware of issues and challenges that other team members face, and it takes action to remove them. Everyone knows the project's current status and what the other team members are working on.

Contraindications

Don't let the daily stand-up stifle communication. Some teams find themselves waiting for the stand-up rather than going over and talking to someone when they need to. If you find this happening, eliminating the stand-up for a little while may actually improve communication.

> Communicate issues as soon as they come up.

Beware of leaders who dominate the stand-up. As reviewer Jonathan Clarke so aptly put it, the ideal leader is "a charismatic but impatient colleague who will hurry and curtail speakers." The stand-up is a meeting of equals—no one person should dominate.

Alternatives

If you can't conduct a daily stand-up meeting, you need to stay in touch in some other way. If your team sits together, the resulting natural communication may actually be sufficient. Watch for unpleasant surprises that more communication can prevent.

Another alternative is the traditional weekly status meeting. I find these more effective when team members submit their statuses to a single moderator who can present collated information in 10 or 15 minutes. However, I've also seen this approach fall apart quickly.

Further Reading

"It's Not Just Standing Up: Patterns for Daily Stand-up Meetings" [Yip], at *http://www.martinfowler.com/articles/itsNotJustStandingUp.html*, is a nice collection of patterns for stand-up meetings.

"Stand-Up Meeting Antipatterns" [Miller], at *http://fishbowl.pastiche.org/2003/11/19/standup_meeting_antipatterns*, takes the opposite approach and describes common antipatterns and their solutions.

Coding Standards

Audience
Programmers

We embrace a joint aesthetic.

Back in the days of the telegraph, as the story goes, telegraph operators could recognize each other on the basis of how they keyed their dots and dashes. Each operator had a unique style, or *fist*, that experts could recognize easily. Programmers have style, too. We each have our own way of producing code. We refine our style over years until we think it's the most readable, the most compact, or the most informative it can be.

Individual style is great when you're working alone. In team software development, however, the goal is to create a collective work that is greater than any individual could create on his own. Arguing about whose style is best gets in the way; it's easier to work together in a single style.

XP suggests creating a *coding standard*: guidelines to which all developers agree to adhere when programming.

Beyond Formatting

I once led a team of four programmers who had widely differing approaches to formatting. When we discussed coding standards, I catalogued three different approaches to braces and tabs. Each approach had its own vigorous defender. I didn't want us to get bogged down in arguments, so I said that people could use whatever brace style they wanted.

The result was predictable: we had three different approaches to formatting in our code. I even saw two different ways of indenting within a single, short method.

You know what surprised me? It wasn't that bad. Sure, the layout was ugly, and I would have preferred consistency, but the code was still readable. In the end, the *rest* of our coding standard mattered much more than formatting.

We all agreed that clearly named variables and short methods were important. We agreed to use assertions to make our code fail fast, not to optimize without measurements, and never to pass null references between objects. We agreed on how we should and shouldn't handle exceptions, what to do about debugging code, and when and where to log events. These standards helped us far more than a consistent formatting style would have because each one had a concrete benefit. Perhaps that's why we were able to agree on them when we couldn't agree on formatting styles.

Don't get me wrong: a consistent formatting standard is good. If you can agree on one, do! However, when you're putting together your coding standard, don't fall into the trap of arguing about formatting. There are more important issues.

How to Create a Coding Standard

Creating a coding standard is an exercise in building consensus. It may be one of the first things that programmers do as a team. Over time, you'll amend and improve the standards. The most important thing you may learn from creating the coding standard is how to disagree constructively.

> The most important thing you will learn is how to disagree.

To that end, I recommend applying two guidelines:

1. Create the minimal set of standards you can live with.
2. Focus on consistency and consensus over perfection.

Hold your first discussion of coding standards during the first iteration. The project will typically start out with some discussion of stories and vision, then some release planning and iteration planning (see "Go!" in Chapter 4). After iteration planning, customers and testers will continue working on the release plan. That's a great time for programmers to talk about coding standards.

The best way to start your coding standard is often to select an industry-standard style guide for your language. This will take care of formatting questions and allow you to focus on design-related questions. If you're not sure what it should encompass, starting points include:

- Development practices (start with the practices in Chapter 9 and Chapter 7)
- Tools, keybindings, and IDE
- File and directory layout
- Build conventions
- Error handling and assertions
- Approach to events and logging
- Design conventions (such as how to deal with null references)

Limit your initial discussion to just one hour. Write down what you agree on. If you disagree about something, move on. You can come back to it later.

> Focus on agreements.

> **NOTE**
> I like to write each item that we agree upon on a flip chart so we can tape it to a wall in our open workspace. If you can find a neutral observer to take notes (such as your project manager), so much the better.

If you have trouble, take a step back and talk about your goals for the software and the results you would like to see. Agree about these issues first, even if you disagree about specific approaches. You will have many opportunities to improve your standard. Make the most important decisions now, and move on.

Depending on your team, this may be a contentious discussion. If that's the case, consider bringing in a professional facilitator to redirect the discussion to your team goals when the things get heated. Your HR department might be able to provide someone, or you can use an outside consultant.

Plan to hold another one-hour coding standard meeting a few days later, and another one a few weeks after that. The long break will allow you to learn to work together and to try out your ideas in practice. If there's still disagreement, experiment with one approach or the other, then revisit the issue.

Hold these initial meetings as often as they're useful. After that, change the standard at any time. Just stand up, announce your intention to the team, and, if everybody agrees, change the flip chart. Retrospectives are another good time to discuss changes to the coding standard.

Ally
Retrospectives (p. 91)

Over time, some of the items in the standard will become second nature. Cross them off to make room for more important issues. As you work together, you will recognize ways in which new standards can help. Add these new standards to the list in the same way as before, as long as everybody agrees to try them.

No matter what standards you choose, someone will be probably unhappy with some guideline even with a consensus-based approach. You'll probably find some practices jarring and grating at first. Over time, you'll get used to it. Coding standards are, in many ways, an aesthetic choice: it doesn't really matter what the standard is, as long as it's consistent and thoughtful. One of the marks of a professional is the willingness to put aside personal aesthetics for a team aesthetic.

Dealing with Disagreement

It's possible to pressure a dissenter into accepting a coding standard she doesn't agree with, but it's probably not a good idea. Doing so is a good way to create resentment and discord.

Instead, remember that few decisions are irrevocable in agile development; mistakes are opportunities to learn and improve. Ward Cunninghman put it well:[*]

> It was a turning point in my programming career when I realized that I didn't have to win every argument. I'd be talking about code with someone, and I'd say, "I think the best way to do it is A." And they'd say, "I think the best way to do it is B." I'd say, "Well no, it's really A." And they'd say, "Well, we want to do B." It was a turning point for me when I could say, "Fine. Do B. It's not going to hurt us that much if I'm wrong. It's not going to hurt us that much if I'm right and you do B, because, we can correct mistakes. So [let's] find out if it's a mistake."

Go ahead and leave the contested item out of the standard. Maybe lack of standardization in that area will lead to a mess. If it does, the team will learn from the experience and you can change the standard.

Adhering to the Standard

People make mistakes. Pair programming helps developers catch mistakes and maintain self-discipline. It provides a way to discuss formatting and coding questions not addressed by the guidelines. It's an also an excellent way to improve the standard; it's much easier to suggest an improvement when you can talk it over with someone first.

Allies

Pair Programming (p. 71)
Collective Code Ownership (p. 191)

Collective code ownership also helps people adhere to the standard, because many different people will edit the same piece of code. Code tends to settle on the standard as a result.

There are less effective approaches. Some teams use automated tools to check their source code for adherence to the coding standard. Others program their version control system to reformat files upon

---

[*] *http://en.wikiquote.org/wiki/Ward_Cunningham*

check-in. I don't like either approach; to me, the latter says that you don't trust people to make good decisions on their own, and the former tends to raise false warnings.

I've also heard of teams who elevate their coding standards to requirements and punish infractions. The idea of enforcing a coding standard leaves a bad taste in my mouth. Your teammates are presumably professionals who pride themselves on doing good work. No coding standard can substitute for professional judgment. Try not to get too upset when you see people deviating from the standard.

> Assume your colleagues are professional and well-meaning.

Assume your colleagues are professional and well-meaning. If someone is not following the standard, assume that there's a good reason—even if all the evidence is to the contrary. Your challenge is to find that reason and address it. This approach shows respect for others and will improve others' respect for you.

> **NOTE**
> Before you do anything, ask yourself whether the coding standard was really a team effort. If everybody agreed to every item, they should have no problem following the standard.

Start by talking with your colleague alone to see if there's a disagreement. Take an attitude of collaborative problem solving: instead of saying, "Why aren't you propagating exceptions like we agreed?" ask, "What do you think about the 'propagate exceptions' standard we agreed on? Should we keep it?" Give objections full consideration, raise them with the rest of the team, and consider changing the standard.

If the objector agrees with the standard but isn't applying it, it's possible that the standard isn't appropriate in every situation. Ask about specific cases you've noticed. Again, be collaborative, not confrontational. Say something like, "I think we're on the same page regarding the importance of propagating exceptions. In that case, can you explain what's happening in this method? I don't understand why this code doesn't propagate the exception here."

During this discussion, you may learn that the objector doesn't understand the standard. By this time, you should be in a good situation to discuss the standard and what it means. If he's a junior programmer and needs more help, coordinate with the rest of the team to make sure he gets plenty of pairing time with experienced developers.

There is another possibility for teams new to XP. Switching to XP is a big change and can make people feel like they've lost control; sometimes they react by picking small things that they refuse to change. An obstinate desire to stick with a particular coding standard, regardless of the wishes of the rest of the team, might be a symptom of this reaction.

In this case, your best solution may be to let the infractions slide for several months. Over time, as team members become more comfortable with the changes in their environment, they'll relax and be more willing to compromise.

Questions

We have legacy code that doesn't fit our standard. Should we fix it?

Leave old code alone if it works and you don't need to read or touch it otherwise. It's expensive and risky to spend a lot of time fixing legacy code upfront. Instead, as you modify and refactor those sections of code, bring them up to the new coding standards. When you fix a bug, add a feature, or improve abstraction and factoring, use the new standards on everything you modify.

You can also use an automated tool to perform large-scale formatting changes. Don't spend too much time on this, but if you can do it easily, you might as well. I prefer to integrate immediately before and after such an operation because reformatting changes tend to disguise other changes. Be aware that making such large-scale changes can render your version control system's change history much more difficult to read.

Results

When you agree on coding standards and conventions, you improve the maintainability and readability of your code. You can take up different tasks in different subsystems with greater ease. Pair programming moves much more smoothly, and you look for ways to improve the expressability and robustness of your code as you write it.

Contraindications

Don't allow coding standards to become a divisive issue for your team.

Alternatives

Some teams work together so well that they don't need a written coding standard; their coding standard is implicit.

If you have a new team, however, create a written coding standard even if everybody gets along well. New teams often go through an initial honeymoon period in which team members are reluctant to disagree with each other. Eventually, disagreements will come out. It's much better to create a standard before problems escalate.

Iteration Demo

Audience
Product Manager, Whole Team

We keep it real.

An XP team produces working software every week, starting with the very first week.

Sound impossible? It's not. It's merely difficult. It takes a lot of discipline to keep that pace. Programmers need discipline to keep the code clean so they can continue to make progress. Customers need discipline to fully understand and communicate one set of features before starting another. Testers need discipline to work on software that changes daily.

The rewards for this hard work are significantly reduced risk, a lot of energy and fun, and the satisfaction of doing great work and seeing progress. The biggest challenge is keeping your momentum.

The *iteration demo* is a powerful way to do so. First, it's a concrete demonstration of the team's progress. The team is proud to show off its work, and stakeholders are happy to see progress.

Second, the demos help the team be honest about its progress. Iteration demos are open to all stakeholders, and some companies even invite external customers to attend. It's harder to succumb to the temptation to push an iteration deadline "just one day" when stakeholders expect a demo.

> Iteration demos help keep the team honest.

Finally, the demo is an opportunity to solicit regular feedback from the customers. Nothing speaks more clearly to stakeholders than working, usable software. Demonstrating your project makes it and your progress immediately visible and concrete. It gives stakeholders an opportunity to understand what they're getting and to change direction if they need to.

Regular delivery is central to successful XP. The iteration demo is a concrete indication of that progress. When schedule problems occur (they always do), an iteration demo makes it harder to avoid reality—and facing reality gives you the opportunity to *manage* it.

How to Conduct an Iteration Demo

Anybody on the team can conduct the iteration demo, but I recommend that the product manager do so. He has the best understanding of the stakeholders' point of view and speaks their language. His leadership also emphasizes the role of the product manager in steering the product.

Invite anybody who's interested. The whole team, key stakeholders, and the executive sponsor should attend as often as possible. Include real customers when appropriate. Other teams working nearby and people who are curious about the XP process are welcome as well. If you can't get everyone in a room, use a teleconference and desktop-sharing software.

> **NOTE**
> If you have a particularly large audience, you may need to set some ground rules about questions and interruptions to prevent the demo from taking too long. I tell attendees that the product manager will be available for further discussion after the meeting.

The entire demo should take about 10 minutes. (After all, it's only been a week since the last one.) If it runs long, I look for ways to bring it to a close before it reaches half an hour.

Because this meeting is so short, I highly recommend starting on time, even if some people aren't present. This will send the message that you value attendees' time as well as the available time to work on the project. Both the product manager and the demo should be available for further discussion and exploration after the meeting.

Once everyone is together, briefly describe the features scheduled for the iteration and their value to the project. If the plan changed during the middle of the iteration, explain what happened. Don't sugarcoat or gloss over problems. Full disclosure will raise your credibility. By neither simplifying nor exaggerating problems, you demonstrate your team's ability to deal with problems professionally. Here is an example:

> Calmly describe problems and how you handled them.

> Last week, we scheduled five stories in the area of online bookings. These stories revolved around adding polish to our flight reservation system. That system was already functionally complete, but we want it to be more impressive and usable for our customers.

> We finished all the stories we had planned, but we had to change the itinerary story, as I'll show you in a moment. It turned out to have some performance problems, so we had to find another solution. It's not exactly what we had planned, but we're happy with the result and we don't intend to spend any more time on it.

After your introduction, go through the list of stories one at a time. Read the story, add any necessary explanation, and demonstrate that the story is finished. Use customer tests to demonstrate stories without a user interface.

Ally
Customer Tests (p. 278)

> Demonstrator: Our first story was to automatically fill in the user's billing information if they put in their frequent flyer number. First, I'll bring up the front page... click "reservations"... type in our test frequent flyer number... and there, you can see that the billing information fills in automatically.

> Audience member: What if they fill in the billing information first?

> Demonstrator: In that case, the billing information is left unchanged. [Demonstrates.]

If you come to a story that didn't work out as planned, provide a straightforward explanation. Don't be defensive; simply explain what happened.

> Demonstrator: Our next story involves the itinerary. As I mentioned, we had to change this story. You may remember that our original story was to show flight segments on an animated globe. The programmers had some concerns about performance, so they did a test and it turned out that rendering the globe would double our datacenter costs.

> Audience member: Why is it so expensive?

> Programmer: Many animations are unique, and we have to render them on the server. As a result, the server has to render a custom animated .GIF for each person. Because it's 3-D, it takes a lot of CPU, which means we would need more powerful hardware in the datacenter. We might be able to cache some of the .GIFs, but we'd need to take a close look at usage stats before we could say whether that would work.

> Demonstrator: We didn't want to spend time on performance optimizations, and the increased hardware cost wasn't worth it. None of our competitors have a map of flight segments at all,

so we decided a simpler 2-D map would be good enough. We had already used up some of our time for this story, though, and we didn't have enough time left to animate the map. After seeing the result [*demonstrates*] we decided it was good enough for now. We intend to move on to new features rather than spending more time on the itinerary.

Once the demo is complete, tell stakeholders how they can run the software themselves. Make an installer available on the network, or provide a server for stakeholder use, or something similar. You can also cut short side discussions by directing people to the sample installation.

Two Key Questions

At the end of the demo, ask your executive sponsor two key questions:[*]

1. Is our work to date satisfactory?
2. May we continue?

These questions help keep the project on track and remind your sponsor to speak up if she's unhappy. You should be communicating well enough with your sponsor that her answers are never a surprise.

> **NOTE**
> Your sponsor isn't likely to attend all the demos, although that's preferable. You can increase the likelihood of her attending by keeping the demo short. If she doesn't come at all, the product manager should conduct a private demo—and ask the two key questions—at least once per month.

Sometimes, she may answer "no" to the first question, or she may answer "yes" but be clearly reluctant. These are early indicators that something is going wrong. After the demo, talk with your sponsor and find out what she's unhappy about. Take immediate action to correct the problem.

> **NOTE**
> Sometimes your sponsor will be unhappy because she wants the team to go faster. See "Estimating" in Chapter 8 for a discussion of how to improve your velocity. "Risk Management," also in Chapter 8, has a discussion of what to do when you can't meet your sponsor's expectations.

In rare cases, the executive sponsor will answer "no" to the second question. You should never hear this answer—it indicates a serious breakdown in communication.

If you do hear this answer, you're done. Meet with your sponsor after the demo and confirm that she wants the team to stop. Let her know that you're prepared to ship what was demonstrated today and you'd like one final week to wrap things up. Try to find out what went wrong, and include your sponsor in the project retrospective, if possible.

---

[*] Thanks to Joshua Kerievsky of Industrial Logic for introducing me to this technique.

Weekly Deployment Is Essential

The iteration demo isn't just a dog and pony show; it's a way to prove that you're making real progress every iteration. Always provide an actual release that stakeholders can try for themselves after the demo. Even if they are not interested in trying a demo release, create it anyway; with a good automated build, it takes only a moment. If you can't create a release, your project may be in trouble.

One of the biggest schedule risks in software is the hidden time between "we're done" and "we've shipped." Teams often have to spend several extra weeks (or months) after the end of the planned schedule to make their product buildable and shippable. Releasing a usable demo every iteration mitigates this risk.

If you're starting a new codebase, be sure that the code is deployable every iteration. This will help stave off technical debt. The weekly rhythm of iteration demos and stakeholder releases is an excellent way to keep the code releasable. Chapter 7 describes how to do so.

If you're working on a legacy codebase, weekly deployment may not yet be possible. Your build system may be incomplete, you may not have an adequate demo environment, or the installer may not yet be written. If so, this indicates a large chunk of technical debt. See "Applying XP to an Existing Project" in Chapter 4 for suggestions on how to address this problem while continuing to satisfy stakeholders.

Questions

What do we do if the stakeholders keep interrupting and asking questions during the demo?

A certain number of questions is normal, particularly when you start giving demos. Over time, as stakeholders adapt to the weekly rhythm, you should see fewer interruptions.

For the first month or so, you can establish goodwill by ignoring the half-hour guideline and answering every question. After the first month, the product manager can politely ask stakeholders to direct further questions to him after the meeting.

What do we do if stakeholders keep nitpicking our choices?

Nitpicking is also normal, particularly in the beginning. It's usually a sign of genuine interest in the product, so don't take it too personally. Write the ideas down on cards, as with any story, and have the product manager prioritize them after the meeting. Resist the temptation to address, prioritize, or begin designing solutions in the meeting. Not only does this extend the meeting, it reduces the discipline of the normal planning practices.

If nitpicking continues after the first month, it may be a sign that the on-site customers are missing something. Take a closer look at the complaints to see if there's a deeper problem. Root-cause analysis may help.

> **Ally**
> Root-Cause Analysis (p. 88)

The stakeholders are excited by what they see and want to add a bunch of features. They're good ideas, but we don't have time for them—we need to move on to another part of the product. What should we do?

Don't say "no" during the iteration demo. Don't say "yes," either. Simply thank the stakeholders for their suggestions, and write them down as stories. After the demo is over, the product manager should take a close look at the suggestions and their value relative to the overall vision. If they don't fit into the schedule, she should make that decision and communicate it to the stakeholders.

We completely blew this iteration and don't have anything to show. What do we do?

It will be hard, but you need to be honest about what happened. Take responsibility as a team (rather than blaming individuals or functional groups), try not to be defensive, and let stakeholders know what you're doing to prevent the same thing from happening again. Here is an example:

> This week, I'm afraid we have nothing to show. We planned to work on flight tracking this week, but we underestimated the difficulty of interfacing with the backend airline systems. We discovered that we need our own test environment for the systems because our suppliers' systems are unreliable.
>
> We identified this problem early in the iteration, and we thought we could work around it. We did, but not in time to finish any stories. We should have replanned the iteration and created smaller stories that we could finish as soon as we encountered this issue. Now we know, and we'll be more proactive about replanning next time.
>
> The problems with interfacing with the airlines' systems will affect many of our stories. To prevent further surprises, we've revised our estimates. This pushes our best-case release date out by three weeks, which uses up most of our risk buffer. We're still on target for our scheduled release, but we'll have to cut features if we encounter any other major problems between now and then.
>
> I'm sorry for the bad news and welcome any suggestions. We can take a few questions now, and I'll be available for further discussion after we finish planning the upcoming iteration.

Results

When you conduct a weekly iteration demo and demo release, you instill trust in stakeholders, and the team is confident in its ability to deliver. You share problems forthrightly, which allows you to manage them and helps prevent them from ballooning out of control.

Contraindications

Because the iteration demo is highly visible, you may be tempted to fake a demo. You might show a user interface that doesn't have any logic behind it, or purposefully avoid showing an action that has a significant defect.

Instead, be clear about the software's limitations and what you intend to do about them. Faking progress leads stakeholders to believe that you have greater capacity than you actually do. They'll expect you to continue at the inflated rate, and you'll steadily fall behind. For more on the dangers

> Inability to demo is a clear danger sign.

of overpromoting, see "Organizational Strategy #6: Be Honest," earlier in this chapter.

If you can't demonstrate progress weekly, it's a clear sign that your project is in trouble. Slow down for a week, and figure out what's going wrong. Ask your mentor for help. The problem may be as simple as trying to do too much work.

Some teams hold a demo every week but can't actually *deploy* software for stakeholder use every week. This is a common indicator of technical debt. It reflects a deficiency in the team's build process and its ability to get stories "done done."

Allies

Ten-Minute Build (p. 177)

"Done Done" (p. 156)

Alternatives

The iteration demo is a clear indication of your ability to deliver: either you have the ability to demonstrate new features every week, or you don't. Your executive sponsor either gives you permission to continue, or he doesn't. I'm not aware of any alternatives that provide such valuable feedback.

Some teams conduct real releases at the end of each iteration rather than a demo. This is a great addition to the practice, if you can do it.

Reporting

Audience
Coaches, Upper Management

We inspire trust in the team's decisions.

You're part of a whole team. Everybody sits together. An informative workspace clearly tracks your progress. All the information you need is at your fingertips. Why do you need reports?

Actually, *you* don't need them. The people who aren't on your team, particularly upper management and stakeholders, do. They have a big investment in you and the project, and they want to know how well it's working.

Types of Reports

Progress reports are exactly that: reports on the progress of the team, such as an iteration demo or a release plan. Although progress reports seem to exist so that stakeholders can monitor and correct the team's direction, that's not their purpose. Instead, good progress reports allow stakeholders to trust the team's decisions.

Management reports are for upper management. They provide high-level information that allows management to analyze trends and set goals. It's not information you can pick up by casually lingering in an open workspace for an hour or two every month; it includes trends in throughput or defect rates.

What kinds of reports do you need to build trust and satisfy strategic needs? It depends on the stakeholders. Some stakeholders are hands-off and just want to see progress toward a goal; others want to know more details so they can build broader knowledge. You may need to produce a variety of reports for different audiences.

Be careful, though—reports take time and energy away from development, so don't produce every report you can imagine. Provide just enough reporting to satisfy key stakeholders. The project manager and product manager should combine their knowledge of stakeholders to gauge the proper level of reporting. The best way to know, of course, is to ask.

The range of reports you can produce is as broad as your imagination. The following sections list some that I've found particularly useful or, contrarily, common and unhelpful. The first set of reports are a normal byproduct of the whole team's work. The rest are usually the project manager's responsibility, though they depend on some input from the rest of the team.

Progress Reports to Provide

XP teams have a pronounced advantage when it comes to reporting progress: they make observable progress every week, which removes the need for guesswork. Furthermore, XP teams create several progress reports as a normal byproduct of their work.

Useful *and* free? There's little not to like about these four reports.

Vision statement

Your on-site customers should create and update a vision statement that describes what you're doing, why you're doing it, and how you'll know if you're successful. This provides important context for other reports. Post it prominently and reference it in conversation.

Ally
Vision (p. 201)

Weekly demo

Nothing is as powerful at demonstrating progress as working software. Invite stakeholders to the weekly iteration demo. They probably won't attend every week, but the mere fact that you hold weekly demos will build confidence in your work.

Ally
Iteration Demo (p. 138)

Release and iteration plans

The release and iteration planning boards already posted in your workspace provide great detail about progress. (See Figure 8-4, a release planning board, and Figure 8-9, an iteration planning board.) Invite stakeholders to look at them any time they want detailed status information.

For off-site stakeholders, consider using a webcam or regularly posted digital photos to broadcast the plans.

Burn-up chart

A *burn-up chart* is an excellent way to get a bird's-eye view of the project (see Figure 8-7). It shows progress and predicts a completion date. Most teams produce a burn-up chart when they update their release plan.

Progress Reports to Consider

If your stakeholders want more information, consider providing one or more of the following reports. Avoid providing them by default; each takes time that you could spend on development instead.

> Only produce reports that are strictly necessary.

Roadmap

Some stakeholders may want more detail than the vision statement provides, but not the overwhelming detail of the release and iteration plans. For these stakeholders, consider maintaining a document or slide deck that summarizes planned releases and the significant features in each one.

Status email

A weekly status email can supplement the iteration demo. I like to include a list of the stories completed for each iteration and their value. I also include our current range of probable completion scope and dates, and I explain any changes from the previous report.

If you added or removed stories from the schedule, explain that here, too. An honest appraisal of your work is part of an accurate status report.

Management Reports to Consider

Whereas progress reports demonstrate that the team will meet its goals, management reports demonstrate that the team is working well. As with progress reports, report only what you must.

Productivity

Software development productivity is notoriously difficult to measure [Fowler 2003]. It sounds simple—productivity is the amount of production over time—but in software, we don't have an objective way to measure production. What's the size of a feature?

NOTE

We can measure the *software's* size by counting function points or lines of code, but that's akin to measuring cell phone features in cubic inches.

Instead of trying to measure features, measure the team's impact on the business. Create an objective measure of value, such as return on investment. You can base it on revenue, cost savings, or some other valuable result.

Coming up with an objective measure of value is the most difficult part of reporting productivity. I can't provide specific guidance because the metric depends on what's important to your business. Your product manager and upper management should be able to help create this measure.

Once you have a measure, track its value every iteration. Until the team releases software to production, this number will trend downward, below zero. The team will be incurring costs but not generating value. After a release, the trend should turn upward.

The primary complaint I hear about this metric is that it's partially outside of the team's control. What if the sales staff doesn't sell the software? What if the business users aren't interested in the software?

These are valid concerns, but they ignore the reality of organizational success. For your team to achieve an organizational success, not just a technical success, your software must provide business value. This productivity metric reflects that fact.

To score well on this metric, you should have a team that includes on-site customers. These customers will figure out what customers or users want and show key stakeholders how to sell or use the software. By doing so, they will help turn technically excellent software into truly valuable software.

Ally
Real Customer Involvement (p. 120)

Throughput

Throughput is the number of features the team can develop in a particular amount of time. To avoid difficult questions such as "What's a feature?," measure the amount of time between the moment the team agrees to develop some idea and the moment that idea is in production and available for general use. The less time, the better.

Defects

Anyone can produce software quickly if it doesn't have to work. Consider counterbalancing your throughput report with defect counts.

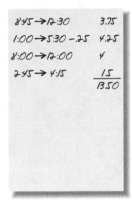

Figure 6-5. Time tracking example

One of the biggest challenges of counting defects is figuring out the difference between a defect and intentional behavior. Decide who will arbitrate these discussions early so you can avoid arguments.

When you count the defects is just as important as *how* you count them. On an XP team, finding and fixing defects is a normal part of the process. To avoid overcounting defects, wait until you have marked a story as "done done" and completed its iteration before marking something as a defect.

Ally
_____
"Done Done" (p. 156)

Time usage

If the project is under time pressure—and projects usually are—stakeholders may want to know that the team is using its time wisely. Often, when the team mentions its velocity, stakeholders question it. "Why does it take 6 programmers a week to finish 12 days of work? Shouldn't they finish 30 days of work in that time?"

Although I prefer that stakeholders trust the team to schedule its tasks wisely, that trust takes time to develop. In the beginning, I often produce a report that shows how the programmers are using their time. This report requires that programmers track their time in detail, so I stop producing it as soon as possible, typically after a month or two. To keep the burden low, I ask programmers to write their times on the back of each iteration task card (see Figure 6-5) and hand them in to the project manager for collating into these categories:

- Unaccounted and nonproject work (time spent on other projects, administration, company-wide meetings, etc.)
- Out of office (vacation and sick days)
- Improving skills (training, research time, etc.)
- Planning (time spent in planning activities, including the retrospective and iteration demo)
- Developing (time spent testing, coding, refactoring, and designing)

Graph the total time in each category in an area chart with "Developing" on the bottom and "Unaccounted" on top. I mark the bottom three categories green; the fourth yellow; and the top white (see Figure 6-6).

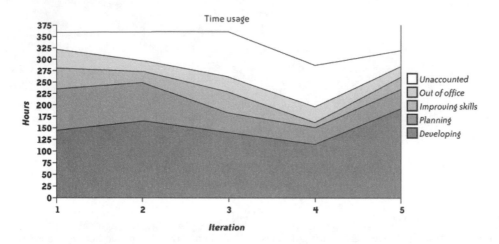

Figure 6-6. Time usage report

Once the report is in place, stakeholders may still wonder why velocity doesn't match effort. Explain that velocity includes a scaling factor to account for estimate error and overhead. See "Explaining Estimates" in Chapter 8 for more ideas.

Reports to Avoid

Some reports, although common, don't provide useful information. "Estimating" in Chapter 8 provides suggestions for explaining your estimates and velocity.

NOTE

If a stakeholder asks you for one of these reports, don't flatly refuse. Instead, find out why she wants the report and see if there's a better way to meet her need.

Source lines of code (SLOC) and function points

Source lines of code (SLOC) and its language-independent cousin, *function points*, are common approaches to measuring software size. Unfortunately, they're also used for measuring productivity. As with a fancy cell phone, however, software's *size* does not necessarily correlate to *features* or *value*.

Well-designed code is modular; it supports multiple features without duplication. The better the design, the less duplication, and thus the fewer lines of code. This sort of careful design takes time and effort, but results in fewer bugs and software that's easier to change.

Reporting SLOC (or function points) encourages your team to produce more lines of code per day. Rather than increasing its productivity, your team is most likely to spend less time on design quality. SLOC production will go up, true, but design quality will go down. Research shows that the more

> Reporting SLOC encourages defects and high costs.

lines of code a program has, the more defects it is likely to have and the more it will cost to develop.

All in all, SLOC and function points are flawed productivity metrics. They can be useful for end-of-project comparisons to industry averages, but avoid using it in a weekly report.

Number of stories

Some people think they can use the number of stories delivered each iteration as a measure of productivity. Don't do that. Stories have nothing to do with productivity.

A normal-sized team will typically work on 4 to 10 stories every iteration. To achieve this goal, they combine and split stories as needed. A team doing this job well will deliver a consistent number of stories each iteration regardless of its productivity.

Velocity

If a team estimates its stories in advance, an improvement in velocity *may* result from an improvement in productivity. Unfortunately, there's no way to differentiate between productivity changes and inconsistent estimates. Because you can artificially improve velocity by incurring technical debt, I strongly recommend against using velocity as a measure of productivity.

> Never compare velocity across teams.

Above all, never compare velocity across teams. Different teams will have different ways of estimating. Their velocities have nothing in common.

> NOTE
>
> Measuring the *variation* in velocity may produce interesting information for discussion in the retrospective (see "Retrospectives" in Chapter 5), but the information is too ambiguous to report outside the team.

Code quality

There's no substitute for developer expertise in the area of code quality. The available code quality metrics, such as cyclomatic code complexity, all require expert interpretation. There is no single set of metrics that clearly shows design or code quality. The metrics merely recommend areas that deserve further investigation.

Avoid reporting code quality metrics. They are a useful tool for developers but they're too ambiguous for reporting to stakeholders.

Questions

What do you mean, "Progress reports are for stakeholder trust"? Shouldn't we also report when we need help with something?

Absolutely. However, progress reports are for status; you shouldn't assume that anyone actually reads them. Sometimes their existence is enough to satisfy stakeholders that you're on track.

When you need a stakeholder's help, whether to learn more about the business priorities or to overcome a hurdle, ask for it. Don't rely on stakeholders to notice something in the reports.

> Talk to stakeholders directly when you need their help.

What if some of our stakeholders want to micromanage us?

The product manager and project manager should manage the stakeholders. They should give them what they need while shielding the team from their micromanagement. They need to be tactful, yet firm.

Isn't this just busywork? We have an informative workspace, stand-up meetings, and iteration demos. Stakeholders and managers can visit any time. Why do they need reports?

If your stakeholders attend your meetings *and* get sufficient value out of them, you probably don't need reports. In that case, the project manager should talk to stakeholders about cancelling unnecessary reports.

Until you reach that point, don't assume that writing solid code, delivering working software, and meeting real business needs will make everyone realize your value as a team. Sometimes you just need to staple a cover page to your TPS report in order to fit in.

What if programmers don't want to track their time for the time usage report? They say they have better things to do.

They're right—tracking time is a wasteful activity. However, the team has to balance the need to satisfy stakeholders with the need to use its time wisely.

You can make this decision easier to swallow in two ways. First, don't mandate the report unilaterally. Instead, discuss the reasons to produce reports as a team and come to a joint conclusion about which reports to provide. Keep in mind that some team members have greater practical insight about the consequences of reporting, or of not reporting, than others.

Second, do everything you can to keep the time-tracking burden low. When it's time to produce the report, the project manager should collate the data rather than asking programmers to do so.

Why should the project manager do all the grunt work for the reports? Shouldn't he delegate that work?

The project manager's job is to help the team work smoothly. He should never add to the workload of the people on the critical path. Instead, he should remove roadblocks from the path, and reports are one of those roadblocks.

Our organization measures employees individually based on the contents of certain reports. What do we do?

XP teams produce work as a team, not individually, so this is a difficult situation. First, the project manager should review the evaluation policy with HR and upper management. If there is any flexibility in the process, take advantage of it.

If there's no flexibility, work within the review process as much as you can. Highlight teamwork wherever possible. When the team implements a particularly valuable feature, be sure to mention everyone's contribution.

Results

Appropriate reporting will help stakeholders trust that your team is doing good work. Over time, the need for reports will decrease, and you will be able to report less information less frequently.

Contraindications

Time spent on reports is time *not* spent developing. Technically speaking, reports are wasteful because they don't contribute to development progress. As a result, I prefer to produce as few reports as possible.

Computerized planning may seem to make reporting easier. Unfortunately, it tends to do so at the expense of collaborative, dynamic planning (see "The Planning Game" in Chapter 8), and an informative workspace. That's backward: it optimizes a wasteful activity at the expense of productive activities.

> Don't let reporting compromise the benefits of card-based planning.

To avoid creating reports manually, I use the iteration demo, planning boards, and the burn-up chart as my only reports whenever I can. They are a normal part of the process and require no extra effort to produce. I use webcams or a digital camera to broadcast the boards if necessary.

I prefer not to report time usage, as it's time-consuming to produce and programmers don't like to collect the data, but I usually have to. While I only report it when I sense concern from important stakeholders about the team's velocity, that concern is typical for companies new to XP. Reevaluate this need about once a month, and stop producing the time usage report as soon as you can.

Alternatives

Frequent communication can sometimes take the place of formal reporting. If this option is available to you, it's a better option.

Further Reading

Why Does Software Cost So Much? [DeMarco 1995] contains an essay titled "Mad About Measurement" that discusses challenges of measuring performance, and includes a brief investigation into the results of reporting cyclomatic code complexity.

"Cannot Measure Productivity" [Fowler 2003] discusses the challenges of measuring software development productivity in more detail than I do here. *http://www.martinfowler.com/bliki/ CannotMeasureProductivity.html*.

CHAPTER 7

Releasing

What is the value of code? Agile developers value "working software over comprehensive documentation."[*] Does that mean a requirements document has no value? Does it mean unfinished code has no value?

Like a rock at the top of a hill, code has *potential*—potential energy for the rock and potential value for the code. It takes a push to realize that potential. The rock has to be pushed onto a slope in order to gain kinetic energy; the software has to be pushed into production in order to gain value.

It's easy to tell how much you need to push a rock. Big rock? Big push. Little rock? Little push. Software isn't so simple—it often looks ready to ship long before it's actually done. It's my experience that teams underestimate how hard it will be to push their software into production.

To make things more difficult, software's potential value changes. If nothing ever pushes that rock, it will sit on top of its hill forever; its potential energy won't change. Software, alas, sits on a hill that undulates. You can usually tell when your hill is becoming a valley, but if you need weeks or months to get your software rolling, it might be sitting in a ditch by the time you're ready to push.

In order to meet commitments and take advantage of opportunities, you must be able to push your software into production within minutes. This chapter contains 6 practices that give you leverage to turn your big release push into a 10-minute tap:

- *"done done"* ensures that completed work is ready to release.
- *No bugs* allows you to release your software without a separate testing phase.
- *Version control* allows team members to work together without stepping on each other's toes.
- A *ten-minute build* builds a tested release package in under 10 minutes.
- *Continuous integration* prevents a long, risky integration phase.
- *Collective code ownership* allows the team to solve problems no matter where they may lie.

[*] The Agile Manifesto, *http://www.agilemanifesto.org/*.

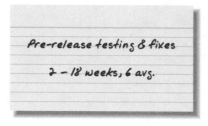

Figure 7-1. A sample card

- Post-hoc *documentation* decreases the cost of documentation and increases its accuracy.

"RELEASING" MINI-ÉTUDE

The purpose of this étude is to examine pushing software into production. If you're new to agile development, you may use it to create a map of all the steps involved in releasing software, even if you're not currently using XP. If you're an experienced agile practitioner, review Chapter 13 and use this étude to help you modify your process to remove communication bottlenecks.

Conduct this étude for a timeboxed half-hour every day for as long as it is useful. Expect to feel rushed by the deadline at first. If the étude becomes stale, discuss how you can change it to make it interesting again.

You will need red and green index cards, an empty table or magnetic whiteboard for your *value stream map*,[*] and writing implements for everyone.

Step 1. Start by forming heterogeneous pairs—have a programmer work with a customer, a customer work with a tester, and so forth, rather than pairing by job description. Work with a new partner every day.

Step 2. (Timebox this step to 10 minutes.) Within pairs, consider all the activities that have to happen between the time someone has an idea and when you can release it to real users or customers. Count an iteration as one activity, and group together any activities that take less than a day. Consider time spent waiting as an activity, too. If you can't think of anything new, pick an existing card and skip to Step 3.

Choose at least one task, and write it on a *red* card. Reflect on all the times you have performed this activity. If you have released software, use your experience; do not speculate. How long did it take? Think in terms of calendar time, not effort. Write three times down on the card: the *shortest* time you can remember, the *longest* time you can remember, and the *typical* time required. (See Figure 7-1.)

Step 3. (Timebox this step to 10 minutes.) Discuss things that your team can do to *reduce* the time required for this activity or to *eliminate* it entirely. Choose just one idea and write it on a *green* card.

Step 4. (Timebox this step to 15 minutes.) As a team, discuss your cards and place them on the table or whiteboard in a value stream map. Place activities (red cards) that must happen first before activities that can happen afterward. (See Figure 7-2.) If you're using a whiteboard, draw arrows between the cards to make the flow of work more clear. Place green cards underneath red cards.

Consider these discussion questions:

---

[*] The value stream map was inspired by [Poppendieck & Poppendieck].

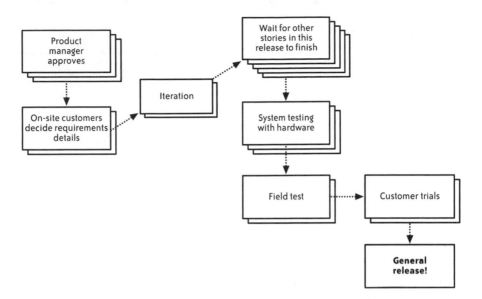

Figure 7-2. A sample value stream map

- At which step does work pile up?
- Which results surprise you?
- Who is the constraint in the overall system? How can you improve the performance of the overall system?
- Are there green cards with ideas you can adopt now?

"Done Done"

We're done when we're production-ready.

Audience
Whole Team

"Hey, Liz!" Rebecca sticks her head into Liz's office. "Did you finish that new feature yet?"

Liz nods. "Hold on a sec," she says, without pausing in her typing. A flurry of keystrokes crescendos and then ends with a flourish. "Done!" She swivels around to look at Rebecca. "It only took me half a day, too."

"Wow, that's impressive," says Rebecca. "We figured it would take at least a day, probably two. Can I look at it now?"

"Well, not quite," says Liz. "I haven't integrated the new code yet."

"OK," Rebecca says. "But once you do that, I can look at it, right? I'm eager to show it to our new clients. They picked us precisely because of this feature. I'm going to install the new build on their test bed so they can play with it."

Liz frowns. "Well, I wouldn't show it to anybody. I haven't tested it yet. And you can't install it anywhere—I haven't updated the installer or the database schema generator."

"I don't understand," Rebecca grumbles. "I thought you said you were done!"

"I am," insists Liz. "I finished coding just as you walked in. Here, I'll show you."

"No, no, I don't need to see the code," Rebecca says. "I need to be able to show this to our customers. I need it to be finished. *Really* finished."

"Well, why didn't you say so?" says Liz. "This feature is done—it's all coded up. It's just not *done* done. Give me a few more days."

Production-Ready Software

Wouldn't it be nice if, once you finished a story, you never had to come back to it? That's the idea behind *"done done."* A completed story isn't a lump of unintegrated, untested code. It's ready to deploy.

> You should able to deploy the software at the end of any iteration.

Partially finished stories result in hidden costs to your project. When it's time to release, you have to complete an unpredictable amount of work. This destabilizes your release planning efforts and prevents you from meeting your commitments.

To avoid this problem, make sure all of your planned stories are "done done" at the end of each iteration. You should be able to deploy the software at the end of any iteration, although normally you'll wait until more features have been developed.

What does it take for software to be "done done"? That depends on your organization. I often explain that a story is only complete when the customers can use it as they intended. Create a checklist that shows the story completion criteria. I write mine on the iteration planning board:

- Tested (all unit, integration, and customer tests finished)
- Coded (all code written)
- Designed (code refactored to the team's satisfaction)
- Integrated (the story works from end to end—typically, UI to database—and fits into the rest of the software)
- Builds (the build script includes any new modules)
- Installs (the build script includes the story in the automated installer)
- Migrates (the build script updates database schema if necessary; the installer migrates data when appropriate)
- Reviewed (customers have reviewed the story and confirmed that it meets their expectations)
- Fixed (all known bugs have been fixed or scheduled as their own stories)
- Accepted (customers agree that the story is finished)

Some teams add "Documented" to this list, meaning that the story has documentation and help text. This is most appropriate when you have a technical writer as part of your team.

Ally
The Whole Team (p. 28)

Other teams include "Performance" and "Scalability" in their "done done" list, but these can lead to premature optimization. I prefer to schedule performance, scalability, and similar issues with dedicated stories (see "Performance Optimization" in Chapter 9).

How to Be "Done Done"

XP works best when you make a little progress on every aspect of your work every day, rather than reserving the last few days of your iteration for getting stories "done done." This is an easier way to work, once you get used to it, and it reduces the risk of finding unfinished work at the end of the iteration.

> Make a little progress on every aspect of your work every day.

Use test-driven development to combine testing, coding, and designing. When working on an engineering task, make sure it integrates with the existing code. Use continuous integration and keep the 10-minute build up-to-date. Create an engineering task (see "Incremental Requirements" in Chapter 9 for more discussion of customer reviews) for updating the installer, and have one pair work on it in parallel with the other tasks for the story.

Allies
Test-Driven Development (p. 285)
Continuous Integration (p. 183)
Ten-Minute Build (p. 177)

Just as importantly, include your on-site customers in your work. As you work on a UI task, show an on-site customer what the screen will look like, even if it doesn't work yet (see "Customer review" in Chapter 9). Customers often want to tweak a UI when they see it for the first time. This can lead to a surprising amount of last-minute work if you delay any demos to the end of the iteration.

Similarly, as you integrate various pieces, run the software to make sure the pieces all work together. While this shouldn't take the place of testing, it's a good check to help prevent you from missing anything. Enlist the help of the testers on occasion, and ask them to show you exploratory testing techniques. (Again, this review doesn't replace real exploratory testing.)

Ally
Exploratory Testing (p. 341)

Throughout this process, you may find mistakes, errors, or outright bugs. When you do, fix them right away—then improve your work habits to prevent that kind of error from occurring again.

Ally
No Bugs (p. 160)

When you believe the story is "done done," show it to your customers for final acceptance review. Because you reviewed your progress with customers throughout the iteration, this should only take a few minutes.

Making Time

This may seem like an impossibly large amount of work to do in just one week. It's easier to do if you work on it throughout the iteration rather than saving it up for the last day or two. The real secret, though, is to make your stories small enough that you can completely finish them all in a single week.

Many teams new to XP create stories that are too large to get "done done." They finish all the coding, but they don't have enough time to completely finish the story—perhaps the UI is a little off, or a bug snuck through the cracks.

Remember, *you* are in control of your schedule. *You* decide how many stories to sign up for and how big they are. Make any story smaller by splitting it into multiple parts (see "Stories" in Chapter 8) and only working on one of the pieces this iteration.

Creating large stories is a natural mistake, but some teams compound the problem by thinking, "Well, we really *did* finish the story, except for that one little bug." They give themselves credit for the story, which inflates their velocity and perpetuates the problem.

If you have trouble getting your stories "done done," don't count those stories toward your velocity (see "Velocity" in Chapter 8). Even if the story only has a few minor UI bugs, count it as a zero when calculating your velocity. This will lower your velocity, which will help you choose a more

> If a story isn't "done done," don't count it toward your velocity.

manageable amount of work in your next iteration. ("Estimating" in Chapter 8 has more details about using velocity to balance your workload.)

You may find this lowers your velocity so much that you can only schedule one or two stories in an iteration. This means that your stories were too large to begin with. Split the stories you have, and work on making future stories smaller.

Questions

How does testers' work fit into "done done"?

In addition to helping customers and programmers, testers are responsible for nonfunctional testing and exploratory testing. Typically, they do these only *after* stories are "done done." They may perform some nonfunctional tests, however, in the context of a specific performance story.

Ally
Exploratory Testing (p. 341)

Regardless, the testers are part of the team, and everyone on the team is responsible for helping the team meet its commitment to deliver "done done" stories at the end of the iteration. Practically speaking, this usually means that testers help customers with customer testing, and they may help programmers and customers review the work in progress.

What if we release a story we think is "done done," but then we find a bug or stakeholders tell us they want changes?

If you can absorb the change with your iteration slack, go ahead and make the change. Turn larger changes into new stories.

Ally

Slack (p. 246)

This sort of feedback is normal—expect it. The product manager should decide whether the changes are appropriate, and if they are, he should modify the release plan. If you are constantly surprised by stakeholder changes, consider whether your on-site customers truly reflect your stakeholder community.

Results

When your stories are "done done," you avoid unexpected batches of work and spread wrap-up and polish work throughout the iteration. Customers and testers have a steady workload through the entire iteration. The final customer acceptance demonstration takes only a few minutes. At the end of each iteration, your software is ready to demonstrate to stakeholders with the scheduled stories working to their satisfaction.

Contraindications

This practice may seem advanced. It's not, but it does require self-discipline. To be "done done" every week, you must also work in iterations and use small, customer-centric stories.

Allies

Iterations (p. 41)
Stories (p. 253)
Sit Together (p. 112)
Incremental Design and Architecture (p. 321)
Test-Driven Development (p. 285)

In addition, you need a whole team—one that includes customers and testers (and perhaps a technical writer) in addition to programmers. The whole team must sit together. If they don't, the programmers won't be able to get the feedback they need in order to finish the stories in time.

Finally, you need incremental design and architecture and test-driven development in order to test, code, and design each story in such a short timeframe.

Alternatives

This practice is the cornerstone of XP planning. If you aren't "done done" at every iteration, your velocity will be unreliable. You won't be able to ship at any time. This will disrupt your release planning and prevent you from meeting your commitments, which will in turn damage stakeholder trust. It will probably lead to increased stress and pressure on the team, hurt team morale, and damage the team's capacity for energized work.

The alternative to being "done done" is to fill the end of your schedule with make-up work. You will end up with an indeterminate amount of work to fix bugs, polish the UI, create an installer, and so forth. Although many teams operate this way, it will damage your credibility and your ability to deliver. I don't recommend it.

No Bugs

We confidently release without a dedicated testing phase.

Let's cook up a bug pie. First, start with a nice, challenging language. How about C? We'll season it with a dash of assembly.

Next, add extra bugs by mixing in concurrent programming. Our old friends Safety and Liveness are happy to fight each other over who provides the most bugs. They supplied the Java multithreading library with bugs for years!

Now we need a really difficult problem domain. How about real-time embedded systems?

To top off this disaster recipe, we need the right kind of programmers. Let's see... experts... no... senior developers... no... aha! Novices! Just what we need.

Take your ingredients—C, real-time embedded systems, multitasking, and don't forget the novices—add a little assembly for seasoning, shake well, and bake for three years. (I do love me a bug pie.)

Here's how it turns out:

> The GMS team delivered this product after three years of development [60,638 lines of code], having encountered a total of 51 defects during that time. The open bug list never had more than two items at a time. Productivity was measured at almost three times the level for comparable embedded software teams. The first field test units were delivered after approximately six months into development. After that point, the software team supported the other engineering disciplines while continuing to do software enhancements.[*]

These folks had everything stacked against them—except their coach and her approach to software development. If they can do it, so can you.

How Is This Possible?

If you're on a team with a bug count in the hundreds, the idea of "no bugs" probably sounds ridiculous. I'll admit: "no bugs" is an ideal to strive for, not something your team will necessarily achieve.

However, XP teams *can* achieve dramatically lower bug rates. [Van Schooenderwoert]'s team averaged one and a half bugs per month in a very difficult domain. In an independent analysis of a company practicing a variant of XP, QSM Associates reported an average reduction from 2,270 defects to 381 defects [Mah].

You might think improvements like this are terribly expensive. They're not. In fact, agile teams tend to have above-average productivity.[†]

Evidence for these results is as yet anecdotal. Scientific studies of complete software development methodologies are rare due to the large number of variables involved. While there are organizations that draw performance conclusions by aggregating hundreds of projects, none that I am aware of have enough data to draw conclusions on agile projects in general, let alone XP specifically. (QSM Associates

---

[*] "Embedded Agile Project by the Numbers with Newbies" [Van Schooenderwoert].

[†] See, for example, [Van Schooenderwoert], [Mah], and [Anderson 2006].

is a well-regarded example of such an organization; as of June 2006, they only had data from a few agile projects.[*])

In the absence of conclusive proof, how can you know if your team will achieve these results? There's only one way to know for sure: try it and see. It doesn't take superpowers. Teams of novices coached by an experienced developer have done it. All you need is *commitment* to follow the XP practices rigorously and *support* from your organization to do so.

How to Achieve Nearly Zero Bugs

Many approaches to improving software quality revolve around finding and removing more defects[†] through traditional testing, inspection, and automated analysis.

The agile approach is to *generate fewer defects*. This isn't a matter of finding defects earlier; it's a question of not generating them at all.

For example, [Van Schooenderwoert] delivered 21 bugs to customers. Working from Capers Jones' data, Van Schooenderwoert says that a "best in class" team building their software would have generated 460 defects, found 95 percent of them, and delivered 23 to their customer.[‡] In contrast, Van Schooenderwoert's team generated 51 defects, found 59 percent of them, and delivered 21 to their customer. At 0.22 defects per function point, this result far exceeds Capers Jones' best-in-class expectation of two defects per function point.

To achieve these results, XP uses a potent cocktail of techniques:

1. *Write fewer bugs* by using a wide variety of technical and organizational practices.
2. *Eliminate bug breeding grounds* by refactoring poorly designed code.
3. *Fix bugs quickly* to reduce their impact, write tests to prevent them from reoccurring, then fix the associated design flaws that are likely to breed more bugs.
4. *Test your process* by using exploratory testing to expose systemic problems and hidden assumptions.
5. *Fix your process* by uncovering categories of mistakes and making those mistakes impossible.

This may seem like a lot to do, but most of it comes naturally as part of the XP process. Most of these activities improve productivity by increasing code quality or by removing obstacles. If you do them as part of XP, you won't have to do many of the other more expensive activities that other teams perform, such as an exhaustive upfront requirements gathering phase, disruptive code inspections, or a separate bug-fixing phase.

Ingredient #1: Write Fewer Bugs

Don't worry—I'm not going to wave my hands and say, "Too many bugs? No problem! Just write fewer bugs!" To stop writing bugs, you have to take a rigorous, thoughtful approach to software development.

---

[*] Personal communication with Michael Mah of QSM Associates.

[†] I use "defect" synonymously with "bug."

[‡] An "average" team would have generated 1,035, found 80 percent, and delivered 207.

Start with test-driven development (TDD), which is a proven technique for reducing the number of defects you generate [Janzen & Saiedian]. It leads to a comprehensive suite of unit and integration tests, and perhaps more importantly, it structures your work into small, easily verifiable steps. Teams using TDD report that they rarely need to use a debugger.

Allies

Test-Driven Development
(p. 285)

Energized Work (p. 79)

Pair Programming (p. 71)

Sit Together (p. 112)

Customer Tests (p. 278)

Exploratory Testing (p. 341)

Iteration Demo (p. 138)

Coding Standards (p. 133)

"Done Done" (p. 156)

To enhance the benefits of test-driven development, work sensible hours and program all production code in pairs. This improves your brainpower, which helps you make fewer mistakes and allows you to see mistakes more quickly. Pair programming also provides positive peer pressure, which helps you maintain the self-discipline you need to follow defect-reduction practices.

Test-driven development helps you eliminate coding defects, but code isn't your only source of defects. You can also produce good code that does the wrong thing. To prevent these requirements-oriented defects, work closely with your stakeholders. Enlist on-site customers to sit with your team. Use customer tests to help communicate complicated domain rules. Have testers work with customers to find and fix gaps in their approach to requirements. Demonstrate your software to stakeholders every week, and act on their feedback.

Supplement these practices with good coding standards and a "done done" checklist. These will help you remember and avoid common mistakes.

Ingredient #2: Eliminate Bug Breeding Grounds

Writing fewer bugs is an important first step to reducing the number of defects your team generates. If you accomplish that much, you're well ahead of most teams. Don't stop now, though. You can generate even fewer defects.

Even with test-driven development, your software will accumulate technical debt over time. Most of it will be in your design, making your code defect-prone and difficult to change, and it will tend to congregate in specific parts of the system. According to [Boehm], about 20 percent of the modules in a program are typically responsible for about 80 percent of the errors.

These design flaws are unavoidable. Sometimes a design that looks good when you first create it won't hold up over time. Sometimes a shortcut that seems like an acceptable compromise will come back to bite you. Sometimes your requirements change and your design will need to change as well.

Technical debt breeds bugs.

Whatever its cause, technical debt leads to complicated, confusing code that's hard to get right. It breeds bugs. To generate fewer defects, pay down your debt.

Although you could dedicate a week or two to fixing these problems, the best way to pay off your debt is to make small improvements every week. Keep new code clean by creating simple designs and refactoring as you go. Use the slack in each iteration to pay down debt in old code.

Allies

Simple Design (p. 314)

Refactoring (p. 303)

Slack (p. 246)

Ingredient #3: Fix Bugs Now

Programmers know that the longer you wait to fix a bug, the more it costs to fix [McConnell 1996, p. 75]. In addition, unfixed bugs probably indicate further problems. Each bug is the result of a flaw in your system that's likely to breed more mistakes. Fix it now and you'll improve both quality and productivity.

To fix the bug, start by writing an automated test that demonstrates the bug. It could be a unit test, integration test, or customer test, depending on what kind of defect you've found. Once you have a failing test, fix the bug. Get a green bar.

Don't congratulate yourself yet—you've fixed the problem, but you haven't solved the underlying cause. Why did that bug occur? Discuss the code with your pairing partner. Is there a design flaw that made this bug possible? Can you change an API to make such bugs more obvious? Is there some way to refactor the code that would make this kind of bug less likely? Improve your design. If you've identified a systemic problem, discuss it with the rest of your team in your next stand-up meeting or iteration retrospective. Tell people what went wrong so they can avoid that mistake in the future.

Fixing bugs quickly requires the whole team to participate. Programmers, use collective code ownership so that any pair can fix a buggy module. Customers and testers, personally bring new bugs to the attention of a programmer and help him reproduce it. These actions are easiest when the whole team sits together.

Allies

Collective Code Ownership (p. 191)

Sit Together (p. 112)

In practice, it's not possible to fix every bug right away. You may be in the middle of working on something else when you find a bug. When this happens to me, I ask my navigator to write the problem on our to-do list. We come back to it 10 or 20 minutes later, when we come to a good stopping point.

Some bugs are too big to fix while you're in the middle of another task. For these, I write the bug on a story card and announce it to the team. (Some teams use red story cards for this purpose.) We collectively decide if there's enough slack in the iteration to fix the bug and still meet our other commitments. If there is, we create tasks for the newly created story and pairs volunteer for them as normal. Sometimes your only task will be "fix the bug." I use the story card as its own task card when this happens.

Ally

Slack (p. 246)

If there *isn't* enough slack to fix the bug, estimate the cost to fix it and ask your product manager to decide whether to fix it in this release. If it's important enough to fix, schedule it into the very next iteration.

NOTE

Although you may wish to fix every bug right away, you need to consider its cost and value before doing so. Some bugs are expensive to fix but have limited impact; these are often not worth fixing. However, because bugs generally become more expensive to fix over time, you should typically only choose between "fix" (as soon as possible) or "don't fix" (until a later release).

DON'T PLAY THE BUG BLAME GAME

FEATURE

—*License plate seen on a Volkswagon Beetle*

If you tell a programmer there's a bug in his software, you're likely to get a prickly response: "That's not a bug, it's a feature!" or "What did you do wrong?"

I suspect this is because "bug" usually means "you screwed up."[*] Arguing about whether something is a bug often seems to be a fancy approach to finger-pointing. Some folks have taken this to a high art, making elaborate distinctions between bugs, defects, faults, errors, issues, anomalies, and of course, unintentional features. I prefer to avoid formal categorizations. What really matters is whether you will *do* or *not do* something, regardless of whether that something is fixing a bug or implementing a feature.

Mistakes do occur, of course, and we want to prevent those mistakes. Pointing fingers is counterproductive. The *whole team*—on-site customers, testers, and programmers—is responsible for delivering valuable software. Regardless of who made the mistake, the whole team is responsible for preventing it from reaching stakeholders. To that end, when I think about bugs, I focus on what the team delivers, not where the bug came from.

NOTE

A *bug* or *defect* is any behavior of your software that will unpleasantly surprise important stakeholders.

Before you yell "bug!", however, there are a few things to know:

- If the team finds and fixes a problem as part of its normal work—in other words, before a story is "done done"—it's not a bug.
- If the on-site customers have intentionally decided that the software should behave this way, it's not a bug. (Some of your software's behavior will be unpleasant to stakeholders—you can't please all people all the time—but hopefully it won't be a surprise.)

Remembering these things won't help you settle contract disputes, so don't use them for formal bug categorization. Instead, change the way you think about bugs. Stop worrying about who made what mistake, and start focusing on what you can do, as a team, to increase value by delivering fewer bugs.

Ingredient #4: Test Your Process

These practices will dramatically cut down the number of bugs in your system. However, they only prevent bugs you expect. Before you can write a test to prevent a problem, you have to realize the problem can occur.

Exploratory testing, in the hands of a good—some may say diabolical—tester, is an invaluable way to broaden your understanding of the types of problems that can occur. An exploratory tester uses her intuition and experience to tell her what kinds of problems programmers and customers have the most trouble considering. For example, she might unplug her network cable in the middle of an operation or perform a SQL injection attack on your database.

Ally
Exploratory Testing (p. 341)

If your team has typical adversarial relationships between programmers, customers, and testers, these sorts of unfair tests might elicit bitter griping from programmers. Remember, though—you're all in this together. The testers expose holes in your thought process and, by doing so, save you from having to

---

[*] Thanks to Ron Jeffries for this insight.

make uncomfortable apologies to stakeholders or from dramatic failures in production. Congratulate your testers on their ingenuity—and as you write tests, remember the problems they have exposed.

Exploratory testing is a very effective way of finding unexpected bugs. It's so effective that the rest of the team might start to get a little lazy.

Don't rely on exploratory testing to find bugs in your software. (Really!) Your primary defense against bugs is test-driven development and all the other good practices I've mentioned. Instead, use exploratory testing to test your *process*. When an exploratory test finds a bug, it's a sign that your work habits—your process—have a hole in them. Fix the bug, then fix your process.

> Think of exploratory testing as testing your process, not your software.

Testers, only conduct exploratory testing on stories that the team agrees are "done done." Programmers and customers, if your testers find any problems, think of them as bugs. Take steps to prevent them from occurring, just as you would for any other bug. Aim for a defect rate of under one or two bugs per month *including* bugs found in exploratory testing.

A good exploratory tester will find more bugs than you expect. To make the bug rate go down, fix your process.

Ingredient #5: Fix Your Process

Some bugs occur because we're human. (D'oh!) More often, bugs indicate an unknown flaw in our approach. When the number of bugs you generate gets low enough, you can do something usually associated with NASA's Space Shuttle software: root-cause analysis and process improvement on every bug.

> **NOTE**
> Even if your defect count isn't low enough to allow you to do root-cause analysis of every bug, consider randomly picking a bug each iteration for further analysis.

When you fix a bug, start by writing an automated test and improving your design to make the bug less likely. This is the beginning of root-cause analysis, but you can go even further.

As you write the test and fix the design, ask questions. Why was there no test preventing this bug? Why does the design need fixing? Use the "five whys" technique to consider the root cause. Then, as a team, discuss possible root causes and decide how best to change your work habits to make that kind of bug more difficult.

> **Ally**
> Root-Cause Analysis (p. 88)

MAKING MISTAKES IMPOSSIBLE

The best way to fix your process is to make mistakes impossible. For example, if you have a problem with UI field lengths being inconsistent with database field lengths, you could change your design to base one value off the other.

The next best solution is to find mistakes automatically. For example, you could write a test to check all UI and database fields for consistency and run that test as part of every build.

The least effective approach (but better than nothing!) is to add a manual step to your process. For example, you could add "check modified database/UI fields for length consistency" to your "done done" checklist.

Next, ask yourselves if the root cause of *this* bug could also have led to *other* bugs you haven't yet found. Testers, ask yourselves if this type of mistake reveals a blind spot in the team's thinking. Perform additional testing to explore these questions.

Invert Your Expectations

If you follow these practices, bugs should be a rarity. Your next step is to treat them that way. Rather than shrugging your shoulders when a bug occurs—"Oh yeah, another bug, that's what happens in software"—be shocked and dismayed. "That's our fourth bug this month! Why do we have so many bugs?"

I'm not so naïve as to suggest that the power of belief will eliminate bugs, but if you're already close, the shift in attitude will help you make the leap from *reducing* bugs to *nearly eliminating* bugs. You'll spend more energy on discovering and fixing root causes.

For this reason, I recommend that new XP teams not install a bug database. If you're only generating a bug or two per month, you don't need a database to keep track of your bugs; you can just process them as they come in. Explicitly *not* providing a database helps create the attitude that bugs are abnormal. It also removes the temptation to use the database as a substitute for direct, personal communication.

Depending on your industry, you may need a formal way to track defects so a database may be appropriate. However, I never assume a database will be necessary until the requirements of the situation *prove* it. Even then, I look for ways to use our existing process to meet the regulatory or organizational requirements. Although some shudder at the informality, archiving red bug cards in a drawer may suffice.

Even if you are able to eliminate your bug database, you still need to be able to reproduce bugs. You may need screenshots, core dumps, and so forth. If you fix bugs as soon as they come in, you may be able to work directly out of your email inbox. Otherwise, you can keep this information in the same place that you keep other requirements details. (See "Incremental Requirements" in Chapter 9.)

Questions

If novices can do this, what's stopping management from firing everybody and hiring novices?

All else remaining equal, experienced developers will always produce better results and more quickly than novices. If you have the option to bring high-quality people into your team, do it.

The point is that these practices are within the grasp of average teams—even teams of novices, as long as they have an experienced coach. They won't achieve zero bugs, but they are likely to achieve better results than they would otherwise.

How do we prevent security defects and other challenging bugs?

The approach I've described only prevents bugs you think to prevent. Security, concurrency, and other difficult problem domains may introduce defects you never considered.

In this situation, using exploratory testing to test and fix your process is even more important. You may need to hire a specialist tester, such as a security expert, to probe for problems and teach the team how to prevent such problems in the future.

How long should we spend working on a bug before we convert it into a story?

It depends on how much slack you have left in the iteration. Early in the iteration, when there's still a lot of slack, I might spend as much as four pair-hours on a defect. Later, when there's less slack, I might only spend 10 minutes on it.

Ally

Slack (p. 246)

Bugs are usually harder to find than to fix, so enlist the help of the testers. The fix often takes mere minutes once you've isolated the problem.

If our guideline is to fix bugs as soon as we find them, won't we have the unconscious temptation to overlook bugs?

Perhaps. This is one reason we pair: pairing helps us maintain our team discipline. If you find yourself succumbing to the temptation to ignore a bug, write it on a story card rather than let it slide by. Tell the rest of the team about the bug, and ask somebody to volunteer to fix it.

If we don't find any bugs, how do we know that our testers are doing exploratory testing correctly?

It's a bit of conundrum: the team is supposed to prevent bugs from occurring in "done done" stories, so exploratory testing shouldn't find anything. Yet if exploratory testing doesn't find anything, you could be testing the wrong things.

If bugs are particularly devastating for your project, ask an independent testing group to test a few of your iteration releases. If they don't find anything surprising, then you can have confidence in your exploratory testing approach.

This is probably overkill for most teams. If you're following the practices and your testers haven't found anything, you can comfortably release your software. Reevaluate your approach if your stakeholders or customers find a significant bug.

We have a large amount of legacy code. How can we adopt this policy without going mad?

Most legacy code doesn't have any tests and is chock-full of bugs. You can dig your way out of this hole, but it will take a lot of time and effort. See "Applying XP to an Existing Project" in Chapter 4 for details.

Results

When you produce nearly zero bugs, you are confident in the quality of your software. You're comfortable releasing your software to production without further testing at the end of any iteration. Stakeholders, customers, and users rarely encounter unpleasant surprises, and you spend your time producing great software instead of fighting fires.

Contraindications

"No Bugs" depends on the support and structure of all of XP. To achieve these results, you need to practice nearly all of the XP practices rigorously:

- All the "Thinking" practices are necessary (Pair Programing, Energized Work, Informative Workspace, Root-Cause Analysis, and Retrospectives); they help you improve your process, and they help programmers notice mistakes as they code.

- All the "Collaborating" practices except "Reporting" are necessary (Trust, Sit Together, Real Customer Involvement, Ubiquitous Language, Stand-Up Meetings, Coding Standards, and Iteration

Demo); most help prevent requirements defects, and the rest help programmers coordinate with each other.

- All the "Releasing" practices except "Documentation" are necessary ("Done Done," No Bugs, Version Control, Ten-Minute Build, Continuous Integration, and Collective Code Ownership); most help keep the code organized and clean. "Done Done" helps prevent inadvertent omissions.

- All the "Planning" practices except "Risk Management" are necessary (Vision, Release Planning, The Planning Game, Iteration Planning, Slack, Stories, and Estimating); they provide structure and support for the other practices.

- All the "Developing" practices except "Spike Solutions" are necessary (Test-Driven Development, Refactoring, Simple Design, Incremental Design and Architecture, Performance Optimization, Customer Reviews, Customer Testing, Exploratory Testing); they improve design quality, reduce requirements defects, and provide a way for testers to be involved in defect prevention as well as defect detection.

If you aren't using all these practices, don't expect dramatic reductions in defects. Conversely, if you have a project that's in XP's sweet spot (see "Is XP Right for Us?" in Chapter 4) and you're using all the XP practices, more than a few bugs per month may indicate a problem with your approach to XP. You need time to learn the practices, of course, but if you don't see improvements in your bug rates within a few months, consider asking for help (see "Find a Mentor" in Chapter 2).

Alternatives

You can also reduce bugs by using more and higher quality testing (including inspection or automated analysis) to find and fix a higher percentage of bugs. However, testers will need some time to review and test your code, which will prevent you from being "done done" and ready to ship at the end of each iteration.

Further Reading

"Embedded Agile Project by the Numbers with Newbies" [Van Schooenderwoert] expands on the embedded C project described in the introduction.

Version Control

We keep all our project artifacts in a single, authoritative place.

Audience
Programmers

To work as a team, you need some way to coordinate your source code, tests, and other important project artifacts. A *version control system* provides a central repository that helps coordinate changes to files and also provides a history of changes.

A project without version control may have snippets of code scattered among developer machines, networked drives, and even removable media. The build process may involve one or more people scrambling to find the latest versions of several files, trying to put them in the right places, and only succeeding through the application of copious caffeine, pizza, and stress.

A project *with* version control uses the version control system to mediate changes. It's an orderly process in which developers get the latest code from the server, do their work, run all the tests to confirm their code works, then check in their changes. This process, called *continuous integration*, occurs several times a day for each pair.

Ally
Continuous Integration (p. 183)

NOTE

If you aren't familiar with the basics of version control, start learning now. Learning to use a version control system effectively may take a few days, but the benefits are so great that it is well worth the effort.

VERSION CONTROL TERMINOLOGY

Different version control systems use different terminology. Here are the terms I use throughout this book:

Repository
> The repository is the master storage for all your files and and their history. It's typically stored on the version control server. Each standalone project should have its own repository.

Sandbox
> Also known as a working copy, a sandbox is what team members work out of on their local development machines. (Don't ever put a sandbox on a shared drive. If other people want to develop, they can make their own sandbox.) The sandbox contains a copy of all the files in the repository from a particular point in time.

Check out
> To create a sandbox, check out a copy of the repository. In some version control systems, this term means "update and lock."

Update
> Update your sandbox to get the latest changes from the repository. You can also update to a particular point in the past.

Lock
> A lock prevents anybody from editing a file but you.

Check in or commit
> Check in the files in your sandbox to save them into the repository.

Revert

> Revert your sandbox to throw away your changes and return to the point of your last update. This is handy when you've broken your local build and can't figure out how to get it working again. Sometimes reverting is faster than debugging, especially if you have checked in recently.

Tip or head

> The tip or head of the repository contains the latest changes that have been checked in. When you update your sandbox, you get the files at the tip. (This changes somewhat when you use branches.)

Tag or label

> A tag or label marks a particular time in the history of the repository, allowing you to easily access it again.

Roll back

> Roll back a check-in to remove it from the tip of the repository. The mechanism for doing so varies depending on the version control system you use.

Branch

> A branch occurs when you split the repository into distinct "alternate histories," a process known as *branching*. All the files exist in each branch, and you can edit files in one branch independently of all other branches.

Merge

> A merge is the process of combining multiple changes and resolving any conflicts. If two programmers change a file separately and both check it in, the second programmer will need to merge in the first person's changes.

Concurrent Editing

If multiple developers modify the same file without using version control, they're likely to accidentally overwrite each other's changes. To avoid this pain, some developers turn to a *locking model* of version control: when they work on a file, they lock it to prevent anyone else from making changes. The files in their sandboxes are read-only until locked. If you have to check out a file in order to work on it, then you're using a locking model.

While this approach solves the problem of accidentally overwriting changes, it can cause other, more serious problems. A locking model makes it difficult to make changes. Team members have to carefully coordinate who is working on which file, and that stifles their ability to refactor and make other beneficial changes. To get around this, teams often turn to strong code ownership, which is the worst of the code ownership models because only one person has the authority to modify a particular file. Collective code ownership is a better approach, but it's very hard to do if you use file locking.

> **Ally**
>
> Collective Code Ownership
> (p. 191)

Instead of a locking model, use a *concurrent model* of version control. This model allows two people to edit the same file simultaneously. The version control system automatically merges their changes—nothing gets overwritten accidentally. If two people edit the exact same lines of code, the version control system prompts them to merge the two lines manually.

Automatic merges may seem risky. They *would* be risky if it weren't for continuous integration and the automated build. Continuous integration reduces the scope of merges to a manageable level, and the build, with its comprehensive test suite, confirms that merges work properly.

Allies

Continuous Integration (p. 183)

Ten-Minute Build (p. 177)

Time Travel

One of the most powerful uses of a version control system is the ability to go back in time. You can update your sandbox with all the files from a particular point in the past.

This allows you to use *diff debugging*. When you find a challenging bug that you can't debug normally, go back in time to an old version of the code when the bug didn't exist. Then go forward and backward until you isolate the exact check-in that introduced the bug. You can review the changes in that check-in alone to get insight into the cause of the bug. With continuous integration, the number of changes will be small.

NOTE

A powerful technique for diff debugging is the *binary chop*, in which you cut the possible number of changes in half with each test. If you know that version 500 doesn't have the bug and your current version, 700, does, then check version 600. If the bug is present in version 600, it was introduced somewhere between 500 and 599, so now check version 550. If the bug is *not* present in version 600, it was introduced somewhere between version 601 and 700, so check version 650. By applying a bit of logic and halving the search space each time, you can quickly isolate the exact version.

A bit of clever code could even automate this search with an automated test.[*]

Time travel is also useful for reproducing bugs. If somebody reports a bug and you can't reproduce it, try using the same version of the code that the reporter is using. If you can reproduce the behavior in the old version but not in the current version, especially with a unit test, you can be confident that the bug is and will remain fixed.

Whole Project

It should be obvious that you should store your source code in version control. It's less obvious that you should store everything else in there, too. Although most version control systems allow you to go back in time, it doesn't do you any good unless you can build the exact version you had at that time. Storing the whole project in version control—including the build system—gives you the ability to re-create old versions of the project in full.

As much as possible, keep all your tools, libraries, documentation, and everything else related to the project in version control. Tools and libraries are particularly important. If you leave them out, at some point you'll update one of them, and then you'll no longer be able to go back to a time before the update. Or, if you do, you'll have to painstakingly remember which version of the tool you *used* to use and manually replace it.

---

[*] Thanks to Andreas Kö for demonstrating this.

For similar reasons, store the entire project in a single repository. Although it may seem natural to split the project into multiple repositories—perhaps one for each deliverable, or one for source code and one for documentation—this approach increases the opportunities for things to get out of sync.

Perform your update and commit actions on the whole tree as well. Typically, this means updating or committing from the top-level directory. It may be tempting to commit only the directory you've been working in, but that leaves you vulnerable to the possibility of having your sandbox split across two separate versions.

The only project-related artifact I *don't* keep in version control is generated code. Your automated build should re-create generated code automatically.

> Leave generated code out of the repository.

There is one remaining exception to what belongs in version control: code you plan to throw away. Spike solutions (see "Spike Solutions" in Chapter 9), experiments, and research projects may remain unintegrated, unless they produce concrete documentation or other artifacts that will be useful for the project. Check in only the useful pieces of the experiment. Discard the rest.

Customers and Version Control

Customer data should go in the repository, too. That includes documentation, notes on requirements (see "Incremental Requirements" in Chapter 9), technical writing such as manuals, and customer tests (see "Customer Tests" in Chapter 9).

When I mention this to programmers, they worry that the version control system will be too complex for customers to use. Don't underestimate your customers. While it's true that some version control systems are very complex, most have user-friendly interfaces. For example, the TortoiseSvn Windows client for the open-source Subversion version control system is particularly nice.

Even if your version control system is somewhat arcane, you can always create a pair of simple shell scripts or batch files—one for update and one for commit—and teach your customers how to run them. If you sit together, you can always help your customers when they need to do something more sophisticated, such as time travel or merging.

Keep It Clean

One of the most important ideas in XP is that you keep the code clean and ready to ship. It starts with your sandbox. Although you have to break the build in your sandbox in order to make progress, confine it to your sandbox. *Never* check in code that breaks the build. This allows anybody to update at any time without worrying about breaking their build—and that, in turn, allows everyone to work smoothly and share changes easily.

> Always check in code that builds and passes all tests.

> **NOTE**
> You can even minimize broken builds in your sandbox. With good test-driven development, you're never more than five minutes away from a working build.

Because your build automatically creates a release, any code that builds is theoretically ready to release. In practice, the code may be clean but the software itself won't be ready for the outside world. Stories will be half-done, user interface elements will be missing, and some things won't entirely work.

By the end of each iteration, you will have finished all these loose ends. Each story will be "done done," and you will deploy the software to stakeholders as part of your iteration demo. This software represents a genuine increment of value for your organization. Make sure you can return to it at any time by *tagging* the tip of the repository. I usually name mine "Iteration X," where X is the number of the iterations we have conducted.

Not every end-of-iteration release to stakeholders gets released to customers. Although it contains completed stories, it may not have enough to warrant a release. When you conduct an actual release, add another tag to the end-of-iteration build to mark the release. I usually name mine "Release Y," where Y is the number of releases we have conducted.

NOTE

Although your build should theoretically work from any sandbox, save yourself potential headaches by performing release builds from a new, pristine sandbox. The first time you spend an hour discovering that you've broken a release build by accidentally including an old file, you'll resolve never to do it again.

To summarize, your code goes through four levels of completion:

1. *Broken.* This only happens in your sandbox.
2. *Builds and passes all tests.* All versions in your repository are at least at this level.
3. *Ready to demo to stakeholders.* Any version marked with the "Iteration X" tag is ready for stakeholders to try.
4. *Ready to release to real users and customers.* Any version marked with the "Release Y" tag is production-ready.

Single Codebase

One of the most devastating mistakes a team can make is to duplicate their codebase. It's easy to do. First, a customer innocently requests a customized version of your software. To deliver this version quickly, it seems simple to duplicate the codebase, make the changes, and ship it. Yet that *copy and paste customization* doubles the number of lines of code that you need to maintain.

I've seen this cripple a team's ability to deliver working software on a timely schedule. It's nearly impossible to recombine a duplicated codebase without heroic and immediate action. That one click doesn't just lead to technical debt; it leads to indentured servitude.

> Duplicating your codebase will cripple your ability to deliver.

Unfortunately, version control systems actually make this mistake easier to make. Most of these systems provide the option to *branch* your code—that is, to split the repository into two separate lines of development. This is essentially the same thing as duplicating your codebase.

Branches have their uses, but using them to provide multiple customized versions of your software is risky. Although version control systems provide mechanisms for keeping multiple branches synchronized, doing so is tedious work that steadily becomes more difficult over time. Instead, design your code to support multiple configurations. Use a plug-in architecture, a configuration file, or factor out a common library or framework. Top it off with a build and delivery process that creates multiple versions.

Appropriate Uses of Branches

Branches work best when they are short-lived or when you use them for small numbers of changes. If you support old versions of your software, a branch for each version is the best place to put bug fixes and minor enhancements for those versions.

Some teams create a branch in preparation for a release. Half the team continues to perform new work, and the other half attempts to stabilize the old version. In XP, your code shouldn't require stabilization, so it's more useful to create such a branch at the point of release, not in preparation for release.

> **NOTE**
> To eliminate the need for a branch entirely, automatically migrate your customers and users to the latest version every time you release.

Branches can also be useful for continuous integration and other code management tasks. These *private branches* live for less than a day. You don't need private branches to successfully practice XP, but if you're familiar with this approach, feel free to use it.

Questions

Which version control system should I use?

There are plenty of options. In the open source realm, Subversion is popular and particularly good when combined with the TortoiseSvn frontend. Of the proprietary options, Perforce gets good reviews, although I haven't tried it myself.

Avoid Visual SourceSafe (VSS). VSS is a popular choice for Microsoft teams, but it has numerous flaws and problems with repository corruption—an unacceptable defect in a version control system.

Your organization may already provide a recommended version control system. If it meets your needs, use it. Otherwise, maintaining your own version control system isn't much work and requires little of a server besides disk space.

Should we really keep all our tools and libraries in version control?

Yes, as much as possible. If you install tools and libraries manually, two undesirable things will happen. First, whenever you make an update, everyone will have to manually update their computer. Second, at some point in the future you'll want to build an earlier version, and you'll spend several hours struggling to remember which versions of which tools you need to install.

Some teams address these concerns by creating a "tools and libraries" document and putting it in source control, but it's a pain to keep such a document up-to-date. Keeping your tools and libraries in source control is a simpler, more effective method.

Some tools and libraries require special installation, particularly on Windows, which makes this strategy more difficult. They don't all need installation, though—some just come with an installer because it's a cultural expectation. See if you can use them without installing them, and try to avoid those that you can't easily use without special configuration.

For tools that require installation, I put their install packages in version control, but I don't install them automatically in the build script. The same is true for tools that are useful but not necessary for the build, such as IDEs and diff tools.

How can we store our database in version control?

Rather than storing the database itself in version control, set up your build to initialize your database schema and migrate between versions. Store the scripts to do this in version control.

Ally

Ten-Minute Build (p. 177)

How much of our core platform should we include in version control?

In order for time travel to work, you need to be able to exactly reproduce your build environment for any point in the past. In theory, everything required to build should be in version control, including your compiler, language framework, and even your database management system (DBMS) and operating system (OS). Unfortunately, this isn't always practical. I include as much as I can, but I don't usually include my DBMS or operating system.

Some teams keep an image of their entire OS and installed software in version control. This is an intriguing idea, but I haven't tried it.

With so many things in version control, how can I update as quickly as I need to?

Slow updates may be a sign of a poor-quality version control system. The speed of better systems depends on the number of files that have *changed*, not the total number of files in the system.

One way to make your updates faster is to be selective about what parts of your tools and libraries you include. Rather than including the entire distribution—documentation, source code, and all—include only the bare minimum needed to build. Many tools only need a handful of files to execute. Include distribution package files in case someone needs more details in the future.

How should we integrate source code from other projects? We have read-only access to their repositories.

If you don't intend to change their code and you plan on updating infrequently, you can manually copy their source code into your repository.

If you have more sophisticated needs, many version control systems will allow you to integrate with other repositories. Your system will automatically fetch their latest changes when you update. It will even merge your changes to their source code with their updates. Check your version control system's documentation for more details.

Be cautious of making local changes to third-party source code; this is essentially a branch, and it incurs the same synchronization challenges and maintenance overhead that any long-lived branch does. If you find yourself making modifications beyond vendor-supplied configuration files, consider pushing those changes upstream, back to the vendor, as soon as possible.

We sometimes share code with other teams and departments. Should we give them access to our repository?

Certainly. You may wish to provide read-only access unless you have well-defined ways of coordinating changes from other teams.

Results

With good version control practices, you are easily able to coordinate changes with other members of the team. You easily reproduce old versions of your software when you need to. Long after your project has finished, your organization can recover your code and rebuild it when they need to.

Contraindications

You should always use some form of version control, even on small one-person projects. Version control will act as a backup and protect you when you make sweeping changes.

Concurrent editing, on the other hand, can be dangerous if an automatic merge fails and goes undetected. Be sure you have a decent build if you allow concurrent edits. Concurrent editing is also safer and easier if you practice continuous integration and have good tests.

Allies
Ten-Minute Build (p. 177)
Continuous Integration (p. 183)
Test-Driven Development (p. 285)

Alternatives

There is no practical alternative to version control.

You may choose to use file locking rather than concurrent editing. Unfortunately, this approach makes refactoring and collective code ownership very difficult, if not impossible. You can alleviate this somewhat by keeping a list of proposed refactorings and scheduling them, but the added overhead is likely to discourage people from suggesting significant refactorings.

Further Reading

Pragmatic Version Control Using Subversion [Mason] is a good introduction to the nuts and bolts of version control that specifically focuses on Subversion.

Source Control HOWTO [Sink], at *http://www.ericsink.com/scm/source_control.html*, is a helpful introduction to version control for programmers with a Microsoft background.

Software Configuration Management Patterns: Effective Teamwork, Practical Integration [Berczuk & Appleton] goes into much more detail about the ways in which to use version control.

Ten-Minute Build

Audience
Programmers

We eliminate build and configuration hassles.

Here's an ideal to strive for. Imagine you've just hired a new programmer. On the programmer's first day, you walk him over to the shiny new computer you just added to your open workspace.

"We've found that keeping everything in version control and having a really great automated build makes us a lot faster," you say. "Here, I'll show you. This computer is new, so it doesn't have any of our stuff on it yet."

You sit down together. "OK, go ahead and check out the source tree." You walk him through the process and the source tree starts downloading. "This will take a while because we have all our build tools and libraries in version control, too. Don't worry—like any good version control system, it brings down changes, so it's only slow the first time. We keep tools and libraries in version control because it allows us to update them easily. Come on, let me show you around the office while it downloads."

After giving him the tour, you come back. "Good, it's finished," you say. "Now watch this—this is my favorite part. Go to the root of the source tree and type build."

The new programmer complies, then watches as build information flies by. "It's not just building the source code," you explain. "We have a complex application that requires a web server, multiple web services, and several databases. In the past, when we hired a new programmer, he would spend his first couple of weeks just configuring his workstation. Test environments were even worse. We used to idle the whole team for days while we wrestled with problems in the test environment. Even when the environment worked, we all had to share one environment and we couldn't run tests at the same time.

"All that has changed. We've automated all of our setup. Anybody can build and run all the tests on their own machine, any time they want. I could even disconnect from the network right now and it would keep building. The build script is doing everything: it's configuring a local web server, initializing a local database... everything.

"Ah! It's almost done. It's built the app and configured the services. Now it's running the tests. This part used to be really slow, but we've made it much faster lately by improving our unit tests so we could get rid of our end-to-end tests."

Suddenly, everything stops. The cursor blinks quietly. At the bottom of the console is a message: BUILD SUCCESSFUL.

"That's it," you say proudly. "Everything works. I have so much confidence in our build and tests that I could take this and install it on our production servers today. In fact, we could do that right now, if we wanted to, just by giving our build a different command.

"You're going to enjoy working here." You give the new programmer a friendly smile. "It used to be hell getting even the simplest things done. Now, it's like butter. Everything just works."

Automate Your Build

What if you could build and test your entire product—or create a deployment package—at any time, just by pushing a button? How much easier would that make your life?

Producing a build is often a frustrating and lengthy experience. This frustration can spill over to the rest of your work. "Can we release the software?" "With a few days of work." "Does the software work?" "My piece does, but I can't build everything." "Is the demo ready?" "We ran into a problem with the build—tell everyone to come back in an hour."

Sadly, build automation is easy to overlook in the rush to finish features. If you don't have an automated build, start working on one now. It's one of the easiest things you can do to make your life better.

> Automating your build is one of the easiest ways to improve morale and increase productivity.

How to Automate

There are plenty of useful build tools available, depending on your platform and choice of language. If you're using Java, take a look at Ant. In .NET, NAnt and MSBuild are popular. Make is the old standby for C and C++. Perl, Python, and Ruby each have their preferred build tools as well.

Your build should be comprehensive but not complex. In addition to compiling your source code and running tests, it should configure registry settings, initialize database schemas, set up web servers, launch processes—everything you need to build and test your software from scratch without human intervention. Once you get the basics working, add the ability to create a production release, either by creating an install file or actually deploying to servers.

> NOTE
>
> Construct your build so that it provides a single, unambiguous result: SUCCESS or FAILURE. You will run the build dozens of times per day. Manual checks are slow, error-prone, and—after the umpteenth time—seriously annoying.

A key component of a successful automated build is the *local build*. A local build will allow you to build and test at any time without worrying about other people's activities. You'll do this every few minutes in XP, so independence is important. It will also make your builds run faster.

> You should be able to build even when disconnected from the network.

Be cautious of IDEs and other tools that promise to manage your build automatically. Their capability often begins and ends with compiling source code. Instead, take control of your build script. Take the time to understand exactly how and why it works and when to change it. Rather than starting with a pre-made template, you might be better off creating a completely new script. You'll learn more, and you'll be able to eliminate the complexity a generic script adds.

The details are up to you. In my build scripts, I prefer to have all autogenerated content go into a single directory called *build/*. The output of each major step (such as compiling source code, running tests, collating files into a release, or building a release package) goes into a separate directory under *build/*. This structure allows me to inspect the results of the build process and—if anything goes wrong—wipe the slate clean and start over.

When to Automate

At the start of the project, in the very first iteration, set up a bare-bones build system. The goal of this first iteration is to produce the simplest possible product that exercises your entire system. That includes delivering a working—if minimal—product to stakeholders.

Because the product is so small and simple at this stage, creating a high-quality automated build is easy. Don't try to cover all the possible build scenarios you need in the future. Just make sure you can build, test, and deploy this one simple product—even if it does little more than "Hello, world!" At this stage, deployment might be as simple as creating a *.zip* file.

> Use the build script to configure the integration machine. Don't configure it manually.

Once you have the seed of your build script, it's easy to improve. Every iteration, as you add features that require more out of your build, improve your script. Use your build script every time you integrate. To make sure it stays up-to-date, never configure the integration machine manually. If you find that something needs configuration, modify the build script to configure it for you.

Ally

Continuous Integration (p. 183)

Automating Legacy Projects

If you want to add a build script to an existing system, I have good news and bad news. The good news is that creating a comprehensive build script is one of the easiest ways to improve your life. The bad news is that you probably have a bunch of technical debt to pay off, so it won't happen overnight.

As with any agile plan, the best approach is to work in small stages that provide value as soon as possible. If you have a particularly complex system with lots of components, work on one component at a time, starting with the one that's most error-prone or frustrating to build manually.

Once you've picked the right component to automate, start by getting it to compile. That's usually an easy step, and it allows you to make progress right away.

Next, add the ability to run unit tests and make sure they pass. You probably compile and run unit tests in your IDE already, so this may not seem like a big improvement. Stick with it; making your build script able to prove itself is an important step. You won't have to check the results manually anymore.

Your next step depends on what's causing you the most grief. What is the most annoying thing about your current build process? What configuration issue springs up to waste a few hours every week? Automate that. Repeat with the next-biggest annoyance until you have automated everything. Once you've finished this, congratulations! You've eliminated all your build annoyances. You're ahead of most teams: you have a good build script.

Now it's time to make a *great* build script. Take a look at how you deploy. Do you create a release package such as an installer, or do you deploy directly to the production servers? Either way, start automating the biggest annoyances in your deployment process, one at a time. As before, repeat with the next-biggest annoyance until you run out of nits to pick.

This won't happen overnight, but try to make progress every week. If you can solve one annoyance every week, no matter how small, you'll see noticeable improvement within a month. As you work on other things, try not to add new debt. Include all new work in the build script from the beginning.

Ten Minutes or Less

A great build script puts your team way ahead of most software teams. After you get over the rush of being able to build the whole system at any time you want, you'll probably notice something new: the build is slow.

With continuous integration, you integrate every few hours. Each integration involves two builds: one on your machine and one on the integration machine. You need to wait for both builds to finish before continuing because you can never let the build break in XP. If the build breaks, you have to roll back your changes.

A 10-minute build leads to a 20-minute integration cycle. That's a pretty long delay. I prefer a 10- or 15-minute integration cycle. That's about the amount of time it takes to stretch my legs, get some coffee, and talk over our work with my pairing partner.

The easiest way to keep the build under 5 minutes (with a 10-minute maximum) is to keep the build times down from the beginning. One team I worked with started to look for ways to speed up the build whenever it exceeded 100 seconds.

Many new XP teams make the mistake of letting their build get too long. If you're in that boat, don't worry. You can fix long build times in the same agile way you fix all technical debt: piece by piece, focusing on making useful progress at each step.

For most teams, their tests are the source of a slow build. Usually it's because their tests aren't focused enough. Look for common problems: are you writing end-to-end tests when you should be writing unit tests and integration tests? Do your unit tests talk to a database, network, or file system?

> Slow tests are the most common cause of slow builds.

You should be able to run about 100 unit tests per second. Unit tests should comprise the majority of your tests. A fraction (less than 10 percent) should be integration tests, which checks that two components synchronize properly. When the rest of your tests provide good coverage, only a handful—if any—need to be end-to-end tests. See "Speed Matters in Chapter 9 for more information.

Although tests are the most common cause of slow builds, if compilation speed becomes a problem, consider optimizing code layout or using a compilation cache or incremental compilation. You could also use a distributed compilation system or take the best machine available for use as the build master. Don't forget to take advantage of the dependency evaluation features of your build tool: you don't need to rebuild things that haven't changed.

In the worst-case scenario, you may need to split your build into a "fast" build that you run frequently and a "slow" build that an integration server runs when you check in (see "Continuous Integration," later in this chapter). Be careful—this approach leads to more build failures than a single, fast build does. Keep working on making your build faster.

Questions

Who's responsible for maintaining the build script?

All the programmers are responsible for maintaining the script. As the codebase evolves, the build script should evolve with it.

At first, one person will probably be more knowledgeable about the script than others. When you need to update the script, pair with this person and learn all you can.

The build script is the center of your project automation universe. The more you know about how to automate your builds, the easier your life will become and the faster you'll be able to get work done.

We have a configuration management (CM) department that's responsible for maintaining our builds. We aren't allowed to modify the script ourselves. What do we do?

You need to be able to update your scripts continuously to meet your specific needs. It's unlikely that anybody can be more responsive to your needs than you are. If the CM department is a bottleneck, ask your project manager for help. He may be able to give you control over the scripts.

Alternatively, you might be able to use a two-stage build in which you run your own scripts privately before handing over control to the CM department.

How do we find time to improve our build?

Improving your build directly improves your productivity and quality of life. It's important enough to include in every iteration as part of your everyday work. The best way to do this is to include enough slack in your iteration for taking care of technical debt such as slow builds. If a particular story will require changes to the build script, include that time in your story estimate.

Ally

Slack (p. 246)

Should we really keep all our tools and libraries in version control?

Yes, as much as possible. See "Version Control" earlier in this chapter for details.

Does the build have to be under 10 minutes? We're at 11.

Ten minutes is a good rule of thumb. Your build is too long when pairs move on to other tasks before the integration cycle completes.

We use an IDE with an integrated build system. How can we automate our build process?

Many IDEs use an underlying build script that you can control. If not, you may be better off using a different IDE. Your other alternative is to have a separate command line–based build system, such as Ant, NAnt, or make. You risk duplicating information about dependencies, but sometimes that cost is worthwhile.

We have different target and development environments. How do we make this build work?

If possible, use a cross compiler. If that doesn't work, consider using a cross-platform build tool. The benefits of testing the build on your development platform outweigh the initial work in creating a portable system.

How can we build our entire product when we rely on third-party software and hardware?

Even if your product relies on yet-to-be-built custom hardware or unavailable third-party systems, you still need to build and test your part of the product. If you don't, you'll discover a ton of integration and bug-fixing work when the system becomes available.

A common solution for this scenario is to build a simulator for the missing system, which allows you to build integration tests. When the missing system becomes available, the integration tests help you determine if the assumptions you built into the simulator were correct.

Missing components add risk to your project, so try to get your hands on a test system as soon as possible.

How often should we build from scratch?

At least once per iteration. Building from scratch is often much slower than an incremental build, so it depends on how fast the build is and how good your build system is. If you don't trust your build system, build from scratch more often. You can set up a smoke-testing system that builds the project from scratch on every check-in.

My preference is to reduce build times so that incremental builds are unnecessary, or to fix the bugs in the build system so I trust the incremental builds. Even so, I prefer to build from scratch before delivering to customers.

Results

With a good automated build, you can build a release any time you want. When somebody new joins the team, or when you need to wipe a workstation and start fresh, it's a simple matter of downloading the latest code from the repository and running the build.

When your build is fast and well-automated, you build and test the whole system more frequently. You catch bugs earlier and, as a result, spend less time debugging. You integrate your software frequently without relying on complex background build systems, which reduces integration problems.

Contraindications

Every project should have a good automated build. Even if you have a system that's difficult to build, you can start chipping away at the problem today.

Some projects are too large for the 10-minute rule to be effective. Before you assume this is true for your project, take a close look at your build procedures. You can often reduce the build time much more than you realize.

Alternatives

If the project truly is too large to build in 10 minutes, it's probably under development by multiple teams or subteams. Consider splitting the project into independent pieces that you can build and test separately.

If you can't build your system in less than 10 minutes (yet), establish a maximum acceptable threshhold and stick to it. Drawing this line helps identify a point beyond which you will not allow more technical debt to accumulate. Like a sink full of dishes two hours before a dinner party, the time limit is a good impetus to do some cleaning.

Continuous Integration

Audience
Programmers

We keep our code ready to ship.

Most software development efforts have a hidden delay between when the team says "we're done" and when the software is actually ready to ship. Sometimes that delay can stretch on for months. It's the little things: merging everyone's pieces together, creating an installer, prepopulating the database, building the manual, and so forth. Meanwhile, the team gets stressed out because they forgot how long these things take. They rush, leave out helpful build automation, and introduce more bugs and delays.

Continuous integration is a better approach. It keeps everybody's code integrated and builds release infrastructure along with the rest of the application. The ultimate goal of continuous integration is to be able to deploy all but the last few hours of work at any time.

> The ultimate goal is to be able to deploy at any time.

Practically speaking, you won't actually release software in the middle of an iteration. Stories will be half-done and features will be incomplete. The point is to be *technologically* ready to release even if you're not *functionally* ready to release.

Why It Works

If you've ever experienced a painful multiday (or multiweek) integration, integrating every few hours probably seems foolish. Why go through that hell so often?

Actually, short cycles make integration *less* painful. Shorter cycles lead to smaller changes, which means there are fewer chances for your changes to overlap with someone else's.

That's not to say collisions don't happen. They do. They're just not very frequent because everybody's changes are so small.

> **NOTE**
> Collisions are most likely when you're making wide-ranging changes. When you do, let the rest of the team know beforehand so they can integrate their changes and be ready to deal with yours.

How to Practice Continuous Integration

In order to be ready to deploy all but the last few hours of work, your team needs to do two things:

1. Integrate your code every few hours.
2. Keep your build, tests, and other release infrastructure up-to-date.

To integrate, update your sandbox with the latest code from the repository, make sure everything builds, then commit your code back to the repository. You can integrate any time you have a successful build. With test-driven development, that should happen every few minutes. I integrate whenever I make a significant change to the code or create something I think the rest of the team will want right away.

Ally
Test-Driven Development (p. 285)

Each integration should get as close to a real release as possible. The goal is to make preparing for a release such an ordinary occurrence that, when you actually do ship, it's a nonevent.[*] Some teams that use continuous integration automatically burn an installation CD every time they integrate. Others create a disk image or, for network-deployed products, automatically deploy to staging servers.

> Toss out your recent changes and start over when you get badly stuck.

Never Break the Build

When was the last time you spent hours chasing down a bug in your code, only to find that it was a problem with your computer's configuration or in somebody else's code? Conversely, when was the last time you spent hours blaming your computer's configuration (or somebody else's code), only to find that the problem was in code you just wrote?

On typical projects, when we integrate, we don't have confidence in the quality of our code *or* in the quality of the code in the repository. The scope of possible errors is wide; if anything goes wrong, we're not sure where to look.

Reducing the scope of possible errors is the key to developing quickly. If you have total confidence that your software worked five minutes ago, then only the actions you've taken in the last five minutes could cause it to fail now. That reduces the scope of the problem so much that you can often figure it out just by looking at the error message—there's no debugging necessary.

To achieve this, agree as a team never to break the build. This is easier than it sounds: you can actually guarantee that the build will never break (well, almost never) by following a little script.

> Agree as a team never to break the build.

The Continuous Integration Script

To guarantee an always-working build, you have to solve two problems. First, you need to make sure that what works on *your* computer will work on *anybody's* computer. (How often have you heard the phrase, "But it worked on my machine!"?) Second, you need to make sure nobody gets code that hasn't been proven to build successfully.

To do this, you need a spare development machine to act as a central integration machine. You also need some sort of physical object to act as an integration token. (I use a rubber chicken. Stuffed toys work well, too.)

---

[*] ... except for the release party, of course.

With an integration machine and integration token, you can ensure a working build in several simple steps.

To update from the repository

1. Check that the integration token is available. If it isn't, another pair is checking in unproven code and you need to wait until they finish.
2. Get the latest changes from the repository. Others can get changes at the same time, but don't let anybody take the integration token until you finish.

Run a full build to make sure everything compiles and passes tests after you get the code. If it doesn't, something went wrong. The most common problem is a configuration issue on your machine. Try running a build on the integration machine. If it works, debug the problem on your machine. If it doesn't work, find the previous integrators and beat them about the head and shoulders, if only figuratively.

To integrate

1. Update from the repository (follow the previous script). Resolve any integration conflicts and run the build (including tests) to prove that the update worked.
2. Get the integration token and check in your code.
3. Go over to the integration machine, get the changes, and run the build (including tests).
4. Replace the integration token.

If the build fails on the integration machine, you have to fix the problem before you give up the integration token. The fastest way to do so is to roll back your changes. However, if nobody is waiting for the token, you can just fix the problem on your machine and check in again.

Avoid fixing problems manually on the integration machine. If the build worked on your machine, you probably forgot to add a file or a new configuration to the build script. In either case, if you correct the problem manually, the next people to get the code won't be able to build.

CONTINUOUS INTEGRATION SERVERS

There's a lively community of open-source *continuous integration servers* (also called *CI servers*). The granddaddy of them all is CruiseControl, pioneered by ThoughtWorks employees.

A continuous integration server starts the build automatically after check-in. If the build fails, it notifies the team. Some people try to use a continuous integration server instead of the continuous integration script discussed earlier. This doesn't quite work because without an integration token, team members can accidentally check out code that hasn't yet been proven to work.

Another common mistake is using a continuous integration server to shame team members into improving their build practices. Although the "wow factor" of a CI server can sometimes inspire people to do so, it only works if people are really willing to make an effort to check in good code. I've heard many reports of people who tried to use a CI server to enforce compliance, only to end up fixing all the build failures themselves while the rest of the team ignored their strong-arming.

If your team sits together and has a fast build, you don't need the added complexity of a CI server. Simply walk over to the integration machine and start the build when you check in. It only takes a few seconds—less time than it takes for a CI server to notice your check-in—and gives you an excuse to stretch your legs.

If you do install a CI server, don't let it distract you. Focus on mastering the *practice* of continuous integration, not the *tool*. Integrate frequently, never break the build, and keep your release infrastructure up-to-date.

Introducing Continuous Integration

The most important part of adopting continuous integration is getting people to agree to integrate frequently (every few hours) and never to break the build. Agreement is the key to adopting continuous integration because there's no way to force people not to break the build.

> Get the team to agree to continuous integration rather than imposing it on them.

If you're starting with XP on a brand-new project, continuous integration is easy to do. In the first iteration, install a version control system. Introduce a 10-minute build with the first story, and grow your release infrastructure along with the rest of your application. If you are disciplined about continuing these good habits, you'll have no trouble using continuous integration throughout your project.

If you're introducing XP to an existing project, your tests and build may not yet be good enough for continuous integration. Start by automating your build (see "Ten-Minute Build" earlier in this chapter), then add tests. Slowly improve your release infrastructure until you can deploy at any time.

Dealing with Slow Builds

The most common problem facing teams practicing continuous integration is slow builds. Whenever possible, keep your build under 10 minutes. On new projects, you should be able to keep your build under 10 minutes all the time. On a legacy project, you may not achieve that goal right away. You can still practice continuous integration, but it comes at a cost.

Ally

Ten-Minute Build (p. 177)

When you use the integration script discussed earlier, you're using *synchronous integration*—you're confirming that the build and tests succeed before moving on to your next task. If the build is too slow, synchronous integration becomes untenable. (For me, 20 or 30 minutes is too slow.) In this case, you can use *asynchronous integration* instead. Rather than waiting for the build to complete, start your next task immediately after starting the build, without waiting for the build and tests to succeed.

The biggest problem with asynchronous integration is that it tends to result in broken builds. If you check in code that doesn't work, you have to interrupt what you're doing when the build breaks half an hour or an hour later. If anyone else checked out that code in the meantime, their build won't work either. If the pair that broke the build has gone home or to lunch, someone else has to clean up the mess. In practice, the desire to keep working on the task at hand often overrides the need to fix the build.

If you have a very slow build, asynchronous integration may be your only option. If you must use this, a continuous integration server is the best way to do so. It will keep track of what to build and will automatically notify you when the build has finished.

Over time, continue to improve your build script and tests (see "Ten-Minute Build" earlier in this chapter). Once the build time gets down to a reasonable number (15 or 20 minutes), switch to synchronous integration. Continue

> Switch to synchronous integration when you can.

improving the speed of the build and tests until synchronous integration feels like a pleasant break rather than a waste of time.

Multistage Integration Builds

Some teams have sophisticated tests, measuring such qualities as performance, load, or stability, that simply cannot finish in under 10 minutes. For these teams, multistage integration is a good idea.

A *multistage integration* consists of two separate builds. The normal 10-minute build, or *commit build*, contains all the normal items necessary to prove that the software works: unit tests, integration tests, and a handful of end-to-end tests (see "Test-Driven Development" in Chapter 9 for more about these types of tests). This build runs synchronously as usual.

In addition to the regular build, a slower *secondary build* runs asynchronously. This build contains the additional tests that do not run in a normal build: performance tests, load tests, and stability tests.

Although a multistage build is a good idea for a mature project with sophisticated testing, most teams I encounter use multistage integration as a workaround for a slow test suite. I prefer to improve the test suite instead; it's more valuable to get better feedback more often.

> Prefer improved tests to a multistage integration.

If this is the case for you, a multistage integration might help you transition from asynchronous to synchronous integration. However, although a multistage build is better than completely asynchronous integration, don't let it stop you from continuing to improve your tests. Switch to fully synchronous integration when you can; only synchronous integration guarantees a known-good build.

Questions

I know we're supposed to integrate at least every four hours, but what if our current story or task takes longer than that?

You can integrate at any time, even when the task or story you're working on is only partially done. The only requirement is that the code builds and passes its tests.

What should we do while we're waiting for the integration build to complete?

Take a break. Get a cup of tea. Perform ergonomic stretches. Talk with your partner about design, refactoring opportunities, or next steps. If your build is under 10 minutes, you should have time to clear your head and consider the big picture without feeling like you're wasting time.

Ally

Ten-Minute Build (p. 177)

Isn't asynchronous integration more efficient than synchronous integration?

Although asynchronous integration may seem like a more efficient use of time, in practice it tends to disrupt flow and leads to broken builds. If the build fails, you have to interrupt your new task to roll back and fix the old one. This means you must leave your new task half-done, switch contexts (and sometimes partners) to fix the problem, then switch back. It's wasteful and annoying.

> Synchronous integration reduces integration problems.

Instead of switching gears in the middle of a task, many teams let the build remain broken for a few hours while they finish the new task. If other people integrate during this time, the existing failures hide any new failures in their integration. Problems compound and cause a vicious cycle: painful integrations lead to longer broken builds, which lead to more integration problems, which lead to more painful integrations. I've seen teams that practice asynchronous integration leave the build broken for days at a time.

Remember, too, that the build should run in under 10 minutes. Given a fast build, the supposed inefficiency of synchronous integration is trivial, especially as you can use that time to reflect on your work and talk about the big picture.

Are you saying that asynchronous integration will never work?

You can make asynchronous integration work if you're disciplined about keeping the build running fast, checking in frequently, running the build locally before checking in, and fixing problems as soon as they're discovered. In other words, do all the good things you're supposed to do with continuous integration.

Synchronous integration makes you confront these issues head on, which is why it's so valuable. Asynchronous integration, unfortunately, makes it all too easy to ignore slow and broken builds. You don't have to ignore them, of course, but my experience is that teams using asynchronous integration have slow and broken builds much more often than teams using synchronous integration.

Ron Jeffries said it best:[*]

> When I visit clients with asynchronous builds, I see these things happening, I think it's fair to say invariably:
>
> 1. The "overnight" build breaks at least once when I'm there;
> 2. The build lamp goes red at least once when I'm there, and stays that way for more than an hour.
>
> With a synchronous build, once in a while you hear one pair say "Oh, shjt."
>
> I'm all for more automation. But I think an asynch build is like shutting your eyes right when you drive through the intersection.

Our version control system doesn't allow us to roll back quickly. What should we do?

The overriding rule of the known-good build is that you must *know the build works* when you put the integration token back. Usually, that means checking in, running the build on the integration machine, and seeing it pass. Sometimes—we hope not often—it means rolling back your check-in, running the old build, and seeing that pass instead.

Ally
Version Control (p. 169)

If your version control system cannot support this, consider getting one that does. Not being able to revert easily to a known-good point in history is a big danger sign. You need to be able to revert a broken build with as much speed and as little pain as possible so you can get out of the way of other people waiting to integrate. If your version control can't do this for you, create an automated script that will.

One way to script this is to check out the older version to a temporary sandbox. Delete all the files in the regular sandbox except for the version control system's metadata files, then copy all the nonmetadata files over from the older version. This will allow you to check in the old version on top of the new one.

---

[*] Via the art of agile mailing list, *http://tech.groups.yahoo.com/group/art-of-agile/message/365.*

We rolled back our check-in, but the build is still failing on the integration machine. What do we do now?

Oops—you've almost certainly exposed some sort of configuration bug. It's possible the bug was in your just-integrated build script, but it's equally possible there was a latent bug in one of the previous scripts and you accidently exposed it. (Lucky you.)

Either way, the build has to work before you give up the integration token. Now you debug the problem. Enlist the help of the rest of the team if you need to; a broken integration machine is a problem that affects everybody.

Why do we need an integration machine? Can't we just integrate locally and check in?

In theory, if the build works on your local machine, it should work on any machine. In practice, don't count on it. The integration machine is a nice, pristine environment that helps prove the build will work anywhere. For example, I occasionally forget to check in a file; watching the build fail on the integration machine when it passed on mine makes my mistake obvious.

Nothing's perfect, but building on the integration machine does eliminate the majority of cross-machine build problems.

I seem to always run into problems when I integrate. What am I doing wrong?

One cause of integration problems is infrequent integration. The less often you integrate, the more changes you have to merge. Try integrating more often.

Another possibility is that your code tends to overlap with someone else's. Try talking more about what you're working on and coordinating more closely with the pairs that are working on related code.

If you're getting a lot of failures on the integration machine, you probably need to do more local builds before checking in. Run a full build (with tests) before you integrate to make sure your code is OK, then another full build (with tests) afterward to make sure the integrated code is OK. If that build succeeds, you shouldn't have any problems on the integration machine.

I'm constantly fixing the build when other people break it. How can I get them to take continuous integration seriously?

It's possible that your teammates haven't all bought into the idea of continuous integration. I often see teams in which only one or two people have any interest in continuous integration. Sometimes they try to force continuous integration on their teammates, usually by installing a continuous integration server without their consent. It's no surprise that the team reacts to this sort of behavior by ignoring broken builds. In fact, it may actually *decrease* their motivation to keep the build running clean.

Talk to the team about continuous integration before trying to adopt it. Discuss the trade-offs as a group, collaboratively, and make a group decision about whether to apply it.

If your team has agreed to use continuous integration but is constantly breaking the build anyway, perhaps you're using asynchronous integration. Try switching to synchronous integration, and follow the integration script exactly.

Results

When you integrate continuously, releases are a painless event. Your team experiences fewer integration conflicts and confusing integration bugs. The on-site customers see progress in the form of working code as the iteration progesses.

Contraindications

Don't try to force continuous integration on a group that hasn't agreed to it. This practice takes everyone's willful cooperation.

Using continuous integration without a version control system and a 10-minute build is *painful*.

Allies

Version Control (p. 169)
Ten-Minute Build (p. 177)

Synchronous integration becomes frustrating if the build is longer than 10 minutes and too wasteful if the build is very slow. My threshhold is 20 minutes. The best solution is to speed up the build.

A physical integration token only works if all the developers sit together. You can use a continuous integration server or an electronic integration token instead, but be careful to find one that's as easy to use and as obvious as a physical token.

Integration tokens don't work at all for very large teams; people spend too much time waiting to integrate. Use private branches in your version control system instead. Check your code into a private branch, build the branch on an integration machine—you can have several—then promote the branch to the mainline if the build succeeds.

Alternatives

If you can't perform synchronous continuous integration, try using a CI server and asynchronous integration. This will likely lead to more problems than synchronous integration, but it's the best of the alternatives.

If you don't have an automated build, you won't be able to practice asynchronous integration. Delaying integration is a very high-risk activity. Instead, create an automated build as soon as possible, and start practicing one of the forms of continuous integration.

Some teams perform a daily build and smoke test. Continuous integration is a more advanced version of the same practice; if you have a daily build and smoke test, you can migrate to continuous integration. Start with asynchronous integration and steadily improve your build and tests until you can use synchronous integration.

Collective Code Ownership

We are all responsible for high-quality code.

There's a metric for the risk imposed by concentrating knowledge in just a few people's heads—it's called the *truck number*. How many people can get hit by a truck before the project suffers irreparable harm?

It's a grim thought, but it addresses a real risk. What happens when a critical person goes on holiday, stays home with a sick child, takes a new job, or suddenly retires? How much time will you spend training a replacement?

Collective code ownership spreads responsibility for maintaining the code to all the programmers. Collective code ownership is exactly what it sounds like: everyone shares reponsibility for the quality of the code. No single person claims ownership over any part of the system, and anyone can make any necessary changes anywhere.

In fact, improved code quality may be the most important part of collective code ownership. Collective ownership allows—no, *expects*—everyone to fix problems they find. If you encounter duplication, unclear names, or even poorly designed code, it doesn't matter who wrote it. It's *your* code. Fix it!

> Fix problems no matter where you find them.

Making Collective Ownership Work

Collective code ownership requires letting go of a little bit of ego. Rather than taking pride in *your* code, take pride in *your team's* code. Rather than complaining when someone edits your code, enjoy how the code improves when you're not working on it. Rather than pushing your personal design vision, discuss design possibilities with the other programmers and agree on a shared solution.

Collective ownership requires a joint commitment from team members to produce good code. When you see a problem, fix it. When writing new code, don't do a half-hearted job and assume somebody else will fix your mistakes. Write the best code you can.

> Always leave the code a little better than you found it.

On the other hand, collective ownership means you don't have to be perfect. If you've produced code that works, is of reasonable quality, and you're not sure how to make it better, don't hesitate to let it go. Someone else will improve it later, if and when it needs it.

Working with Unfamiliar Code

If you're working on a project that has *knowledge silos*—in other words, little pockets of code that only one or two people understand—then collective code ownership might seem daunting. How can you take ownership of code that you don't understand?

To begin, take advantage of pair programming. When somebody picks a task involving code you don't understand, volunteer to pair with him. When you work on a task, ask the local expert to pair with you. Similarly, if you need to work on some unfamiliar code, take advantage of your shared workspace to ask a question or two.

Allies

Pair Programming (p. 71)
Sit Together (p. 112)

Rely on your inference skills as well. You don't need to know exactly what's happening in every line of code. In a well-designed system, all you need to know is what each package (or namespace) is responsible for. Then you can infer high-level class responsibilities and method behaviors from their names. (See "Refactoring" in Chapter 9.)

NOTE

Inferring high-level design from a brief review of the code is a black-belt design skill that's well worth learning. Take advantage of every opportunity to practice. Check your inferences by asking an expert to summarize class responsibilities and relationships.

Rely on the unit tests for further documentation and as your safety net. If you're not sure how something works, change it anyway and see what the tests say. An effective test suite will tell you when your assumptions are wrong.

As you work, look for opportunities to refactor the code. I often find that refactoring code helps me understand it. It benefits the next person, too; well-factored code tends toward simplicity, clarity, and appropriate levels of abstraction.

Ally

Refactoring (p. 303)

If you're just getting started with XP, you might not yet have a great set of unit tests and the design might be a little flaky. In this case, you may not be able to infer the design, rely on unit tests, or refactor, so pairing with somebody who knows the code well becomes more important. Be sure to spend time introducing unit tests and refactoring so that the next person can take ownership of the code without extra help.

Hidden Benefits

"Of course nobody can understand it... it's job security!"

—Old programmer joke

It's not easy to let a great piece of code out of your hands. It can be difficult to subsume the desire to take credit for a particularly clever or elegant solution, but it's necessary so your team can take advantage of all the benefits of collaboration.

It's also good for you as a programmer. Why? The whole codebase is yours—not just to modify, but to support and improve. You get to expand your skills. Even if you're an absolute database guru, you don't have to write only database code throughout the project. If writing a little UI code sounds interesting, find a programming partner and have at it.

You also don't have to carry the maintenance burden for a piece of code someone assigned you to write. Generally, the pair that finds a bug fixes the bug. They don't need your permission. Even better, they don't necessarily need your help; they may know the code now as well as you did when you wrote it.

It's a little scary at first to come into work and not know exactly what you'll work on, but it's also freeing. You no longer have long subprojects lingering overnight or over the weekend. You get variety and challenge and change. Try it—you'll like it.

Questions

We have a really good UI designer/database programmer/scalability guru. Why not take advantage of those skills and specialties?

Please do! Collective code ownership shares knowledge and improves skills, but it won't make everyone an expert at everything.

Don't let specialization prevent you from learning other things, though. If your specialty is databases and the team is working on user interfaces this week, take on a user interface task. It can only improve your skills.

How can everyone learn the entire codebase?

People naturally gravitate to one part of the system or another. They become experts in particular areas. Everybody gains a general understanding of the overall codebase, but each person only knows the details of what he's worked with recently.

The tests and simple design allow this approach to work. Simple design and its focus on code clarity make it easier to understand unfamiliar code. The tests act both as a safety net and as documentation.

Doesn't collective ownership increase the possibility of merge conflicts?

It does, and so it also requires continuous integration. Continuous integration decreases the chances of merge conflicts.

In the first week or two of the project, when there isn't much code, conflicts are more likely. Treat the code gently for the first couple of iterations. Talk together frequently and discuss your plans. As you progress, the codebase will grow, so there will be more room to make changes without conflict.

> **Ally**
>
> Continuous Integration (p. 183)

We have some pretty junior programmers, and I don't trust them with my code. What should we do?

Rather than turning your junior programmers loose on the code, make sure they pair with experienced members of the team. Keep an eye on their work and talk through design decisions and trade-offs. How else will they learn your business domain, learn your codebase, or mature as developers?

Different programmers on our team are responsible for different projects. Should the team collectively own all these projects?

If you have combined programmers working on several projects into a single team (as described in the discussion of team size in "Is XP Right for Us?" in Chapter 4), then yes, the whole team should take responsibility for all code. If your programmers have formed multiple separate teams, then they usually should not share ownership across teams.

Results

When you practice collective code ownership, you constantly make minor improvements to all parts of the codebase, and you find that the code you've written improves without your help. When a team member leaves or takes a vacation, the rest of the team continues to be productive.

Contraindications

Don't use collective code ownership as an excuse for *no* code ownership. Managers have a saying: "Shared responsibility is no responsibility at all." Don't let that happen to your code. Collective code ownership doesn't mean someone else is responsible for the code; it means *you* are responsible for the code—all of it. (Fortunately, the rest of the team is there to help you.)

Collective code ownership requires good communication. Without it, the team cannot maintain a shared vision, and code quality will suffer. Several XP practices help provide this communication: a team that includes experienced designers, sitting together, and pair programming.

> **Allies**
> Sit Together (p. 112)
> Pair Programming (p. 71)

Although they are not strictly necessary, good design and tests make collective code ownership easier. Proceed with caution unless you use test-driven development, simple design, and agree on coding standards. To take advantage of collective ownership's ability to improve code quality, the team must practice relentless refactoring.

> **Allies**
> Test-Driven Development (p. 285)
> Simple Design (p. 314)
> Coding Standards (p. 133)
> Refactoring (p. 303)

To coordinate changes, you must use continuous integration and a concurrent model of version control.

Alternatives

A typical alternative to collective code ownership is *strong code ownership*, in which each module has a specific owner and only that person may make changes. A variant is *weak code ownership*, in which one person owns a module but others can make changes as long as they coordinate with the owner. Neither approach, however, shares knowledge or enables refactoring as well as collective ownership does.

> **Allies**
> Continuous Integration (p. 183)
> Version Control (p. 169)

If you cannot use collective code ownership, you need to adopt other techniques to spread knowledge and encourage refactoring. Pair programming may be your best choice. Consider holding weekly design workshops to review the overall design and to brainstorm improvements.

> **Ally**
> Pair Programming (p. 71)

I recommend against strong code ownership. It encourages rigid silos of knowledge, which makes you vulnerable to any team member's absence. Weak code ownership is a better choice, although it still doesn't provide the benefits of collective ownership.

Documentation

We communicate necessary information effectively.

The word *documentation* is full of meaning. It can mean written instructions for end-users, or detailed specifications, or an explanation of APIs and their use. Still, these are all forms of *communication*—that's the commonality.

Communication happens all the time in a project. Sometimes it helps you get your work done; you ask a specific question, get a specific answer, and use that to solve a specific problem. This is the purpose of *work-in-progress documentation*, such as requirements documents and design documents.

Other communication provides business value, as with *product documentation*, such as user manuals and API documentation. A third type—*handoff documentation*—supports the long-term viability of the project by ensuring that important information is communicated to future workers.

Work-In-Progress Documentation

In XP, the whole team sits together to promote the first type of communication. Close contact with domain experts and the use of ubiquitous language create a powerful oral tradition that transmits information when necessary. There's no substitute for face-to-face communication. Even a phone call loses important nuances in conversation.

XP teams also use test-driven development to create a comprehensive test suite. When done well, this captures and communicates details about implementation decisions as unambiguous, executable design specifications that are readable, runnable, and modifiable by other developers. Similarly, the team uses customer testing to communicate information about hard-to-understand domain details. A ubiquitous language helps further reveal the intent and purpose of the code.

The team does document some things, such as the vision statement and story cards, but these act more as reminders than as formal documentation. At any time, the team can and should jot down notes that help them do their work, such as design sketches on a whiteboard, details on a story card, or hard-to-remember requirements in a wiki or spreadsheet.

In other words, XP teams don't need traditional written documentation to do their work. The XP practices support work-in-progress communication in other ways—ways that are actually more effective than written documentation.

Product Documentation

Some projects need to produce specific kinds of documentation to provide business value. Examples include user manuals, comprehensive API reference documentation, and reports. One team I worked with created code coverage metrics—not because they needed them, but because senior management wanted the report to see if XP would increase the amount of unit testing.

Because this documentation carries measurable business value but isn't otherwise necessary for the team to do its work, schedule it in the same way as all customer-valued work: with a story. Create, estimate, and prioritize stories for product documentation just as you would any other story.

Allies
Stories (p. 253)
The Planning Game (p. 219)

Handoff Documentation

If you're setting the code aside or preparing to hand off the project to another team (perhaps as part of final delivery), create a small set of documents recording big decisions and information. Your goal is to summarize the most important information you've learned while creating the software—the kind of information necessary to sustain and maintain the project.

Besides an overview of the project and how it evolved in design and features, your summary should include nonobvious information. Error conditions are important. What can go wrong, when might it occur, and what are the possible remedies? Are there any traps or sections of the code where the most straightforward approach was inappropriate? Do certain situations reoccur and need special treatment?

This is all information you've discovered through development as you've learned from writing the code. In clear written form, this information helps mitigate the risk of handing the code to a fresh group.

As an alternative to handoff documentation, you can gradually migrate ownership from one team to another. Exploit pair programming and collective code ownership to move new developers and other personnel onto the project and to move the previous set off in phases. Instead of a sharp break (or big thud) as one team's involvement ends and the other begins, the same osmotic communication that helps a team grow can help transition, repopulate, or shrink a team.

Allies
Pair Programming (p. 71)
Collective Code Ownership (p. 191)

Questions

Isn't it a risk to reduce the amount of documentation?

It could be. In order to reduce documentation, you have to replace it with some other form of communication. That's what XP does.

Increasing the amount of written communication also increases your risk. What if that information goes out of date? How much time does someone need to spend updating that documentation, and could that person spend that time updating the tests or refactoring the code to communicate that information more clearly?

The real risk is in decreasing the amount and accuracy of appropriate communication for your project, not in favoring one medium of communication. Favoring written communication may decrease your agility, but favoring spoken communication may require more work to disseminate information to the people who need it.

Results

When you communicate in the appropriate ways, you spread necessary information effectively. You reduce the amount of overhead in communication. You mitigate risk by presenting only necessary information.

Contraindications

Alistair Cockburndescribes a variant of Extreme Programming called "Pretty Adventuresome Programming":[*]

---

[*] http://c2.com/cgi/wiki?PrettyAdventuresomeProgramming. (*http://c2.com/cgi/wiki?PrettyAdventuresomeProgramming*)

A PrettyAdventuresomeProgrammer says:

"Wow! That ExtremeProgramming stuff is neat! We almost do it, too! Let's see...

"Extreme Programming requires:

- You do pair programming.
- You deliver an increment every three* weeks.
- You have a user on the team full time.
- You have regression unit tests that pass 100% of the time.
- You have automated acceptance tests which define the behavior of the system.

"As a reward for doing those,

- You don't put comments in the code.
- You don't write any requirements or design documentation.

"Now on this project, we're pretty close...

- well, actually a couple of our guys sit in the basement, a couple on the 5th floor, and a couple 2 hours drive from here, so we don't do pair programming,
- and actually, we deliver our increments every 4-6 months,
- we don't have users anywhere in sight,
- and we don't have any unit tests,

"but at least we don't have any design documentation,* and we don't comment our code much! So in a sense, you're right, we're almost doing ExtremeProgramming!"

Those people aren't doing XP, they are doing PAP [Pretty Adventuresome Programming]. PAP is using XP (in name) to legitimize not doing the things one doesn't want to do, without doing the XP practices that protects one from not doing the other things. E.g., changing the code all the time, but not writing unit tests; not writing documentation, but not writing clear code either. Not...(almost anything)... but not sitting close together. etc.*

In other words, continue to create documentation until you have practices in place to take its place. You have to be rigorous in your practice of XP in order to stop writing work-in-progress documentation. Particularly important is a whole team (with all the team roles filled—see "The XP Team" in Chapter 3) that sits together.

Ally
Sit Together (p. 112)

Some organizations value written documentation so highly that you can't eliminate work-in-progress documents. In my experience, these organizations usually aren't interested in trying XP. If yours is like that, but it wants to do XP anyway, talk with management about why those documents are important and whether XP can replace them. Perhaps handoff documents are an acceptable compromise. If not,

---

* Most teams now use one- or two-week iterations. I recommend one-week iterations for new teams; see "Iteration Planning" in Chapter 8.

* Emphasis in original.

* Alistair later added, "I am interested in having available a sarcasm-filled, derisively delivered phrase to hit people with who use XP as an excuse for sloppy, slap-dash development. I, of all people, think it actually is possible to turn dials to different numbers [Alistair means that you don't have to go as far as XP does to be successful], but I have no patience with people who slap the XP logo on frankly sloppy development."

don't eliminate work-in-progress documents. Either schedule the documents with stories or include the cost of creating and updating documents in your estimates.

Alternatives

If you think of documents as *communication mechanisms* rather than simply printed paper, you'll see that there are a wide variety of alternatives for documentation. Different media have different strengths. Face-to-face conversations are very high bandwidth but can't be referenced later, whereas written documents are very low bandwidth (and easily misunderstood) but can be referred to again and again.

Alistair Cockburn suggests an intriguing alternative to written documents for handoff documentation: rather than creating a design overview, use a video camera to record a whiteboard conversation between an eloquent team member and a programmer who doesn't understand the system. Accompany the video with a table of contents that provides timestamps for each portion of the conversation.

CHAPTER 8

Planning

Today I talked to a friend who wanted to know how I organized software projects. His team has grown rapidly, and their attempts to create and manage detailed plans are spiraling out of control. "It just doesn't scale," he sighed.

The larger your project becomes, the harder it is to plan everything in advance. The more chaotic your environment, the more likely it is that your plans will be thrown off by some unexpected event. Yet in this chaos lies opportunity.

Rather than trying to plan for every eventuality, embrace the possibilities that change brings you. This attitude is very different from facing change with clenched jaws and white knuckles. In this state of mind, we welcome surprise. We marvel at the power we have to identify and take advantage of new opportunities. The open horizon stretches before us. We know in which direction we need to travel, and we have the flexibility in our plan to choose the best way to get there. We'll know it when we find it.

This approach may sound like it's out of control. It would be, except for eight practices that allow you to control the chaos of endless possibility:

- *Vision* reveals where the project is going and why it's going there.
- *Release Planning* provides a roadmap for reaching your destination.
- *The Planning Game* combines the expertise of the whole team to create achievable plans.
- *Risk Management* allows the team to make and meet long-term commitments.
- *Iteration Planning* provides structure to the team's daily activities.
- *Slack* allows the team to reliably deliver results every iteration.
- *Stories* form the line items in the team's plan.
- *Estimating* enables the team to predict how long its work will take.

"PLANNING" MINI-ÉTUDE

The purpose of this étude is to discuss the effect of change on value. If you're new to agile development, you may use it to better understand the purpose of your project and how each story adds value. If you're an experienced agile practitioner, review Chapter 14 and use this étude to help you adapt your plans.

Conduct this étude for a timeboxed half-hour every day for as long as it is useful. Expect to feel rushed by the deadline at first. If the étude becomes stale, discuss how you can change it to make it interesting again.

You will need three different colors of index cards, an empty table or whiteboard, and writing implements.

Step 1. Start by forming pairs. Try for heterogenous pairs.

Step 2. (Timebox this step to five minutes.) Within your pair, choose an unimplemented story and discuss why it's valuable to the customer. Write the primary reason on an index card.

Step 3. (Timebox this step to five minutes.) Within your pair, brainstorm ideas that would provide even more value, whether by changing the existing story or by creating a new story. Write one idea on an index card of a different color.

Step 4. (Timebox this step to five minutes.) Still within your pair, devise an experiment that would prove whether your new idea would work in practice—*without actually trying the idea itself.* What can you do to test the concept behind your idea? Write the test on an index card of a third color.

Step 5. (Timebox this step to 15 minutes.) Return to the group. Choose three pairs. Give each pair five minutes to lead a discussion of their findings. Post the resulting cards on the table or whiteboard for as long as you perform this étude.

Discussion questions may include:

- What types of value are there in the cards?
- What would be hard to do? What would be easy?
- How well does your work reflect the potential value of the project?
- Which concrete experiments should you conduct in the next iteration?

Vision

We know why our work is important and how we'll be successful.

Audience
Product Manager, Customers

Vision. If there's a more derided word in the corporate vocabulary, I don't know what it is. This word brings to mind bland corporate-speak: "Our vision is to serve customers while maximizing stakeholder value and upholding the family values of our employees." Bleh. Content-free baloney.

Don't worry—that's not what you're going to do.

Product Vision

Before a project is a project, someone in the company has an idea. Suppose it's someone in the Wizzle-Frobitz company.* "Hey!" he says, sitting bolt upright in bed. "We could frobitz the wizzles so much better if we had some software that sorted the wizzles first!"

Maybe it's not quite that dramatic. The point is, projects start out as ideas focused on results. Sell more hardware by bundling better software. Attract bigger customers by scaling more effectively. Open up a new market by offering a new service. The idea is so compelling that it gets funding, and the project begins.

Somewhere in the transition from idea to project, the compelling part—the *vision* of a better future—often gets lost. Details crowd it out. You have to hire programmers, domain experts, and interaction designers. You must create stories, schedule iterations, and report on progress. Hustle, people, hustle!

That's a shame, because nothing matters more than delivering the vision. The goal of the entire project is to frobitz wizzles better. If the details are perfect (the wizzles are sorted with elegance and precision) but the vision is forgotten (the wizzle sorter doesn't work with the frobitzer), then the software will probably fail. Conversely, if you ship something that helps frobitz wizzles better than anything else, does it really matter *how* you did it?

Where Visions Come From

Sometimes the vision for a project strikes as a single, compelling idea. One person gets a bright idea, evangelizes it, and gets approval to pursue it. This person is a *visionary*.

More often, the vision isn't so clear. There are multiple visionaries, each with their own unique idea of what the project should deliver.

Either way, the project needs a single vision. Someone must unify, communicate, and promote the vision to the team and to stakeholders. That someone is the product manager.

Identifying the Vision

Like the children's game of telephone, every step between the visionaries and the product manager reduces the product manager's ability to accurately maintain and effectively promote the vision.

---

* Not a real company.

If you only have one visionary, the best approach is to have that visionary act as product manager. This reduces the possibility of any telephone-game confusion. As long as the vision is both worthwhile and achievable, the visionary's day-to-day involvement as product manager greatly improves the project's chances of delivering an impressive product.

If the visionary isn't available to participate fully, as is often the case, someone else must be the product manager. Ask the visionary to recommend a trusted lieutenant or protégé: someone who has regular interaction with the visionary and understands how he thinks.

Frequently, a project will have multiple visionaries. This is particularly common in custom software development. If this is the case on your project, you need to help the visionaries combine their ideas into a single, cohesive vision.

Before you go too far down that road, however, ask yourself whether you actually have multiple projects. Is each vision significantly different? Can you execute them serially, one vision at a time, as separate projects built by the same team on a single codebase? If you can, that may be your best solution.

If you can't tease apart the visions (do try!), you're in for a tough job. In this case, the role of the product manager must change. Rather than being a visionary himself, the product manager *facilitates* discussion between multiple visionaries. The best person for the job is one who understands the business well, already knows each of the visionaries, and has political savvy and good facilitation skills.

It might be more accurate to call this sort of product manager a *product facilitator* or *customer coach*, but I'll stick with *product manager* for consistency.

Documenting the Vision

After you've worked with visionaries to create a cohesive vision, document it in a vision statement. It's best to do this collaboratively, as doing so will reveal areas of disagreement and confusion. Without a vision statement, it's all too easy to gloss over disagreements and end up with an unsatisfactory product.

Once created, the vision statement will help you maintain and promote the vision. It will act as a vehicle for discussions about the vision and a touchpoint to remind stakeholders why the project is valuable.

Don't forget that the vision statement should be a *living* document: the product manager should review it on a regular basis and make improvements. However, as a fundamental statement of the project's purpose, it may not change much.

How to Create a Vision Statement

The vision statement documents three things: *what* the project should accomplish, *why* it is valuable, and the project's *success criteria*.

The vision statement can be short. I limit mine to a single page. Remember, the vision statement is a clear and simple way of describing why the project deserves to exist. It's not a roadmap; that's the purpose of release planning.

Ally

Release Planning (p. 206)

In the first section—*what* the project should accomplish—describe the problem or opportunity that the project will address, expressed as an end result. Be specific, but not prescriptive. Leave room for the team to work out the details.

Here is a real vision statement describing "Sasquatch," a product developed by two entrepreneurs who started a new company:

Sasquatch helps teams collaborate over long distance. It enables the high-quality team dynamics that occur when teams gather around a table and use index cards to brainstorm, prioritize, and reflect.

Sasquatch's focus is *collaboration* and *simplicity*. It is not a project management tool, a tracking tool, or a retrospectives tool. Instead, it is a free-form sandbox that can fulfill any of these purposes. Sasquatch assumes that participants are well-meaning and create their own rules. It does not incorporate mechanisms to enforce particular behaviors among participants.

Sasquatch exudes *quality*. Customers find it a joy to use, although they would be hard-pressed to say why. It is full of small touches that make the experience more enjoyable.

Collaboration, simplicity, and quality take precedence over breadth of features. Sasquatch development focuses on polishing existing features to a high gloss before adding new ones.

In the second section, describe *why* the project is valuable.

Sasquatch is valuable to our customers because long-distance collaboration is so difficult without it. Even with desktop sharing tools, one person becomes the bottleneck for all discussion. Teams used to the power of gathering around a table chafe at these restrictions. Sasquatch gives everyone an opportunity to participate. It makes long-distance collaboration effective and even enjoyable.

Sasquatch is valuable to us because it gives us an opportunity to create an entrepreneurial product. Sasquatch's success will allow us to form our own product company and make a good living doing work that we love.

In the final section, describe the project's *success criteria*: how you will know that the project has succeeded and when you will decide. Choose concrete, clear, and unambiguous targets:

We will deploy Sasquatch in multiple stages with increasing measures of success at each stage.

In the first stage, we will demonstrate a proof-of-concept at a major Agile event. We will be successful if we attract a positive response from agile experts.

In the second stage, we will make a Sasquatch beta available for free use. We will be successful if at least 10 teams use it on a regular basis for real-world projects within 6 months.

In the third stage, we will convert Sasquatch to a pay service. We will be successful if it grosses at least $1,000 in the first three months.

In the fourth stage, we will rely on Sasquatch for our income. We will be successful if it meets our minimum monthly income requirements within one year of accepting payment.

Promoting the Vision

After creating the vision statement, post it prominently as part of the team's informative workspace. Use the vision to evangelize the project to stakeholders and to explain the priority (or deprioritization) of specific stories.

Ally

Informative Workspace (p. 83)

Be sure to include the visionaries in product decisions. Invite them to release planning sessions. Make sure they see iteration demos, even if that means a private showing. Involve them in discussions with real customers. Solicit their feedback about progress, ask for their help in improving the plan, and give them opportunities to write stories. They can even be an invaluable resource in company politics, as successful visionaries are often senior and influential.

Including your visionaries may be difficult, but make the effort; distance between the team and its visionaries decreases the team's understanding of the product it's building. While the vision statement is necessary and valuable, a visionary's personal passion and excitement for the product communicates far more clearly. If the team interacts with the visionary frequently, they'll understand the product's purpose better and they'll come up with more ideas for increasing value and decreasing cost.

NOTE

When I'm faced with an inaccessible visionary, I don't assume that the problem is insurmountable. Because the participation of the visionaries is so valuable, I take extra steps to include visionaries in any way I can. I don't take organizational structures for granted, and I push to remove barriers.

If the visionaries cannot meet with the team at all, then the product manager will have to go to them to share the plan, get feedback, and conduct private demos. This is the least effective way of involving the visionaries, and you must decide if the product manager understands the vision well enough to act in their stead. Ask your mentor for help making this decision. If you conclude that the product manager doesn't understand the vision well, talk with your executive sponsor about the risks of continuing, and consider that your team may be better off doing something else until the visionaries are available.

Questions

Discussing the vision has led to contentious arguments. Should we stop talking about our vision?

Even if there are big disagreements about the vision, you should still pursue a unified vision. Otherwise, the final product will be just as fragmented and unsatisfactory as the vision is. You may benefit from engaging the services of a professional facilitator to help mediate the discussions.

Our organization already has a template for vision statements. Can we use it?

Certainly. Be sure you cover *what*, *why*, and *success criteria*. Find a way to fit those topics into the template. Keep your vision statement to a single page if you can.

Our visionary finds it very difficult to communicate a cohesive vision. What can we do when it changes?

Rapidly shifting goals tend to be common with entrepreneurial visionaries. It isn't due to lack of vision or consistency; instead, your visionary sees a variety of opportunities and changes direction to match.

If the vision is constantly changing, this may be a sign that what you think of as the vision is just a temporary strategy in a larger, overarching vision. Take your concerns to the visionary and stakeholders and try to identify that larger vision.

If you succeed in discovering the larger vision, adaptive release planning (see "Adapt Your Plans" later in this chapter) can help you keep up with your visionary. Adaptive planning's emphasis on learning and on taking advantage of opportunities will fit in perfectly with your visionary's entrepreneurial spirit.

> **Allies**
>
> Release Planning (p. 206)
> The Planning Game (p. 219)

Your visionary may continue to shift direction more quickly than you can implement her ideas. Wild and unpredictable shifts make it difficult to develop software effectively. The planning game helps; stick with the normal mechanism of scheduling and implementing stories. Your product manager should act as a buffer in this case, protecting the team from rapid shifts and explaining to your visionary what the team can reasonably accomplish.

Can individual iterations and releases have smaller visions?

Of course! This works particularly well with release planning—it can be a great way to help customers choose the priority of stories as they plan their next release.

I'm less fond of visions for iteration planning, just because iterations are so short and simple that the extra effort usually isn't worth it.

Results

When your project has a clear and compelling vision, prioritizing stories is easy. You can easily see which stories to keep and which to leave out. Programmers contribute to planning discussions by suggesting ways to maximize value while minimizing development cost. Your release plan incorporates small releases that deliver value.

When the visionary promotes the vision well, everyone understands why the project is important to the company. Team members experience higher morale, stakeholders trust the team more, and the organization supports the project.

Contraindications

Always pursue a unified vision for your projects, even at the risk of discovering there isn't one. If the project isn't worth doing, it's better to cancel it now than after spending a lot of money.

Alternatives

Some project communities are so small and tightly knit that everyone knows the vision. However, even these teams can benefit from creating a one-page vision statement. The only alternative to a clear vision is a confusing one—or no vision at all.

Further Reading

Some of the ideas in this section were inspired by the "Mastering Projects" workshop presented by True North pgs, Inc. If you have the opportunity to attend their workshop, take advantage of it.

Release Planning

We plan for success.

Imagine you've been freed from the shackles of deadlines. "Maximize our return on investment," your boss says. "We've already talked about the vision for this project. I'm counting on you to work out the details. Create your own plans and set your own release dates—just make sure we get a good return on our investment."

Now what?

One Project at a Time

First, work on only one project at a time. Many teams work on several projects simultaneously, which is a mistake. Task-switching has a substantial cost: "[T]he minimum penalty is 15 percent... Fragmented knowledge workers may look busy, but a lot of their busyness is just thrashing" [DeMarco 2002]. Working on one project at a time allows you to release each project as you complete it, which increasees the total value of your work.

Consider a team that has two projects. In this simplified example, each project has equal value; when complete, each project will yield $$ in value every month. Each project takes three months to complete.

NOTE

Although I'm describing value in dollar signs, money isn't the only source of value. Value can be intangible as well.

In Scenario A (see Figure 8-1), the team works on both projects simultaneously. To avoid task-switching penalties, they switch between projects every month. They finish Project 1 after five months and Project 2 after six. At the end of the seventh month, the team has earned $$$$$$.

In Scenario B, the team works on just one project at a time. They release Project 1 at the end of the third month. It starts making money while they work on Project 2, which they complete after the sixth month, as before. Although the team's productivity didn't change—the projects still took six months—they earned more money from Project 1. By the end of the seventh month, they earned $$$$$$$$$$. That's nearly twice as much value with no additional effort.

Something this easy ought to be criminal. What's really astounding is the number of teams that work on simultaneous projects anyway.

Release Early, Release Often

Releasing early is an even better idea when you're working on a single project. If you group your most valuable features together and release them first, you can achieve startling improvements in value.

Consider another example team. This team has just one project. In Scenario A (see Figure 8-2), they build and release it after six months. The project is worth $$$$ per month, so at the end of the seventh month, they've earned $$$$$.

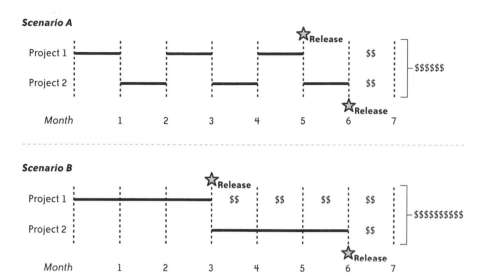

Figure 8-1. Effects of multitasking on value

In Scenario B, the team groups the most valuable features together, works on them first, and releases them after three months. The first release starts making $$$ per month. They then work on the remaining features and release them at the end of the sixth month. As before, their productivity hasn't changed. All that's changed is their release plan. Yet due to the income from the first release, the team has made $$$$$$$$$$$$$$ by the end of the end of the seventh month—nearly *triple* that of Scenario A with its single release.

These scenarios are necessarily simplified. *Software by Numbers* [Denne & Cleland-Huang] has a more sophisticated example that uses real numbers and calculates value over the entire life of the product (see Table 8-1). In their example, the authors convert a five-year project with two end-of-project releases (Scenario A) into five yearly releases ordered by value (Scenario B). As before, the team's productivity remains the same.

Table 8-1. Realistic example of frequent releases

	Scenario A	Scenario B
Total Cost	$4.3 million	$4.712 million
Revenue	$5.6 million	$7.8 million
Investment	$2.76 million	$1.64 million
Payback	$1.288 million	$3.088 million
Net Present Value @ 10%	$194,000	$1.594 million
Internal Rate of Return	12.8%	36.3%

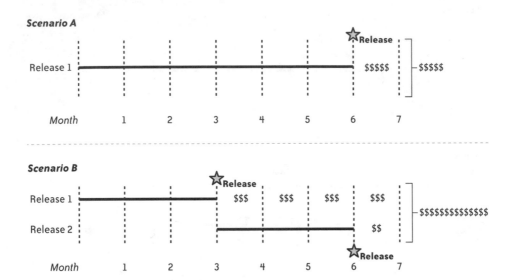

Figure 8-2. Effect of frequent releases on value

Scenario A is a marginal investment somewhat equivalent to obtaining a 12.8 percent interest rate. It requires an investment of $2.76 million and yields profits of $1.288 million. Considering the risk of software development, the investors can put that money to better use elsewhere. The project should not be funded.

Scenario B—the same project released more often—is an excellent investment somewhat equivalent to obtaining a 36.3 percent interest rate. Although Scenario B costs more because it conducts more releases, those releases allow the project to be self-funding. As a result, it requires a smaller investment of $1.64 million and yields profits of $3.088 million. This project is well worth funding.

Look at these results again. Each of these examples shows dramatic increases in value. Yet *nothing changed* except the order in which the teams released their features!

BENEFITS FOR PROGRAMMERS

Frequent releases are good for the organization. What's it worth to developers? Releases are painful, with flag days and repository freezes and rushes to complete, right?

Slow down. Breathe. Frequent releases can actually make your life easier.

By delivering tested, working, valuable software to your stakeholders regularly, you increase trust. Your stakeholders request a feature and soon see results. There's quick feedback between planning a release and getting the software. You will also get feedback *from* stakeholders more quickly. This allows you to learn and adapt.

There are technical benefits, too. One secret of XP is that doing hard things often and in small doses takes away most of the risk and almost all the pain. If you have the discipline to set up the necessary infrastructure to make a release at any point (with continuous integration and a 10-minute build), doing so takes only slightly more work than checking in your code and running the complete test suite.

Imagine eliminating all the stress of tracking down changes from a dozen branches and trying to merge multiple new features simultaneously to make a demo for a trade show next week that you just found out about on Thursday morning—because you can make a release at any time. Life is much better this way.

How to Release Frequently

Releasing frequently doesn't mean setting aggressive deadlines. In fact, aggressive deadlines *extend* schedules rather than reducing them [McConnell 1996, p. 220]. Instead, release more often by including less in each release. Minimum marketable features [Denne & Cleland Huang] are an excellent tool for doing so.

A minimum marketable feature, or MMF, is the smallest set of functionality that provides value to your market, whether that market is internal users (as with custom software) or external customers (as with commercial software). MMFs provide value in many ways, such as competitive differentiation, revenue generation, and cost savings.

As you create your release plan, think in terms of stakeholder value. Sometimes it's helpful to think of stories and how they make up a single MMF. Other times, you may think of MMFs that you can later decompose into stories. Don't forget the *minimum* part of minimum marketable feature—try to make each feature as small as possible.

Once you have minimal features, group them into possible releases. This is a brainstorming exercise, not your final plan, so try a variety of groupings. Think of ways to minimize the number of features needed in each release.

The most difficult part of this exercise is figuring out how to make small releases. It's one thing for a *feature* to be marketable, and another for a whole *release* to be marketable. This is particularly difficult when you're launching a new product. To succeed, focus on what sets your product apart, not the features it needs to match the competition.

An Example

Imagine you're the product manager for a team that's creating a new word processor. The market for word processors is quite mature, so it might seem impossible to create a small first release. There's so much to do just to *match* the competition, let alone to provide something new and compelling. You need basic formatting, spellchecking, grammar checking, tables, images, printing... the list goes on forever.

Approaching a word processor project in this way is daunting to the point where it may seem like a worthless effort. Rather than trying to match the competition, focus on the features that make your word processor unique. Release those features first—they probably have the most value.

Suppose that the competitive differentiation for your word processor is its powerful collaboration capabilities and web-based hosting. The first release might have four features: basic formatting, printing, web-based hosting, and collaboration. You could post this first release as a technical preview to start generating buzz. Later releases could improve on the base features and justify charging a fee: tables, images, and lists in one release, spellchecking and grammar checking in another, and so on.

If this seems foolish, consider Writely, the online word processing application. It doesn't have the breadth of features that Microsoft Word does, and it probably won't for many years. Instead, it focuses on what sets it apart: collaboration, remote document editing, secure online storage, and ease of use.*

According to venture capitalist Peter Rip, the developers released the first alpha of Writely *two weeks* after they decided to create it.† How much is releasing early worth? Ask Google. Ten months later, they bought Writely,‡ even though Writely *still* didn't come close to Microsoft Word's feature set.§ Writely is now known as Google Docs.

CUSTOMERS AND FREQUENT RELEASES

"Our customers don't want releases that frequently!"

This may be true. Sometimes your customers won't accept releases as frequently as you deliver them. They may have regulatory requirements that necessitate rigorous testing and certification before they can install new versions.

Sometimes resistance to frequent releases comes from the hidden costs of upgrading. Perhaps upgrades require a difficult or costly installation process. Perhaps your organization has a history of requiring a series of hotfixes before a new release is stable.

Whatever the reason, the key to making frequent releases is to decrease the real or perceived costs of upgrading. Add an upgrade feature that notifies users of new versions and installs them automatically. Provide well-tested upgrade utilities that automatically convert user data.

Hosted applications, such as web applications, provide the ultimate in release flexibility. These allow you to release at any time, possibly without users even noticing. Some XP teams with hosted software and a mature set of existing features actually release *every day*.

Adapt Your Plans

If such significant results are possible from frequent releases, imagine what you could accomplish if you could also increase the value of each release. This is actually pretty easy: after each release, collect stakeholder feedback, cancel work on features that turned out to be unimportant, and put more effort into those features that stakeholders find most valuable.

With XP, you can change your plans more often than once per release. XP allows you to adjust your plan every iteration. Why? To react to unexpected challenges quickly. More importantly, it allows you to take advantage of opportunities. Where do these opportunities come from? You *create* them.

The beginning of every software project is when you know the least about what will make the software valuable. You might know a lot about its value, but you will always know *more* after you talk with stakeholders, show them demos, and conduct actual releases. As you continue, you will discover that

---

* *http://www.writely.com/.*

† "Writely is the seed of a Big idea," *http://earlystagevc.typepad.com/earlystagevc/2005/09/writely_is_the_.html.*

‡ "Writely—The Back Story," *http://earlystagevc.typepad.com/earlystagevc/2006/03/sam_steve_and_j.html.*

§ "Only in a bubble is Google's web WP an Office-killer," *http://www.theregister.co.uk/2006/03/10/google_writely_analysis/.*

some of your initial opinions about value were incorrect. No plan is perfect, but if you change your plan to reflect what you've learned—if you adapt—you create more value.

To increase the value of your software, create opportunities to learn. Think of your plan as a plan for *learning* as much as it is a plan for *implementation*. Focus on what you don't know. What are you uncertain about? What might be a good idea? Which good ideas can you prove in practice? Don't just speculate— create experiments. Include a way of testing each uncertainty.

For example, if you were creating a collaborative online word processor, you might not be sure how extensive your support for importing Microsoft Word documents should be. Some sort of support is necessary, but how much? Supporting all possible Word documents would take a long time to implement and prevent you from adding other, possibly more valuable features. Too little support could damage your credibility and cause you to lose customers.

To test this uncertainty, you could add a rudimentary import feature to your software (clearly marked "experimental"), release it, and have it create a report on the capabilities needed to support the types of documents that real users try to import. The information you gather will help you adapt your plan and increase your product's value.

> **NOTE**
> Web users are used to "beta" web applications, so releasing an experimental feature is possible in that context. A project with less forgiving users may require the use of a pre-release program, focus groups, or some other feedback mechanism.

Keep Your Options Open

To take the most advantage of the opportunities you create, build a plan that allows you to release at any time. Don't get me wrong—the point is not to *actually* release all the time, but to *enable* you to release at any time.

Why do this? It allows you to keep your options open. If an important but completely new opportunity comes along, you can release what you have and immediately change directions to take advantage of the opportunity. Similarly, if there's some sort of disaster, such as the project's surprise cancellation, you can release what you have anyway. At any time, you should be able to release a product that has value proportional to the investment you've made.

> At any time, you should be able to release a product that has value proportional to the investment you've made.

To release at any time, build your plan so that each story stands alone. Subsequent stories can build on previous stories, but each one should be releasable on its own. For example, one item in your plan might be "Provide login screen," and the next might be "Allow login screen to have client-specific branding." The second item enhances the first, but the first is releasable on its own.

Suppose you're creating a system that gets data from a user, validates the data, and writes it to a database. You might initially create a story for each step: "Get data," "Validate data," and "Write data to database." These are sometimes called *horizontal stripes*. This is an easy way to create stories, but it prevents you from releasing, or even effectively reviewing, the software until you finish all three stories. It gives you less flexibility in planning, too, because the three stories form an all-or-nothing clump in your schedule.

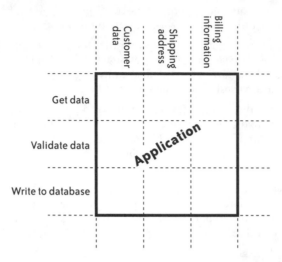

Figure 8-3. Horizontal and vertical stripes

A better approach is to create stories that do all three tasks but provide narrower individual utility. For example, you might create the stories "Process customer data," "Process shipping address," and "Process billing information." These are *vertical stripes* (see Figure 8-3).

Don't worry too much if you have trouble making your stories perfectly releasable. It takes practice. Releasable stories give you more flexibility in planning, but a few story clumps in your plan won't hurt much. With experience, you'll learn to make your plans less lumpy.

How to Create a Release Plan

There are two basic types of plans: *scopeboxed* plans and *timeboxed* plans. A scopeboxed plan defines the features the team will build in advance, but the release date is uncertain. A timeboxed plan defines the release date in advance, but the specific features that release will include are uncertain.

NOTE

Some people try to fix the release date *and* features. This can only end in tears; given the uncertainty and risk of software development, making this work requires adding a huge amount of padding to your schedule, sacrificing quality, working disastrous amounts of overtime, or all of the above.

Timeboxed plans are almost always better. They constrain the amount of work you can do and force people to make difficult but important prioritization decisions. This requires the team to identify cheaper, more valuable alternatives to some requests. Without a timebox, your plan will include more low-value features.

To create your timeboxed plan, first choose your release dates. I like to schedule releases at regular intervals, such as once per month and no more than three months apart.

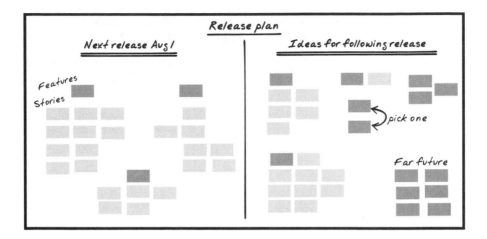

Figure 8-4. A release planning board

NOTE

Does it seem odd to set the release date before deciding on features or estimates? Don't worry—you'll constrain your plan to fit into the time available.

Now flesh out your plan by using your project vision to guide you in brainstorming minimum marketable features. Decompose these into specific stories, and work with the programmers to get estimates. Using the estimates as a guide, prioritize the stories so that the highest-value, lowest-cost stories are done first. (For more details, see "The Planning Game" later in this chapter.)

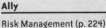

Allies

Vision (p. 201)
Stories (p. 253)
Estimating (p. 260)

NOTE

To brainstorm features and stories, use the vision to guide you, turn to interaction designers for ideas, and involve stakeholders as appropriate. Classic requirements gathering techniques may also help; see "Further Reading" at the end of this section for suggestions.

The end result will be a single list of prioritized stories. Using your velocity, risk factors, and story estimates, you can predict how many stories each release will include (see "Risk Management" later this chapter). With that information as a guide, discuss options for reducing costs and splitting stories so that each release provides a lot of value.

Ally

Risk Management (p. 224)

This final list of stories is your release plan. Post it prominently (I use a magnetic whiteboard—see Figure 8-4) and refer to it during iteration planning. Every week, consider what you've learned from stakeholders and discuss how you can use that information to improve your plan.

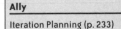

Ally

Iteration Planning (p. 233)

"DONE DONE" AND RELEASE PLANNING

"Done done" applies to release planning as well as to stories. Just as you shouldn't postpone tasks until the end of an iteration, don't postpone stories until the end of a release.

Every feature should be "done done" before you start on the next feature. This means you need to schedule stories for reports, administration interfaces, security, performance, scalability, UI polish, and installers as appropriate. In particular, schedule bug-fix stories right away unless you've decided that they're not worth fixing in this release.

Ally

No Bugs (p. 160)

Planning at the Last Responsible Moment

It takes a lot of time and effort to brainstorm stories, estimate them, and prioritize them. If you're adapting your plan as you go, some of that effort will be wasted. To reduce waste, plan at the last responsible moment. The *last responsible moment* is the last moment at which you can responsibly make a decision (see "XP Concepts" in Chapter 3). In practice, this means that the further away a particular event is, the less detail your release plan needs to contain.

Another way to look at this is to think in terms of planning horizons. Your *planning horizon* detemines how far you look into the future. Many projects try to determine every requirement for the project up front, thus using a planning horizon that extends to the end of the project.

To plan at the last responsible moment, use a tiered *set* of planning horizons. Use long planning horizons for general plans and short planning horizons for specific, detailed plans, as shown in Figure 8-5.

Your planning horizons depend on your situation and comfort level. The more commitments you need to make to stakeholders, the longer your detailed planning horizons should be. The more uncertain your situation is, or the more likely you are to learn new things that will change your plan, the shorter your planning horizons should be. If you aren't sure which planning horizons to use, ask your mentor for guidance. Here are some good starting points:

- Define the *vision* for the entire project.
- Define the *release date* for the next two releases.
- Define the *minimum marketable features* for the current release, and start to place features that won't fit in this release into the next release.
- Define all the *stories* for the current feature and most of the current release. Place stories that don't fit into the next release.
- *Estimate and prioritize* stories for the current iteration and the following three iterations.
- Determine *detailed requirements and customer tests* for the stories in the current iteration.

Allies

Vision (p. 201)
Stories (p. 253)
Estimating (p. 260)
Customer Tests (p. 278)

ADAPTIVE PLANNING IN ACTION

A few years ago, my wife and I took a two-month trip to Europe. It was easily the biggest, most complicated trip we've taken. We knew we couldn't plan it all in advance, so we used an adaptive approach.

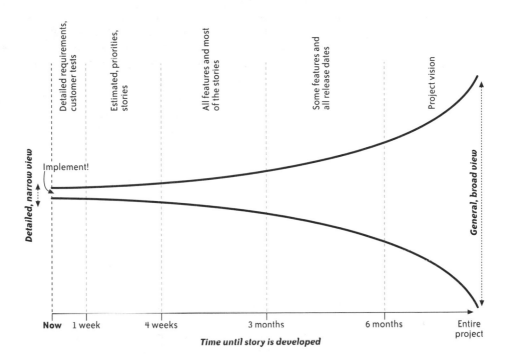

Figure 8-5. *Planning horizons*

We started with our vision for the trip. No, we didn't write a vision statement (she won't let me be that geeky), but we did agree that our goal for the trip was to visit a wide variety of European cities instead of going to one place and staying there. We discussed the countries we wanted to see, but we didn't make any decisions that would commit us to visiting a particular set.

We identified the last responsible moment for various decisions in our trip. Airline tickets generally get more expensive over time, so we booked our flight to London months in advance and made plans to stay with relatives there at the beginning and end of our trip. Hotels, however, only need a few days' notice. (In fact, too much advance notice means they might lose your reservation.)

We also took steps that would give us more options. We found a good guidebook that covered all of Europe. We purchased a EuroRail pass, which allowed us to use Europe's excellent rail system to travel through the continent. Although we thought we knew which countries we intended to visit, we spent extra money for a pass that would allow us to visit any European country.

With these general decisions made, we left the details for the last responsible moment. While on the trip, a few days before leaving for our next destination, we decided which country and city to visit next. We stopped by the train station, looked up departure times, and made reservations when necessary. We looked up candidate hotels in our guidebook and emailed the three most promising, then went back to enjoying the current city. The next day, we confirmed one of the hotel reservations. On the last day, we lazed about, picked a time to leave from list of train departure times, then boarded the train. We would arrive in the new city four or five hours later, drop off our belongings at the hotel, and go explore... then start the process over by thinking about the next city and country.

This approach not only gave us flexibility, it was *easy* and *relaxing*. Because we only made our reservations a day or two in advance, no hotel ever lost or confused our reservations. If we found that we particularly enjoyed a city, we stayed longer. If we didn't like it, we left early. On previous vacations, we had been slaves to a pre-planned itinerary, fretting over details for the entire trip. On this much longer and more complicated trip, we only had to think about the details for our next few days.

The flexibility also allowed us to experience things that we never would have otherwise. In Italy, we discovered that our intention to go to Turkey would eat up a huge amount of time in travel. We exploited our EuroRail passes and went to northern Europe instead and ended up having some of our most memorable experiences in cities we had never expected to visit.

By creating a rough plan in advance, keeping our options open, and making detailed decisions at the last responsible moment, we had a much better vacation than we would have had otherwise. Similarly, when you use adaptive planning in software development, unpredictable opportunities arise and allow you to increase the value of your software.

Adaptive Planning and Organizational Culture

Does the idea of spending two months travelling in a foreign country without advance hotel reservations seem scary? In practice, it was easy and relaxing, but when I tell the story of our adaptively planned trip to Europe (see the "Adaptive Planning in Action" sidebar), audiences get nervous.

Organizations often have a similar reaction to adaptive planning. An adaptive plan works to achieve a vision. However, just as my wife and I achieved our vision—"have fun visiting a lot of European cities"—but didn't know exactly which cities we would visit, an adaptive team will achieve its vision even though it cannot say exactly what it will deliver.

Ally
Vision (p. 201)

No aspect of agile development challenges organizational culture more than the transition to adaptive planning. It requires changes not only to the development team, but to reporting, evaluation, and executive oversight. The choice of adaptive planning extends to surprisingly diverse parts of the project community, and people often have a shocked or emotional reaction to the idea.

As a result, you may not be able to influence a change to adaptive planning. Unless you have executive support, any change that does occur will probably be slow and gradual. Even *with* executive support, this change is difficult.

> Work within your organization's culture.

You can work within your organization's culture to do adaptive planning under the radar. Use adaptive planning, but set your planning horizons to match the organization's expectations. Generally, estimating and prioritizing stories for the remainder of the current release is enough. This works best if you have small, frequent releases.

As your stakeholders and executives gain trust in your ability to deliver, you may be able to shorten your detailed planning horizons and migrate further toward an adaptive plan.

Questions

I thought we were supposed to release every week. Is this different?

You may be confusing iterations with releases. Although the team should release software to internal stakeholders every week as part of the iteration demo, you may not choose to release to end-users or real customers that often.

Weekly releases are a great choice if you have the opportunity. Your ability to do so will depend on your business needs.

If we don't plan the entire project in detail, what should we tell our stakeholders about our plans?

Although you may not plan out all the details of your project in advance, you should have plenty of detail to share with stakeholders. You should always know the overall vision for the project. Depending on your planning horizons, you will probably have a list of the features for the next release as well as a planned date for that release. You will also have specific, estimated stories for near-term work.

If your stakeholders need more information or predictability, you may need longer planning horizons. In any event, be sure to let stakeholders know that this is your *current* plan and that it is subject to change if you find better ways of meeting the project vision.

Planning at the last responsible moment means we can't show exactly what we'll deliver. Doesn't that require too much trust from stakeholders?

Any development effort requires that the organization trust the team to do its job. If stakeholders require a detailed plan in order to trust you, use longer planning horizons that allow you to provide the plan they desire.

If we use short planning horizons, how can we be sure we'll deliver on the project vision?

If you're not sure you can deliver on the project vision, focus your plan on discovering whether you can. You may need to extend your planning horizons or create a small, limited-availability release to test crucial concepts. The details depend on your situation, so if you're not sure what to do, ask your mentor for guidance.

No matter your decision, clearly convey your concern to stakeholders, and let them know how you intend to address the uncertainty.

Results

When you create, maintain, and communicate a good release plan, the team and stakeholders all know where the project is heading. The plan shows how the team will meet the project vision, and team members are confident the plan is achievable. You complete features and release high-quality software regularly and consistently.

If you are adapting your plan well, you consistently seek out opportunities to learn new things about your plan, your product, and your stakeholders. As you learn, you modify your plan to take advantage of new insights. Stakeholders and the team agree that each release is better than originally planned.

Contraindications

Not all of these ideas are appropriate for everyone. I've put the easiest ones first, but even the easy ones have limitations.

Working on one project at a time is an easy, smart way to increase your return on investment. Despite its usefulness, working on one project at a time is anathema to some organizations. Proceed with caution.

Releasing frequently requires that your customers and users be able to accept more frequent releases. This is a no-brainer for most web-based software because users don't have to do anything to get updates. Other software might require painful software rollouts, and some even require substantial testing and certification. That makes frequent releases more difficult.

Adaptive planning requires that your organization define project success in terms of value rather than "delivered on time, on budget, and as specified." This can be a tough idea for some organizations to swallow. You may be able to assuage fears about adaptive plans by committing to a specific release date but leaving the details of the release unspecified.

Keeping your options open—that is, being ready to release, and thus change directions, at any time—requires a sophisticated development approach. Practices such as test-driven development, continuous integration, and incremental design and architecture help.

> **Allies**
> Test-Driven Development (p. 285)
> Continuous Integration (p. 183)
> Incremental Design and Architecture (p. 321)

Tiered planning horizons require a cohesive vision and regular updates to the plan. Use them when you can reliably revisit the plan at least once per iteration. Be sure your team includes a product manager and on-site customers who are responsible for maintaining the plan.

Finally, be cautious of plans without a predefined release date or a release date more than three months in the future. Without the checkpoint and urgency of a near-term release, these plans risk wandering off course.

Alternatives

The classic alternative to adaptive release planning is *predictive release planning*, in which the entire plan is created in advance. This can work in stable environments, but it tends to have trouble reacting to changes.

If you don't use incremental design and architecture, [Denne & Cleland-Huang] provide a sophisticated Incremental Funding Methodology that shows how to prioritize technical infrastructure alongside features. However, XP's use of incremental design neatly sidesteps this need.

> **Ally**
> Incremental Design and Architecture (p. 321)

Finally, teams with an established product and a relatively small need for changes and enhancements don't always need a release plan. Rather than thinking in terms of features or releases, these teams work from a small story backlog and release small enhancements every iteration. In some cases, they conduct daily deployment. You could think of this as an adaptive plan with a very short planning horizon.

Further Reading

Software by Numbers [Denne & Cleland-Huang] provides a compelling and detailed case for conducting frequent releases.

Agile Software Development Ecosystems [Highsmith] has an excellent discussion of adaptive planning in Chapter 15.

Lean Software Development [Poppendieck & Poppendieck] discusses postponing decisions and keeping your options open in Chapter 3.

The Planning Game

Our plans take advantage of both business and technology expertise.

You may know when and what to release, but how do you actually construct your release plan? That's where *the planning game* comes in.

In economics, a *game* is something in which "players select actions and the payoffs depend on the actions of all players."[*] The study of these games "deals with strategies for maximizing gains and minimizing losses... [and are] widely applied in the solution of various decision making problems."[†]

That describes the planning game perfectly. It's a structured approach to creating the best possible plan given the information available.

The planning game is most notable for the way it maximizes the amount of information contributed to the plan. It is strikingly effective. Although it has limitations, if you work within them, I know of no better way to plan.

How to Play

XP assumes that customers have the most information about *value*: what best serves the organization. Programmers have the most information about *costs*: what it will take to implement and maintain those features. To be successful, the team needs to maximize value while minimizing costs. A successful plan needs to take into account information from both groups, as every decision to *do* something is also a decision *not* to do something else.

Accordingly, the planning game requires the participation of both customers and programmers. (Testers may assist, but they do not have an explicit role in the planning game.) It's a *cooperative game*; the team as a whole wins or loses, not individual players.

Because programmers have the most information about costs—they're most qualified to say how long it will take to implement a story—they *estimate*.

Because customers have the most information about value—they're most qualified to say what is important—they *prioritize*.

Neither group creates the plan unilaterally. Instead, both groups come together, each with their areas of expertise, and play the planning game:

1. Anyone creates a story or selects an unplanned story.
2. Programmers estimate the story.
3. Customers place the story into the plan in order of its relative priority.
4. The steps are repeated until all stories have been estimated and placed into the plan.

Allies
Stories (p. 253)
Estimating (p. 260)

---

[*] Deardorff's Glossary of International Economics, *http://www-personal.umich.edu/~alandear/glossary/g.html*.

[†] Dictionary definition of "game theory," *http://dictionary.reference.com/search?q=game theory&x=0&y=0*.

The planning game doesn't always follow this neat and orderly format. As long as programmers estimate and customers prioritize, the details aren't important. For example, the programmers may estimate a stack of stories all at once for the customers to prioritize later. Typically, most stories are created at the beginning of each release, during initial release planning sessions, as the team brainstorms what to include.

During the planning game, programmers and customers may ask each other questions about estimates and priorities, but each group has final say over its area of expertise.

The result of the planning game is a plan: a single list of stories in priority order. Even if two stories are of equivalent priority, one must come before the other. If you're not sure which to put first, pick one at random.

Overcoming disagreements

Release planning is always a difficult process because there are many more stories to do than there is time available to do them. Also, each stakeholder has his own priorities, and balancing these desires is challenging. Tempers rise and the discussion gets heated—or worse, some people sit back and tune out, only to complain later. This struggle is natural and happens on *any* project, XP or not, that tries to prioritize conflicting needs.

My favorite way to plan is to gather the team, along with important stakeholders, around a large conference table. Customers write stories on index cards, programmers estimate them, and customers place them on the table in priority order. One end of the table represents the stories to do first, and the other end represents stories to do last. The plan tends to grow from the ends toward the middle, with the most difficult decisions revolving around stories that are neither critical nor useless.

Ally
Stories (p. 253)

Using index cards and spreading them out on a table allows participants to point to stories and move them around. It reduces infighting by demonstrating the amount of work to be done in a visible way. The conversation focuses on the cards and their relative priorities rather than on vague discussions of principles or on "must have/not important" distinctions.

> Use index cards to focus disagreements away from individuals.

ON DISAPPOINTMENT

The planning game is certain to give you information that makes you unhappy. You may feel tempted to blame the messenger and stop playing the planning game, or stop using XP altogether. That would be a mistake. As David Schmaltz of True North pgs says, every project has a fixed amount of disappointment associated with it. You can either use the planning game to dole out the disappointment in measured doses... or save it all up for the end.

How to Win

When customers and programmers work directly together throughout this process, something amazing happens. I call it *the miracle of collaboration*. It really is a miracle because time appears out of nowhere.

Like all miracles, it's not easy to achieve. When programmers give an estimate, customers often ask a question that causes every programmer's teeth to grind: "Why does it cost so much?"

The instictive reaction to this question is defensive: "It costs so much because software development is hard, damn it! Why are you questioning me!?"

Programmers, there's a better way to react. Reword the customer's question in your head into a simple request for information: "Why is this expensive?" Answer by talking about what's easy and what's difficult.

For example, imagine that a product manager requests a toaster to automatically pop up the toast when it finishes. The programmers reply that the feature is very expensive, and when the product manager asks why, the programmers calmly answer, "Well, popping up the toast is easy; that's just a spring. But detecting when the toast is done—that's new. We'll need an optical sensor and some custom brownness-detecting software."

This gives the product manager an opportunity to ask, "What about all those other toasters out there? How do they know when the toast is done?"

The programmers respond, "They use a timer, but that doesn't really detect when the toast is done. It's just a kludge."

Now the product manager can reply, "That's OK! Our customers don't want a super toaster. They just want a regular toaster. Use a timer like everyone else."

"Oh, OK. Well, that won't be expensive at all."

When you have honest and open dialog between customers and programmers, the miracle of collaboration occurs and extra time appears out of nowhere. Without communication, customers tend not to know what's easy and what's not, and they end up planning stories that are difficult to implement. Similarly, programmers tend not to know what customers think is important, and they end up implementing stories that aren't valuable.

With collaboration, the conflicting tendencies can be reconciled. For example, a customer could ask for something unimportant but difficult, and the programmers could point out the expense and offer easier alternatives. The product manager could then change directions and save time. Time appears out of nowhere. It's the miracle of collaboration.

Questions

Won't programmers pad their estimates or slack off if they have this much control over the plan?

In my experience, programmers are highly educated professionals with high motivation to meet customer expectations. [McConnell 1996] validates this experience: "Software developers like to work. The best way to motivate developers is to provide an environment that makes it easy for them to focus on what they like doing most, which is developing software... [Developers] have high achievement motivation: they will work to the objectives you specify, but you have to tell them what those objectives are" [McConnell 1996, pp. 255-256].

Although programmer estimates may be higher than you like, it's most likely because they want to set realistic expectations. If the estimates do turn out to be too high, the team will achieve a higher velocity and automatically do more each iteration to compensate.

Won't customers neglect important technical issues if they have this much control over the plan?

Customers want to ship a solid, usable product. They have to balance that desire with the desire to meet crucial market windows. As a result, they may sometimes ask for options that compromise important technical capabilities. They do so because they aren't aware of the nuances of technical trade-offs in the same way that programmers are.

As a programmer, you are most qualified to make decisions on technical issues, just as the customers are most qualified to make decisions on business issues. When the customers ask for an explanation of an estimate, don't describe the technical options. Instead, *interpret* the technology and describe the options in terms of business impact.

Rather than describing the options like this:

> We're thinking about using a Mark 4 Wizzle-Frobitz optical sensor here for optimal release detection. We could use a Mark 1 spring-loaded countdown timer, too. We'd have to write some custom software to use the Mark 4, but it's very sophisticated, cutting-edge stuff and it will allow us to detect the exact degree of brownness of the bread. The Mark 1 is ancient tech without dynamic detection abilities, but it won't take any extra time to implement. Which would you prefer?

Try this instead:

> We have two choices for popping up toast. We can use either an optical sensor or a timer. The optical sensor will allow us to toast the bread to the user's exact preference, but it will increase our estimate by three days. The timer won't take any extra time but the user is more likely to have undercooked or burned toast. Which would you prefer?

If a technical option simply isn't appropriate, don't mention it, or mention your decision in passing as part of the cost of doing business:

> Because this is the first iteration, we need to install a version control system. We've included that cost in the estimate for our first story.

Our product manager doesn't want to prioritize. He says everything is important. What can we do?

Be firm. Yes, everything is important, but something has to come first and something will come last. Someone has to make the tough schedule decisions. That's the product manager's job.

Results

When you play the planning game well, both customers and programmers feel that they have contributed to the plan. Any feelings of pressure and stress are focused on the constraints of the plan and possible options, rather than on individuals and groups. Programmers suggest technical options for reducing scope while maintaining the project vision. Customers ruthlessly prioritize the stories that best serve the vision.

Ally
Vision (p. 201)

Contraindications

The planning game is an easy, effective approach that relies on many of XP's simplifying assumptions, such as:

- Customer-centric stories
- Story dependencies that customers can manage effectively (in practice, this means no technical dependencies and simple business dependencies)
- Customers capable of making wise prioritization decisions
- Programmers capable of making consistent estimates

Allies

Stories (p. 253)
The Whole Team (p. 28)
Estimating (p. 260)

If these conditions are not true on your team, you may not be able to take advantage of the planning game.

The planning game also relies on the programmers' abilities to implement design and architecture incrementally. Without this capability, the team will find itself creating technical stories or strange story dependencies that make planning more difficult.

Ally

Incremental Design and
Architecture (p. 321)

Finally, the planning game assumes that the team has a single dominant constraint (for more information about the theory of constraints, see "XP Concepts" in Chapter 3). It's very rare for a system to exhibit two constraints simultaneously, so this shouldn't be a problem. Similarly, the planning game assumes that the programmers are the constraint. If this isn't true for your team, discuss your options with your mentor.

Alternatives

There are a wide variety of project planning approaches. The most popular seems to be Gantt charts that assume task-based plans and schedule what each individual person will do.

In contrast to that approach, the planning game focuses on what the *team produces*, not on what *individuals do*. The team has the discretion to figure out how to produce each story and organizes itself to finish the work on time.

This focus on results, rather than on tasks, combined with the planning game's ability to balance customer and programmer expertise, makes it the most effective approach to software planning I've experienced. However, if you wish to use another approach to planning, you can do so. Talk with your mentor about how to make your preferred approach to planning work with the rest of the XP practices.

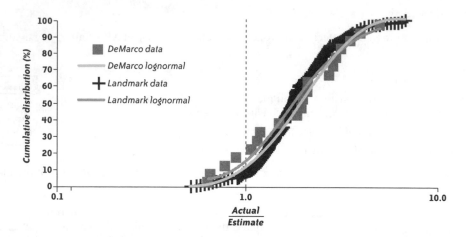

Figure 8-6. An example of historical project data

Risk Management

We make and meet long term commitments.

<table>
<tr><td>**Audience**</td></tr>
<tr><td>Project Manager, Whole Team</td></tr>
</table>

The following statement is *nearly* true:

> Our team delivers a predictable amount of work every iteration. Because we had a velocity of 14 story points last week, we'll deliver 14 story points this week, and next week, and the next. By combining our velocity with our release plan, we can commit to a specific release schedule!

Good XP teams do achieve a stable velocity. Unfortunately, velocity only reflects the issues the team *normally* faces. Life always has some *additional* curve balls to throw. Team members get sick and take vacations; hard drives crash, and although the backups worked, the restore doesn't; stakeholders suddenly realize that the software you've been showing them for the last two months needs some major tweaks before it's ready to use.

Despite these uncertainties, your stakeholders need schedule commitments that they can rely upon. *Risk management* allows you to make and meet these commitments.

A Generic Risk-Management Plan

Every project faces a set of common risks: turnover, new requirements, work disruption, and so forth. These risks act as a multiplier on your estimates, doubling or tripling the amount of time it takes to finish your work.

How much of a multiplier do these risks entail? It depends on your organization. In a perfect world, your organization would have a database of the type shown in Figure 8-6.[*] It would show the chance of completing before various risk multipliers.

---

[*] Reprinted from [Little].

Because most organizations don't have this information available, I've provided some generic risk multipliers instead. (See Table 8-2.) These multipliers show your chances of meeting various schedules. For example, in a "Risky" approach, you have a 10 percent chance of finishing according to your estimated schedule. Doubling your estimates gives you a 50 percent chance of on-time completion, and to be virtually certain of meeting your schedule, you have to quadruple your estimates.

Table 8-2. Generic risk multipliers

	Process approach		
Percent chance	Rigorous[a]	Risky[b]	Description
10%	x1	x1	Almost impossible ("ignore")
50%	x1.4	x2	50-50 chance ("stretch goal")
90%	x1.8	x4	Virtually certain ("commit")

[a] These figures are based on [DeMarco & Lister's] RISKOLOGY simulator, version 4a, available from *http://www.systemsguild.com/riskology.html*. I used the standard settings but turned off productivity variance, as velocity would automatically adjust for that risk.

[b] These figures are based on [Little].

If you use the XP practices—in particular, if you're strict about being "done done" every iteration, your velocity is stable, and you fix all your bugs each iteration—then your risk is lowered. Use the risk multiplier in the "Rigorous" column. On the other hand, if you're *not* strict about being "done done" every iteration, if your velocity is unstable, or if you postpone bugs and other work for future iterations, then use the risk multiplier in the "Risky" column.

Allies

"Done Done" (p. 156)
No Bugs (p. 160)

> **NOTE**
>
> These risk multipliers illustrate an important difference between risky and rigorous appraoches. Both can get lucky and deliver according to their estimates. Risky approaches, however, take a lot longer when things go wrong. They require much more padding in order to make and meet commitments.

Although these numbers come from studies of hundreds of industry projects, those projects didn't use XP. As a result, I've guessed somewhat at how accurately they apply to XP. However, unless your company has a database of prior projects to turn to, they are your best starting point.

Project-Specific Risks

Using the XP practices and applying risk multipliers will help contain the risks that are common to all projects. The generic risk multipliers include the normal risks of a flawed release plan, ordinary requirements growth, and employee turnover. In addition to these risks, you probably face some that are specific to your project. To manage these, create a *risk census*—that is, a list of the risks your project faces that focuses on your project's *unique* risks.

[DeMarco & Lister 2003] suggest starting work on your census by brainstorming catastrophes. Gather the whole team and hand out index cards. Remind team members that during this exercise, negative thinking is not only OK, it's necessary. Ask them to consider ways in which the project could fail. Write several questions on the board:*

1. What about the project keeps you up at night?

2. Imagine it's a year after the project's disastrous failure and you're being interviewed about what went wrong. What happened?

3. Imagine your best dreams for the project, then write down the opposite.

4. How could the project fail without anyone being at fault?

5. How could the project fail if it were the stakeholders' faults? The customers' faults? Testers? Programmers? Management? Your fault? Etc.

6. How could the project succeed but leave one specific stakeholder unsatisfied or angry?

Write your answers on the cards, then read them aloud to inspire further thoughts. Some people may be more comfortable speaking out if a neutral facilitator reads the cards anonymously.

Once you have your list of catastrophes, brainstorm scenarios that could lead to those catastrophes. From those scenarios, imagine possible root causes. These root causes are your risks: the causes of scenarios that will lead to catastrophic results.

> **Ally**
> Root-Cause Analysis (p. 88)

For example, if you're creating an online application, one catastrophe might be "extended downtime." A scenario leading to that catastrophe would be "excessively high demand," and root causes include "denial of service attack" and "more popular than expected."

After you've finished brainstorming risks, let the rest of the team return to their iteration while you consider the risks within a smaller group. (Include a cross-section of the team.) For each risk, determine:

- Estimated probability—I prefer "high," "medium," and "low."

- Specific impact to project if it occurs—dollars lost, days delayed, and project cancellation are common possibilities.

You may be able to discard some risks as unimportant immediately. I ignore unlikely risks with low impact and all risks with negligible impact. Your generic risk multipler accounts for those already.

For the remainder, decide whether you will *avoid* the risk by not taking the risky action; *contain* it by reserving extra time or money, as with the risk multiplier; or *mitigate* it by taking steps to reduce its impact. You can combine these actions. (You can also *ignore* the risk, but that's irresponsible now that you've identified it as important.)

For the risks you decide to handle, determine transition indicators, mitigation and contingency activities, and your risk exposure.

- *Transition indicators* tell you when the risk will come true. It's human nature to downplay upcoming risks, so choose indicators that are objective rather than subjective. For example, if your risk is "unexpected popularity causes extended downtime," then your transition indicator might be "server utilization trend shows upcoming utilization over 80 percent."

- *Mitigation* activities reduce the impact of the risk. Mitigation happens in advance, regardless of whether the risk comes to pass. Create stories for them and add them to your release plan. To

---

* Based on [DeMarco & Lister 2003, p. 117]

continue the example, possible stories include "support horizontal scalability" and "prepare load balancer."

- *Contingency* activities also reduce the impact of the risk, but they are only necessary if the risk occurs. They often depend on mitigation activities that you perform in advance. For example, "purchase more bandwidth from ISP," "install load balancer," and "purchase and prepare additional frontend servers."

- *Risk exposure* reflects how much time or money you should set aside to contain the risk. To calculate this, first estimate the numerical probability of the risk and then multiply that by the impact. When considering your impact, remember that you will have already paid for mitigation activities, but contingency activities are part of the impact. For example, you might believe that downtime due to popularity is 35 percent likely, and the impact is three days of additional programmer time and $20,000 for bandwidth, colocation fees, and new equipment. Your total risk exposure is $7,000 and one day.

Some risks have a 100 percent chance of occurring. These are no longer risks—they are reality. Update your release plan to deal with them.

Other risks can kill your project if they occur. For example, a corporate reorganization might disband the team. Pass these risks on to your executive sponsor as assumptions or requirements. ("We assume that, in the event of a reorg, the team will remain intact and assigned to this project.") Other than documenting that you did so, and perhaps scheduling some mitigation stories, there's no need to manage them further.

For the remaining risks, update your release plan to address them. You will need stories for mitigation activities, and you may need stories to help you monitor transition indicators. For example, if your risk is "unexpected popularity overloads server capacity," you might schedule the story "prepare additional servers in case of high demand" to mitigate the risk, and "server load trend report" to help you monitor the risk.

You also need to set aside time, and possibly money, for contingency activities. Don't schedule any contingency stories yet—you don't know if you'll need them. Instead, add up your risk exposure and apply dollar exposure to the budget and day exposure to the schedule. Some risks will occur and others won't, but on average, the impact will be equal to your risk exposure.

MONITORING RISKS

One of the hardest things about project-specific risks is remembering to follow up on them. It's human nature to avoid unpleasant possibilities. The best way I've found to monitor risks is to assign someone to track them. The project manager is a good choice for this role, but you can choose anybody on the team. However, choose someone who's not the team's constraint. It's more important for them to do things that no one else can do.

Every week, review your project-specific risks and check the transition indicators. Consider whether the risks are still applicable, and ask yourself if any new risks have come to light.

NOTE
I write project-specific risks on yellow cards and put them on the release planning board.

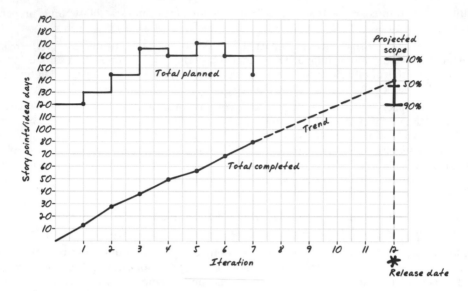

Figure 8-7. A burn-up chart

How to Make a Release Commitment

With your risk exposure and risk multipliers, you can predict how many story points you can finish before your release date. Start with your timeboxed release date from your release plan. (Using scopeboxed release planning? See the "Predicting Release Dates" sidebar.) Figure out how many iterations remain until your release date and subtract your risk exposure. Multiply by your velocity to determine the number of points remaining in your schedule, then divide by each risk multiplier to calculate your chances of finishing various numbers of story points.

Ally

Release Planning (p. 206)

```
risk_adjusted_points_remaining = (iterations_remaining - risk_exposure) * velocity / risk_multiplier
```

For example, if you're using a rigorous approach, your release is 12 iterations away, your velocity is 14 points, and your risk exposure is one iteration, you would calculate the range of possibilities as:

```
points remaining = (12 - 1) * 14 = 154 points
10 percent chance: 154 / 1 = 154 points
50 percent chance: 154 / 1.4 = 110 points
90 percent chance: 154 / 1.8 = 86 points
```

In other words, when it's time to release, you're 90 percent likely to have finished 86 more points of work, 50 percent likely to have finished 110 more points, and only 10 percent likely to have finished 154 more points.

You can show this visually with a *burn-up chart*, shown in Figure 8-7.* Every week, note how many story points you have completed, how many total points exist in your next release (completed plus remaining stories), and your range of risk-adjusted points remaining. Plot them on the burn-up chart as shown in the figure.

---

* According to John Brewer (*http://tech.groups.yahoo.com/group/extremeprogramming/message/81856*), the burn-up chart was created by Phil Goodwin as a variant of Scrum's burn-down charts. I've modified it further to include risk-based commitments.

Use your burn-up chart and release plan to provide stakeholders with a list of features you're committing to deliver on the release date. I commit to delivering features that are 90 percent likely to be finished, and I describe features between 50 and 90 percent likely as *stretch goals*. I don't mention features that we're less than 50 percent likely to complete.

PREDICTING RELEASE DATES

I recommend using timeboxed plans with a fixed release date—they're less risky. However, you can predict a release date for a given set of stories. To do so, start with the total number of points in the stories you want to deliver. Divide by your velocity to get the number of iterations required to finish those stories, then multiply by each risk multiplier. Finish by adding your risk exposure to each risk-adjusted prediction.

```
risk_adjusted_iterations_remaining = (points_remaining / velocity * risk_multiplier) + risk_exposure
```

Success over Schedule

The majority of this discussion of risk management has focused on managing the risk to your *schedule* commitments. However, your real goal should be to deliver an organizational success—to deliver software that provides substantial value to your organization, as guided by the success criteria in your project vision.

> Success is more than a delivery date.

Ally
Vision (p. 201)

Taking too long can put that success at risk, so rapid delivery *is* important. Just don't forget about the real goal. As you evaluate your risks, think about the risk to the success of the *project*, not just the risk to the *schedule*. Take advantage of adaptive release planning. Sometimes you're better off taking an extra month to deliver a great result, rather than just a good one.

Ally
Release Planning (p. 206)

When Your Commitment Isn't Good Enough

Someday, someone will ask you to commit to a schedule that your predictions show is impossible to achieve. The best way to make the schedule work is to reduce scope or extend the release date. If you can't do so personally, ask your manager or product manager to help.

If you can't change your plan, you may be able to improve your velocity (see "Estimating" later in this chapter). This is a long shot, so don't put too much hope in it.

It's also possible that your pessimistic predictions are the result of using a risky process. You can improve the quality of your predictions by being more rigorous in your approach. Make sure you're "done done" every iteration and include enough slack to have a stable velocity. Doing so will decrease your velocity, but it will also decrease your risk and allow you to use risk multipliers from the "Rigorous" column, which may lead to a better overall schedule.

Allies
"Done Done" (p. 156)
Slack (p. 246)

Typically, though, your schedule is what it is. If you can't change scope or the date, you can usually change little else. As time passes and your team builds trust with stakeholders, people may become more interested in options for reducing scope or extending the delivery date. In the meantime, don't promise to take on more work than you can deliver. Piling on work will increase technical debt and hurt the schedule. Instead, state the team's limitations clearly and unequivocally.

Ally
Trust (p. 102)

If that isn't satisfactory, ask if there's another project the team can work on that will yield more value. Don't be confrontational, but don't give in, either. As a leader, you have an obligation to the team—and to your organization—to tell the truth.

In some organizations, inflexible demands to "make it work" are questionable attempts to squeeze more productivity out of the team. Sadly, applying pressure to a development team tends to reduce quality without improving productivity. In this sort of organization, as the true nature of the schedule becomes more difficult to ignore, management tends to respond by laying on pressure and "strongly encouraging" overtime.

Look at the other projects in the organization. What happens when they are late? Does management respond rationally, or do they respond by increasing pressure and punishing team members?

If it's the latter, decide now whether you value your job enough to put up with the eventual pressure. If not, start looking for other job opportunities immediately. (Once the pressure and mandatory overtime begin, you may not have enough time or energy for a job hunt.) If your organization is large enough, you may also be able to transfer to another team or division.

As a tool of last resort, *if* you're ready to resign *and* you're responsible for plans and schedules, it's entirely professional to demand respect. One way to do so is to say, "Because you no longer trust my advice with regard to our schedule, I am unable to do the job you hired me to do. My only choice is to resign. Here is my resignation letter."

This sometimes gets the message through when nothing else will work, but it's a big stick to wield, and it could easily cause resentment. Be careful. "Over my dead body!" you say. "Here's your noose," says the organization.

Questions

What should we tell our stakeholders about risks?

It depends how much detail each stakeholder wants. For some, a commitment and stretch goal may be enough. Others may want more detailed information.

Be sure to share your risk census and burn-up chart with your executive sponsor and other executives. Formally transfer responsibility for the project assumptions (those risks that will kill the project if they come true). Your assumptions are the executives' risks.

Your risk multipliers are too high. Can I use a lower multiplier?

Are your replacement multipliers based on objective data? Is that data representative of the project you're about to do? If so, go ahead and use them. If not, be careful. You can lower the multiplier, but changing the *planned* schedule won't change the *actual* result.

We're using a scopeboxed plan, and our stakeholders want a single delivery date rather than a risk-based range. What should we do?

Your project manager or product manager might be able to help you convince the organization to accept a risk-based range of dates. Talk with them about the best way to present your case.

If you must have a single date, pick a single risk multiplier to apply. Which one you choose depends on your organization. A higher risk multiplier improves your chances of success but makes the schedule look worse. A lower risk multiplier makes the schedule look better but reduces your chances of meeting that schedule.

Many organizations have acclimated to slipping delivery dates. Managers in these organizations intuitively apply an informal risk multiplier in their head when they hear a date. In this sort of organization, applying a large risk multiplier might make the schedule seem ridiculously long.

Consider other projects in your organization. Do they usually come in on time? What happens if they don't? Talk with your project manager and product manager about management and stakeholder expectations. These discussions should help you choose the correct risk multiplier for your organization. Remember, though, using a risk-based *range* of dates is a better option, and using a timeboxed schedule is better than using a scopeboxed schedule.

Results

With good risk management, you deliver on your commitments even in the face of disruptions. Stakeholders trust and rely on you, knowing that when they need something challenging yet valuable, they can count on you to deliver it.

Contraindications

Use risk management only for external commitments. Within the team, focus your efforts on achieving the unadjusted release plan as scheduled. Otherwise, your work is likely to expand to meet the deadline. Figure 8-8[*] shows how a culture of doubling estimates at one company prevented most projects from finishing early without reducing the percentage of projects that finished late.

Be careful of using risk management in an organization that brags that "failure is not an option." You may face criticism for looking for risks. You may still be able to present your risk-derived schedule as a commitment or stretch goal, but publicizing your risk census may be a risk itself.

Alternatives

Risk management is primarily an organizational decision rather than an individual team decision. If your organization has already institutionalized risk management, they may mandate a different approach. Your only trouble may be integrating it into XP's simultaneous phases; to do so, use this description as a starting point and consider asking your mentor (see "Find a Mentor" in Chapter 2) for advice specific to your situation.

Some organizations add a risk buffer to individual estimates rather than the overall project schedule. As Figure 8-8 illustrates, this tends to lead to waste.

---

[*] Reprinted from [Little].

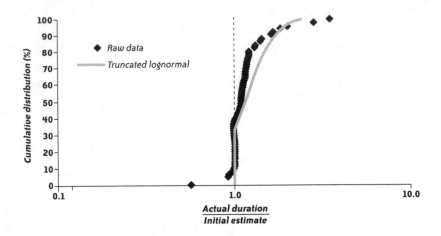

Figure 8-8. Just double the estimate

Further Reading

Waltzing with Bears: Managing Risk on Software Projects [DeMarco & Lister 2003] provides more detail and considers risk management from an organizational perspective. My favorite quote comes from the back cover: "If there's no risk on your next project, don't do it."

Iteration Planning

We stop at predetermined, unchangeable time intervals and compare reality to plan.

Iterations are the heartbeat of an XP project. When an iteration starts, stories flow in to the team as they select the most valuable stories from the release plan. Over the course of the iteration, the team breathes those stories to life. By the end of the iteration, they've pumped out working, tested software for each story and are ready to begin the cycle again.

Allies

Stories (p. 253)
Release Planning (p. 206)

Iterations are an important safety mechanism. Every week, the team stops, looks at what it's accomplished, and shares those accomplishments with stakeholders. By doing so, the team coordinates its activities and communicates its progress to the rest of the organization. Most importantly, iterations counter a common risk in software projects: the tendency for work to take longer than expected.

The Iteration Timebox

Programming schedules die in inches. At first you're on schedule: "I'll be done once I finish this test." Then you're limping: "I'll be done as soon as I fix this bug." Then gasping: "I'll be done as soon as I research this API flaw... no, really." Before you know it, two days have gone by and your task has taken twice as long as you estimated.

Death by inches sneaks up on a team. Each delay is only a few hours, so it doesn't feel like a delay, but they multiply across the thousands of tasks in a project. The cumulative effects are devastating.

Iterations allow you to avoid this surprise. Iterations are exactly one week long and have a strictly defined completion time. This is a *timebox*: work ends at a particular time regardless of how much you've finished. Although the iteration timebox doesn't *prevent* problems, it *reveals* them, which gives you the opportunity to correct the situation.

In XP, the iteration demo marks the end of the iteration. Schedule the demo at the same time every week. Most teams schedule the demo first thing in the morning, which gives them a bit of extra slack the evening before for dealing with minor problems.

Allies

Iteration Demo (p. 138)
Slack (p. 246)

The Iteration Schedule

Iterations follow a consistent, unchanging schedule:

- Demonstrate previous iteration (up to half an hour)
- Hold retrospective on previous iteration (one hour)
- Plan iteration (half an hour to four hours)
- Commit to delivering stories (five minutes)
- Develop stories (remainder of iteration)
- Prepare release (less than 10 minutes)

Allies

Iteration Demo (p. 138)
Retrospectives (p. 91)
Ten-Minute Build (p. 177)

Many teams start their iterations on Monday morning and end Friday evening, but I prefer iterations that start on Wednesday morning. This allows people to leave early on Friday or take Monday off without missing important events. It also allows the team to conduct releases before the weekend.

> Choose an iteration start time that works for your team, and stick with it.

How to Plan an Iteration

After the iteration demo and retrospective are complete, iteration planning begins. Start by measuring the velocity of the previous iteration. Take all the stories that are "done done" and add up their original estimates. This number is the amount of story points you can reasonably expect to complete in the upcoming iteration.

Ally
"Done Done" (p. 156)

> **NOTE**
> Be sure to use *estimated* time, not actual time, when calculating velocity. This allows the velocity to account for interruptions and other overhead.

With your velocity in hand, you can select the stories to work on this iteration. Ask your customers to select the most important stories from the release plan. Select stories that exactly add up to the team's velocity. You may need to split stories (see "Stories" later in this chapter) or include one or two less important stories to make the estimates add up perfectly.

Ally
Release Planning (p. 206)

> **NOTE**
> Avoid using the iteration planning meeting for extensive release planning. Do the bulk of your release planning during the previous iteration.

Because the iteration planning meeting takes stories from the front of the release plan, you should have already estimated and prioritized those stories. As a result, selecting stories for the iteration plan should only take a few minutes, with perhaps 10 or 15 minutes more to explain:

Product Manager: OK, here we are again. What is it this time? Iteration 23? [Writes "Iteration 23" at top of the blank iteration planning whiteboard.] What was our velocity in the previous iteration?

Programmer: [Counts up stories.] Fourteen, same as usual.

Product Manager: [Writes "Velocity: 14" on the whiteboard.] OK, let's roll the release planning board in here. [Helps drag the planning board over, then points at it.] The other customers and I had some tough decisions to make after our recent release. Our users love what we've been doing, which is good, and they're making all kinds of suggestions, which is also good, but some of their ideas could easily derail us, which is not so good. Anyway, you don't need to worry about that. Bottom line is that we're sticking with the same plan as before, at least for this next iteration. So, let's see, 14 points... [starts picking stories off of the release planning board] 3... 5... 6, 7... 10... 12... 14. [He puts them on the table.] All right, everybody, that's our iteration. Good luck—I have to go talk with our division VP. Mary's going to stick around to answer any questions you have about these stories. I'll be back this afternoon if you need anything.

Mary: Good luck, Brian. *[The product manager leaves.]* We've talked about these stories before, so I'll just refresh your memory...

After you have chosen the stories for the iteration, everybody but the programmers can leave the meeting, although anybody is welcome to stay if she likes. At least one customer should stick around to answer programmer questions and to keep an ear out for misunderstandings.

> **NOTE**
> The team's constraint determines how much the team can do in each iteration (see "XP Concepts" in Chapter 3 for more about the Theory of Constraints). This book assumes programmers are the constraint, so the iteration plan is based entirely on programmer tasks and estimates. Other team members may conduct their own iteration planning sessions if they wish, but it isn't required.

At this point, the real work of iteration planning begins. Start by breaking down the stories into engineering tasks.

Engineering tasks are concrete tasks for the programmers to complete. Unlike stories, engineering tasks don't need to be customer-centric. Instead, they're programmer-centric. Typical engineering tasks include:

- Update build script
- Implement domain logic
- Add database table and associated ORM objects
- Create new UI form

Brainstorm the tasks you need in order to finish all the iteration's stories. Some tasks will be specific to a single story; others will be useful for multiple stories. Focus only on tasks that are necessary for completing the iteration's stories. Don't worry about all-hands meetings, vacations, or other interruptions.

> **NOTE**
> Some nonprogramming stories, such as a story to estimate a stack of other stories, can't be broken into tasks. Reestimate the story in terms of ideal hours (see "Estimating" later in this chapter) and leave it at that.

Brainstorming tasks is a *design* activity. If everybody has the same ideas about how to develop the software, it should go fairly quickly. If not, it's a great opportunity for discussion before coding begins. You don't need to go into too much detail. Each engineering task should take a pair one to three hours to complete. (This translates into about two to six hours of estimated effort.) Let pairs figure out the details of each task when they get to them.

As each team member has an idea for a task, he should write it down on a card, read it out loud, and put it on the table. Everybody can work at once. You'll be able to discard duplicate or inappropriate tasks later.

As you work, take advantage of your on-site customer's presence to ask about the detailed requirements for each story. What do the customers expect when the story is done?

Amy, John, Kim, Fred, Belinda, and Joe continue planning. Mary, one of the on-site customers, sits off to the side, working on email.

"OK, here we are again," deadpans John, mimicking their product manager.

Amy snickers. "These stories look pretty straightforward to me. Obviously, we need to implement new domain logic for each story. This warehouse stocking story looks like it will affect the warehouse and SKU classes." She takes an index card and writes, "Update warehouse and SKU classes for warehouse stocking."

"Speaking of products, now that we're going to be storing the weight of each SKU, we need to update the SKU class for that, too," says Belinda. She takes another card and writes, "Update SKU class to include weight." She pauses to consider. "Maybe that's too small to be a task."

Joe speaks up. "That weight story is mostly a UI change at this point. We'll need to update the SKU configuration screen and the administration screen. We can put weight into the SKU class at the same time." He starts writing another task card.

"Wait a second, Joe." Mary looks up from her email. "Did you say that the weight issue was only a UI change?"

"That's right," says Joe.

"That's not entirely true," says Mary. "Although we mostly need to add the ability to enter weight into the system for later use, we do want it to show up on our inventory report."

"Oh, good to know," says Joe. He writes, "Update inventory report with SKU weight" on a task card.

Kim and Fred have been talking off to the side. Now they speak up. "We've made some cards for the database changes we'll need this iteration," Kim says. "Also, I think we need to update our build script to do a better job of updating schemas, so I wrote a task card for that, too."

"Sounds good," says John. "Now, I think these other stories also need domain logic changes..."

After you've finished brainstorming tasks, spread them out on the table and look at the whole picture. Are these tasks enough to finish all the stories? Are there any duplicates or overlaps? Is anybody uncertain about how the plan works with the way the software is currently designed? Discuss and fix any problems.

Next, estimate the tasks. As with brainstorming, this can occur in parallel, with individual programmers picking up cards, writing estimates, and putting them back. Call out the estimates as you finish them. If you hear somebody call out an estimate you disagree with, stop to discuss it and come to consensus.

> Finish brainstorming before you start estimating.

Estimate the tasks in *ideal hours*. How long would the task take if you had perfect focus on the task, suffered no interruptions, and could have the help of anybody on the team? Estimate in person-hours as well: a task that takes a pair two hours is a four-hour estimate. If any of the tasks are bigger than six hours of effort, split them into smaller tasks. Combine small tasks that are less than an hour or two.

Finally, stop and take a look at the plan again. Does anybody disagree with any of the estimates? Does everything still fit together?

As a final check, add up the estimates and compare them to the total task estimates from your previous iteration. Using this plan, can you commit to delivering all the stories? Is there enough slack in the plan for dealing with unexpected problems?

Ally

Slack (p. 246)

> **NOTE**
>
> Comparing the total of your task estimates to last week's total will help you get a feel for whether the iteration is achievable. The two numbers don't need to match exactly.
>
> Don't bother comparing your estimate to the actual number of hours you'll be working. There are too many variables outside of your control, such as estimate accuracy, interruptions, and nonproject meetings, for there to be a useful corollation.

You may discover that you aren't comfortable committing to the plan you have. If so, see if there are any tasks you can remove or simplify. Discuss the situation with your on-site customers. Can you replace a difficult part of a story with something easier but equally valuable? If not, split or remove a story.

Ally

Stories (p. 253)

Similarly, if you feel that you can commit to doing more, add a story to the plan.

Continue to adjust the plan until the team is ready to commit to delivering its stories. With experience, you should be able to make plans that don't need adjustment.

The Commitment Ceremony

Commitment is a bold statement. It means that you're making a promise to your team and to stakeholders to deliver all the stories in the iteration plan. It means that you think the plan is achievable and that you take responsibility, as part of the team, for delivering the stories.

Hold a little ceremony at the end of the iteration planning meeting. Gather the whole team together—customers, testers, and programmers—and ask everyone to look at the stories. Remind everybody that the team is about to commit to delivering these stories at the end of the iteration. Ask each person, in turn, if he can commit to doing so. Wait for a verbal "yes."

> Openly discuss problems without pressuring anybody to commit.

It's OK to say "no." If anybody seems uncomfortable saying "yes" out loud, remind them that "no" is a perfectly fine answer. If somebody does say no, discuss the reason as a team and adjust the plan accordingly.

Commitment is important because it helps the team consistently deliver iterations as promised, which is the best way to build trust in the team's ability. Commitment gives people an opportunity to raise concerns before it's too late. As a pleasant side effect, it helps the team feel motivated to work together to solve problems during the iteration.

Ally

Trust (p. 102)

After the Planning Session

After you finish planning the iteration, work begins. Decide how you'll deliver on your commitment. In practice, this usually means that programmers volunteer to work on a task and ask for someone to pair with them. As pairs finish their tasks, they break apart. Individuals pick up new tasks from the board and form new pairs.

> **Ally**
> Pair Programming (p. 71)

Other team members each have their duties as well. This book assumes that programmers are the constraint in the system (see "XP Concepts" in Chapter 3 for more about the Theory of Constraints), so other team members may not have a task planning board like the programmers do. Instead, the customers and testers keep an eye on the programmers' progress and organize their work so it's ready when the programmers need it. This maximizes the productivity of the whole team.

As work continues, revise the iteration plan to reflect the changing situation. (Keep track of your original task and story estimates, though, so you can use them when you plan the next iteration.) Remember that your commitment is to deliver *stories*, not tasks, and ask whether your current plan will succeed in that goal.

> Every team member is responsible for the successful delivery of the iteration's stories.

At the end of the iteration, release your completed software to stakeholders. With a good 10-minute build, this shouldn't require any more than a button press and a few minutes' wait. The following morning, start a new iteration by demonstrating what you completed the night before.

> **Ally**
> Ten-Minute Build (p. 177)

Dealing with Long Planning Sessions

Iteration planning should take anywhere from half an hour to four hours. Most of that time should be for discussion of engineering tasks. For established XP teams, assuming they start their iteration demo first thing in the morning, planning typically ends by lunchtime.

New teams often have difficulty finishing planning so quickly. This is normal during the first several iterations. It will take a little while for you to learn your problem space, typical approaches to design problems, and how best to work together.

If iteration planning still takes a long time after the first month or so, look for ways to speed it up. One common problem is spending too much time doing release planning during the iteration planning meeting. Most release planning should happen during the previous iteration, primarily among customers, while the programmers work on stories. Picking stories for the iteration plan should be a simple matter of taking stories from the front of the release plan. It should only take a few minutes because you won't estimate or discuss priorities.

NOTE

The team may have a few new stories as a result of stakeholder comments during the iteration demo. In general, though, the customers should have already prioritized most of the stories.

Long planning sessions also result from spending a lot of time trying to break down the stories into engineering tasks. This may be a result of doing too much design work. Although iteration planning *is* a design activity, it's a very high-level one. Most of the real design work will happen during the iteration

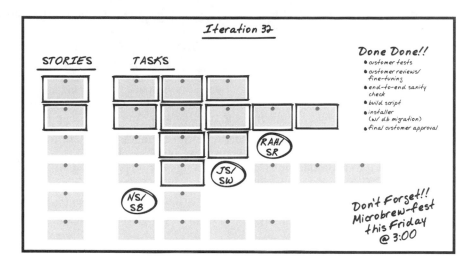

Figure 8-9. An iteration planning board

as pairs work on specific tasks. If you spend much time discussing possible design details, ask yourself whether you really need to solve these problems in order to come up with good engineering tasks.

If you find that team members don't understand the existing design, or if you have long discussions about how it works, you may lack shared design understanding. Remedy this problem with collective code ownership and more pair programming.

Allies

Collective Code Ownership (p. 191)

Pair Programming (p. 71)

If you find yourselves speculating about possible design choices, your problem may be a result of trying to make your design too general. Remember to keep the design simple. Focus on the requirements that you have today. Trust pairs doing test-driven development to make good decisions on their own.

Design speculation can also occur when you don't understand the requirements well. Take advantage of the on-site customer in your meeting. Ask him to explain the details of each story and why the system needs to behave in a particular way.

Allies

Simple Design (p. 314)

Test-Driven Development (p. 285)

Tracking the Iteration

Like your release plan, your iteration plan should be a prominent part of your informative workspace. Put your stories and tasks on a magnetic whiteboard, as shown in Figure 8-9. When you start work on a task, take it off of the whiteboard and clip it to your workstation. (Mark your initials on the whiteboard so people know where the task went.) As you finish each task, put it back on the board and circle it with a green marker.

Ally

Sit Together (p. 112)

Ally

Informative Workspace (p. 83)

One of the difficulties in iteration planning is identifying that things are going wrong in time to fix them. I take a brief look at our progress every day. Is there a task that's been in progress for more than a day? It might be a problem. If it's halfway through the iteration, are about half the cards marked green? If not, we might not finish everything on time.

After the iteration ends, take your cards down from the board, add a card on top with some vital statistics (iteration number, dates, whatever else you think is relevant), clip them together, and file them in a drawer. Alternatively, you can just throw them away. You're unlikely to come back to the cards, but most teams prefer archiving them just in case.

When Things Go Wrong

Does making a big deal out of commitment mean that you always deliver everything as promised? No, of course not. Commitment is about working around problems and doing what's necessary to deliver the iteration's stories—but sometimes a problem comes up that you can't work around.

When you discover a problem that threatens your iteration commitment, first see if there's any way you can change your plan so that you still meet your commitments. Would using some of your iteration slack help? Is there an engineering task that you can simplify or postpone? Discuss your options as a team and revise your plan.

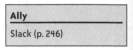
Ally
Slack (p. 246)

Sometimes the problem will be too big to absorb. In this case, you'll usually need to reduce the scope of the iteration. Typically, this involves splitting or removing a story. As a team, discuss your options and make the appropriate choice.

NOTE

Always stay in control of your iteration, even if you have to change your plan to do so. Any iteration that delivers all of the stories in the current plan—even if you changed the plan—is a success.

Under no circumstances, however, should you change the iteration deadline.

After changing the plan, the customers should reestablish trust with stakeholders by explaining what happened, why, and what the team is doing to prevent this sort of problem in the future.

Despite your best efforts, you may have a bad week and end up with nothing at all to demonstrate to your stakeholders. Some teams declare a *lost iteration* when this happens. They roll back their code and use their previous velocity as if the lost iteration never happened. Every team makes mistakes, so this is a fine approach as long as it happens rarely (less than once per quarter). If it happens more often, something is wrong. Ask your mentor for help.

Partially Done Work

At the end of the iteration, every story should be "done done." Partially completed stories should be rare: they reflect a planning problem. That said, they will happen occasionally, particularly when you're new to XP.

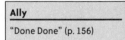
Ally
"Done Done" (p. 156)

Some teams think that the best way to handle partially completed stories is to delete all the code for uncompleted stories and deliver only what's completely done. This sounds harsh, but it's a good idea. "With true timeboxing, the software is either accepted or thrown away at the timebox deadline. That makes it clear that the quality level must be acceptable at all times. The success of timeboxing depends on being able to meet tight schedules by limiting the product's scope, not its quality." [McConnell 1996, p. 581]

If you follow this practice, you probably won't throw away much code—the iteration is only a week long. Starting fresh may require you to rewrite code, but you'll retain everything you learned when you wrote it the first time. The second attempt will often produce better code and you may even finish more quickly.

> You may delete code, but you won't delete what you've learned.

If you think this is extreme, as long as you know you will definitely work on that story during the next iteration, it's OK to keep the code. However, if you will not *immediately* continue to work on that story, it's best to delete the code. Get it out of your way. It's technical debt and baggage. If you ever need it, you can always get it out of version control.

Ally

Version Control (p. 169)

Emergency Requests

It's inevitable: you're on the third day of the iteration, everything is going well, and a customer comes up to you and says, "Pat, we really need to get this story in." What do you do?

As a programmer, it's very tempting to tell your customer to take a hike—right over the edge of a cliff. Changing direction in the middle of an iteration, after all, means an interruption in concentration, delays, and lost work.

On the other hand, responsiveness to business needs is a core agile value, so suppress that homicidal urge, smile, and provide your customer with options.

You can change the iteration schedule under the condition that you take out as much work as you add. In other words, if you're adding a two-point story to the plan, a two-point story needs to come out of the plan.

In addition, you may only replace stories that you haven't started yet. A two-point story that's half-done isn't a two-point story anymore—but it's not a one-point story, either. It's too difficult to tell how much work you have left on a story until it's "done done," and replacing it will lead to technical debt in the form of half-finished code.

Before making any changes, however, remember that your next planning meeting is less than a week away. Rather than inserting chaos into the team's work, ask yourself how much of an emergency you're really facing. Maybe it can wait until the next planning meeting. After all, it's only a day or three away.

The Batman

Dealing with an emergency request every now and then is fine—it's a great way for the team to be responsive. On the other hand, an emergency in every iteration means that something is wrong.

After the second or third iteration in a row with an emergency request, take a look at what's happening. Perhaps your on-site customers need to be more disciplined about release planning. Perhaps stakeholders need stronger reminders that requests can wait until the next iteration. Often the requests will die down as your organization adapts to the iteration heartbeat.

In some cases, however, the team has a legitimate need to provide ongoing support for ad hoc requests. If this is true for your team, sacrifice a programmer to be the batman.

"Batman" is a military term as well as a comic book character: it refers to a soldier assigned to deal with chores so that officers can focus on officering. On an XP team, the *batman* deals with organizational emergencies and support requests so the other programmers can focus on programmering. The batman has no other duties: he doesn't work on stories or the iteration plan.

Rotate a new programmer into the batman role every iteration to prevent burn-out. If the load is particularly high, you may need two or more batmen per iteration.

Depending on your situation, you may be better off using daily iterations rather than a batman. A daily iteration allows you to postpone all emergencies until the next morning, which enables the team to focus better (see the "Daily Iterations" sidebar). It's appropriate for teams that primarily deal with small ad hoc issues, such as bug fixes and minor enhancements, and don't have a long-term release plan.

DAILY ITERATIONS

If you have a particularly chaotic environment, you probably won't be able to use a lot of the XP practices. However, iterations—particularly daily iterations—can be a great way to bring structure to this environment.

One team I worked with was struggling under a crushing load of support requests. They had resorted to *firefighting*: they responded to whichever request seemed like the biggest emergency.

We instituted a simple daily iteration—nothing else—in which the team prioritized outstanding support requests using the planning game. They deferred any new requests that came in during the day until the next planning game. That was acceptable because the team planned every morning.

Ally
The Planning Game (p. 219)

The results were remarkable. Productivity increased, morale shot up, and the team actually found itself with free time. Daily iterations helped the team tame the chaos and, in so doing, dramatically improved their effectiveness.

If you find yourself struggling with firefighting, daily iterations might help your team, too.

Questions

How should we schedule time for fixing bugs?

You should fix bugs as soon as you find them, preferably as you work on each task. This time is part of the overhead of your iteration. Don't batch them up for fixing later, even if "later" is as soon as the end of the iteration.

Ally
No Bugs (p. 160)

Some bugs will be too big to absorb into your iteration slack. Create story cards for these and schedule them as soon as possible—or decide that they aren't worth fixing at all.

Ally

Slack (p. 246)

If we don't estimate stories during iteration planning, when do we estimate stories?

Estimate new stories as they appear throughout the iteration. If this is too much of an interruption, batch up the stories and estimate them at a particular time every day.

If you have a lot of stories to estimate, as often happens near the beginning of a project, schedule time for estimation with a story.

All the available tasks depend on tasks that other pairs are working on right now. What should I work on?

This happens less frequently than you might think; breaking stories into engineering tasks helps modularize the design. However, it does happen.

It's OK to have two pairs working on the same class. In this case, discuss the issue and come to agreement about the names of the class and the public methods that both pairs will be using. Then pick one pair to write the class. The other pair creates the exact same class but, instead of writing real code, they stub in some hardcoded return values.

When you integrate, replace the fake class with the real one and make sure the tests still pass.

What should the batman do when there are no outstanding support requests?

Whatever she likes, as long as she can easily put it aside when a support request comes in. Don't try to squeeze every last drop of efficiency out of the batman; doing so will likely slow the team down and make the batman's job even more tedious.

Results

When you use iterations well, your team has a consistent, predictable velocity. Stakeholders know what to expect from the team and trust that it will deliver on its commitments. The team discovers mistakes quickly and deals with them while still meeting its commitments. Rarely, the team meets its commitments by replanning, changing its commitments, and communicating these changes to stakeholders.

Contraindications

XP's iterations assume the use of customer-centric stories. To successfully deliver software in such a short timescale, the team must use simultaneous phases as well as simple design and incremental design and architecture. If you don't use these practices, XP-style iterations probably won't work for you.

Allies

Stories (p. 253)
Simple Design (p. 314)
Incremental Design and Architecture (p. 321)

In order to achieve a consistent velocity and deliver on commitments, your iteration must include slack. Never artificially inflate your velocity. Similarly, don't use commitment as a club. Never force team members to commit to a plan they don't agree with.

Ally

Slack (p. 246)

Energized work is also important. Without it, the team will have trouble maintaining equilibrium and a stable velocity.

Ally

Energized Work (p. 79)

Finally, there's little value to a strict iteration schedule unless you pay close attention to the feedback cycles of velocity, planning, and frequent releases. A disciplined iteration schedule may improve predictability and estimation, but you must notice and react to changes in order to take advantage of it.

Ally

Release Early, Release Often (p. 206)

Alternatives

Some methods use longer iterations that release to real customers, not just to internal stakeholders, at the end of each iteration. Other methods use independent phases instead of simultaneous phases and iterations. Either of these approaches can work, but most of XP's practices assume the presence of short iterations. If you don't use XP-style iterations, talk with your mentor about whether XP will work in your situation.

Some established XP teams don't use engineering tasks at all. Instead, they use very small stories that can each be finished in less than a day. This approach works best for established products. Other teams use engineering tasks but don't estimate them. Either approach can work well, but they're advanced techniques. I recommend explicitly creating and estimating engineering tasks to start.

Iteration length

Throughout this book, I've assumed that your team uses one-week iterations. However, iterations may be of any length. Many teams prefer two-week iterations.

I've found that shorter iteration lengths are better for teams new to XP. Teams seem to mature in their understanding of XP based on how many *iterations* they've undertaken rather than how many *weeks* they've experienced. As a result, shorter iterations means more rapid improvement for a team new to XP.

Short iterations allow the team to practice core XP skills more frequently. A short iteration leads to more planning, more internal releases, more iteration demos, and more retrospectives. They reduce the team's ability to use overtime to cover up scheduling flaws, which helps the team learn to estimate and plan well.

One-week iterations also make decisions easier by reducing schedule risk. If a discussion is taking too long, you can say, "This may not be perfect, but we'll review it again next week." This makes planning and retrospectives easier.

On the other hand, one-week iterations put more pressure on the team. This makes energized work more difficult and can limit refactoring. Velocity is less stable in one-week iterations, because even one holiday represents a big loss of time for the iteration.

Allies

Energized Work (p. 79)
Refactoring (p. 303)

I prefer one-week iterations for new teams. For established teams that are comfortable with all the XP practices, I prefer two-week iterations. Two-week iterations are a little less stressful and lead to a more stable velocity.

Three and four-week iterations seem too long to me. They don't provide enough feedback to the team or the larger organization. However, if you think that a longer iteration would be useful for your team, please try it. Be careful: longer iterations are more sensitive to mistakes, because it takes longer to expose and to recover from those mistakes.

Don't use longer iterations if you feel that you need more time to get your work done. Longer iterations won't change the amount of time you have; they only change how often you check your progress. If you have difficulty getting your work done, *shorten* your iteration length (to a minimum of

Shorten your iteration length if you're having trouble with XP.

one week) and look at what you're doing to support energized work. Be sure to reduce your workload in each iteration proportionally. Shortening your iteration length will reduce the amount of work you have to do each iteration and will help you identify problems in your process.

Ally
Energized Work (p. 79)

Some teams base their iterations on a number of business days rather than a calendar. For example, rather than having a seven calendar-day iteration, the team's iterations are five business days long. This is helpful for one-week iterations because it reduces the impact of holidays on the team's velocity. However, I don't recommend business-day iterations because they're harder to schedule with stakeholders. The regular

Ally
Trust (p. 102)

heartbeat of the XP team is an excellent way to generate trust, and business-day iterations don't have the same impact. It's nice to know that Wednesday is *always* the start of a new iteration.

Further Reading

Agile Estimating and Planning [Cohn] and *Planning Extreme Programming* [Beck & Fowler] each provide alternative ways of approaching iteration planning.

Slack

Audience
Programmers, Coaches

We deliver on our iteration commitments.

Imagine that the power cable for your workstation is just barely long enough to reach the wall receptacle. You can plug it in if you stretch it taut, but the slightest vibration will cause the plug to pop out of the wall and the power to go off. You'll lose everything you were working on.

Ally
Iterations (p. 41)

I can't afford to have my computer losing power at the slightest provocation. My work's too important for that. In this situation, I would move the computer closer to the outlet so that it could handle some minor bumps. (Then I would tape the cord to the floor so people couldn't trip over it, install an uninterruptable power supply, and invest in a continuous backup server.)

Your project plans are also too important to be disrupted by the slightest provocation. Like the power cord, they need slack.

How Much Slack?

The amount of slack you need doesn't depend on the number of problems you face. It depends on the *randomness* of problems. If you always experience exactly 20 hours of problems in each iteration, your velocity will automatically compensate. However, if you experience between 20 and 30 hours of problems in each iteration, your velocity will bounce up and down. You need 10 hours of slack to stabilize your velocity and to ensure that you'll meet your commitments.

These numbers are just for illustration. Instead of measuring the number of hours you spend on problems, take advantage of velocity's feedback loop (see "Estimating" later in this chapter for more about velocity). If your velocity bounces around a lot, stop signing up for more stories than your velocity allows. This will cause your velocity to settle at a lower number that incorporates enough slack for your team. On the other hand, if your velocity is rock solid, try reducing slack by committing to a small extra story next iteration.

How to Introduce Slack

One way to introduce slack into your iterations might be to schedule no work on the last day or two of your iteration. This would give you slack, but it would be pretty wasteful. A better approach is to schedule useful, important work that isn't time-critical—work you can set aside in case of an emergency. *Paying down technical debt* fits the bill perfectly.

> **NOTE**
> Only the constraint needs slack. The rest of the team organizes their work around the constraint's schedule, resulting in slack for the entire team. ("XP Concepts" in Chapter 3 discusses the Theory of Constraints in more detail.)
>
> In this book, I've assumed that programmers are your team's constraint. If that isn't true for your team, you will need slack that is appropriate for your constraint. Talk to your mentor (see "Find a Mentor" in Chapter 2) about how to modify this advice for your specific situation.

Even the best teams inadvertantly accumulate technical debt. Although you should always make your code as clean as you can, some technical debt will slip by unnoticed.

Rather than doing the bare minimum necessary to keep your head above water, be generous in refactoring and cleaning up technical debt in existing code. Every iteration, look for opportunities to make existing code better. Make this part of your everyday work. Every time I find myself scratching my head over a variable or method name, I change it. If I see some code that's no longer in use, I delete it.

Ally
Refactoring (p. 303)

In addition to these small improvements, look for opportunities to make larger changes. Perhaps the code uses primitives rather than introducing a new type, or perhaps a class needs to have some of its responsibilities extracted into a new class.

> **NOTE**
> I notice technical debt most when I navigate during pair programming. When a problem slows us down and I find myself feeling irritated, that inspires me to suggest that we fix it.

Paying down technical debt directly increases team productivity, so I spend a lot of time on it throughout the iteration. I usually spend about eight hours per week paying down technical debt, but other members of my teams spend only a few hours. A good rule of thumb is to spend 10 percent of the iteration on technical debt.

Don't spend all your time on a single problem. Refactor throughout the iteration—an hour encapsulating a structure here, two hours fixing class responsibilities there. Each refactoring should address a specific, relatively small problem. Sometimes you'll fix only part of a larger problem—

> Perform big refactorings incrementally.

that's OK as long as it makes the code better. If your team pays down technical debt every week, you'll have the opportunity to see and fix remaining problems in the future.

As you fix technical debt, focus on fixes that make your current work easier. Don't go looking for technical debt that's unrelated to stories you're currently working on. If you consistently relate your improvements to your current work, you'll automatically put the most effort into the most frequently modified and most valuable parts of the system.

Research Time

To keep up with their constantly expanding field, programmers must continually improve their skills. In doing so, they will often learn things that enhance their work on the project.

Dedicated *research time* is an excellent way to encourage learning and add additional slack into your iterations. To introduce it, set aside half a day for each programmer to conduct self-directed research on a topic of his choice. Be completely hands-off. I recommend only two rules: don't spend this time on project stories or tasks, and don't modify any project code.

> **NOTE**
> If you're concerned about people goofing off, provide lunch the next day and ask that people share what they've done in informal peer discussion. This is a good way to share knowledge anyway.

I've introduced this technique to several teams, and it's paid dividends each time. Two weeks after introducing research time at one organization, the product manager told me that research time was the most valuable time the team spent, and suggested that we double it.

Research time works because programmers are typically motivated by a desire to do good work, particularly when they're self-directed. Most programmers have a natural desire to make their lives easier and to impress their colleagues. As a result, the work done in research time often has a surprisingly high return for the project.

Research time is particularly valuable for XP teams. The continuous drumbeat of iteration deadlines is great for reducing risk and motivating the team to excel, but it can lead to tunnel vision. Dedicated research time gives programmers a chance to widen their ranges, which often leads to insights about how to develop more effectively.

NOTE

I schedule research time for the morning of the penultimate day of the iteration. This is late enough in the iteration that we can use the time as slack if we need to, but not so late to distract programmers with the upcoming deadline. Mornings are better than afternoons because it's harder to start on time when production code is occupying your attention.

For research time to be effective, you must focus. Half a day can go by very quickly. It's easy to think of research time as a catch-all for postponed meetings. Be strict about avoiding interruptions and enlist the help of the project manager. Ignore your email, turn off your IM, and use your web browser only for specific research.

When you first adopt research time, you might have trouble deciding what to work on. Think about what has puzzled you recently. Would you like to learn more about the details of your UI framework? Is there a programming language you've wanted to try but your organization doesn't use? Has real-time networking always fascinated you?

As you do your research, create spike solutions—small standalone programs—that demonstrate what you've learned. Avoid trying to make software that's generally useful; that will reduce the amount of time available to pursue core ideas. If something turns out to deserve further work, create and schedule a story for it.

Ally
Spike Solutions (p. 331)

When Your Iteration Commitment Is at Risk

Research time and paying down technical debt are important tasks that enhance your programmers' skills and allow them to deliver more quickly. Paying down technical debt, in particular, should be part of every iteration. However, if your iteration commitments are at risk, it's OK to set these two tasks aside *temporarily* in order to meet those commitments.

Use refactoring as a shock absorber

Before starting a big refactoring to pay down technical debt, consider the iteration plan and think about the kinds of problems the team has encountered. If the iteration is going smoothly, go ahead and refactor. If you've encountered problems or you're a little behind schedule, shrug your shoulders and work on meeting your iteration commitment instead. You'll have another opportunity to fix the problem later. By varying the amount of time you spend paying down technical debt, you can ensure that most iterations come in exactly on time.

> **NOTE**
> Continue refactoring *new* code as you write it. It's OK to defer cleaning up existing technical debt temporarily, but incurring new technical debt will hurt your productivity.

Incur a little voluntary overtime

Every iteration experiences a few bumps. Varying the time you spend paying down technical debt is your first line of defense. Rarely, though, a problem sneaks past. In this case, if family commitments permit, I voluntarily work a few extra hours. Overtime is unusual in the companies I work with, so an extra hour a day once in a while isn't a big deal. Another programmer or two will often volunteer to do the same.

Ally

Energized Work (p. 79)

> **NOTE**
> Be careful not to overuse overtime. Overuse will sap team members' ability to do good work. You can use it to clean up after small problems, but each programmer should only contribute an hour or so per day, and only voluntarily.

Cancel research time

Some problems will be too significant to clean up in overtime. In this case, consider cancelling research time in order to address the problem. First, though, take a second look at whether you need to replan the iteration instead (see "Iteration Planning" earlier in this chapter). When problems are big, even cancelling research time may not be enough.

Don't Cross the Line

Slack is a wonderful tool. It helps you meet your commitments and gives you time to perform important, nonurgent tasks that improve your productivity.

Be careful, though. Although slack is a wonderful way to handle transitory problems, it can also disguise systemic problems. If you rely on slack to finish your stories in every iteration, that time isn't really slack—it's required.

To return to the power cord example, suppose that your workstation is on a jiggly desk. Every time you type, the desk jiggles a bit and the power cord pops out. You could add just enough slack to the cord to handle your typing, but that wouldn't really be slack; it's necessary to use the computer at all. If anything else happens while you're typing—say, Bob from marketing gives you a friendly slap on the back—the cord will still pop out.

If you work overtime, cancel research time, or don't pay down any technical debt for two or three iterations in a row, you've overcommitted and have no slack. Congratulate yourself for delivering on your commitments anyway. Now add slack by reducing your velocity.

> If you consistently use most of your slack, you've overcommitted.

Making enough time for these nonurgent tasks is difficult. With a deadline rushing head-first toward you, it's difficult to imagine spending any time that doesn't directly contribute to getting stories out the door. New XP teams especially struggle with this. Don't give up. Slack is essential to meeting commitments, and that is the key to successful XP.

Reducing the Need for Slack

In my experience, there are two big sources of randomness on XP teams: customer unavailability and technical debt. Both lead to an unpredictable environment, make estimating difficult, and require you to have more slack in order to meet your commitments.

If programmers have to wait for customer answers as they work, you can reduce the need for slack by making customers more available to answer programmer questions. They may not like that—customers are often surprised by the amount of time XP needs from them—but if you explain that it will help improve velocity, they may be more interested in helping.

On the other hand, if programmers often encounter unexpected *technical* delays, such as surprising design problems, difficulty integrating, or unavailability of a key staging environment, then your need for slack is due to too much technical debt. Fortunately, using your slack to pay down technical debt will automatically reduce the amount of slack you need in the future.

Questions

If our commitment is at risk, shouldn't we stop pair programming or using test-driven development? Meeting our commitment is most important, right?

First, pair programming and test-driven development (TDD) should allow you to deliver more quickly, not more slowly. However, they do have a learning curve— particularly TDD—so it's true that avoiding TDD might allow you to meet your commitments in the early stages of your project.

Allies
Pair Programming (p. 71)
Test-Driven Development (p. 285)

However, you shouldn't use them as slack. Pair programming, test-driven development, and similar practices maintain your capability to deliver high-quality code. If you don't do them, you will immediately incur technical debt and hurt your productivity. You may meet this iteration's commitments, but you'll do so at the expense of the next iteration. If your existing slack options aren't enough, you need to replan your iteration, as discussed in"Iteration Planning" earlier in this chapter.

In contrast, paying down technical debt, going home on time, and conducting research *enhance* your capability to deliver. Using them as slack once in a while won't hurt.

Research time sounds like professional development. Shouldn't programmers do that on their own time?

In my experience, research time pays dividends within a few months. It's worthwhile even without an explicit policy of encouraging professional development.

However, if research time isn't appropriate for your organization, you can increase the amount of time you spend paying down technical debt instead.

Should we pair program during research time?

You can if you want, but you don't have to. Treat it as you would any other spike.

Shouldn't a project have just one buffer at the end of the project rather than a lot of little buffers?

Ally
Spike Solutions (p. 331)

The book *Critical Chain* [Goldratt 1997] argues for creating a single buffer at the end of a project rather than padding each estimate. It's good advice, and adding slack to each iteration might seem to contradict that.

However, an XP team makes a commitment to deliver every week. In a sense, an XP team conducts a series of one-week projects, each with a commitment to stakeholders and its own small buffer protecting that commitment. This commitment is necessary for stakeholder trust, to take advantage of feedback, and to overcome the inherently high risk of software projects. Without it, the project would drift off course.

XP avoids *Parkinson's Law* ("work expands to fill the time available") and *Student Syndrome* ("work is delayed until its deadline") by performing important but nonurgent tasks in the buffer.

Results

When you incorporate slack into your iterations, you consistently meet your iteration commitments. You rarely need overtime. In addition, by spending so much time paying down technical debt, your code steadily improves, increasing your productivity and making further enhancements easier.

Contraindications

The danger of thinking of these tasks as slack is thinking they aren't important. They're actually *vital*, and a team that doesn't perform these tasks will slow down over time. They're just not time-critical like your iteration commitment is. Don't use slack as an excuse to set aside these tasks indefinitely.

In addition, never incur technical debt in the name of slack. If you can't meet your iteration commitments while performing standard XP tasks, replan the iteration instead. Practices you should never use as slack include test-driven development, refactoring new code, pair programming, and making sure stories are "done done."

Allies
Test-Driven Development (p. 285)
Refactoring (p. 303)
Pair Programming (p. 71)
"Done Done" (p. 156)

Finally, don't use try to use iteration slack to meet release commitments. There isn't enough iteration slack to make a meaningful difference to your release commitments—in fact, removing slack from your iterations could easily add so much chaos to your process that productivity actually goes down. Use risk management to provide slack for your release commitments.

Ally
Risk Management (p. 224)

Alternatives

Slack allows you to be "done done" and meet your iteration commitments. It enables a consistent velocity. It provides an opportunity for extra refactoring. It reduces technical debt and increases team capability. I'm not aware of any alternatives that provide all these benefits.

Rather than including slack at the iteration level, some teams add a safety buffer to every estimate. As [Goldratt 1997] explains, this leads to delays and often doesn't improve the team's ability to meet their commitments.

Many organizations, however, choose not to include any slack in their plans. It's no coincidence that these organizations have trouble meeting commitments. They also waste a lot of time thrashing around as they attempt to achieve the unachievable.

Reading groups

Some teams form a reading group rather than conducting research time. This is an excellent alternative to research time, particularly for teams that are interested in discussing fundamental ideas rather than exploring new technologies.

One way to do so is to take turns reading sections of a book or an article out loud and then discussing them. This approach has the advantage of not requiring advance preparation, which promotes more active participation. One person should act as facilitator and inspire discussion by asking questions about each section.

A reading group can easily spend half a day per week in productive conversation. To take this book as an example, you could probably discuss one or two practice sections per session.

Silver stories

Other teams schedule *silver stories* for slack. These are less-important stories that the team can set aside if they need extra time. I prefer to pay down technical debt instead because teams often neglect this crucial task.

The difficulty with silver stories is that you need to set aside slack tasks at a moment's notice. If you do that to a silver story, you'll leave behind technical debt in the form of half-done code. If you use silver stories, be sure to delete all code related to the story if you have to put it aside.

I've also observed that silver stories hurt programmer morale. If the team needs to use some slack, they don't finish all the stories on the board. Even though the silver stories were bonus stories, it doesn't feel like that in practice. In contrast, *any* time spent paying down technical debt directly improves programmers' quality of life. That's a win.

Further Reading

Slack: Getting Past Burnout, Busywork, and the Myth of Total Efficiency [DeMarco 2002] provides a compelling case for providing slack throughout the organization.

The Goal and *Critical Chain* [Goldratt 1992 and 1997] are two business novels that make the case for using slack (or "buffers"), instead of padding estimates, to protect commitments and increase throughput.

"Silicon Valley Patterns Study of Domain-Driven Design" (*http://domaindrivendesign.org/discussion/ siliconvalleypatterns/index.html*) is an interesting transcript of some meetings of a long-running and highly successful reading group.

Stories

Audience
Whole Team

We plan our work in small, customer-centric pieces.

Stories may be the most misunderstood entity in all of XP. They're not requirements. They're not use cases. They're not even narratives. They're much simpler than that.

Stories are for planning. They're simple one- or two-line descriptions of work the team should produce. Alistair Cockburn calls them "promissory notes for future conversation."* Everything that stakeholders want the team to produce should have a story, for example:

Ally

Release Planning (p. 206)

- "Warehouse inventory report"
- "Full-screen demo option for job fair"
- "TPS report for upcoming investor dog-and-pony show"
- "Customizable corporate branding on user login screen"

This isn't enough detail for the team to implement and release working software, nor is that the intent of stories. A story is a placeholder for a detailed discussion about requirements. Customers are responsible for having the requirements details available when the rest of the team needs them.

Ally

Incremental Requirements (p. 273)

Although stories are short, they still have two important characteristics:

1. Stories represent *customer value* and are written in the customers' terminology. (The best stories are actually written by customers.) They describe an end-result that the customer values, not implementation details.

2. Stories have clear *completion criteria*. Customers can describe an objective test that would allow programmers to tell when they've successfully implemented the story.

The following examples are *not* stories:

- "Automate integration build" does not represent customer value.
- "Deploy to staging server outside the firewall" describes implementation details rather than an end-result, and it doesn't use customer terminology. "Provide demo that customer review board can use" would be better.
- "Improve performance" has no clear completion criteria. Similarly, "Make it fast enough for my boss to be happy" lacks *objective* completion criteria. "Searches complete within one second" is better.

Story Cards

Write stories on index cards.

---

* *http://c2.com/cgi/wiki?UserStory.*

This isn't the result of some strange Luddittian urge on the part of XP's creators; it's a deliberate choice based on the strengths of the medium. You see, physical cards have one feature that no conglomeration of pixels has: they're tactile. You can pick them up and move them around. This gives them power.

During release planning, customers and stakeholders gather around a big table to select stories for the next release. It's a difficult process of balancing competing desires. Index cards help prevent these disputes by visually showing priorities, making the scope of the work more clear, and directing conflicts toward the plan rather than toward personalities, as discussed in "The Planning Game" earlier in this chapter.

Ally

Release Planning (p. 206)

Story cards also form an essential part of an informative workspace. After the planning meeting, move the cards to the release planning board—a big, six-foot whiteboard, placed prominently in the team's open workspace (see Figure 8-4). You can post hundreds of cards and still see them all clearly. For each iteration, place the story cards to finish during the iteration on the iteration planning board (another big whiteboard; see Figure 8-9) and move them around to indicate your status and progress. Both of these boards are clearly visible throughout the team room and constantly broadcast information to the team.

Ally

Informative Workspace (p. 83)

Index cards also help you be responsive to stakeholders. When you talk with a stakeholder and she has a suggestion, invite her to write it down on a blank index card. I always carry cards with me for precisely this purpose. Afterward, take the stakeholder and her card to the product manager. They can walk over to the release planning board and discuss the story's place in the overall vision. Again, physical cards focus the discussion on relative priorities rather than on contentious "approved/disapproved" decisions.

> Use index cards to be more responsive to stakeholder suggestions.

If the product manager and stakeholder decide to add the story to the release plan, they can take it to the programmers right away. A brief discussion allows the programmers to estimate the story. Developers write their estimate—and possibly a few notes—on the card, and then the stakeholder and product manager place the card into the release plan.

Ally

Estimating (p. 260)

Physical index cards enable these ways of working in a very easy and natural way that's surprisingly difficult to replicate with computerized tools. Although you *can* use software, index cards just work better: they're easier to set up and manipulate, make it easier to see trends and the big picture, and allow you to change your process with no configuration or programming.

> Index cards are simpler and more effective than computerized tools.

Most people are skeptical about the value of index cards at first, so if you feel that way, you're not alone. The best way to evaluate the value of physical story cards is to try them for a few months, then decide whether to keep them.

Customer-Centricity

Stories need to be *customer-centric*. Write them from the on-site customers' point of view, and make sure they provide something that customers care about. On-site customers are in charge of priorities in the planning game, so if a story has no customer value, your customers won't—and shouldn't—include it in the plan.

Ally
The Planning Game (p. 219)

> NOTE
>
> A good way to ensure that your stories are customer-centric is to ask your customers to write the stories themselves.

One practical result of customer-centric stories is that you won't have stories for technical issues. There should be no "Create a build script" story, for example—customers wouldn't know how to prioritize it. Although programmers can tell customers where the technical stories belong in the plan, that disrupts the balance of power over the scope of the project and can leave customers feeling disenfranchised.

Instead, include any technical considerations in the estimate for each story. If a story requires that the programmers create or update a build script, for example, include that cost when estimating for that story.

> NOTE
>
> Including technical costs in stories, rather than having dedicated technical stories, requires incremental design and architecture.

Customer-centric stories aren't necessarily always valuable to the end-user, but they should always be valuable to the on-site customers. For example, a story to produce a tradeshow demo doesn't help end-users, but it helps the customers sell the product.

Splitting and Combining Stories

Although stories can start at any size, it is difficult to estimate stories that are too large or too small. Split large stories; combine small ones.

The right size for a story depends on your velocity. You should be able to complete 4 to 10 stories in each iteration. Split and combine stories to reach this goal. For example, a team with a velocity of 10 days per iteration might split stories with estimates of more than 2 days and combine stories that are less than half a day.

> Select story sizes such that you complete 4 to 10 each iteration.

Combining stories is easy. Take several similar stories, staple their cards together, and write your new estimate on the front.

Splitting stories is more difficult because it tempts you away from vertical stripes and releasable stories (discussed in "Release Planning" earlier in this chapter). It's easiest to just create a new story for each step in the previous story. Unfortunately, this approach leads to story clumps. Instead, consider the *essence* of the story. Peel away all the other issues and write them as new stories. [Cohn] has an excellent chapter on how to do this in his book *Agile Estimating and Planning*. He summarizes various options for splitting stories:

- Split large stories along the boundaries of the data supported by the story.
- Split large stories based on the operations that are performed within the story.
- Split large stories into separate CRUD (Create, Read, Update, Delete) operations.
- Consider removing cross-cutting concerns (such as security, logging, error handling, and so on) and creating two versions of the story: one with and one without support for the cross-cutting concern.
- Consider splitting a large story by separating the functional and nonfunctional (performance, stability, scalability, and so forth) aspects into separate stories.
- Separate a large story into smaller stories if the smaller stories have different priorities.

Special Stories

Most stories will add new capabilities to your software, but any action that requires the team's time and is not a part of their normal work needs a story.

Documentation stories

XP teams need very little documentation to do their work (see "Documentation" in Chapter 7), but you may need the team to produce documentation for other reasons. Create documentation stories just like any other: make them customer-centric and make sure you can identify specific completion criteria. An example of a documentation story is "Produce user manual."

> **Ally**
> Documentation (p. 195)

"Nonfunctional" stories

Performance, scalability, and stability—so-called *nonfunctional* requirements—should be scheduled with stories, too. Be sure that these stories have precise completion criteria. See "Performance Optimization" in Chapter 9 for more.

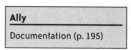

> **Ally**
> Performance Optimization (p. 335)

Bug stories

Ideally, your team will fix bugs as soon as they find them, before declaring a story "done done." Nobody's perfect, though, and you will miss some bugs. Schedule these bugs with story cards, such as "Fix multiple-user editing bug." Schedule them as soon as possible to keep your code clean and reduce your need for bug-tracking software.

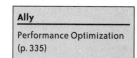

> **Allies**
> No Bugs (p. 160)
> "Done Done" (p. 156)

Bug stories can be difficult to estimate. Often, the biggest timesink in debugging is figuring out what's wrong, and you usually can't estimate how long that will take. Instead, provide a timeboxed estimate: "We'll spend up to a day investigating this bug. If we haven't fixed it by then, we'll schedule another story."

Spike stories

Sometimes programmers won't be able to estimate a story because they don't know enough about the technology required to implement the story. In this case, create a story to research that technology. An example of a research story is "Figure out how to estimate 'Send HTML' story." Programmers will often use a *spike solution* (see "Spike Solutions" in Chapter 9) to research the technology, so these sorts of stories are typically called *spike stories*.

> **Ally**
> Spike Solutions (p. 331)

Word these stories in terms of the goal, not the research that needs to be done. When programmers work on a research story, they only need to do enough work to make their estimate for the real story. They shouldn't try to figure out all the details or solve the entire problem.

Programmers can usually estimate how long it will take to *research* a technology even if they don't know the technology in question. If they can't estimate the research time, timebox the story as you do with bug stories. I find that a day is plenty of time for most spike stories, and half a day is sufficient for most.

Estimating

Other than spike stories, you normally don't need to schedule time for the programmers to estimate stories—you can just ask them for an estimate at any time. It's part of the overhead of the iteration, as are support requests and other unscheduled interruptions. If your programmers feel that estimating is too much of an interruption, try putting new story cards in a pile for the programmers to estimate when it's convenient.

Sometimes you'll have a large number of new stories to estimate. In this case, it might be worth creating a story card for estimating those stories.

Meetings

Like estimating, most meetings are part of the normal overhead of the iteration. If you have an unusual time commitment, such as training or an off-site day, you can reserve time for it with a story.

Architecture, design, refactoring, and technical infrastructure

Don't create stories for technical details. Technical tasks are part of the cost of implementing stories and should be part of the estimates. Use incremental design and architecture to break large technical requirements into small pieces that you can implement incrementally.

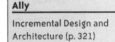

Ally

Incremental Design and Architecture (p. 321)

Questions

Are index cards really more effective than computerized tools? What about reporting?

See our discussion of reporting ("Reporting" in Chapter 6) for more information.

What about backups? Won't the cards get lost?

If you exercise reasonable care, you're unlikely to lose cards. The only time I've seen a team lose their cards was when they created them and then left them in an ignored pile somewhere on their boss' desk for six months.

That said, there's always the possibility of fire or other disaster. If the risk of losing cards is too great for you, consider taking a digital photo of the release planning board every week or so. An eight-megapixel camera has sufficient resolution to capture a six-foot whiteboard and all the detail on the cards.

Why do you recommend sizing stories so that we can complete 4 to 10 stories per iteration?

If you only have a few stories in an iteration, it's harder to see that you're making progress, which increases the risk that you won't see problems in time to correct them. In addition, if something goes wrong and you can't finish a story, it will represent a large percentage of your work. Too many stories, on the other hand, increase your planning and estimating burden. Each story becomes smaller, making it harder to see the big picture.

An average of 6 stories per iteration leads to a 3-month release plan (the maximum I recommend) consisting of 78 stories. That's a nice number. It gives you flexibility in planning without overwhelming you with details.

Our customers understand programming. Can we create programmer-centric technical stories?

It's much more difficult to create customer-centric stories than programmer-centric stories, so it's tempting to find excuses for avoiding them. "Our customers don't mind if we have programmer-centric stories" is one such excuse. Try to avoid it.

Even if your customers really do have the ability to prioritize programmer-centric stories, customer-centric stories lead to better plans. Remember, your goal is to create stories that allow you to release the software at any time. Programmer-centric stories usually don't have that property.

If your customers *are* programmers—if you're writing software *for* programmers, such as a library or framework—then your stories should use a programmer-centric language (see "Ubiquitous Language" in Chapter 6). Even so, they should reflect your customers' perspective. Create stories about your customers' needs, not your plans to fulfill their needs.

How can we encourage stakeholders to use stories for requesting features?

When a stakeholder asks you for a feature, take out an index card and invite him to write it down so it can be scheduled. For electronic requests, an on-site customer should follow up, either by speaking to the requester in person or creating the story card himself.

If stakeholders refuse to use stories, the product manager can manage this relationship by providing stakeholders what they want to see and translating stakeholders' wishes into stories for the team.

Results

When you use stories well, the on-site customers understand all the work they approve and schedule. You work on small, manageable, and independent pieces and can deliver complete features frequently. The project always represents the best possible value to the customer at any point in time.

Contraindications

Stories are no replacement for requirements. You need another way of getting details, whether through expert customers on-site (the XP way) or a requirements document (the traditional way).

Be very cautious of using customer-centric stories without also using most of the XP development practices (see Chapter 9). Customer-centric stories depend on the ability to implement infrastructure incrementally with incremental design and architecture. Without this ability, you're likely to incur greater technical debt.

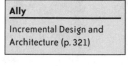

Ally

Incremental Design and Architecture (p. 321)

Physical index cards are only appropriate if the team sits together, or at least has a common area in which they congregate. Experienced distributed teams often keep physical index cards at the main site and copy the cards into the electronic system. This is an administrative headache, but for these teams, the benefits of physical cards make the added work worthwhile.

Ally

Sit Together (p. 112)

Some organizations are skittish about using informal planning tools. If important members of your organization require a formal Gantt chart, you may need to provide it. Your project manager can help you make this decision. As with a distributed team, you may find it valuable to use physical cards as your primary source, then duplicate the information into the tool.

Alternatives

For teams that don't use stories, the main distinction between stories and the line items in most plans is that stories are customer-centric. If you can't use customer-centric stories for some reason, customers cannot participate effectively in the planning game. This will eliminate one of its primary benefits: the ability to create better plans by blending information from both customers and programmers. Unfortunately, no alternative practice will help.

Another distinctive feature of stories is the use of index cards. Physical cards offer many benefits over electronic tools, but you can still use electronic tools if necessary. Some teams track their stories using spreadsheets, and others use dedicated agile planning tools. None of these approaches, however, provide the benefits of physical index cards.

Further Reading

Agile Estimating and Planning [Cohn] discusses options for splitting stories in Chapter 12.

Estimating

We provide reliable estimates.

Programmers often consider estimating to be a black art—one of the most difficult things they must do. Many programmers find that they consistently estimate too low. To counter this problem, they pad their estimates (multiplying by three is a common approach), but sometimes even these rough guesses are too low.

Are good estimates possible? Of course! You just need to focus on your strengths.

What Works (and Doesn't) in Estimating

One reason estimating is so difficult is that programmers can rarely predict how they will spend their time. A task that requires eight hours of uninterrupted concentration can take two or three days if the programmer must deal with constant interruptions. It can take even longer if the programmer works on another task at the same time.

Part of the secret to making good estimates is to predict the effort, not the calendar time, that a project will take. Make your estimates in terms of *ideal engineering days* (often called *story points*), which are the number of days a task would take if you focused on it entirely and experienced no interruptions.

> Estimate in ideal time.

Using ideal time alone won't lead to accurate estimates. I've asked some teams I've worked with to measure exactly how long each task takes them (one team gave me 18 months of data), and even though we estimated in ideal time, the estimates were never accurate.

Still, they were *consistent*. For example, one team always estimated their stories at about 60 percent of the time they actually needed. This may not sound very promising. How useful can inaccurate estimates be, especially if they don't correlate to calendar time? Velocity holds the key.

Velocity

Although estimates are almost never accurate, they are *consistently* inaccurate. While the estimate accuracy of *individual* estimates is all over the map—one estimate might be half the actual time, another might be 20 percent more than the actual time—the estimates *are* consistent in aggregate. Additionally, although each iteration experiences a different set of interruptions, the amount of time required for the interruptions also tends to be consistent from iteration to iteration.

As a result, you can reliably convert estimates to calendar time if you aggregate all the stories in an iteration. A single scaling factor is all you need.

This is where velocity comes in. Your *velocity* is the number of story points you can complete in an iteration. It's a simple yet surprisingly sophisticated tool. It uses a feedback loop, which means every iteration's velocity reflects what the team actually achieved in the previous iteration.

> **NOTE**
> To predict your next iteration's velocity, add the *estimates* of the stories that were "done done" in the previous iteration.

This feedback leads to a magical effect. When the team underestimates their workload, they are unable to finish all their stories by the iteration deadline. This causes their velocity to go down, which in turn reduces the team's workload, allowing them to finish everything on time the following week.

Similarly, if the team overestimates their workload, they find themselves able to finish more stories by the iteration deadline. This causes their velocity to go up, which increases the team's workload to match their capacity.

Velocity is an extremely effective way of balancing the team's workload. In a mature XP team, velocity is stable enough to predict schedules with a high degree of accuracy (see "Risk Management" earlier in this chapter).

Velocity and the Iteration Timebox

Velocity relies upon a strict iteration timebox. To make velocity work, *never* count stories that aren't "done done" at the end of the iteration. *Never* allow the iteration deadline to slip, not even by a few hours.

You may be tempted to cheat a bit and work longer hours, or to slip the iteration deadline, in order to finish your stories and make your velocity a little higher. Don't do that! Artificially raising velocity sabotages the equilibrium of the feedback cycle. If you continue to do it, your velocity will gyrate out of control, which will likely reduce your capacity for energized work in the process. This will further damage your equilibrium and your ability to meet your commitments.

> **Ally**
> Energized Work (p. 79)

NOTE

One project manager wanted to add a few days to the beginning of an iteration so his team could "hit the ground running" and have a higher velocity to show to stakeholders. By doing so, he set the team up for failure: they couldn't keep that pace in the following iteration. Remember that velocity is for predicting schedules, not judging productivity. See "Reporting" in Chapter 6 for ideas about what to report to stakeholders.

Velocity tends to be unstable at the beginning of a project. Give it three or four iterations to stabilize. After that point, you should achieve the same velocity every iteration, unless there's a holiday during the iteration. Use your iteration slack to ensure that you consistently meet your commitments every iteration. I look for deeper problems if the team's velocity changes more than one or twice per quarter.

> **Ally**
> Slack (p. 246)

TIPS FOR ACCURATE ESTIMATES

You can have accurate estimates if you:

1. Estimate in terms of ideal engineering days (story points), not calendar time
2. Use velocity to determine how many story points the team can finish in an iteration
3. Use iteration slack to smooth over surprises and deliver on time every iteration
4. Use risk management to adjust for risks to the overall release plan

---

How to Make Consistent Estimates

There's a secret to estimating: experts automatically make consistent estimates.[*] All you
have to do is use a consistent estimating technique. When you estimate, pick a single,
optimistic value. How long will the story take if you experience no interruptions, can
pair with anyone else on the team, and everything goes well? There's no need to pad
your estimates or provide a probabilistic range with this approach. Velocity
automatically applies the appropriate amount of padding for short-term estimates and risk management
adds padding for long-term estimates.

Ally
Risk Management (p. 224)

There are two corollaries to this secret. First, if you're an
expert but you don't trust your ability to make estimates,
relax. You automatically make good estimates. Just imagine
the work you're going to do and pick the first number that
comes into your head. It won't be right, but it *will* be
consistent with your other estimates. That's sufficient.

> To make a good estimate, go with
> your gut.

Second, if you're not an expert, the way to make good estimates is to become an expert. This isn't as
hard as it sounds. An expert is just a beginner with lots of experience. To become an expert, make a lot
of estimates with relatively short timescales and pay attention to the results. In other words, follow the
XP practices.

All the programmers should participate in estimating. At least one customer should be present to answer
questions. Once the programmers have all the information they need, one programmer will suggest an
estimate. Allow this to happen naturally. The person who is most comfortable will speak first. Often
this is the person who has the most expertise.

NOTE

I assume that programmers are your constraint in this book (see "Theory of
Constraints" in Chapter 3), which means they should be the only ones estimating
stories. The system constraint determines how quickly you can deliver your final
product, so only the constraint's estimates are necessary. If programmers aren't the
constraint on your team, talk with your mentor about how to adjust XP for your
situation.

If the suggested estimate doesn't sound right, or if you don't understand where it came from, ask for
details. Alternatively, if you're a programmer, provide your own estimate and explain your reasoning.
The ensuing discussion will clarify the estimate. When all the programmers confirm an estimate, write
it on the card.

NOTE

If you don't know a part of the system well, practice making estimates for that part of
the system in your head, then compare your estimate with those of the experts. When
your estimate is different, ask why.

---

[*] Unless you have a lot of technical debt. If you do, add more iteration slack (see "Slack" earlier in this chapter) to compensate for
the inconsistency.

At first, different team members will have differing ideas of how long something should take. This will lead to inconsistent estimates. If the team makes estimates as a group, programmers will automatically synchronize their estimates within the first several iterations.

Comparing your estimates to the actual time required for each story or task may also give you the feedback you need to become more consistent. To do so, track your time as described in "Time usage" in Chapter 6.

How to Estimate Stories

Estimate stories in story points. To begin, think of a story point as an ideal day.

NOTE
It's OK to estimate in half-points, but quarter-points shouldn't be necessary.

When you start estimating a story, imagine the engineering tasks you will need to implement it. Ask your on-site customers about their expectations, and focus on those things that would affect your estimate. If you encounter something that seems expensive, provide the customers with less costly alternatives.

As you gain experience with the project, you will begin to make estimates intuitively rather than mentally breaking them down into engineering tasks. Often, you'll think in terms of similar stories rather than ideal days. For example, you might think that a particular story is a typical report, and typical reports are one point. Or you might think that a story is a complicated report, but not twice as difficult as a regular report, and estimate it at one and a half points.

Sometimes you will need more information to make an accurate estimate. In this case, make a note on the card. If you need more information from your customers, write "??" (for "unanswered questions") in place of the estimate. If you need to research a piece of technology further, write "Spike" in place of the estimate and create a spike solution story (see "Spike Solutions" in Chapter 9).

The team has gathered to estimate stories. Mary, one of the on-site customers, starts the discussion. Amy, Jo, and Kim are all programmers.

Mary: Here's our next story. *[She reads the story card aloud, then puts it on the table.]* "Report on parts inventory in warehouse."

Amy: We've done so many reports by now that a new one shouldn't be too much trouble. They're typically one point each. We already track parts inventory, so there's no new data for us to manage. Is there anything unusual about this report?

Mary: I don't think so. We put together a mock-up. *[She pulls out a printout and hands it to Amy.]*

Amy: This looks pretty straightforward. *[She puts the paper on the table. The other programmers take a look.]*

Joe: Mary, what's this age column you have here?

Mary: That's the number of business days since the part entered the warehouse.

Joe: You need business days, not calendar days?

Mary: That's right.

Joe: What about holidays?

Mary: We only want to count days that we're actually in operation. No weekends, holidays, or scheduled shutdowns.

Kim: Joe, I see what you're getting at. Mary, that's going to increase our estimate because we don't currently track scheduled shutdowns. We would need a new UI, or a data feed, in order to know that information. It could add to the complexity of the admin screens, and you and Brian have said that ease of admin is important to you. Do you really need age to be that accurate?

Mary: Hmm. Well, the exact number isn't that important, but if we're going to provide a piece of information, I would prefer it to be accurate. What about holidays—can you do that?

Kim: Can we assume that the holidays will be the same every year?

Mary: Not necessarily, but they won't change very often.

Kim: OK, then we can put them in the config file for now rather than creating a UI for them. That would make this story cheaper.

Mary: You know, I'm going to need to look into this some more. This field isn't that important and I don't think it's going to be worth the added administration burden. Rather than business days, let's just make it the number of calendar weeks. I'll make a separate story for dealing with business days. *[She takes a card and writes, "Report part inventory age in business days, not calendar weeks. No holidays, weekends, or scheduled shutdowns."]*

Kim: Sounds good. That should be pretty easy then, because we already track when the part went into the warehouse. What about the UI?

Mary: All we need to do is add it to the list of reports on the reporting screen.

Kim: I think I'm ready to estimate. *[Looks at other programmers.]* This looks like a pretty standard report to me. It's another specialization for our reporting layer with a few minor logic changes. I'd say it's one point.

Joe: That's what I was thinking, too. Anybody else?

[The other programmers nod.]

Joe: One point. *[He writes "1" on the story card.]* Mary, I don't think we can estimate the business day story you just created until you know what kind of UI you want for it.

Mary: That's fair. *[Writes "??" on the business day card.]* Our next story...

How to Estimate Iteration Tasks

During iteration planning, programmers create engineering tasks that allow them to deliver the stories planned for the iteration. Each engineering task is a concrete, technical task such as "update build script" or "implement domain logic."

Estimate engineering tasks in ideal hours rather than ideal days. When you think about the estimate, be sure to include everything necessary for the task to be "done done"— testing, customer review, and so forth. See "Iteration Planning" earlier in this chapter for more information.

Ally
Iteration Planning (p. 233)

Ally
"Done Done" (p. 156)

When Estimating Is Difficult

If the programmers understand the requirements and are experts in the required technology, they should be able to estimate a story in less than a minute. If the programmers need to discuss the technology, or if they need to ask questions of the customers, then estimating may take longer. I look for ways to bring discussions to a close if an estimate takes longer than five minutes, and I look for deeper problems if every story involves detailed discussion.

One common cause of slow estimating is inadequate customer preparation. To make their estimates, programmers often ask questions the customers haven't considered. In some cases, customers will disagree on the answer and need to work it out.

A *customer huddle*—in which the customers briefly discuss the issue, come to a decision, and return—is one way to handle this. Another way is to write "??" in place of the estimate and move on to the next story. The customers then work out the details at their own pace, and the programmers estimate the story later.

Expect the customers to be unprepared for programmer questions during the first several iterations. Over time, they will learn to anticipate most of the questions programmers will ask.

Programmer inexperience can also cause slow estimating. If the programmers don't understand the problem domain well, they will need to ask a lot of questions before they can make an estimate. As with inadequate customer preparation, this problem will go away in time. If the programmers don't understand the *technology*, however, immediately create a spike story (see "Spike stories" earlier in this chapter) and move on.

> **Ally**
> Spike Solutions (p. 331)

Some programmers try to figure out all the details of the requirements before making an estimate. However, only those issues that would change the estimate by a half-point or more are relevant. It takes practice to figure out which details are important and which you can safely ignore.

This sort of overattention to detail sometimes occurs when a programmer is reluctant to make estimates. A programmer who worries that someone will use her estimate against her in the future will spend too much time trying to make her estimate perfect rather than settling on her first impression.

Programmer reluctance may be a sign of organizational difficulties or excessive schedule pressure, or it may stem from past experiences that have nothing to do with the current project. In the latter case, the programmers usually come to trust the team over time.

> **Ally**
> Trust (p. 102)

To help address these issues during the estimation phase, ask leading questions. For example:

- Do we need a customer huddle on this issue?
- Should we mark this "??" and come back to it later?
- Should we make a spike for this story?
- Do we have enough information to estimate this story?
- Will that information change your estimate?
- We've spent five minutes on this story. Should we come back to it later?

Explaining Estimates

It's almost a law of physics: customers and stakeholders are invariably disappointed with the amount of features their teams can provide. Sometimes they express that disappointment out loud. The best way to deal with this is to ignore the tone and treat the comments as straightforward requests for information.

In fact, a certain amount of back-and-forth is healthy: it helps the team focus on the high-value, low-cost elements of the customers' ideas. (See "How to Win" earlier in this chapter.)

One common customer response is, "Why does that cost so much?" Resist the urge to defend yourself and your sacred honor, pause to collect your thoughts, then list the issues you considered when coming up with the estimate. Suggest options for reducing the cost of the story by reducing scope.

Your explanation will usually satisfy your customers. In some cases, they'll ask for more information. Again, treat these questions as simple requests. If there's something you don't know, admit it, and explain why you made your estimate anyway. If a question reveals something that you haven't considered, change your estimate.

Be careful, though: the questions may cause you to doubt your estimate. Your initial, gut-feel estimate is most likely correct. Only change your estimate if you learn something genuinely new. Don't change it just because you feel pressured. As the programmers who will be implementing the stories, you are the most qualified to make the estimates. Be polite, but firm:

> Politely but firmly refuse to change your estimates when pressured.

> I'm sorry you don't like these estimates. We believe our estimates are correct, but if they're too pessimistic, our velocity will automatically increase to compensate. We have a professional obligation to you and this organization to give you the best estimates we know how, even if they are disappointing, and that's what we're doing.

If a customer reacts with disbelief or browbeats you, he may not realize how disrespectful he's being. Sometimes making him aware of his behavior can help:

> From your body language and the snort you just made, I'm getting the impression that you don't respect or trust our professionalism. Is that what you intended?

Customers and stakeholders may also be confused by the idea of story points. I start by providing a simplified explanation:

> A story point is an estimation technique that automatically compensates for overhead and estimate error. Our velocity is 10, which means we can accomplish 10 points per week.

If the questioner pushes for more information, I explain all the details of ideal days and velocity. That often inspires concern: "If our velocity is 10 ideal days and we have 6 programmers, shouldn't our velocity be 30?"

You can try to explain that ideal days aren't the same as developer days, but that has never worked for me. Now I just offer to provide detailed information:

> Generally speaking, our velocity is 10 because of estimate error and overhead. If you like, we'll perform a detailed audit of our work next week and tell you exactly where the time is going. Would that be useful?

("Reporting" in Chapter 6 discusses time usage reports in detail.)

These questions often dissipate as customers and stakeholders gain trust in the team's ability to deliver. If they don't, or if the problems are particularly bad, enlist the help of your project manager to defuse the situation. "Team Strategy #1: Customer-Programmer Empathy" in Chapter 6 has further suggestions.

How to Improve Your Velocity

Your velocity can suffer for many reasons. The following options might allow you to improve your velocity.

Pay down technical debt

The most common technical problem is excessive technical debt (see "Technical Debt"). This has a greater impact on team productivity than any other factor does. Make code quality a priority and your velocity will improve dramatically. However, this isn't a quick fix. Teams with excessive technical debt often have months—or even years—of cleanup ahead of them. Rather than stopping work to pay down technical debt, fix it incrementally. Iteration slack is the best way to do so, although you may not see a noticeable improvement for several months.

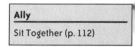

Ally

Slack (p. 246)

Improve customer involvement

If your customers aren't available to answer questions when programmers need them, programmers have to either wait or make guesses about the answers. Both of these hurt velocity. To improve your velocity, make sure that a customer is always available to answer programmer questions.

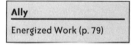

Ally

Sit Together (p. 112)

Support energized work

Tired, burned-out programmers make costly mistakes and don't put forth their full effort. If your organization has been putting pressure on the team, or if programmers have worked a lot of extra hours, shield the programmers from organizational pressure and consider instituting a no-overtime policy.

Ally

Energized Work (p. 79)

Offload programmer duties

If programmers are the constraint for your team—as this book assumes—then hand any work that other people can do *to* other people. Find ways to excuse programmers from unnecessary meetings, shield them from interruptions, and have somebody else take care of organizational bureaucracy such as time sheets and expense reports. You could even hire an administrative assistant for the team to handle all non-project-related matters.

Provide needed resources

Most programming teams have all the resources they need. However, if your programmers complain about slow computers, insufficient RAM, or unavailability of key materials, get those resources for them. It's always surprising when a company nickle-and-dimes its software teams. Does it make sense to save $5,000 in equipment costs if it costs your team half an hour per programmer every day? A team of six programmers will recoup that cost within a month. And what about the opportunity costs of delivering fewer features?

Add programmers (carefully)

Velocity is related to the number of programmers on your team, but unless your project is woefully understaffed and experienced personnel are readily available, adding people won't make an immediate difference. As [Brooks] famously said, "Adding people to a late project only makes it later." Expect new employees to take a month or two to be productive. Pair programming, collective code ownership, and a shared workspace will help reduce that time, though adding junior programmers to the team can actually *decrease* productivity.

Allies

Pair Programming (p. 71)
Collective Code Ownership (p. 191)
Sit Together (p. 112)

Likewise, adding to large teams can cause communication challenges that decrease productivity. Six programmers is my preferred size for an XP team, and I readily add good programmers to reach that number. Past 6, I am very cautious about adding programmers, and I avoid team sizes greater than 10 programmers.

Questions

How do we modify our velocity if we add or remove programmers?

If you add or remove only one person, try leaving your velocity unchanged and see what happens. Another option is to adjust your velocity proportionally to the change. Either way, your velocity will adjust to the correct number after another iteration.

How can we have a stable velocity? Team members take vacations, get sick, and so forth.

Your iteration slack should handle minor variations in people's availability. If a large percentage of the team is away, as during a holiday, your velocity may go down for an iteration. This is normal. Your velocity should return to normal in the next iteration.

Ally

Slack (p. 246)

If you have a small number of programmers—four or fewer—you may find that even one day of absence is enough to affect your velocity. In this case, you may wish to use two-week iterations. See the end of "Iteration Planning" earlier in this chapter for a discussion of the trade-offs.

What should we use as our velocity at the beginning of the project?

For your first iteration, just make your best guess. Set your velocity for the following iteration based on what you actually complete. Expect your velocity to take three or four iterations to stabilize.

Your organization may want you to make release commitments before your velocity has stabilized. The best approach is to say, "I don't have a schedule estimate yet, but we're working on it. I can promise you an estimate in three or four weeks. We need the time to calibrate the developers' estimates to what they actually produce."

Isn't it a waste of time for all the programmers to estimate stories together?

It does take a lot of programmer-hours for all the programmers to estimate together, but this isn't wasted time. Estimating sessions are not just for estimation—they're also a crucial first step in communicating and clarifying requirements. Programmers ask questions and clarify details, which often leads to ideas the customers haven't considered. Sometimes this collaboration reduces the overall cost of the project. (See "The Planning Game" earlier in this chapter.)

All the programmers need to be present to ensure they understand what they will be building. Having the programmers together also increases estimate accuracy.

What if we don't ask the right questions of the customer and miss something?

Sometimes you will miss something important. If Joe hadn't asked Mary about the age column, the team would have missed a major problem and their estimate would have been wrong. These mistakes happen. Information obvious to customers isn't always obvious to programmers.

Although you cannot *prevent* these mistakes, you can reduce them. If all the programmers estimate together, they're more likely to ask the right questions. Mistakes will also decrease as the team becomes more experienced in making estimates. Customers will learn what details to provide, and programmers will learn which questions to ask.

In the meantime, don't worry unless you encounter these surprises often. Address unexpected details when they come up. (See "Iteration Planning" earlier in this chapter.)

If unexpected details frequently surprise you, and the problem doesn't improve with experience, ask your mentor for help.

When should we reestimate our stories?

Story estimates don't need to be accurate, just self-consistent. As a result, you only need to reestimate a story when your understanding of it changes in a way that affects its difficulty or scope.

To make our estimates, we made some assumptions about the design. What if the design changes?

XP uses incremental design and architecture, so the whole design gradually improves over time. As a result, your estimates will usually remain consistent with each other.

Allies
Refactoring (p. 303)
Incremental Design and Architecture (p. 321)

How do we deal with technical dependencies in our stories?

With proper incremental design and architecture, technical dependencies should be rare, although they can happen. I typically make a note in the estimate field: "Six (four if story Foo done first)."

If you find yourself making more than a few of these notes, something is wrong with your approach to incremental design. Ask your mentor for help.

What if we want to get a rough estimate of project length—without doing release planning—before the project begins?

[DeMarco 2002] has argued that organizations set project deadlines based on the value of the project. In other words, the project is only worth doing if you can complete it before the deadline. (Some organizations play games with deadlines in order to compensate for expected overruns, but assume the deadline is accurate in this discussion.)

If this is true—and it coincides with my experience—then the estimate for the project isn't as important as whether you can finish it before the deadline.

To judge whether a project is worth pursuing, gather the project visionary, a seasoned project manager, and a senior programmer or two (preferably ones that would be on the project). Ask the visionary to describe the project's goals and deadline, then ask the project manager and programmers if they think it's possible. If it is, then you should gather the team and perform some real estimating, release planning, and risk management by conducting the first three or four iterations of the project.

Allies
Release Planning (p. 206)
Risk Management (p. 224)

This approach takes about four weeks and yields a release date that you can commit to. [McConnell 2005] provides additional options that are faster but less reliable.

Results

When you estimate well, your velocity is consistent and predictable with each iteration. You make commitments and meet them reliably. Estimation is fast and easy, and you can estimate most stories in a minute or two.

Contraindications

This approach to estimating assumes that programmers are the constraint (see "XP Concepts" in Chapter 3 for more about the Theory of Constraints). It also depends on fixed-length iterations , small stories, and tasks. If these conditions aren't present, you need to use a different approach to estimating.

This approach also requires trust: developers need to believe they can give accurate estimates without being attacked, and customers and stakeholders need to believe the developers are providing honest estimates. That trust may not be present at first, but if it doesn't develop, you'll run into trouble.

Ally
Trust (p. 102)

Regardless of your approach to estimating, never use missed estimates to attack developers. This is a quick and easy way to destroy trust.

Alternatives

There are many approaches to estimating. The one I've described has the benefit of being both accurate and simple. However, its dependency on release planning for long-term estimates makes it labor-intensive for initial project estimates. See [McConnell] for other options.

Further Reading

Agile Estimating and Planning [Cohn] describes a variety of approaches to agile estimation.

Software Estimation: Demystifying the Black Art [McConnell 2005] provides a comprehensive look at traditional approaches to estimation.

CHAPTER 9

Developing

Imagine you've given up the world of software to become a master chef. After years of study and practice, you've reached the top of your profession. One day you receive the ultimate invitation: to cook for 500 attendees at a $10,000-a-plate fundraiser.

A limo takes you from your chartered plane to the venue, and you and your cooks walk confidently into a kitchen... only to stop in shock. The kitchen is a mess: rotting food, unwashed cooking implements, standing water in the sinks. It's the morning of the event. You have 12 hours.

What do you do? You roll up your sleeves and start cleaning. As soon as the first space is clear, a few cooks begin the longest and most complicated food preparation. Others head to the market to get fresh ingredients. The rest keep cleaning. Working around the mess will take too long.

It's a lesson you've learned from software over and over again.

Software development requires the cooperation of everyone on the team. Programmers are often called "developers," but in reality everyone on the team is part of the development effort. When you share the work, customers identify the next requirements while programmers work on the current ones. Testers help the team figure out how to stop introducing bugs. Programmers spread the cost of technical infrastructure over the entire life of the project. Above all, everyone helps keep everything clean.

The best way I know to reduce the cost of writing software is to improve the internal quality of its code and design. I've never seen high quality on a well-managed project fail to repay its investment. It always reduces the cost of development in the short term as well as in the long term. On a successful XP project, there's an amazing feeling—the feeling of being absolutely safe to change absolutely anything without worry.

Here are nine practices that keep the code clean and allow the entire team to contribute to development:

- *Incremental Requirements* allows the team to get started while customers work out requirements details.
- *Customer Tests* help communicate tricky domain rules.

- *Test-Driven Development* allows programmers to be confident that their code does what they think it should.
- *Refactoring* enables programmers to improve code quality without changing its behavior.
- *Simple Design* allows the design to change to support any feature request, no matter how surprising.
- *Incremental Design and Architecture* allows programmers to work on features in parallel with technical infrastructure.
- *Spike Solutions* use controlled experiments to provide information.
- *Performance Optimization* uses hard data to drive optimization efforts.
- *Exploratory Testing* enables testers to identify gaps in the team's thought processes.

"DEVELOPING" MINI-ÉTUDE

The purpose of this étude is to practice reflective design. If you're new to agile development, you may use it to understand your codebase and identify design improvements, even if you're not currently using XP. If you're an experienced agile practitioner, review Chapter 15 and use this étude to discover process changes that will help your team improve its approach to design.

Conduct this étude for a timeboxed half-hour every day for as long as it is useful. Expect to feel rushed by the deadline at first. If the étude becomes stale, discuss how you can change it to make it interesting again.

This étude is for programmers only. You will need pairing workstations, paper, and writing implements.

Step 1. Form pairs. Try to pair with someone you haven't paired with recently.

Step 2. (Timebox this step to 15 minutes.) Look through your code and choose a discrete unit to analyze. Pick something that you have not previously discussed in the larger group. You may choose a method, a class, or an entire subsystem. Don't spend too long picking something; if you have trouble deciding, pick at random.

Reverse-engineer the design of the code by reading it. Model the design with a flow diagram, UML, CRC cards, or whatever technique you prefer. Identify any flaws in the code and its design, and discuss how to fix them. Create a new model that shows what the design will look like after it has been fixed.

If you have time, discuss specific refactoring steps that will allow you to migrate from the current design to your improved design in small, controlled steps.

Step 3. (Timebox this step to 15 minutes.) Within the entire group of programmers, choose three pairs to lead a discussion based on their findings. Each pair has five minutes.

Consider these discussion questions:

- Which sections of the code did you choose?
- What was your initial reaction to the code?
- What are the benefits and drawbacks of the proposals?
- Which specific refactorings can you perform based on your findings?

Incremental Requirements

Audience
Customers

We define requirements in parallel with other work.

A team using an up-front requirements phase keeps their
requirements in a requirements document. An XP team doesn't have a requirements phase and story
cards aren't miniature requirements documents, so where do requirements come from?

The Living Requirements Document

In XP, the on-site customers sit with the team. They're expected to have all the
information about requirements at their fingertips. When somebody needs to know
something about the requirements for the project, she asks one of the on-site customers
rather than looking in a document.

Ally
Sit Together (p. 112)

Face-to-face communication is much more effective than written communication, as [Cockburn]
discusses, and it allows XP to save time by eliminating a long requirements analysis phase. However,
requirements work is still necessary. The on-site customers need to understand the requirements for
the software before they can explain it.

The key to successful requirements analysis in XP is *expert customers*. Involve real
customers, an experienced product manager, and experts in your problem domain (see
"The XP Team" in Chapter 3 and "Real Customer Involvement" in Chapter 6). Many
of the requirements for your software will be intuitively obvious to the right customers.

Ally
Real Customer Involvement (p. 120)

> **NOTE**
> If you have trouble with requirements, your team may not include the right customers.

Some requirements will necessitate even expert customers to consider a variety of options or do some
research before making a decision. Customers, you can and should include other team members in your
discussions if it helps clarify your options. For example, you may wish to include a programmer in your
discussion of user interface options so you can strike a balance between an impressive UI and low
implementation cost.

Write down any requirements you might forget. These notes are primarily for your use
as customers so you can easily answer questions in the future and to remind you of the
decisions you made. They don't need to be detailed or formal requirements documents;
keep them simple and short. When creating screen mock-ups, for example, I often
prefer to create a sketch on a whiteboard and take a digital photo. I can create and
photograph a whiteboard sketch in a fraction of the time it takes me to make a mock-up using an
electronic tool.

Ally
Version Control (p. 169)

> **NOTE**
> Some teams store their requirements notes in a Wiki or database, but I prefer to use
> normal office tools and check the files into version control. Doing this allows you to
> use all of the tools at your disposal, such as word processors, spreadsheets, and
> presentation software. It also keeps requirements documents synchronized with the
> rest of the project and allows you to travel back in time to previous versions.

Work Incrementally

Work on requirements *incrementally*, in parallel with the rest of the team's work. This makes your work easier and ensures that the rest of the team won't have to wait to get started. Your work will typically parallel your release-planning horizons, discussed in "Release Planning" in Chapter 8).

Vision, features, and stories

Start by clarifying your project vision, then identify features and stories as described in "Release Planning" in Chapter 6. These initial ideas will guide the rest of your requirements work.

> **Allies**
> Vision (p. 201)
> Release Planning (p. 206)

Rough expectations

Figure out what a story means to you and how you'll know it's finished slightly before you ask programmers to estimate it. As they estimate, programmers will ask questions about your expectations; try to anticipate those questions and have answers ready. (Over time, you'll learn what sorts of questions your programmers will ask.) A rough sketch of the visible aspects of the story might help.

> **NOTE**
> Sometimes the best way to create a UI mock-up is to work in collaboration with the programmers. The iteration-planning meeting might be the best time for this work.

Mock-ups, customer tests, and completion criteria

Figure out the details for each story just before programmers start implementing it. Create rough mock-ups that show what you expect the work to look like when it's done. Prepare customer tests that provide examples of tricky domain concepts, and describe what "done done" means for each story. You'll typically wait for the corresponding iteration to begin before doing most of this work.

> **Allies**
> Customer Tests (p. 278)
> "Done Done" (p. 156)

Customer review

While stories are under development, before they're "done done," review each story to make sure it works as you expected. You don't need to exhaustively test the application—you can rely on the programmers to test their work—but you should check those areas in which programmers might think differently than you do. These areas include terminology, screen layout, and interactions between screen elements.

> Only working applications show customers what they're really going to get.

> **NOTE**
> Prior to seeing the application in action, every conversation is theoretical. You can discuss options and costs, but until you have an implementation, everyone can only imagine how the choices will feel. Only working applications show you what you're really going to get.

Some of your findings will reveal errors due to miscommunication or misunderstanding. Others, while meeting your requirements, won't work as well in practice as you had hoped. In either case, the solution is the same: talk with the programmers about making changes. You can even pair with programmers as they work on the fixes.

Many changes will be minor, and the programmers will usually be able to fix them as part of their iteration slack. If there are major changes, however, the programmers may not have time to fix them in the current iteration. (This can happen even when the change seems minor from the customer's perspective.) Create story cards for these changes. Before scheduling such a story into your release plan, consider whether the value of the change is worth its cost.

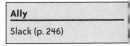

Ally

Slack (p. 246)

Over time, programmers will learn about your expectations for the application. Expect the number of issues you discover to decline each iteration.

A CUSTOMER REVIEW SESSION

By Elisabeth Hendrickson

"Jill, do you have a moment?" Mary asked, walking over to Jill's workstation. "I need to review a story and I was hoping you could show me some of your exploratory testing techniques."

Ally

Exploratory Testing (p. 341)

"Sure, I'd be happy to," Jill said. "What's the charter for our session?"

"I want to explore the Defaults story that Pradeep and Jan are working on," Mary said. "They're not done yet, but they said that the UI is mostly filled in. I wanted to make sure they're going in the right direction."

"OK," Jill said as she wrote "Explore Defaults UI" on a card. "Let's start by setting some explicit defaults in the Preferences page." She navigated to that area of the application, and Mary picked up a notepad, ready to take notes.

Jill reached the Preferences page. "Here are the defaults users can set explicitly," she said, pointing at the screen. "Is this what you were expecting?"

Mary nodded. "We sketched out a mock-up of the screen with the programmers earlier in the iteration. Now that I look at it, though, it seems crowded. I think an icon would be better than those repeated *Set Default* links." She made a note to bring up the issue with the programmers.

"Let's look at the default credit cards next," Jill said. "It's newest."

Mary took the mouse and clicked over to the credit cards screen. "This user has several credit cards, and one has already been marked as the default. We should be able to change it by clicking this radio button," she said, and did so. "Nice! I like how they enabled the *Undo* button when I clicked. But does the save button have to be labeled *Submit*?" She laughed as she made a few notes. "I feel like I'm on the set of a B movie whenever I see that. *Submit to your computer master, puny mortal!*"

Jill grinned. "I never thought of it that way." She paused to consider. "Let's use the zero/one/many heuristic[*] to see what happens when we create a new user with no credit cards." She created a new user, logged in, then navigated back to the Preferences page. The default credit card area on the page showed the heading and no credit cards.

---

[*] See "Exploratory Testing" later in this chapter.

"Hmmm," Mary said, then pointed at the screen. "I hadn't thought about this before, but I'd like to have an *Add New Card* button here. Users will be able to add credit cards both here and on the Payment Method page when they go to check out. I wonder if Pradeep and Jan have time to get that in this iteration?" She made a note to talk to the programmers about the new button.

"In the meantime, we can add a new credit card from the payment screen," Jill said. "I wonder what happens when you add the first card..."

Questions

Our customers don't know what the team should build. What should we do?

Do you have a clear, compelling vision? If so, your customers should know where to start. If you don't, you may not have the right customers on your team. In this case, you can use traditional requirements gathering techniques (see "Further Reading" at the end of this section) to determine the software's requirements, but you're better off involving real experts (see "The XP Team" in Chapter 3 and "Real Customer Involvement" in Chapter 6).

Ally

Vision (p. 201)

What if the customer review finds too many problems for us to deal with?

This is most likely to happen at the beginning of the project, before programmers have learned what the customers like. If this happens to you, spend more time with programmers so that your perspective is captured sooner and more accurately. In some cases, customers should pair with programmers as they work on error-prone areas.

As a programmer, I'm offended by some of the things customers find in their reviews. They're too nitpicky.

Things that can seem nitpicky to programmers—such as the color of the screen background, or a few pixels of alignment in the UI—represent polish and professionalism to customers. This goes both ways: some things that seem important to programmers, such as quality code and refactoring, often seem like unnecessary perfectionism to customers.

Rather than getting upset about these differences of perspective, try to learn what your customers care about and why. As you learn, you will anticipate your customers' needs better, which will reduce the need to make changes.

Results

When customers work out requirements incrementally, programmers are able to work on established stories while customers figure out the details for future stories. Customers have ready answers to requirements questions, which allows estimation and iteration planning to proceed quickly and smoothly. By the time a story is "done done," it reflects the customers' expectations, and customers experience no unpleasant surprises.

Contraindications

In order to incrementally define requirements, the team must include on-site customers who are dedicated to working out requirements details throughout the entire project. Without this dedicated resource, your team will struggle with insufficient and unclear requirements.

Ally
Sit Together (p. 112)

When performing customer reviews, think of them as tools for conveying the customers' perspective rather than as bug-hunting sessions. The programmers should be able to produce code that's nearly bug-free (see "No Bugs" in Chapter 7); the purpose of the review is to bring customers' expectations and programmers' work into alignment.

Ally
No Bugs (p. 160)

Alternatives

The traditional approach to requirements definition is to perform requirements analysis sessions and document the results. This requires an up-front requirements gathering phase, which takes extra time and introduces communication errors.

You can use an up-front analysis phase with XP, but good on-site customers should make that unecessary.

Further Reading

Software Requirements [Wiegers 1999] is a good resource for classic approaches to requirements gathering.

Customer Tests

We implement tricky domain concepts correctly.

Audience
Whole Team

Customers have specialized expertise, or *domain knowledge*, that programmers don't have. Some areas of the application—what programmers call *domain rules*—require this expertise. You need to make sure that the programmers understand the domain rules well enough to code them properly in the application. *Customer tests* help customers communicate their expertise.

Ally
Ubiquitous Language (p. 124)

Don't worry; this isn't as complicated as it sounds. Customer tests are really just examples. Your programmers turn them into automated tests, which they then use to check that they've implemented the domain rules correctly. Once the tests are passing, the programmers will include them in their 10-minute build, which will inform the programmers if they ever do anything to break the tests.

Ally
Ten-Minute Build (p. 177)

To create customer tests, follow the *Describe, Demonstrate, Develop* processes outlined in the next section. Use this process during the iteration in which you develop the corresponding stories.

Describe

At the beginning of the iteration, look at your stories and decide whether there are any aspects that programmers might misunderstand. You don't need to provide examples for everything. Customer tests are for *communication*, not for proving that the software works. (See "No Bugs" in Chapter 7.)

> Customer tests are for communication.

For example, if one of your stories is "Allow invoice deleting," you don't need to explain how invoices are deleted. Programmers understand what it means to delete something. However, you might need examples that show *when* it's OK to delete an invoice, especially if there are complicated rules to ensure that invoices aren't deleted inappropriately.

> **NOTE**
> If you're not sure what the programmers might misunderstand, ask. Be careful, though; when business experts and programmers first sit down to create customer tests, both groups are often surprised by the extent of existing misunderstandings.

Once you've identified potential misunderstandings, gather the team at a whiteboard and summarize the story in question. Briefly describe how the story should work and the rules you're going to provide examples for. It's OK to take questions, but don't get stuck on this step.

For example, a discussion of invoice deletion might go like this:

Customer: One of the stories in this iteration is to add support for deleting invoices. In addition to the screen mock-ups we've given you, we thought some customer tests would be appropriate. Deleting invoices isn't as simple as it appears because we have to maintain an audit trail.

There are a bunch of rules around this issue. I'll get into the details in a moment, but the basic rule is that it's OK to delete invoices that haven't been sent to customers—because presumably that kind of invoice was a mistake. Once an invoice *has* been sent to a customer, it can only be deleted by a manager. Even then, we have to save a copy for auditing purposes.

Programmer: When an invoice *hasn't* been sent and gets deleted, is it audited?

Customer: No—in that case, it's just deleted. I'll provide some examples in a moment.

Demonstrate

After a brief discussion of the rules, provide concrete examples that illustrate the scenario. Tables are often the most natural way to describe this information, but you don't need to worry about formatting. Just get the examples on the whiteboard. The scenario might continue like this:

Customer (cont.): As an example, this invoice hasn't been sent to customers, so an Account Rep can delete it.

Sent	User	OK to delete
N	Account Rep	Y

In fact, anybody can delete it—CSRs, managers, and admins.

Sent	User	OK to delete
N	CSR	Y
N	Manager	Y
N	Admin	Y

But once it's sent, only managers and admins can delete it, and even then it's audited.

Sent	User	OK to delete
Y	Account Rep	N
Y	CSR	N
Y	Manager	Audited
Y	Admin	Audited

Also, it's not a simple case of whether something has been sent or not. "Sent" actually means one of several conditions. If you've done anything that *could* have resulted in a customer seeing the invoice, we consider it "Sent." Now only a manager or admin can delete it.

Sent	User	OK to delete
Printed	Account Rep	N
Exported	Account Rep	N
Posted to Web	Account Rep	N

Sent	User	OK to delete
Emailed	Account Rep	N

> **NOTE**
>
> As you provide examples, be completely specific. It's tempting to create generic examples, such as "This invoice hasn't been sent to customers, so anybody can delete it," but those get confusing quickly and programmers can't automate them. Provide specifics. "This invoice hasn't been sent to customers, so *an account rep* can delete it." This will require you to create more examples—that's a good thing.

Your discussion probably won't be as smooth and clean as in this example. As you discuss business rules, you'll jump back and forth between describing the rules and demonstrating them with examples. You'll probably discover special cases you hadn't considered. In some cases, you might even discover whole new categories of rules you need customer tests for.

One particularly effective way to work is to *elaborate on a theme*. Start by discussing the most basic case and providing a few examples. Next, describe a special case or additional detail and provide a few more examples. Continue in this way, working from simplest to most complicated, until you have described all aspects of the rule.

You don't need to show all possible examples. Remember, the purpose here is to communicate, not to exhaustively test the application. You only need enough examples to show the differences in the rules. A handful of examples per case is usually enough, and sometimes just one or two is sufficient.

Develop

When you've covered enough ground, document your discussion so the programmers can start working on implementing your rules. This is also a good time to evaluate whether the examples are in a format that works well for automated testing. If not, discuss alternatives with the programmers. The conversation might go like this:

> *Programmer:* OK, I think we understand what's going on here. We'd like to change your third set of examples, though—the ones where you say "Y" for "Sent." Our invoices don't have a "Sent" property. We'll calculate that from the other properties you mentioned. Is it OK if we use "Emailed" instead?
>
> *Customer:* Yeah, that's fine. Anything that sends it works for that example.

Don't formalize your examples too soon. While you're brainstorming, it's often easiest to work on the whiteboard. Wait until you've worked out all the examples around a particular business rule (or part of a business rule) before formalizing it. This will help you focus on the business rule rather than formatting details.

In some cases, you may discover that you have more examples and rules to discuss than you realized. The act of creating specific examples often reveals scenarios you hadn't considered. Testers are particularly good at finding these. If you have a lot of issues to discuss, consider letting some or all of the programmers get started on the examples you have while you figure out the rest of the details.

Programmers, once you have some examples, you can start implementing the code using normal test-driven development. Don't use the customer tests as a substitute for writing your own tests. Although it's possible to drive your development with customer tests—in fact, this can feel quite natural and productive—the tests don't provide the fine-grained support that TDD does. Over time, you'll discover holes in your implementation and regression suite. Instead, pick a business rule, implement it with TDD, then confirm that the associated customer tests pass.

> Don't use customer tests as a substitute for test-driven development.

Ally

Test-Driven Development (p. 285)

Focus on Business Rules

One of the most common mistakes in creating customer tests is describing what happens in the user interface rather than providing examples of business rules. For example, to show that an account rep must not delete a mailed invoice, you might make the mistake of writing this:

1. Log in as an account rep
2. Create new invoice
3. Enter data
4. Save invoice
5. Email invoice to customer
6. Check if invoice can be deleted (should be "no")

What happened to the core idea? It's too hard to see. Compare that to the previous approach:

Sent	User	OK to delete
Emailed	Account Rep	N

Good examples focus on the *essence* of your rules. Rather than imagining how those rules might work in the application, just think about what the rules are. If you weren't creating an application at all, how would you describe those rules to a colleague? Talk about *things* rather than *actions*. Sometimes it helps to think in terms of a template: "When (*scenario X*), then (*scenario Y*)."

It takes a bit of practice to think this way, but the results are worth it. The tests become more compact, easier to maintain, and (when implemented correctly) faster to run.

Ask Customers to Lead

Team members, watch out for a common pitfall in customer testing: no customers! Some teams have programmers and testers do all the work of customer testing, and some teams don't involve their customers at all. In others, a customer is present only as a mute observer. Don't forget the "customer" in "customer tests." The purpose of these activities to bring the customer's knowledge and perspective to the team's work. If programmers or testers take the reins, you've lost that benefit and missed the point.

> Remember the "customer" in "customer tests."

In some cases, customers may not be willing to take the lead. Programmers and testers may be able to solve this problem by asking the customers for their help. When programmers need domain expertise, they can ask customers to join the team as they discuss examples. One particularly effective technique is to ask for an explanation of a business rule, pretend to be confused, then hand a customer the whiteboard marker and ask him to draw an example on the board.

NOTE

If customers won't participate in customer testing at all, this may indicate a problem with your relationship with the customers. Ask your mentor (see "Find a Mentor" in Chapter 2) to help you troubleshoot the situation.

TESTERS' ROLE

Testers play an important support role in customer testing. Although the customers should lead the effort, they benefit from testers' technical expertise and ability to imagine diverse scenarios. While customers should generate the initial examples, testers should suggest scenarios that customers don't think of.

On the other hand, testers should be careful not to try to cover every possible scenario. The goal of the exercise is to help the team understand the customers' perspective, not to exhaustively test the application.

Automating the Examples

Programmers may use any tool they like to turn the customers' examples into automated tests. Ward Cunningham's *Fit* (*Framework for Integrated Test*),[*] is specifically designed for this purpose. It allows you to use HTML to mix descriptions and tables, just as in my invoice auditing example, then runs the tables through programmer-created *fixtures* to execute the tests.

NOTE

See *http://fit.c2.com/* or [Mugridge & Cunningham] for details about using Fit. It's available in several languages, including Java, .NET, Python, Perl, and C++.

You may be interested in *FitNesse* at *http://fitnesse.org/*, a variant of Fit. FitNesse is a complete IDE for Fit that uses a Wiki for editing and running tests. (Fit is a command-line tool and works with anything that produces tables in HTML.)

Fit is a great tool for customer tests because it allows customers to review, run, and even expand on their own tests. Although programmers have to write the fixtures, customers can easily add to or modify existing tables to check an idea. Testers can also modify the tests as an aid to exploratory testing. Because the tests are written in HTML, they can use any HTML editor to modify the tests, including Microsoft Word.

Ally

Exploratory Testing (p. 341)

Programmers, don't make Fit too complicated. It's a deceptively simple tool. Your fixtures should work like unit tests, focusing on just a few domain objects. For example, the invoice auditing example would use a custom `ColumnFixture`. Each column in the table corresponds to a variable or method in the fixture. The code is almost trivial (see Example 9-1).

[*] Available free at *http://fit.c2.com/*.

Example 9-1. Example fixture (C#)

```csharp
public class InvoiceAuditingFixture : ColumnFixture
{
    public InvoiceStatus Sent;
    public UserRole User;

    public Permission OkayToDelete() {
        InvoiceAuditer auditer = new InvoiceAuditer(User, InvoiceStatus)
        return auditer.DeletePermission;
    }
}
```

Using Fit in this way requires a ubiquitous language and good design. A dedicated domain layer with *Whole Value* objects[*] works best. Without it, you may have to write end-to-end tests, with all the challenges that entails. If you have trouble using Fit, talk to your mentor about whether your design needs work.

> **Ally**
> Ubiquitous Language (p. 124)

NOTE

I often see programmers try to make a complete library of generic fixtures so that no one need write another fixture. That misses the point of Fit, which is to segregate customer-written examples from programmer implementation. If you make generic fixtures, the implementation details will have to go into the tests, which will make them too complicated and obscure the underlying examples.

Questions

> Most tests can be expressed with a simple `ColumnFixture` or `RowFixture`.

When do programmers run the customer tests?

Once the tests are passing, make them a standard part of your 10-minute build. Like programmers' tests, you should fix them immediately if they ever break.

> **Ally**
> Ten-Minute Build (p. 177)

Should we expand the customer tests when we think of a new scenario?

Absolutely! Often, the tests will continue to pass. That's good news; leave the new scenario in place to act as documentation for future readers. If the new test doesn't pass, talk with the programmers about whether they can fix it with iteration slack or whether you need a new story.

> **Ally**
> Slack (p. 246)

What about acceptance testing (also called functional testing)?

Automated acceptance tests tend to be brittle and slow. I've replaced acceptance tests with customer reviews (see "Customer review" later in this chapter) and a variety of other techniques (see "A Little Lie" in Chapter 3).

> **Ally**
> No Bugs (p. 160)

---

[*] See *Domain-Driven Design* [Evans] for a discussion of domain layers, and see *http://c2.com/ppr/checks.html#1* [Cunningham] for information about *Whole Value*.

Results

When you use customer tests well, you reduce the number of mistakes in your domain logic. You discuss domain rules in concrete, unambiguous terms and often discover special cases you hadn't considered. The examples influence the design of the code and help promote a ubiquitous language. When written well, the customer tests run quickly and require no more maintenance than unit tests do.

> **Ally**
> Ubiquitous Language (p. 124)

Contraindications

Don't use customer tests as a substitute for test-driven development. Customer tests are a tool to help communicate challenging business rules, not a comprehensive automated testing tool. In particular, Fit doesn't work well as a test scripting tool—it doesn't have variables, loops, or subroutines. (Some people have attempted to add these things to Fit, but it's not pretty.) Real programming tools, such as xUnit or Watir, are better for test scripting.

> **Ally**
> Test-Driven Development (p. 285)

In addition, customer tests require domain experts. The real value of the process is the conversation that explores and exposes the customers' business requirements and domain knowledge. If your customers are unavailable, those conversations won't happen.

> **Allies**
> The Whole Team (p. 28)
> Sit Together (p. 112)

Finally, because Fit tests are written in HTML, Fit carries more of a maintenance burden than xUnit frameworks do. Automated refactorings won't extend to your Fit tests. To keep your maintenance costs down, avoid creating customer tests for every business rule. Focus on the tests that will help improve programmer understanding, and avoid further maintenance costs by refactoring your customer tests regularly. Similar stories will have similar tests: consolidate your tests whenever you have the opportunity.

Alternatives

Some teams have testers, not customers, write customer tests. Although this introduces another barrier between the customers' knowledge and the programmers' code, I have seen it succeed. It may be your best choice when customers aren't readily available.

Customer tests don't have to use Fit or FitNesse. Theoretically, you can write them in any testing tool, including xUnit, although I haven't seen anybody do this.

Further Reading

Fit for Developing Software [Mugridge & Cunningham] is the definitive reference for Fit.

"Agile Requirements" [Shore 2005a], online at *http://www.jamesshore.com/Blog/Agile-Requirements.html*, is a series of essays about agile requirements, customer testing, and Fit.

Test-Driven Development

Audience
Programmers

We produce well-designed, well-tested, and well-factored code in small, verifiable steps.

"What programming languages really need is a 'DWIM' instruction," the joke goes. "Do what I mean, not what I say."

Programming is demanding. It requires perfection, consistently, for months and years of effort. At best, mistakes lead to code that won't compile. At worst, they lead to bugs that lie in wait and pounce at the moment that does the most damage.

People aren't so good at perfection. No wonder, then, that software is buggy.

Wouldn't it be cool if there were a tool that alerted you to programming mistakes moments after you made them—a tool so powerful that it virtually eliminated the need for debugging?

There is such a tool, or rather, a technique. It's test-driven development, and it actually delivers these results.

Test-driven development, or TDD, is a rapid cycle of testing, coding, and refactoring. When adding a feature, a pair may perform dozens of these cycles, implementing and refining the software in baby steps until there is nothing left to add and nothing left to take away. Research shows that TDD substantially reduces the incidence of defects [Janzen & Saiedian]. When used properly, it also helps improve your design, documents your public interfaces, and guards against future mistakes.

TDD isn't perfect, of course. (Is anything?) TDD is difficult to use on legacy codebases. Even with greenfield systems, it takes a few months of steady use to overcome the learning curve. Try it anyway—although TDD benefits from other XP practices, it doesn't require them. You can use it on almost any project.

Why TDD Works

Back in the days of punch cards, programmers laboriously hand-checked their code to make sure it would compile. A compile error could lead to failed batch jobs and intense debugging sessions to look for the misplaced character.

Getting code to compile isn't such a big deal anymore. Most IDEs check your syntax as you type, and some even compile every time you save. The feedback loop is so fast that errors are easy to find and fix. If something doesn't compile, there isn't much code to check.

Test-driven development applies the same principle to programmer intent. Just as modern compilers provide more feedback on the syntax of your code, TDD cranks up the feedback on the execution of your code. Every few minutes—as often as every 20 or 30 *seconds*—TDD verifies that the code does what you think it should do. If something goes wrong, there are only a few lines of code to check. Mistakes are easy to find and fix.

TDD uses an approach similar to double-entry bookkeeping. You communicate your intentions twice, stating the same idea in different ways: first with a test, then with production code. When they match, it's likely they were both coded correctly. If they don't, there's a mistake somewhere.

In TDD, the tests are written from the perspective of a class' public interface. They focus on the class' *behavior*, not its *implementation*. Programmers write each test before the corresponding production code. This focuses their attention on creating interfaces that are easy to use rather than easy to implement, which improves the design of the interface.

After TDD is finished, the tests remain. They're checked in with the rest of the code, and they act as living documentation of the code. More importantly, programmers run all the tests with (nearly) every build, ensuring that code continues to work as originally intended. If someone accidentally changes the code's behavior—for example, with a misguided refactoring—the tests fail, signalling the mistake.

How to Use TDD

You can start using TDD today. It's one of those things that takes moments to learn and a lifetime to master.

Imagine TDD as a small, fast-spinning motor. It operates in a very short cycle that repeats over and over again. Every few minutes, this cycle ratchets your code forward a notch, providing code that—although it may not be finished—has been tested, designed, coded, and is ready to check in.

> Every few minutes, TDD provides proven code that has been tested, designed, and coded.

To use TDD, follow the "red, green, refactor" cycle illustrated in Figure 9-1. With experience, unless you're doing a lot of refactoring, each cycle will take fewer than five minutes. Repeat the cycle until your work is finished. You can stop and integrate whenever all your tests pass, which should be every few minutes.

Step 1: Think

TDD uses small tests to force you to write your code—you only write enough code to make the tests pass. The XP saying is, "Don't write any production code unless you have a failing test."

Your first step, therefore, is to engage in a rather odd thought process. Imagine what behavior you want your code to have, then think of a small increment that will require fewer than five lines of code. Next, think of a test—also a few lines of code—that will fail unless that behavior is present.

In other words, think of a test that will force you to add the next few lines of production code. This is the hardest part of TDD because the concept of tests driving your code seems backward, and because it can be difficult to think in small increments.

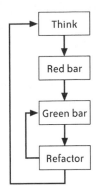

Figure 9-1. The TDD cycle

Pair programming helps. While the driver tries to make the current test pass, the navigator should stay a few steps ahead, thinking of tests that will drive the code to the next increment.

Ally

Pair Programming (p. 71)

Step 2: Red bar

Now write the test. Write only enough code for the current increment of behavior—typically fewer than five lines of code. If it takes more, that's OK, just try for a smaller increment next time.

Code in terms of the class' behavior and its public interface, not how you think you will implement the internals of the class. Respect encapsulation. In the first few tests, this often means you write your test to use method and class names that don't exist yet. This is intentional—it forces you to design your class' interface from the perspective of a user of the class, not as its implementer.

After the test is coded, run your entire suite of tests and watch the new test fail. In most TDD testing tools, this will result in a red progress bar.

This is your first opportunity to compare your intent with what's actually happening. If the test *doesn't* fail, or if it fails in a different way than you expected, something is wrong. Perhaps your test is broken, or it doesn't test what you thought it did. Troubleshoot the problem; you should always be able to predict what's happening with the code.

> **NOTE**
> It's just as important to troubleshoot unexpected *successes* as it is to troubleshoot unexpected *failures*. Your goal isn't merely to have tests that work; it's to remain in control of your code—to always know what the code is doing and why.

Step 3: Green bar

Next, write just enough production code to get the test to pass. Again, you should usually need less than five lines of code. Don't worry about design purity or conceptual elegance—just do what you need to do to make the test pass. Sometimes you can just hardcode the answer. This is OK because you'll be refactoring in a moment.

Run your tests again, and watch all the tests pass. This will result in a green progress bar.

This is your second opportunity to compare your intent with reality. If the test fails, get back to known-good code as quickly as you can. Often, you or your pairing partner can see the problem by taking a second look at the code you just

> When your tests fail and you can't figure out why, revert to known-good code.

wrote. If you can't see the problem, consider erasing the new code and trying again. Sometimes it's best to delete the new test (it's only a few lines of code, after all) and start the cycle over with a smaller increment.

NOTE

Remaining in control is key. It's OK to back up a few steps if that puts you back in control of your code. If you can't bring yourself to revert right away, set a 5- or 10-minute timer. Make a deal with your pairing partner that you'll revert to known-good code if you haven't solved the problem when the timer goes off.

Step 4: Refactor

With all your tests passing again, you can now refactor without worrying about breaking anything. Review the code and look for possible improvements. Ask your navigator if he's made any notes.

<table>
<tr><td>Ally</td></tr>
<tr><td>Refactoring (p. 303)</td></tr>
</table>

For each problem you see, refactor the code to fix it. Work in a series of very small refactorings—a minute or two each, certainly not longer than five minutes—and run the tests after each one. They should always pass. As before, if the test doesn't pass and the answer isn't immediately obvious, undo the refactoring and get back to known-good code.

Refactor as many times as you like. Make your design as good as you can, but limit it to the code's existing behavior. Don't anticipate future needs, and certainly don't add new behavior. Remember, refactorings aren't supposed to change behavior. New behavior requires a failing test.

Step 5: Repeat

When you're ready to add new behavior, start the cycle over again.

Each time you finish the TDD cycle, you add a tiny bit of well-tested, well-designed code. The key to success with TDD is *small increments*. Typically, you'll run through several cycles very quickly, then spend more time on refactoring for a cycle or two, then speed up again.

> The key to TDD is small increments.

With practice, you can finish more than 20 cycles in an hour. Don't focus too much on how fast you go, though. That might tempt you to skip refactoring and design, which are too important to skip. Instead, take very small steps, run the tests frequently, and minimize the time you spend with a red bar.

A TDD Example

I recently recorded how I used TDD to solve a sample problem. The increments are very small—they may even seem ridiculously small—but this makes finding mistakes easy, and that helps me go faster.

As you read, keep in mind that it takes far longer to explain an example like this than to program it. I completed each step in a matter of seconds.

The task

Imagine you need to program a Java class to parse an HTTP query string.[*] You've decided to use TDD to do so.

One name/value pair

Step 1: Think. The first step is to imagine the features you want the code to have. My first thought was, "I need my class to separate name/value pairs into a HashMap." Unfortunately, this would take more than five lines to code, so I needed to think of a smaller increment.

Often, the best way to make the increments smaller is to start with seemingly trivial cases. "I need my class to put *one* name/value pair into a HashMap," I thought, which sounded like it would do the trick.

Step 2: Red Bar. The next step is to write the test. Remember, this is partially an exercise in interface design. In this example, my first temptation was to call the class QueryStringParser, but that's not very object-oriented. I settled on QueryString.

As I wrote the test, I realized that a class named QueryString wouldn't return a HashMap; it would *encapsulate* the HashMap. It would provide a method such as valueFor(name) to access the name/value pairs.

Building that seemed like it would require too much code for one increment, so I decided to have this test to drive the creation of a count() method instead. I decided that the count() method would return the total number of name/value pairs. My test checked that it would work when there was just one pair.

```java
public void testOneNameValuePair() {
    QueryString qs = new QueryString("name=value");
    assertEquals(1, qs.count());
}
```

The code didn't compile, so I wrote a do-nothing QueryString class and count() method.

```java
public class QueryString {
    public QueryString(String queryString) {}
    public int count() { return 0; }
}
```

That gave me the red bar I expected.

---

[*] Pretend you're in an alternate reality without a gazillion libraries that already do this.

Step 3: Green Bar. To make this test pass, I hardcoded the right answer. I could have programmed a better solution, but I wasn't sure how I wanted the code to work. Would it count the number of equals signs? Not all query strings have equals signs. I decided to punt.

```
public int count() { return 1; }
```

Green bar.

NOTE

Note that although I had ideas about how I would finish writing this class, I didn't commit myself to any particular course of action in advance. I remained open to discovering new approaches as I worked.

Step 4: Refactor. I didn't like the QueryString name, but I had another test in mind and I was eager to get to it. I made a note to fix the name on an index card—perhaps HttpQuery would be better. I'd see how I felt next time through the cycle.

Rename QueryString

Step 5: Repeat. Yup.

An empty string

Think. I wanted to force myself to get rid of that hardcoded return 1, but I didn't want to have to deal with multiple query strings yet. My next increment would probably be about the valueFor() method, and I wanted to avoid the complexity of multiple queries. I decided that testing an empty string would require me to code count() properly without making future increments too difficult.

Red Bar. New test.

```
public void testNoNameValuePairs() {
    QueryString qs = new QueryString("");
    assertEquals(0, qs.count());
}
```

Red bar. Expected: <0> but was: <1>. No surprise there.

This inspired two thoughts. First, that I should test the case of a null argument to the QueryString constructor. Second, because I was starting to see duplication in my tests, I should refactor that. I added both notes to my index card.

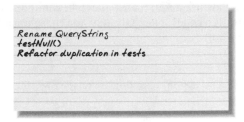

```
Rename QueryString
testNull()
Refactor duplication in tests
```

Green bar. Now I had to stop and think. What was the fastest way for me to get back to a green bar? I decided to check if the query string was blank.

```
public class QueryString {
    private String _query

    public QueryString(string queryString) {
        _query = queryString;
    }

    public int count() {
        if ("".equals(_query)) return 0;
        else return 1;
    }
}
```

Refactor. I double-checked my to-do list . I needed to refactor the tests, but I decided to wait for another test to demonstrate the need. "Three strikes and you refactor," as the saying goes.

It was time to do the cycle again.

testNull()

Think. My list included testNull(), which meant I needed to test the case when the query string is null. I decided to put that in.

Red Bar. This test forced me to think about what behavior I wanted when the value was null. I've always been a fan of code that fails fast, so I decided that a null value was illegal. This meant the code should throw an exception telling callers not to use null values. ("Simple Design," later in this chapter, discusses failing fast in detail.)

```
public void testNull() {
    try {
        QueryString qs = new QueryString(null);
        fail("Should throw exception");
    }
    catch (NullPointerException e) {
        // expected
    }
}
```

Green Bar. Piece of cake.

```
public QueryString(String queryString) {
    if (queryString == null) throw new NullPointerException();

    _query = queryString;
}
```

Refactor. I still needed to refactor my tests, but the new test didn't have enough in common with the old tests to make me feel it was necessary. The production code looked OK, too, and there wasn't anything significant on my index card. No refactorings this time.

NOTE

Although I don't refactor on every cycle, I always stop and seriously consider whether my design needs refactoring.

---

valueFor()

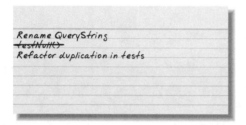

Think. OK, now what? The easy tests were done. I decided to put some meat on the class and implement the valueFor() method. Given a name of a name/value pair in the query string, this method would return the associated value.

As I thought about this test, I realized I also needed a test to show what happens when the name doesn't exist. I wrote that on my index card for later.

Red Bar. To make the tests fail, I added a new assertion at the end of my existing testOneNameValuePair() test.

```
public void testOneNameValuePair() {
    QueryString qs = new QueryString("name=value");
    assertEquals(1, qs.count());
    assertEquals("value", qs.valueFor("name"));
}
```

Green Bar. This test made me think for a moment. Could the split() method work? I thought it would.

```
public String valueFor(String name) {
    String[] nameAndValue = _query.split("=");
    return nameAndValue[1];
}
```

This code passed the tests, but it was incomplete. What if there was more than one equals sign, or no equals signs? It needed proper error handling. I made a note to add tests for those scenarios.

Refactor. The names were bugging me. I decided that QueryString was OK, if not perfect. The qs in the tests was sloppy, so I renamed it query.

Multiple name/value pairs

Think. I had a note reminding me to take care of error handling in valueFor(), but I wanted to tackle something more meaty. I decided to add a test for multiple name/value pairs.

Red Bar. When dealing with a variable number of items, I usually test the case of zero items, one item, and three items. I had already tested zero and one, so now I tested three.

```
public void testMultipleNameValuePairs() {
    QueryString query = new QueryString("name1=value1&name2=value2&name3=value3");
    assertEquals("value1", query.valueFor("name1"));
    assertEquals("value2", query.valueFor("name2"));
    assertEquals("value3", query.valueFor("name3"));
}
```

I could have written an assertion for count() rather than valueFor(), but the real substance was in the valueFor() method. I made a note to test count() next.

Green Bar. My initial thought was that the split() technique would work again.

```
public String valueFor(String name) {
    String[] pairs = _query.split("&");
    for (String pair : pairs) {
        String[] nameAndValue = pair.split("=");
        if (nameAndValue[0].equals(name)) return nameAndValue[1];
    }
    throw new RuntimeException(name + " not found");
}
```

Ewww... that felt like a hack. But the test passed!

NOTE

It's better to get to a green bar quickly than to try for perfect code. A green bar keeps you in control of your code and allows you to experiment with refactorings that clean up your hack.

Refactor: The additions to valueFor() felt hackish. I took a second look. The two issues that bothered me the most were the nameAndValue array and the RuntimeException. An attempt to refactor nameAndValue led to worse code, so I backed out the refactoring and decided to leave it alone for another cycle.

The RuntimeException was worse; it's better to throw a custom exception. In this case, though, the Java convention is to return null rather than throw an exception. I already had a note that I should test the case where name isn't found; I revised it to say that the correct behavior was to return null.

Reviewing further, I saw that my duplicated test logic had reached three duplications. Time to refactor— or so I thought. After a second look, I realized that the only duplication between the tests was that I was constructing a QueryString object each time. Everything else was different, including QueryString's constructor parameters. The tests didn't need refactoring after all. I scratched that note off my list.

In fact, the code was looking pretty good... better than I initially thought, at least. I'm too hard on myself.

Multiple count()

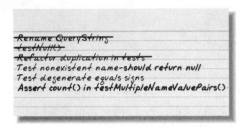

Think. After reviewing my notes, I realized I should probably test degenerate uses of the ampersand, such as two ampersands in a row. I made a note to add tests for that. At the time, though, I wanted to get the count() method working properly with multiple name/value pairs.

Red Bar. I added the count() assertion to my test. It failed as expected.

```
public void testMultipleNameValuePairs() {
    QueryString query = new QueryString("name1=value1&name2=value2&name3=value3");
    assertEquals(3, query.count());
    assertEquals("value1", query.valueFor("name1"));
    assertEquals("value2", query.valueFor("name2"));
    assertEquals("value3", query.valueFor("name3"));
}
```

Green Bar. To get this test to pass, I stole my existing code from valueFor() and modified it. This was blatant duplication, but I planned to refactor as soon as I saw the green bar.

```
public int count() {
    String[] pairs = _query.split("&");
    return pairs.length;
}
```

I was able to delete more of the copied code than I expected. To my surprise, however, it didn't pass! The test failed in the case of an empty query string: expected: <0> but was: <1>. I had forgotten that split() returned the original string when the split character isn't found. My code expected it to return an empty array when no split occurred.

I added a guard clause that took care of the problem. It felt like a hack, so I planned to take a closer look after the tests passed.

```
public int count() {
    if ("".equals(_query)) return 0;
    String[] pairs = _query.split("&");
    return pairs.length;
}
```

Refactor. This time I definitely needed to refactor. The duplication between count() and valueFor() wasn't too strong—it was just one line—but they both parsed the query string, which was a duplication of function if not code. I decided to fix it.

At first, I wasn't sure how to fix the problem. I decided to try to parse the query string into a HashMap, as I had originally considered. To keep the refactoring small, I left count() alone at first and just modified valueFor(). It was a small change.

```
public String valueFor(String name) {
    HashMap<String, String> map = new HashMap<String, String>();

    String[] pairs = _query.split("&");
    for (String pair : pairs) {
        String[] nameAndValue = pair.split("=");
        map.put(nameAndValue[0], nameAndValue[1]);
    }
    return map.get(name);
}
```

NOTE

This refactoring eliminated the exception that I threw when name wasn't found. Technically, it changed the behavior of the program. However, because I hadn't yet written a test for that behavior, I didn't care. I made sure I had a note to test that case later (I did) and kept going.

This code parsed the query string during every call to valueFor(), which wasn't a great idea. I had kept the code in valueFor() to keep the refactoring simple. Now I wanted to move it out of valueFor() into the constructor. This required a sequence of refactorings, as described in "Refactoring," later in this chapter.

I reran the tests after each of these refactorings to make sure that I hadn't broken anything... and in fact, one refactoring did break the tests. When I called the parser from the constructor, testNoNameValuePairs()—the empty query test—bit me again, causing an exception in the parser. I added a guard clause as before, which solved the problem.

After all that refactoring, the tests and production code were nice and clean.

```
public class QueryStringTest extends TestCase {
    public void testOneNameValuePair() {
        QueryString query = new QueryString("name=value");
        assertEquals(1, query.count());
        assertEquals("value", query.valueFor("name"));
    }

    public void testMultipleNameValuePairs() {
        QueryString query = new QueryString("name1=value1&name2=value2&name3=value3");
        assertEquals(3, query.count());
        assertEquals("value1", query.valueFor("name1"));
        assertEquals("value2", query.valueFor("name2"));
        assertEquals("value3", query.valueFor("name3"));
    }

    public void testNoNameValuePairs() {
        QueryString query = new QueryString("");
        assertEquals(0, query.count());
    }

    public void testNull() {
        try {
            QueryString query = new QueryString(null);
            fail("Should throw exception");
        }
```

```
                catch (NullPointerException e) {
                    // expected
                }
            }
        }
    }

    public class QueryString {
        private HashMap<String, String> _map = new HashMap<String, String>();

        public QueryString(String queryString) {
            if (queryString == null) throw new NullPointerException();
            parseQueryString(queryString);
        }

        public int count() {
            return _map.size();
        }

        public String valueFor(String name) {
            return _map.get(name);
        }

        private void parseQueryString(String query) {
            if ("".equals(query)) return;

            String[] pairs = query.split("&");
            for (String pair : pairs) {
                String[] nameAndValue = pair.split("=");
                _map.put(nameAndValue[0], nameAndValue[1]);
            }
        }
    }
```

Your turn

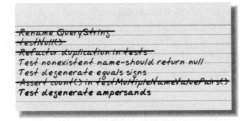

The class wasn't done—it still needed to handle degenerate uses of the equals and ampersand signs, and it didn't fully implement the query string specification yet, either.[*] In the interest of space, though, I leave the remaining behavior as an exercise for you to complete yourself. As you try it, remember to take very small steps and to check for refactorings every time through the cycle.

Testing Tools

To use TDD, you need a testing framework. The most popular are the open source *xUnit* tools, such as *JUnit* (for Java) and *NUnit* (for .NET). Although these tools have different authors, they typically share the basic philosophy of Kent Beck's pioneering SUnit.

---

[*] For example, the semicolon works like the ampersand in query strings.

If your platform doesn't have an xUnit tool, you can build your own. Although the existing tools often provide GUIs and other fancy features, none of that is necessary. All you need is a way to run all your test methods as a single suite, a few assert methods, and an unambiguous pass or fail result when the test suite is done.

Speed Matters

As with programming itself, TDD has myriad nuances to master. The good news is that the basic steps alone—red, green, refactor—will lead to very good results. Over time, you'll fine-tune your approach.

One of the nuances of TDD is test speed—not the frequency of each increment, which is also important, but how long it takes to run all the tests. In TDD, you run the tests as often as one or two times every *minute*. They must be fast. If they aren't, they'll be a distraction rather than a help. You won't run them as frequently, which reduces the primary benefit of TDD: micro-increments of proof.

[Nielsen] reports that users lose interest and switch tasks when the computer makes them wait more than 10 seconds. Computers only seem "fast" when they make users wait less than a second.

Although Nielsen's research explored the area of user interface design, I've found it to be true when running tests as well. If they take more than 10 seconds, I'm tempted to check my email, surf the Web, or otherwise distract myself. Then it takes several minutes for me to get back to work. To avoid this delay, make sure your tests take under 10 seconds to run. Less than a second is even better.

> Make sure your tests take under 10 seconds to run.

An easy way to keep your test times down is to run a subset of tests during the TDD cycle. Periodically run the whole test suite to make sure you haven't accidentally broken something, particularly before integrating and during refactorings that affect multiple classes.

Running a subset does incur the risk that you'll make a mistake without realizing it, which leads to annoying debugging problems later. Advanced practitioners design their tests to run quickly. This requires that they make trade-offs between three basic types of automated tests:

- Unit tests, which run at a rate of hundreds per second
- Focused integration tests, which run at a rate of a handful per second
- End-to-end tests, which often require seconds per test

The vast majority of your tests should be unit tests. A small fraction should be integration tests, and only a few should be end-to-end tests.

Unit Tests

Unit tests focus just on the class or method at hand. They run entirely in memory, which makes them very fast. Depending on your platform, your testing tool should be able to run at least 100 unit tests *per second*.

[Feathers] provides an excellent definition of a unit test:

Unit tests run fast. If they don't run fast, they aren't unit tests.

Other kinds of tests often masquerade as unit tests. A test is not a unit test if:

1. It talks to a database
2. It communicates across a network
3. It touches the file system
4. You have to do special things to your environment (such as editing configuration files) to run it

Tests that do these things are integration tests, not unit tests.

Creating unit tests requires good design. A highly coupled system—a *big ball of mud*, or *spaghetti software*— makes it difficult to write unit tests. If you have trouble doing this, or if Feathers' definition seems impossibly idealistic, it's a sign of problems in your design. Look for ways to decouple your code so that each class, or set of related classes, may be tested in isolation. See "Simple Design" later in this chapter for ideas, and consider asking your mentor for help.

MOCK OBJECTS

Mock objects are a popular tool for isolating classes for unit testing. When using mock objects, your test substitutes its own object (the "mock object") for an object that talks to the outside world. The mock object checks that it is called correctly and provides a pre-scripted response. In doing so, it avoids time-consuming communication to a database, network socket, or other outside entity.

Beware of mock objects. They add complexity and tie your test to the implementation of your code. When you're tempted to use a mock object, ask yourself if there's a way you could improve the design of your code so that a mock object isn't necessary. Can you decouple your code from the external dependency more cleanly? Can you provide the data it needs—in the constructor, perhaps—rather than having it get the data itself?

Mock objects are a useful technique, and sometimes they're the best way to test your code. Before you assume that a mock object is appropriate for your situation, however, take a second look at your design. You might have an opportunity for improvement.

Focused Integration Tests

Unit tests aren't enough. At some point, your code has to talk to the outside world. You can use TDD for that code, too.

A test that causes your code to talk to a database, communicate across the network, touch the file system, or otherwise leave the bounds of its own process is an *integration test*. The best integration tests are *focused integration tests*, which test just one interaction with the outside world.

NOTE

You may think of an integration test as a test that checks that the whole system fits together properly. I call that kind of test an *end-to-end test*.

One of the challenges of using integration tests is the need to prepare the external dependency to be tested. Tests should run exactly the same way every time, regardless of which order you run them in or the state of the machine prior to running them. This is easy with unit tests but harder with integration tests. If you're testing your ability to select data from a database table, that data needs to be in the database.

Make sure each integration test can run entirely on its own. It should set up the environment it needs and then restore the previous environment afterwards. Be sure to do so even if the test fails or an exception is thrown. Nothing is more frustrating than a test suite that intermittently fails.

> Make sure each test is isolated from the others.

Integration tests that don't set up and tear down their test environment properly are common culprits.

NOTE

If you have a test that fails intermittently, don't ignore it, even if you can "fix" the failure by running the tests twice in a row. Intermittent failures are an example of technical debt. They make your tests more frustrating to run and disguise real failures.

You shouldn't need many integration tests. The best integration tests have a narrow focus; each checks just one aspect of your program's ability to talk to the outside world. The number of focused integration tests in your test suite should be proportional to the types of external interactions your program has, not the overall size of the program. (In contrast, the number of unit tests you have *is* proportional to the overall size of the program.)

If you need a lot of integration tests, it's a sign of design problems. It may mean that the code that talks to the outside world isn't cohesive. For example, if all your business objects talk directly to a database, you'll need integration tests for each one. A better design would be to have just one class that talks to the database. The business objects would talk to that class.* In this scenario, only the database class would need integration tests. The business objects could use ordinary unit tests.

End-to-End Tests

In a perfect world, the unit tests and focused integration tests mesh perfectly to give you total confidence in your tests and code. You should be able to make any changes you want without fear, comfortable in the knowledge that if you make a mistake, your tests will catch them.

How can you be sure your unit tests and integration tests mesh perfectly? One way is to write end-to-end tests. End-to-end tests exercise large swaths of the system, starting at (or just behind) the user interface, passing through the business layer, touching the database, and returning. Acceptance tests and functional tests are common examples of end-to-end tests. Some people also call them integration tests, although I reserve that term for focused integration tests.

End-to-end tests can give you more confidence in your code, but they suffer from many problems. They're difficult to create because they require error-prone and labor-intensive setup and teardown procedures. They're brittle and tend to break whenever any part of the system or its setup data changes. They're very slow—they run in seconds or even minutes per test, rather than multiple tests per second. They provide a false sense of security, by exercising so many branches in the code that it's difficult to say which parts of the code are actually covered.

---

* A still better design might involve a persistence layer.

Instead of end-to-end tests, use exploratory testing to check the effectiveness of your unit and integration tests. When your exploratory tests find a problem, use that information to improve your approach to unit and integration testing, rather than introducing end-to-end tests.

Ally

Exploratory Testing (p. 341)

> **NOTE**
>
> Don't use exploratory testing to find bugs; use it to determine if your unit tests and integration tests mesh properly. When you find an issue, improve your TDD strategy.

In some cases, limitations in your design may prevent unit and integration tests from testing your code sufficiently. This often happens when you have legacy code. In that case, end-to-end tests are a necessary evil. Think of them as technical debt: strive to make them unecessary, and replace them with unit and integration tests whenever you have the opportunity.

TDD and Legacy Code

[Feathers] says *legacy code* is "code without tests." I think of it as "code you're afraid to change." This is usually the same thing.

The challenge of legacy code is that, because it was created without tests, it usually isn't designed for testability. In order to introduce tests, you need to change the code. In order to change the code with confidence, you need to introduce tests. It's this kind of chicken-and-egg problem that makes legacy code so difficult to work with.

To make matters worse, legacy code has often accumulated a lot of technical debt. (It's hard to remove technical debt when you're afraid to change existing code.) You may have trouble understanding how everything fits together. Methods and functions may have side effects that aren't apparent.

One way to approach this problem is to introduce end-to-end *smoke tests*. These tests exercise common usage scenarios involving the component you want to change. They aren't sufficient to give you total confidence in your changes, but they at least alert you when you make a big mistake.

With the smoke tests in place, you can start introducing unit tests. The challenge here is finding isolated components to test, as legacy code is often tightly coupled code. Instead, look for ways for your test to strategically interrupt program execution. [Feathers] calls these opportunities *seams*. For example, in an object-oriented language, if a method has a dependency you want to avoid, your test can call a test-specific subclass that overrides and stubs out the offending method.

Finding and exploiting seams often leads to ugly code. It's a case of temporarily making the code worse so you can then make it better. Once you've introduced tests, refactor the code to make it test-friendly, then improve your tests so they aren't so ugly. Then you can proceed with normal TDD.

Adding tests to legacy code is a complex subject that deserves its own book. Fortunately, [Feathers]' *Working Effectively with Legacy Code* is exactly that book.

Questions

What do I need to test when using TDD?

The saying is, "Test everything that can possibly break." To determine if something could possibly break, I think, "Do I have absolute confidence that I'm doing this correctly, and that nobody in the future will inadvertently break this code?"

I've learned through painful experience that I can break nearly anything, so I test nearly everything. The only exception is code without any logic, such as simple accessors and mutators (getters and setters), or a method that only calls another method.

You *don't* need to test third-party code unless you have some reason to distrust it.

How do I test private methods?

As I did in my extended QueryString example, start by testing public methods. As you refactor, some of that code will move into private methods, but the existing tests will still thoroughly test its behavior.

If your code is so complex that you need to test a private method directly, this may be a sign that you should refactor. You may benefit from moving the private methods into their own class and providing a public interface. The "Replace Method with Method Object" refactoring [Fowler 1999, p. 135] may help.

How can I use TDD when developing a user interface?

TDD is particularly difficult with user interfaces because most UI frameworks weren't designed with testability in mind. Many people compromise by writing a very thin, untested translation layer that only forwards UI calls to a presentation layer. They keep all their UI logic in the presentation layer and use TDD on that layer as normal.

There are some tools that allow you to test a UI directly, perhaps by making HTTP calls (for web-based software), or by pressing buttons or simulating window events (for client-based software). These are essentially integration tests, and they suffer similar speed and maintainability challenges as other integration tests. Despite the challenges, these tools can be helpful.

You talked about refactoring your test code. Does anyone really do this?

Yes. I do, and everybody should. Tests are just code. The normal rules of good development apply: avoid duplication, choose good names, factor, and design well.

I've seen otherwise-fine projects go off the rails because of brittle and fragile test suites. By making TDD a central facet of development, you've committed to maintaining your test code just as much as you've committed to maintaining the rest of the code. Take it just as seriously.

Results

When you use TDD properly, you find that you spend little time debugging. Although you continue to make mistakes, you find those mistakes very quickly and have little difficulty fixing them. You have total confidence that the whole codebase is well-tested, which allows you to aggressively refactor at every opportunity, confident in the knowledge that the tests will catch any mistakes.

Contraindications

Although TDD is a very valuable tool, it does have a two- or three-month learning curve. It's easy to apply to toy problems such as the QueryString example, but translating that experience to larger systems takes time. Legacy code, proper unit test isolation, and integration tests are particularly difficult to master. On the other hand, the sooner you start using TDD, the sooner you'll figure it out, so don't let these challenges stop you.

Be careful when applying TDD without permission. Learning TDD could slow you down temporarily. This could backfire and cause your organization to reject TDD without proper consideration. I've found that combining testing time with development time when providing estimates helps alleviate pushback for dedicated developer testing.

Also be cautious about being the only one to use TDD on your team. You may find that your teammates break your tests and don't fix them. It's better to get the whole team to agree to try it together.

Alternatives

TDD is the heart of XP's programming pratices. Without it, all of XP's other technical practices will be much harder to use.

A common misinterpretation of TDD is to design your entire class first, then write all its test methods, then write the code. This approach is frustrating and slow, and it doesn't allow you to learn as you go.

Another misguided approach is to write your tests after you write your production code. This is very difficult to do well—production code must be designed for testability, and it's hard to do so unless you write the tests first. It doesn't help that writing tests after the fact is boring. In practice, the temptation to move on to the next task usually overwhelms the desire for well-tested code.

Although you can use these alternatives to introduce tests to your code, TDD isn't just about testing. It's really about using very small increments to produce high-quality, known-good code. I'm not aware of any alternatives that provide TDD's ability to catch and fix mistakes quickly.

Further Reading

Test-driven development is one of the most heavily explored aspects of Extreme Programming. There are several excellent books on various aspects of TDD. Most are focused on Java and JUnit, but their ideas are applicable to other languages as well.

Test-Driven Development: By Example [Beck 2002] is a good introduction to TDD. If you liked the QueryString example, you'll like the extended examples in this book. The TDD patterns in Part III are particularly good.

Test-Driven Development: A Practical Guide [Astels] provides a larger example that covers a complete project. Reviewers praise its inclusion of UI testing.

JUnit Recipes [Rainsberger] is a comprehensive book discussing a wide variety of testing problems, including a thorough discussion of testing J2EE.

Working Effectively with Legacy Code [Feathers] is a must-have for anybody working with legacy code.

Refactoring

Audience
Programmers

Every day, our code is slightly better than it was the day before.

Entropy always wins. Eventually, chaos turns your beautifully imagined and well-designed code into a big mess of spaghetti.

At least, that's the way it used to be, before refactoring. *Refactoring* is the process of changing the design of your code without changing its behavior—*what* it does stays the same, but *how* it does it changes. Refactorings are also reversible; sometimes one form is better than another for certain cases. Just as you can change the expression $x^2 - 1$ to $(x + 1)(x - 1)$ and back, you can change the design of your code—and once you can do that, you can keep entropy at bay.

Reflective Design

Refactoring enables an approach to design I call *reflective design*. In addition to creating a design and coding it, you can now analyze the design of existing code and improve it. One of the best ways to identify improvements is with *code smells*: condensed nuggets of wisdom that help you identify common problems in design.

A code smell doesn't necessarily mean there's a problem with the design. It's like a funky smell in the kitchen: it could indicate that it's time to take out the garbage, or it could just mean that Uncle Gabriel is cooking with a particularly pungent cheese. Either way, when you smell something funny, take a closer look.

[Fowler 1999], writing with Kent Beck, has an excellent discussion of code smells. It's well worth reading. Here are a summary of the smells I find most often, including some that Fowler and Beck didn't mention.*

Divergent Change and Shotgun Surgery

These two smells help you identify cohesion problems in your code. *Divergent Change* occurs when unrelated changes affect the same class. It's an indication that your class involves too many concepts. Split it, and give each concept its own home.

Shotgun Surgery is just the opposite: it occurs when you have to modify multiple classes to support changes to a single idea. This indicates that the concept is represented in many places throughout your code. Find or create a single home for the idea.

Primitive Obsession and Data Clumps

Some implementations represent high-level design concepts with primitive types. For example, a `decimal` might represent dollars. This is the *Primitive Obsession* code smell. Fix it by encapsulating the concept in a class.

Data Clumps are similar. They occur when several primitives represent a concept as a group. For example, several strings might represent an address. Rather than being encapsulated in a single class, however, the data just clumps together. When you see batches of variables consistently passed around together,

---

* Wannabee Static, Time Dependency, Half-Baked Objects, and Coddling Nulls are new in this book.

you're probably facing a Data Clump. As with Primitive Obsession, encapsulate the concept in a single class.

Data Class and Wannabee Static Class

One of the most common mistakes I see in object-oriented design is when programmers put their data and code in separate classes. This often leads to duplicate data-manipulation code. When you have a class that's little more than instance variables combined with accessors and mutators (getters and setters), you have a *Data Class*. Similarly, when you have a class that contains methods but no meaningful per-object state, you have a *Wannabee Static Class*.

NOTE

One way to detect a Wannabee Static Class is to ask yourself if you could change all of the methods and instance variables into statics (also called class methods and variables) without breaking anything.

Ironically, one of the primary strengths of object-oriented programming is its ability to combine data with the code that operates on that data. Data Classes and Wannabee Statics are twins separated at birth. Reunite them by combining instance variables with the methods that operate on those variables.

Coddling Nulls

Null references pose a particular challenge to programmers: they're occasionally useful, but most they often indicate invalid states or other error conditions. Programmers are usually unsure what to do when they receive a null reference; their methods often check for null references and then return null themselves.

Coddling Nulls like this leads to complex methods and error-prone software. Errors suppressed with null cascade deeper into the application, causing unpredictable failures later in the execution of the software. Sometimes the null makes it into the database, leading to recurring application failures.

Instead of Coddling Nulls, adopt a fail fast strategy (see "Simple Design" later in this chapter). Don't allow null as a parameter to any method, constructor, or property unless it has explicitly defined semantics. Throw exceptions to signify errors rather than returning null. Make sure that any unexpected null reference will cause the code to throw an exception, either as a result of being dereferenced or by hitting an explicit assertion.

Time Dependencies and Half-Baked Objects

Time Dependencies occur when a class' methods must be called in a specific order. *Half-Baked Objects* are a special case of Time Dependency: they must first be constructed, then initialized with a method call, then used.

Time Dependencies often indicate an encapsulation problem. Rather than managing its state itself, the class expects its callers to manage some of its state. This results in bugs and duplicate code in callers. Look for ways to encapsulate the class' state more effectively. In some cases, you may find that your class has too many responsibilities and would benefit from being split into multiple classes.

Analyzing Existing Code

Reflective design requires that you understand the design of existing code. The easiest way to do so is to ask someone else on the team. A conversation around a whiteboard design sketch is a great way to learn.

In some cases, no one on the team will understand the design, or you may wish to dive into the code yourself. When you do, focus on the *responsibilities* and *interactions* of each major component. What is the purpose of this package or namespace? What does this class represent? How does it interact with other packages, namespaces, and classes?

For example, NUnitAsp is a tool for unit testing ASP.NET code-behind logic. One of its classes is HttpClient, which you might infer makes calls to an HTTP (web) server—presumably an ASP.NET web server.

To confirm that assumption, look at the names of the class' methods and instance variables. HttpClient has methods named GetPage, FollowLink, SubmitForm, and HasCookie, along with some USER_AGENT constants and several related methods and properties. In total, it seems pretty clear that HttpClient emulates a web browser.

Now expand that understanding to related elements. Which classes does this class depend on? Which classes depend on this one? What are their responsibilities? As you learn, diagram your growing understanding on a whiteboard.

Creating a *UML sequence diagram*[*] can be helpful for understanding how individual methods interact with the rest of the system. Start with a method you want to understand and look at each line in turn, recursively adding each called method to your sequence diagram. This is fairly time-consuming, so I only recommend it if you're confused about how or why a method works.

NOTE

Round-trip engineering tools will automatically generate UML diagrams by analyzing source code. I prefer to generate my diagrams by hand on a whiteboard. My goal isn't merely to create a diagram—my true goal is to understand the design. Creating the diagram by hand requires me to study the code more deeply, which allows me to learn and understand more.

Although these techniques are useful for understanding the design of unfamiliar code, you shouldn't need them often. You should already have a good understanding of most parts of your software, or be able to talk to someone on the team who does. Unless you're dealing with a lot of legacy code, you should rarely have trouble understanding the design of existing code: your team wrote it, after all. If you find yourself needing these techniques often, something is wrong—ask your mentor for help.

How to Refactor

Reflective design helps you understand what to change; refactoring gives you the ability to make those changes. When you refactor, proceed in a series of small transformations. (Confusingly, each type of transformation is also called a *refactoring*.) Each refactoring is like making a turn on a Rubik's cube. To

---

[*] [Fowler & Scott] is a good resource for learning more about UML.

achieve anything significant, you have to string together several individual refactorings, just as you have to string together several turns to solve the cube.

The fact that refactoring is a sequence of small transformations sometimes gets lost on people new to refactoring. Refactoring isn't rewriting. You don't just change the design of your code; to refactor well, you need to make that change in a series of controlled steps. Each step should only take a few moments, and your tests should pass after each one.

> Refactoring isn't rewriting.

> **Ally**
> Test-Driven Development
> (p. 285)

There are a wide variety of individual refactorings. [Fowler 1999]'s *Refactoring* is the classic work on the subject. It contains an in-depth catalog of refactoring, and is well worth studying—I learned more about good code from reading that book than from any other.

You don't need to memorize all the individual refactorings. Instead, try to learn the mindset behind the refactorings. Work from the book in the beginning. Over time, you'll learn how to refactor intuitively, creating each refactoring as you need it.

NOTE
Some IDEs offer automated refactorings. Although this is helpful for automating some tedious refactorings, learn how to refactor manually, too. There are many more refactoring options available to you than your IDE provides.

Refactoring in Action

Any significant design change requires a sequence of refactorings. Learning how to change your design through a series of small refactorings is a valuable skill. Once you've mastered it, you can make dramatic design changes without breaking anything. You can even do this in pieces, by fixing part of the design one day and the rest of it another day.

To illustrate this point, I'll show each step in the simple refactoring from my TDD example (see the TDD example in "Test-Driven Development" earlier in this chapter). Note how small each step is. Working in small steps enables you to remain in control of the code, prevents confusion, and allows you to work very quickly.

NOTE
Don't let the small scale of this example distract you from the main point: making changes in a series of small, controlled steps. For larger examples, see "Further Reading" at the end of this section.

The purpose of this example was to create an HTTP query string parser. At this point, I had a working, bare-bones parser (see "A TDD Example" earlier in this chapter). Here are the tests:

```
public class QueryStringTest extends TestCase {

    public void testOneNameValuePair() {
        QueryString query = new QueryString("name=value");
        assertEquals(1, query.count());
        assertEquals("value", query.valueFor("name"));
    }
```

```
public void testMultipleNameValuePairs() {
    QueryString query = new QueryString("name1=value1&name2=value2&name3=value3");
    assertEquals(3, query.count());
    assertEquals("value1", query.valueFor("name1"));
    assertEquals("value2", query.valueFor("name2"));
    assertEquals("value3", query.valueFor("name3"));
}

public void testNoNameValuePairs() {
    QueryString query = new QueryString("");
    assertEquals(0, query.count());
}

public void testNull() {
    try {
        QueryString query = new QueryString(null);
        fail("Should throw exception");
    }
    catch (NullPointerException e) {
        // expected
    }
}
}
```

The code worked—it passed all the tests—but it was ugly. Both the count() and valueFor() methods had duplicate parsing code. I wanted to eliminate this duplication and put parsing in just one place.

```
public class QueryString {
    private String _query;

    public QueryString(String queryString) {
        if (queryString == null) throw new NullPointerException();
        _query = queryString;
    }

    public int count() {
        if ("".equals(_query)) return 0;
        String[] pairs = _query.split("&");
        return pairs.length;
    }

    public String valueFor(String name) {
        String[] pairs = _query.split("&");
        for (String pair : pairs) {
            String[] nameAndValue = pair.split("=");
            if (nameAndValue[0].equals(name)) return nameAndValue[1];
        }
        throw new RuntimeException(name + " not found");
    }
}
```

To eliminate the duplication, I needed a single method that could do all the parsing. The other methods would work with the results of the parse rather than doing any parsing of their own. I decided that this parser, called from the constructor, would parse the data into a HashMap.

Although I could have done this in one giant step by moving the body of valueFor() into a parseQueryString() method and then hacking until the tests passed again, I knew from hard-won experience that it was faster to proceed in small steps.

My first step was to introduce HashMap() into valueFor(). This would make valueFor() look just like the parseQueryString() method I needed. Once it did, I could extract out parseQueryString() easily.

```
public String valueFor(String name) {
    HashMap<String, String> map = new HashMap<String, String>();

    String[] pairs = _query.split("&");
    for (String pair : pairs) {
        String[] nameAndValue = pair.split("=");
        map.put(nameAndValue[0], nameAndValue[1]);
    }
    return map.get(name);
}
```

After making this refactoring, I ran the tests. They passed.

NOTE

By removing the `RuntimeException`, I had changed the behavior of the code when the name was not found. That was OK because the `RuntimeException` was just an assertion about an unimplemented feature. I hadn't yet written any tests around it. If I had, I would have changed the code to maintain the existing behavior.

Now I could extract the parsing logic into its own method. I used my IDE's built-in *Extract Method* refactoring to do so.

```
public String valueFor(String name) {
    HashMap<String, String> map = parseQueryString();
    return map.get(name);
}

private HashMap<String, String> parseQueryString() {
    HashMap<String, String> map = new HashMap<String, String>();

    String[] pairs = _query.split("&");
    for (String pair : pairs) {
        String[] nameAndValue = pair.split("=");
        map.put(nameAndValue[0], nameAndValue[1]);
    }
    return map;
}
```

The tests passed again, of course. With such small steps, I'd be surprised if they didn't. That's the point: by taking small steps, I remain in complete control of my changes, which reduces surprises.

I now had a `parseQueryString()` method, but it was only available to `valueFor()`. My next step was to make it available to all methods. To do so, I created a `_map` instance variable and had `parseQueryString()` use it.

```
public class QueryString {
    private String _query;
    private HashMap<String, String> _map = new HashMap<String, String>();

...

    public String valueFor(String name) {
        HashMap<String, String> map = parseQueryString();
        return map.get(name);
    }
```

```
        private HashMap<String, String> parseQueryString() {
            String[] pairs = _query.split("&");
            for (String pair : pairs) {
                String[] nameAndValue = pair.split("=");
                _map.put(nameAndValue[0], nameAndValue[1]);
            }
            return _map;
        }
    }
```

This is a trickier refactoring than it seems. Whenever you switch from a local variable to an instance variable, the order of operations can get confused. That's why I continued to have parseQueryString() return _map, even though it was now available as an instance variable. I wanted to make sure this first step passed its tests before proceeding to my next step, which was to get rid of the unnecessary return.

```
public class QueryString {
    private String _query;
    private HashMap<String, String> _map = new HashMap<String, String>();

...

    public String valueFor(String name) {
        parseQueryString();
        return _map.get(name);
    }

    private void parseQueryString() {
        String[] pairs = _query.split("&");
        for (String pair : pairs) {
            String[] nameAndValue = pair.split("=");
            _map.put(nameAndValue[0], nameAndValue[1]);
        }
    }
}
```

The tests passed again.

Because parseQueryString() now stood entirely on its own, its only relationship to valueFor() was that it had to be called before valueFor()'s return statement. I was finally ready to achieve my goal of calling parseQueryString() from the constructor.

```
public class QueryString {
    private String _query;
    private HashMap<String, String> _map = new HashMap<String, String>();

    public QueryString(String queryString) {
        if (queryString == null) throw new NullPointerException();
        _query = queryString;
        parseQueryString();
    }

...

    public String valueFor(String name) {
        return _map.get(name);
    }

...

}
```

This seemed like a simple refactoring. After all, I moved only *one line* of code. Yet when I ran my tests, they failed. My parse method didn't work with an empty string—a degenerate case that I hadn't yet implemented in valueFor(). It wasn't a problem as long as only valueFor() ever called parseQueryString(), but it showed up now that I called parseQueryString() in the constructor.

NOTE

This shows why taking small steps is such a good idea. Because I had only changed one line of code, I knew exactly what had gone wrong.

The problem was easy to fix with a guard clause.

```java
private void parseQueryString() {
    if ("".equals(_query)) return;

    String[] pairs = _query.split("&");
    for (String pair : pairs) {
        String[] nameAndValue = pair.split("=");
        _map.put(nameAndValue[0], nameAndValue[1]);
    }
}
```

At this point, I was nearly done. The dupliate parsing in the count() method caused all of this mess, and I was ready to refactor it to use the _map variable rather than do its own parsing. It went from:

```java
public int count() {
    if ("".equals(_query)) return 0;
    String[] pairs = _query.split("&");
    return pairs.length;
}
```

to:

```java
public int count() {
    return _map.size();
}
```

I love it when I can delete code.

I reviewed the code and saw just one loose end remaining: the _query instance variable that stored the unparsed query string. I no longer needed it anywhere but parseQueryString(), so I demoted it from an instance variable to a parseQueryString() parameter.

```java
public class QueryString {
    private HashMap<String, String> _map = new HashMap<String, String>();

    public QueryString(String queryString) {
        if (queryString == null) throw new NullPointerException();
        parseQueryString(queryString);
    }

    public int count() {
        return _map.size();
    }

    public String valueFor(String name) {
        return _map.get(name);
    }
```

```
    private void parseQueryString(String query) {
        if ("".equals(query)) return;

        String[] pairs = query.split("&");
        for (String pair : pairs) {
            String[] nameAndValue = pair.split("=");
            _map.put(nameAndValue[0], nameAndValue[1]);
        }
    }
}
```

When you compare the initial code to this code, there's little in common. Yet this change took place as a series of small, careful refactorings. Although it took me a long time to describe the steps, each individual refactoring took a matter of seconds in practice. The whole series occurred in a few minutes.

Questions

How often should we refactor?

Constantly. Perform little refactorings as you use TDD and bigger refactorings every week. Every week, your design should be better than it was the week before. (See "Incremental Design and Architecture" later in this chapter.)

> **Ally**
> Incremental Design and Architecture (p. 321)

Isn't refactoring rework? Shouldn't we design our code correctly from the beginning?

If it were possible to design your code perfectly from the beginning, then refactoring would be rework. However, as anybody who's worked with large systems knows, mistakes always creep in. It isn't possible to design software perfectly. That's why refactoring is important. Rather than bemoan the errors in the design, celebrate your ability to fix them.

What about our database? That's what really needs improvement.

You can refactor databases, too. Just as with normal refactorings, the trick is to proceed in small, behavior-preserving steps. For example, to rename a table, you can create a new table, copy the data from one to the next, update constraints, update stored procedures and applications, then delete the old table.[*] See "Further Reading" at the end of this section for more.

How can we make large design changes without conflicting with other team members?

Take advantage of communication and continuous integration. Before taking on a refactoring that will touch a bunch of code, check in your existing code and let people know what you're about to do. Sometimes other pairs can reduce the chance of integration conflicts by mirroring any renaming you're planning to do. (IDEs with refactoring support make such renaming painless.)

> **Ally**
> Continuous Integration (p. 183)

During the refactoring, I like to use the distributed version control system SVK, built atop Subversion. It allows me to commit my changes to a local repository one at a time, then push all of them to the main repository when I reach the point of integration. This doesn't prevent conflicts with other pairs, but it allows me to checkpoint locally, which reduces my need to disturb anyone else before I finish.

---

[*] These steps assume that the database isn't live during the refactoring. A live refactoring would have a few more steps.

My refactoring broke the tests! They passed, but then we changed some code and now they fail. What happened?

It's possible you made a mistake in refactoring, but if not, it could be a sign of poor tests. They might test the code's *implementation* rather than its *behavior*. Undo the refactoring and take a look at the tests; you may need to refactor them.

Is refactoring tests actually worthwhile?

Absolutely! Too many developers forget to do this and find themselves maintaining tests that are brittle and difficult to change. Tests have to be maintained just as much as production code does, so they're valid targets for refactoring, too.

Exercise caution when refactoring tests. It's easier to unwittingly break a test than it is to break production code because you can make the test pass when it shouldn't. I like to temporarily change my production code to make the tests fail just to show that they still can. Pair programming also helps.

> **Ally**
> Pair Programming (p. 71)

Sometimes it's valuable to leave more duplication in your tests than you would in the code itself. Tests have a documentation value, and reducing duplication and increasing abstraction can sometimes obscure the intent of the tests. This can be a tough judgment call—err on the side of eliminating duplication.

Results

When you use refactoring as an everyday part of your toolkit, the code constantly improves. You make significant design changes safely and confidently. Every week, the code is at least slightly better than it was the week before.

Contraindications

Refactoring requires good tests. Without it, it's dangerous because you can't easily tell whether your changes have modified behavior. When I have to deal with untested legacy code, I often write a few end-to-end tests first to provide a safety net for refactoring.

> **Ally**
> Test-Driven Development (p. 285)

Refactoring also requires collective code ownership. Any significant design changes will require that you change all parts of the code. Collective code ownership makes this possible. Similarly, refactoring requires continuous integration. Without it, each integration will be a nightmare of conflicting changes.

> **Allies**
> Collective Code Ownership (p. 191)
> Continuous Integration (p. 183)

It's possible to spend too much time refactoring. You don't need to refactor code that's unrelated to your present work. Similarly, balance your need to deliver stories with the need to have good code. As long as the code is better than it was when you started, you're doing enough. In particular, if you think the code could be better, but you're not sure how to improve it, it's OK to leave it for someone else to improve later.

Alternatives

There is no real alternative to refactoring. No matter how carefully you design, all code accumulates technical debt. Without refactoring, that technical debt will eventually overwhelm you, leaving you to choose between rewriting the software (at great expense and risk) or abandoning it entirely.

Further Reading

"Clean Code: Args—A Command-line Argument Parser" [Martin 2005] is a rare treasure: a detailed walk-through of an extended refactoring. If you liked my refactoring example but want more, read this article. It's online at *http://www.objectmentor.com/resources/articles/Clean_Code_Args.pdf*.

Refactoring: Improving the Design of Existing Code [Fowler 1999] is the definitive reference for refactoring. It's also a great read. Buy it.

Refactoring to Patterns [Kerievsky] takes Fowler's work one step further, showing how refactorings can string together to achieve significant design changes. It's a good way to learn more about how to use individual refactorings to achieve big results.

Refactoring Databases: Evolutionary Database Design [Ambler & Sadalage] shows how refactoring can apply to database schemas.

Simple Design

Our design is easy to modify and maintain.

> Perfection is achieved, not when there is nothing more to add, but when there is nothing left to take away. —Antoine de Saint-Exupéry, author of *The Little Prince*

> Any intelligent fool can make things bigger, more complex and more violent. It takes a touch of genius and a lot of courage to move in the opposite direction. —Albert Einstein

When writing code, agile developers often stop to ask themselves, "What is the simplest thing that could possibly work?" They seem to be obssessed with simplicity. Rather than anticipating changes and providing extensibility hooks and plug-in points, they create a simple design that anticipates as little as possible, as cleanly as possible. Unintuitively, this results in designs that are ready for *any* change, anticipated or not.

This may seem silly. How can a design be ready for any change? Isn't the job of a good designer or architect to anticipate future changes and make sure the design can be extended to support them? Doesn't *Design Patterns: Elements of Reusable Software* say that the key to maximizing reuse is to anticipate changes and design accordingly?

I'll let Erich Gamma, coauthor of *Design Patterns*, answer these questions. In the following excerpt, Gamma is interviewed by Bill Venners.[*]

> *Venners:* The GoF book [*Design Patterns*] says, "The key to maximizing reuse lies in anticipating new requirements and changes to existing requirements, and in designing your systems so they can evolve accordingly. To design a system so that it's robust to such changes, you must consider how the system might need to change over its lifetime. A design that doesn't take change into account risks major redesign in the future." That seems contradictory to the XP philosophy.

> *Gamma:* It contradicts absolutely with XP. It says you should think ahead. You should speculate. You should speculate about flexibility. Well yes, I matured too and XP reminds us that it is expensive to speculate about flexibility, so I probably wouldn't write this exactly this way anymore. To add flexibility, you really have to be able to justify it by a requirement. If you don't have a requirement up front, then I wouldn't put a hook for flexibility in my system up front.

> But I don't think XP and [design] patterns are conflicting. It's how you use patterns. The XP guys have patterns in their toolbox, it's just that they refactor to the patterns once they need the flexibility. Whereas we said in the book ten years ago, no, you can also anticipate. You start your design and you use them there up-front. In your up-front design you use patterns, and the XP guys don't do that.

> *Venners:* So what do the XP guys do first, if they don't use patterns? They just write the code?

> *Gamma:* They write a test.

---

[*] "Erich Gamma on Flexibility and Reuse: A Conversation with Erich Gamma, Part II," *http://www.artima.com/lejava/articles/reuse.html*.

Venners: Yes, they code up the test. And then when they implement it, they just implement the code to make the test work. Then when they look back, they refactor, and maybe implement a pattern?

Gamma: Or when there's a new requirement. I really like flexibility that's requirement driven. That's also what we do in Eclipse. When it comes to exposing more API, we do that on demand. We expose API gradually. When clients tell us, "Oh, I had to use or duplicate all these internal classes. I really don't want to do that," when we see the need, then we say, OK, we'll make the investment of publishing this as an API, make it a commitment. So I really think about it in smaller steps, we do not want to commit to an API before its time.

BECK ON SIMPLICITY

In the first edition of *Extreme Programming Explained*, Kent Beck described simple design as code that passes its tests and meets four guidelines, with the earlier guidelines taking precedence over the later ones:

1. The system (code and tests together) must communicate everything you want to communicate.

2. The system must contain no duplicate code. (Guidelines 1 and 2 together constitute the Once and Only Once rule).

3. The system should have the fewest possible classes.

4. The system should have the fewest possible methods.

In the second edition, he rephrased the advice:

1. *Appropriate for the intended audience.* It doesn't matter how brilliant and elegant a piece of design is; if the people who need to work with it don't understand it, it isn't simple for them.

2. *Communicative.* Every idea that needs to be communicated is represented in the system. Like words in a vocabulary, the elements of the system communicate to future readers.

3. *Factored.* Duplication of logic or structure makes code hard to understand and modify.

4. *Minimal.* Within the above three constraints, the system should have the fewest elements possible. Fewer elements means less to test, document, and communicate.

Simple doesn't mean *simplistic*. Don't make boneheaded design decisions in the name of reducing the number of classes and methods. A simple design is clean and elegant, not something you throw together with the least thought possible. Here are some points to keep in mind as you strive for simplicity.

> Simple, not simplistic.

You Aren't Gonna Need It (YAGNI)

This pithy XP saying sums up an important aspect of simple design: avoid speculative coding. Whenever you're tempted to add something to your design, ask yourself if it supports the stories and features you're currently delivering. If not, well... you aren't gonna need it. Your design could change. Your customers' minds could change.

Similarly, remove code that's no longer in use. You'll make the design smaller, simpler, and easier to understand. If you need it again in the future, you can always get it out of version control. For now, it's a maintenance burden you don't need.

Ally
Version Control (p. 169)

We do this because excess code makes change difficult. Speculative design, added to make specific changes easy, often turns out to be wrong in some way, which actually makes changes more difficult. It's usually easier to add to a design than to fix a design that's wrong. The incorrect design has code that depends on it, sometimes locking bad decisions in place.

Once and Only Once

Once and only once is a surprisingly powerful design guideline. As Martin Fowler said:[*]

> One of the things I've been trying to do is look for simpler [rules] or rules underpinning good or bad design. I think one of the most valuable rules is avoid duplication. "Once and only once" is the Extreme Programming phrase. The authors of *The Pragmatic Programmer* [Hunt & Thomas] use "don't repeat yourself," or the DRY principle.
>
> You can almost do this as an exercise. Look at some program and see if there's some duplication. Then, without really thinking about what it is you're trying to achieve, just pigheadedly try to remove that duplication. Time and time again, I've found that by simply removing duplication I accidentally stumble onto a really nice elegant pattern. It's quite remarkable how often that is the case. I often find that a nice design can come from just being really anal about getting rid of duplicated code.

There's even more to this idea than removing duplication. Think of it this way:

Express every concept once. (And only once).[†]

In other words, don't just eliminate duplication; make sure that every important concept has an explicit representation in your design. As [Hunt & Thomas] phrase their DRY Principle: "Every piece of knowledge must have a single, unambiguous, authoritative representation within a system."

An effective way to make your code express itself once (and only once) is to be explicit about core concepts. Rather than expressing these concepts with a primitive data type, create a new type. For example, rather than representing dollar amounts with a `decimal` data type, create a `Dollars` class. (See Example 9-2.)

Example 9-2. Simple value type

```
public class Dollars {
    private decimal _dollars;
    public Dollars(decimal dollars) { _dollars = dollars; }
    public decimal AsDecimal() { return _dollars; }
    public boolean Equals(object o) {...}
}
```

Although using basic data types may seem simpler—it's one less class, after all—it actually makes your design more complex. Your code doesn't have a place for the concept. As a result, every time someone works with that concept, the code may need to reimplement basic behavior, such as string parsing and formatting, which results in widespread duplication. This duplication will likely be only fragments of

---

[*] *http://www.artima.com/intv/principlesP.html.*

[†] Thanks to Andrew Black for this insight.

code, but the net weight of those fragments will make your code hard to change. For example, if you decide to change the display of dollar amounts—perhaps you want negative amounts to be red—you must find every little fragment of formatting code and fix it.

Instead, make sure that every concept has a home. Don't generalize; just make sure the basic concept has an explicit representation. Over time, as needed, add code (such as formatting and parsing) to your type. By starting with a simple but explicit representation of the concept, you provide a location for those future changes to congregate. Without it, they will tend to accumulate in other methods and lead to duplication and complex code.

Self-Documenting Code

Simplicity is in the eye of the beholder. It doesn't matter much if *you* think the design is simple; if the rest of your team or future maintainers of your software find it too complicated, then it is.

To avoid this problem, use idioms and patterns that are common for your language and team. It's OK to introduce new ideas, too, but run them past other team members first. Be sure to use names that clearly reflect the intent of your variables, methods, classes, and other entities.

Pair programming will help you create simple code. If you have trouble understanding something your partner wrote, discuss the situation and try to find a better way to express the concept. Before you use a comment to explain something, ask your partner how to make the code express its intent without needing a comment.

Ally
Pair Programming (p. 71)

> **NOTE**
> Comments aren't bad, but they *are* a sign that your code is more complex than it needs to be. Try to eliminate the need for comments when you can. You can't just arbitrarily delete comments, of course—first make the code so expressive that the comments no longer add value.

Isolate Third-Party Components

A hidden source of duplication lies in calls to third-party components. When you have these calls spread throughout your code, replacing or augmenting that component becomes difficult. If you discover that the component isn't sufficient for your needs, you could be in trouble.

To prevent this problem, isolate your third-party components behind an interface that you control. Ask yourself, "When I need to upgrade or change this component, how hard will it be?" In object-oriented languages, consider using the *Adapter pattern* [Gamma et al.] rather than instantiating third-party classes directly. For frameworks that require that you extend their classes, create your own base classes that extend the framework classes, rather than extending the classes directly.

> **NOTE**
> Isolating third-party components also allows you to extend the features of the component and gives you a convenient interface to write tests against if you need to.

Create your adapter incrementally. Instead of supporting every feature of the component in your adapter, support only what you need today. Write the adapter's interface to match your needs, not the interface of the component. This will make it easier to use and to replace when necessary.

Isolating third-party components reduces duplication at the cost of making your code slightly more complex. Some components, such as Java's J2SE or the .NET framework, are so pervasive that isolating them makes little sense. Make the decision to isolate common components according to the risk that you'll need to replace or augment that component. For example, I would use the Java or .NET String class directly, without an adapter, but I might consider isolating .NET's cryptography libraries or elements of the J2EE framework.

Limit Published Interfaces

Published interfaces reduce your ability to make changes. Once the public interface to a class or other module is published so that people outside the team may use it, changing it requires great expense and effort. Because other people might be using the interface, changing it can sabotage their efforts.

Some teams approach design as if every public interface were also a published interface. This *internal publication* assumes that, once defined, a public interface should never change. This is a bad idea—it prevents you from improving your design over time. A better approach is to change your nonpublished interfaces whenever you need, updating callers accordingly.

If your code is used outside your team, then you do need published interfaces. Each one, however, is a commitment to a design decision that you may wish to change in the future. Minimize the number of interfaces you expose to the outside world, and ask if the benefit of having other teams use your code is really worth the cost.* (Sometimes it is, but don't automatically assume so.) Postpone publishing interfaces as long as possible to allow your design to improve and settle.

In some cases, as with teams creating a library for third-party use, the entire purpose of the project is to create a published interface. In that case, your API is your product. Still, the smaller the interface, the better—it's much easier to add new elements to your API than to remove or change incorrect elements. Make the interface as small as is practical.

As Erich Gamma said in the interview, "When it comes to exposing more API [in Eclipse, the open-source Java IDE], we do that on demand. We expose API gradually... when we see the need, then we say, OK, we'll make the investment of publishing this as an API, make it a commitment. So I really think about it in smaller steps, we do not want to commit to an API before its time."

NOTE

When developing a library, you can develop your interface incrementally and then freeze it only when you release. Still, it's probably a good idea to think ahead to future changes and consider whether anything about the API you're about to publish will make those changes difficult.

Fail Fast

One of the pitfalls of simple design is that your design will be incomplete. Some elements won't work because no one has needed them before.

---

* [Brooks] estimated that making code externally reusable increases costs threefold. That estimate probably doesn't apply to modern development, but there's still a nontrivial cost associated with creating reusable components. "Object-oriented" doesn't mean "automatic reuse," despite early claims to the contrary.

To prevent these gaps from being a problem, write your code to *fail fast*. Use assertions to signal the limits of your design; if someone tries to use something that isn't implemented, the assertion will cause his tests to fail.

NOTE

Sometimes you can have more expressive assertions by writing your own assertion facility, rather than using your language's built-in facility. I like to create a class called `Assert` (`Assume` and `Require` are good synonyms if `Assert` is unavailable) and implement class (static) methods such as `notNull(object)`, `unreachableCode()` and `impossibleException (exception)`.

Questions

What if we know we're going to need a feature? Shouldn't we put in a design hook for it?

In XP, the plan can change every week. Unless you're implementing the feature that very week, don't put the hook in. The plan could change, leaving you stuck with unneeded code.

Plus, if you're using incremental design and architecture properly, your code will actually be easier to modify in the future than it is today. Saving the change for later will save time and money.

Ally

Incremental Design and Architecture (p. 321)

What if ignoring a feature will make it harder to implement in the future?

A simple design should make arbitrary changes possible by reducing duplication and limiting the scope of changes. If ignoring a potential feature could make it more difficult, you should look for ways to eliminate that risk without explicitly coding support for the feature. "Incremental Design and Architecture," later in this chapter, has more about risk-driven architecture.

Results

When you create simple designs, you avoid adding support for any features other than the ones you're working on in the current iteration. You finish work more quickly as a result. When you use simple design well, your design supports arbitrary changes easily. Although new features might require a lot of new code, changes to existing code are localized and straightforward.

Contraindications

Simple design requires continuous improvement through refactoring and incremental design and architecture. Without these, your design will fail to evolve with your requirements.

Allies

Refactoring (p. 303)
Incremental Design and Architecture (p. 321)

Don't use simple design as an excuse for poor design. Simplicity requires careful thought. As the Einstein quote at the beginning of this section says, it's a lot easier to create complex designs than simple ones. Don't pretend "simple" means "fastest" or "easiest."

Pair programming and collective code ownership, though not strictly necessary for simple design, will help your team devote the brainpower needed to create truly simple designs.

Allies

Pair Programming (p. 71)
Collective Code Ownership
(p. 191)

Alternatives

Until recently, the accepted best practice in design followed the advice Erich Gamma now disavows: "The key to maximizing reuse lies in anticipating new requirements and changes to existing requirements, and in designing your systems so they can evolve accordingly."

A team can have success with this approach, but it depends on how well they anticipate new requirements. If the team's expectations are too far off, they might need to rewrite a lot of code that was based on bad assumptions. Some changes may affect so much code that they're considered impossible. If you follow this approach, it's best to hire designers who have a lot of experience in your specific industry. They're more likely to correctly anticipate changes.

Further Reading

Martin Fowler has a collection of his excellent IEEE Design columns online at *http://www.martinfowler.com/articles.html#IDAOPDBC*. Many of these columns discuss core concepts that help in creating a simple design.

The Pragmatic Programmer: From Journeyman to Master [Hunt & Thomas] contains a wealth of design information that will help you create simple, flexible designs. *Practices of an Agile Developer* [Subramaniam & Hunt] is its spiritual successor, offering similarly pithy advice, though with less emphasis on design and coding.

Prefactoring [Pugh] also has good advice for creating simple, flexible designs.

"Fail Fast" [Shore 2004b] discusses that concept in more detail. It is available at *http://www.martinfowler.com/ieeeSoftware/failFast.pdf*.

Incremental Design and Architecture

We deliver stories every week without compromising design quality.

XP makes challenging demands of its programmers: every week, programmers should finish 4 to 10 customer-valued stories. Every week, customers may revise the current plan and introduce entirely new stories—with no advance notice. This regimen starts with the first week of the project.

Allies

Iterations (p. 41)
Stories (p. 253)

In other words, as a programmer you must be able to produce customer value, from scratch, in a single week. No advance preparation is possible. You can't set aside several weeks for building a domain model or persistence framework; your customers need you to deliver completed stories.

Fortunately, XP provides a solution for this dilemma: *incremental design* (also called *evolutionary design*) allows you to build technical infrastructure (such as domain models and persistence frameworks) incrementally, in small pieces, as you deliver stories.

How It Works

Incremental design applies the concepts introduced in test-driven development to all levels of design. Like test-driven development, programmers work in small steps, proving each before moving to the next. This takes place in three parts: start by creating the simplest design that could possibly work, incrementally add to it as the needs of the software evolve, and continuously improve the design by reflecting on its strengths and weaknesses.

Ally

Test-Driven Development
(p. 285)

To be specific, when you *first* create a design element—whether it's a new method, a new class, or a new architecture—be completely specific. Create a simple design that solves only the problem you face at the moment, no matter how easy it may seem to solve more general problems.

Ally

Simple Design (p. 314)

This is difficult! Experienced programmers think in abstractions. In fact, the ability to think in abstractions is often a sign of a good programmer. Coding for one specific scenario will seem strange, even unprofessional.

Do it anyway. The abstractions will come. Waiting to make them will enable you to create designs that are simpler and more powerful.

> Waiting to create abstractions will enable you to create designs that are simple and powerful.

The *second* time you work with a design element, modify the design to make it more general—but only general enough to solve the two problems it needs to solve. Next, review the design and make improvements. Simplify and clarify the code.

Ally

Refactoring (p. 303)

The *third* time you work with a design element, generalize it further—but again, just enough to solve the three problems at hand. A small tweak to the design is usually enough. It will be pretty general at this point. Again, review the design, simplify, and clarify.

Continue this pattern. By the *fourth* or *fifth* time you work with a design element—be it a method, a class, or something bigger—you'll typically find that its abstraction is perfect for your needs. Best of all, because you allowed practical needs to drive your design, it will be simple yet powerful.

> **NOTE**
>
> You can see this process in action in test-driven development. TDD is an example of incremental design at the level of methods and individual classes. Incremental design goes further than TDD, however, scaling to classes, packages, and even application architecture.

INCONCEIVABLE!

I have to admit I was very skeptical of incremental design when I first heard about it. I felt that up-front design was the only responsible approach. The first time my team tried incremental design, we mixed up-front design with incremental design. We designed the architecture up-front, feeling it was too important to leave until later. Over time, however, experience showed us that many of those initial design decisions had serious flaws. We used incremental design not only to fix the flaws, but to produce far better alternatives. When I left the project eighteen months later, it had the best design of any code I've ever seen.

That project taught me to trust incremental design. It's different from traditional design approaches, but it's also strikingly effective—and more forgiving of mistakes. Software projects usually succumb to *bit rot* and get more difficult to modify over time. With incremental design, the reverse tends to be true: software actually gets *easier* to modify over time. Incremental design is so effective, it's now my preferred design approach for any project, XP or otherwise.

Continuous Design

Incremental design initially creates every design element—method, class, namespace, or even architecture—to solve a specific problem. Additional customer requests guide the incremental evolution of the design. This requires continuous attention to the design, albeit at different timescales. Methods evolve in minutes; architectures evolve over months.

No matter what level of design you're looking at, the design tends to improve in bursts. Typically, you'll implement code into the existing design for several cycles, making minor changes as you go. Then something will give you an idea for a new design approach, which will require a series of refactorings to support it. [Evans] calls this a *breakthrough* (see Figure 9-2). Breakthroughs happen at all levels of the design, from methods to architectures.

Breakthroughs are the result of important insights and lead to substantial improvements to the design. (If they don't, they're not worth implementing.) You can see a small, method-scale breakthrough at the end of "A TDD Example" earlier in this chapter.

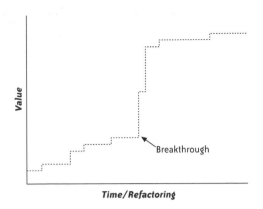

Figure 9-2. Breakthrough

Incrementally Designing Methods

You've seen this level of incremental design before: it's test-driven development. While the driver implements, the navigator thinks about the design. She looks for overly complex code and missing elements, which she writes on her notecard. She thinks about which features the code should support next, what design changes might be necessary, and which tests may guide the code in the proper direction. During the refactoring step of TDD, both members of the pair look at the code, discuss opportunities for improvements, and review the navigator's notes.

Allies

Test-Driven Development (p. 285)
Pair Programming (p. 71)

> **NOTE**
> The roles of driver and navigator aren't as cut-and-dried as I imply. It's OK for drivers to think about design and for navigators to make implementation suggestions.

Method refactorings happen every few minutes. Breakthroughs may happen several times per hour and can take 10 minutes or more to complete.

Incrementally Designing Classes

When TDD is performed well, the design of individual classes and methods is beautiful: they're simple, elegant, and easy to use. This isn't enough. Without attention to the interaction between classes, the overall system design will be muddy and confusing.

During TDD, the navigator should also consider the wider scope. Ask yourself these questions: are there similarities between the code you're implementing and other code in the system? Are class responsibilities clearly defined and concepts clearly represented? How well does this class interact with other classes?

> Nothing clarifies a design issue like working code.

When you see a problem, jot it down on your card. During one of the refactoring steps of TDD—usually, when you're not in the middle of something else—bring up the issue, discuss solutions with your partner, and refactor. If you think your design change will significantly affect other members of the team, take a quick break to discuss it around a whiteboard.

> **NOTE**
>
> Don't let design discussions turn into long, drawn-out disagreements. Follow *the 10-minute rule*: if you disagree on a design direction for 10 minutes, try one and see how it works in practice. If you have a particularly strong disagreement, split up and try both as spike solutions. Nothing clarifies a design issue like working code.

Class-level refactorings happen several times per day. Depending on your design, breakthroughs may happen a few times per week and can take several hours to complete. (Nonetheless, remember to proceed in small, test-verified steps.) Use your iteration slack to complete breakthrough refactorings. In some cases, you won't have time to finish all the refactorings you identify. That's OK; as long as the design is better at the end of the week than it was at the beginning, you're doing enough.

Ally
Slack (p. 246)

> **NOTE**
>
> Avoid creating TODO comments or story/task cards for postponed refactorings. If the problem is common enough for you or others to notice it again, it will get fixed eventually. If not, then it probably isn't worth fixing. There are always more opportunities to refactor than time to do it all; TODOs or refactoring cards add undue stress to the team without adding much value.

Incrementally Designing Architecture

Large programs use overarching organizational structures called *architecture*. For example, many programs segregate user interface classes, business logic classes, and persistence classes into their own namespaces; this is a classic *three-layer architecture*. Other designs have the application pass the flow of control from one machine to the next in an *n-tier architecture*.

These architectures are implemented through the use of recurring patterns. They aren't design patterns in the formal Gang of Four[*] sense. Instead, they're standard conventions specific to your codebase. For example, in a three-layer architecture, every business logic class will probably be part of a "business logic" namespace, may inherit from a generic "business object" base class, and probably interfaces with its persistence layer counterpart in a standard way.

These recurring patterns embody your application architecture. Although they lead to consistent code, they're also a form of duplication, which makes changes to your architecture more difficult.

Fortunately, you can also design architectures incrementally. As with other types of continuous design, use TDD and pair programming as your primary vehicle. While your software grows, be conservative in introducing new architectural patterns: introduce just what you need to for the amount of code you have and the features you support at the moment. Before introducing a new pattern, ask yourself if the duplication is really necessary. Perhaps there's some language feature you can use that will reduce your need to rely on the pattern.

---

[*] The "Gang of Four" is a common nickname for the authors of *Design Patterns*, a book that introduced design patterns to the mainstream.

In my experience, breakthroughs in architecture happen every few months. (This estimate will vary widely depending on your team members and code quality.) Refactoring to support the breakthrough can take several weeks or longer because of the amount of duplication involved. Although changes to your architecture may be tedious, they usually aren't difficult once you've identified the new architectural pattern. Start by trying out the new pattern in just one part of your design. Let it sit for a while—a week or two—to make sure the change works well in practice. Once you're sure it does, bring the rest of the system into compliance with the new structure. Refactor each class you touch as you perform your everyday work, and use some of your slack in each iteration to fix other classes.

<table>
<tr><td>Ally</td></tr>
<tr><td>Slack (p. 246)</td></tr>
</table>

Keep delivering stories while you refactor. Although you could take a break from new development to refactor, that would disenfranchise your customers. Balance technical excellence with delivering value. Neither can take precedence over the other. This may lead to inconsistencies within the code during the changeover, but fortunately, that's mostly an aesthetic problem—more annoying than problematic.

> **Balance technical excellence with delivering value.**

> **NOTE**
> Introducing architectural patterns incrementally helps reduce the need for multiiteration refactorings. It's easier to expand an architecture than it is to simplify one that's too ambitious.

Risk-Driven Architecture

Architecture may seem too essential not to design up-front. Some problems do seem too expensive to solve incrementally, but I've found that nearly everything is easy to change if you eliminate duplication and embrace simplicity. Common thought is that distributed processing, persistence, internationalization, security, and transaction structure are so complex that you *must* consider them from the start of your project. I disagree; I've dealt with all of them incrementally [Shore 2004a].

> **NOTE**
> Two issues that remain difficult to change are choice of programming language and platform. I wouldn't want to make those decisions incrementally!

Of course, no design is perfect. Even with simple design, some of your code will contain duplication, and some will be too complex. There's always more refactoring to do than time to do it. That's where *risk-driven architecture* comes in.

<table>
<tr><td>Ally</td></tr>
<tr><td>Simple Design (p. 314)</td></tr>
</table>

Although I've emphasized designing for the present, it's OK to *think* about future problems. Just don't *implement* any solutions to stories that you haven't yet scheduled.

What do you do when you see a hard problem coming? For example, what if you know that internationalizing your code is expensive and only going to get more expensive? Your power lies in your ability to choose which refactorings to work on. Although it would be inappropriate to implement features your customers haven't asked for, you *can* direct your refactoring efforts toward reducing risk. Anything that improves the current design is OK—so choose improvements that also reduce future risk.

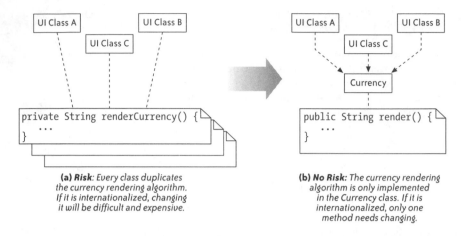

(a) Risk: Every class duplicates the currency rendering algorithm. If it is internationalized, changing it will be difficult and expensive.

(b) No Risk: The currency rendering algorithm is only implemented in the Currency class. If it is internationalized, only one method needs changing.

Figure 9-3. Use risk to drive refactoring

To apply risk-driven architecture, consider what it is about your design that concerns you and eliminate duplication around those concepts. For example, if your internationalization concern is that you always format numbers, dates, and other variables in the local style, look for ways to reduce duplication in your variable formatting. One way to do so is to make sure every concept has its own class (as described in "Once and Only Once" earlier in this chapter), then condense all formatting around each concept into a single method within each class, as shown in Figure 9-3. If there's still a lot of duplication, the Strategy pattern would allow you to condense the formatting code even further.

Limit your efforts to improving your *existing* design. Don't actually implement support for localized formats until your customers ask for them. Once you've eliminated duplication around a concept—for example, once there's only one method in your entire system that renders numbers as strings—changing its implementation will be just as easy later as it is now.

NOTE

A team I worked with replaced an entire database connection pooling library in half a pair-day. Although we didn't anticipate this need, it was still easy because we had previously eliminated all duplication around database connection management. There was just one method in the entire system that created, opened, and closed connections, which made writing our own connection pool manager almost trivially easy.[*]

USING STORIES TO REDUCE RISK

Another great way to reduce technical risk is to ask your customers to schedule stories that will allow you to work on the risky area. For example, to address the number localization risk, you could create a story such as "Localize application for Spain" (or any European country). This story expresses customer value, yet addresses an internationalization risk.

---

[*] We did have to make it thread-safe, so it wasn't entirely trivial.

Your customers have final say over story priorities, however, and their sense of risk and value may not match yours. Don't feel too bad if this happens; you can still use refactorings to reduce your risk.

It's Not Just Coding

Although incremental design focuses heavily on test-driven development and refactoring as an enabler, it isn't about coding. When you use TDD, incremental design, and pair programming well, every pairing session involves a lot of conversation about design. In fact, that's what *all* the (relevant) conversations are about. As Ron Jeffries likes to say, design is so important in XP that we do it *all the time*. Some of the design discussions are very detailed and nitpicky, such as, "What should we name this method?" Others are much higher-level, such as, "These two classes share some responsibilities. We should split them apart and make a third class."

Allies

Test-Driven Development (p. 285)
Refactoring (p. 303)
Pair Programming (p. 71)

Have design discussions away from the keyboard as often as you think is necessary, and use whatever modelling techniques you find helpful. Try to keep them informal and collaborative; sketches on a whiteboard work well. Some people like to use *CRC* (Class, Responsibility, Collaborator) cards.

Some of your discussions will be *predictive*, meaning you'll discuss how you can change your design to support some feature that you haven't yet added to the code. Others will be *reflective*, meaning you'll discuss how to change your design to better support existing features.

NOTE

Beware of getting trapped in *analysis paralysis* and spending too much time trying to figure out a design. If a design direction isn't clear after 10 minutes or so, you probably need more information. Continue using TDD and making those refactorings that are obvious, and a solution will eventually become clear.

Reflective design (discussed in more detail in "Refactoring" earlier in this chapter) is always helpful in XP. I like to sketch UML diagrams on a whiteboard to illustrate problems in the current design and possible solutions. When my teams discover a breakthrough refactoring at the class or architecture level, we gather around a whiteboard to discuss it and sketch our options.

Predictive design is less helpful in XP, but it's still a useful tool. As you're adding a new feature, use it to help you decide which tests to write next in TDD. On a larger scale, use predictive design to consider risks and perform risk-driven architecture.

Ally

Test-Driven Development (p. 285)

The trick to using predictive design in XP is keeping your design simple and focusing only on the features it currently supports. Although it's OK to predict how your design will change when you add new features, you shouldn't actually implement those changes until you're working on the stories in question. When you do, you should keep your mind open to other ways of implementing those features. Sometimes the act of coding with test-driven development will reveal possibilities you hadn't considered.

Given these caveats, I find that I use predictive design less and less as I become more experienced with incremental design. That's not because it's "against the rules"—I'm perfectly happy breaking rules—but because working incrementally and reflectively has genuinely yielded better results for me.

Try it yourself, and find the balance between predictive and reflective design that works best for you.

Questions

Isn't incremental design more expensive than up-front design?

Just the opposite, actually, in my experience. There are two reasons for this. First, because incremental design implements just enough code to support the current requirements, you start delivering features much more quickly with incremental design. Second, when a predicted requirement changes, you haven't coded any parts of the design to support it, so you haven't wasted any effort.

Even if requirements never changed, incremental design would still be more effective, as it leads to design breakthroughs on a regular basis. Each breakthrough allows you to see new possibilities and eventually leads to another breakthrough—sort of like walking through a hilly forest in which the top of each hill reveals a new, higher hill you couldn't see before. This continual series of breakthroughs substantially improves your design.

What if we get the design absolutely wrong and have to backtrack to add a new feature?

Sometimes a breakthrough will lead you to see a completely new way of approaching your design. In this case, refactoring may seem like backtracking. This happens to everyone and is not a bad thing. The nature of breakthroughs—especially at the class and architectural level—is that you usually don't see them until after you've lived with the current design for a while.

Our organization (or customer) requires comprehensive design documentation. How can we satisfy this requirement?

Ask them to schedule it with a story, then estimate and deliver it as you would any other story. Remind them that the design will change over time. The most effective option is to schedule documentation stories for the last iteration.

Ally
Documentation (p. 195)

If your organization requires up-front design documentation, the only way to provide it is to engage in up-front design. Try to keep your design efforts small and simple. If you can, use incremental design once you actually start coding.

Results

When you use incremental design well, every iteration advances the software's features and design in equal measure. You have no need to skip coding for an iteration for refactoring or design. Every week, the quality of the software is better than it was the week before. As time goes on, the software becomes increasingly easy to maintain and extend.

Contraindications

Incremental design requires simple design and constant improvement. Don't try to use incremental design without a commitment to continuous daily improvement (in XP terms, *merciless refactoring*). This requires self-discipline and a strong desire for high-quality code from at least one team member. Because nobody can do that all the time, pair programming, collective code ownership, energized work, and slack are important support mechanisms.

Allies
Refactoring (p. 303)
Simple Design (p. 314)
Pair Programming (p. 71)
Collective Code Ownership (p. 191)
Energized Work (p. 79)
Slack (p. 246)

Test-driven development is also important for incremental design. Its explicit refactoring step, repeated every few minutes, gives pairs continual opportunities to stop and make design improvements. Pair programming helps in this area, too, by making sure that half the team's programmers—as navigators—always have an opportunity to consider design improvements.

Ally

Test-Driven Development (p. 285)

Be sure your team sits together and communicates well if you're using incremental design. Without constant communication about class and architectural refactorings, your design will fragment and diverge. Agree on coding standards so that everyone follows the same patterns.

Allies

Sit Together (p. 112)
Coding Standards (p. 133)

Anything that makes continuous improvement difficult will make incremental design difficult. Published interfaces are an example; because they are difficult to change after publication, incremental design may not be appropriate for published interfaces. (You can still use incremental design for the *implementation* of those interfaces.) Similarly, any language or platform that makes refactoring difficult will also inhibit your use of incremental design.

Ally

Refactoring (p. 303)

Finally, some organizations place organizational rather than technical impediments on refactoring, as with organizations that require up-front design documentation or have rigidly controlled database schemas. Incremental design may not be appropriate in these situations.

Alternatives

If you are uncomfortable with XP's approach to incremental design, you can hedge your bets by combining it with up-front design. Start with an up-front design stage, and then commit completely to XP-style incremental design. Although it will delay the start of your first iteration (and may require some up-front requirements work, too), this approach has the advantage of providing a safety net without incurring too much risk.

NOTE

If you're feeling bold, use XP's iterative design directly, without the safety net. Incremental design is powerful, effective, and inexpensive. The added effort of an up-front design stage isn't necessary.

There are other alternatives to incremental design, but I don't think they would work well with XP. One option is to use another type of incremental design, one more like up-front design, that does some up-front design at the beginning of every iteration, rather than relying on simple design and refactoring to the extent that XP does.

I haven't tried other incremental design approaches with XP because they seem to interact clumsily with XP's short iterations. The design sessions could be too short and small to create a cohesive architecture on their own. Without XP's focus on simple design and merciless refactoring, a single design might not evolve.

Another alternative is to design everything up-front. This could work in an environment with very few requirements changes (or a prescient designer), but it's likely to break down with XP's adaptive plans and tiered planning horizons (see "Release Planning" in Chapter 8).

Further Reading

"Is Design Dead?" [Fowler 2000], online at *http://www.martinfowler.com/articles/designDead.html*, discusses evolutionary design from a slightly skeptical perspective.

"Continuous Design" [Shore 2004a] discusses my experiences with difficult challenges in incremental design, such as internationalization and security. It is available at *http://www.martinfowler.com/ieeeSoftware/continuousDesign.pdf*.

Spike Solutions

We perform small, isolated experiments when we need more information.

You've probably noticed by now that XP values concrete data over speculation. Whenever you're faced with a question, don't speculate about the answer—conduct an experiment! Figure out how you can use real data to make progress.

That's what spike solutions are for, too.

About Spikes

A *spike solution*, or *spike*, is a technical investigation. It's a small experiment to research the answer to a problem. For example, a programmer might not know whether Java throws an exception on arithmetic overflow. A quick 10-minute spike will answer the question.

```
public class ArithmeticOverflowSpike {
    public static void main(String[] args) {
        try {
            int a = Integer.MAX_VALUE + 1;
            System.out.println("No exception: a = " + a);
        }
        catch (Throwable e) {
            System.out.println("Exception: " + e);
        }
    }
}
```

No exception: a = -2147483648

NOTE

Although this example is written as a standalone program, small spikes such as this one can also be written inside your test framework. Although they don't actually call your production code, the test framework provides a convenient way to quickly run the spike and report on the results.

Performing the Experiment

The best way to implement a spike is usually to create a small program or test that demonstrates the feature in question. You can read as many books and tutorials as you like, but it's my experience that nothing helps me understand a problem more than writing working code. It's important to work from a practical point of view, not just a theoretical one.

Writing code, however, often takes longer than reading a tutorial. Reduce that time by writing small, standalone programs. You can ignore the complexities necessary to write production code—just focus on getting something working. Run from the command line or your test framework. Hardcode values. Ignore user input, unless absolutely necessary. I often end up with programs a few dozen lines long that run almost everything from main().

Of course, this approach means you can't reuse this code in your actual production codebase, as you didn't develop it with all your normal discipline and care. That's fine. It's an *experiment*. When you finish, throw it away, check it in as documentation, or share it with your colleagues, but don't treat it as anything other than an experiment.

> Spike solutions clarify technical issues by setting aside the complexities of production code.

NOTE

I discard the spikes I create to clarify a technical question (such as "Does this language throw an exception on arithmetic overflow?"), but generally keep the ones that demonstrate how to accomplish a specific task (such as "How do I send HTML email?"). I keep a separate *spikes/* directory in my repository just for these sorts of spikes.

DESIGN SPIKES

Sometimes you'll need to test an approach to your production code. Perhaps you want to see how a design possibility will work in practice, or you need to see how a persistence framework will work on your production code.

In this case, go ahead and work on production code. Be sure to check in your latest changes before you start the spike, and be careful not to check in any of your spike code.

Scheduling Spikes

Most spikes are performed on the spur of the moment. You see a need to clarify a small technical issue, and you write a quick spike to do so. If the spike takes more than a few minutes, your iteration slack absorbs the cost.

Ally
Slack (p. 246)

If you anticipate the need for a spike when estimating a story, include the time in your story estimate. Sometimes you won't be able to estimate a story at all until you've done your research; in this case, create a spike story and estimate that instead (see "Stories" in Chapter 8).

Questions

Your spike example is terrible! Don't you know that you should never catch Throwable?

Exactly. Production code should never catch Throwable, but a spike isn't production code. Spike solutions are the one time that you can forget about writing good code and focus just on short-term results. (That said, for larger spikes, you may find code that's *too* sloppy is hard to work with and slows you down.)

Should we pair on spikes?

It's up to you. Because spikes aren't production code, even teams with strict pair programming rules don't require writing spikes in pairs.

One very effective way to pair on a spike is to have one person research the technology while the other person codes. Another option is for both people to work independently on separate approaches, each doing their own research and coding, then coming together to review progress and share ideas.

Should we really throw away the code from our spikes?

Unless you think someone will refer to it later, toss it. Remember, the purpose of a spike solution is to give you the information and experience to know *how* to solve a problem, not to produce the code that solves it.

How often should we do spikes?

Perform a spike whenever you have a question about if or how some piece of technology will work.

What if the spike reveals that the problem is more difficult than we thought?

That's good; it gives you more information. Perhaps the customer will reconsider the value of the feature, or perhaps you need to think of another way to accomplish what you want.

Once, a customer asked me for a feature I thought might work in a certain way, but my spike demonstrated that the relevant Internet standard actually prohibited the desired behavior. We came up with a different design for implementing the larger feature.

Results

When you clarify technical questions with well-directed, isolated experiments, you spend less time speculating about how your program will work. You focus your debugging and exploratory programming on the problem at hand rather than on the ways in which your production code might be interacting with your experiment.

Contraindications

Avoid the temptation to create useful or generic programs out of your spikes. Focus your work on answering a specific technical question, and stop working on the spike as soon as it answers that question. Similarly, there's no need to create a spike when you already understand a technology well.

Don't use spikes as an excuse to avoid disciplined test-driven development and refactoring. Never copy spike code into production code. Even if it is exactly what you need, rewrite it using test-driven development so that it meets your production code standards.

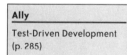

Ally

Test-Driven Development
(p. 285)

Alternatives

Spike solutions are a learning technique based on performing small, concrete experiments. Some people perform these experiments in their production code, which can work well for small experiments (such as the arithmetic overflow example), but it increases the scope of possible error. If something doesn't work as expected, is it because your understanding of the technology is wrong? Is it due to an unseen interaction with the production code or test framework? Standalone spikes eliminate this uncertainty.

For stories that you can't estimate accurately, an alternative to scheduling a spike story is to provide a high estimate. This is risky because some stories will take longer than your highest estimate, and some may not be possible at all.

Another option is to research problems by reading about the underlying theory and finding code snippets in books or online. This is often a good way to get started on a spike, but the best way to really understand what's going on is to create your own spike. Simplify and adapt the example. Why does it work? What happens when you change default parameters? Use the spike to clarify your understanding.

Performance Optimization

Audience
Programmers, Testers

We optimize when there's a proven need.

Our organization had a problem.[*] Every transaction our software processed had a three-second latency. During peak business hours, transactions piled up—and with our recent surge in sales, the lag sometimes became hours. We cringed every time the phone rang; our customers were upset.

We knew what the problem was: we had recently changed our order preprocessing code. I remember thinking at the time that we might need to start caching the intermediate results of expensive database queries. I had even asked our customers to schedule a performance story. Other stories had been more important, but now performance was top priority.

I checked out the latest code and built it. All tests passed, as usual. Carlann suggested that we create an end-to-end performance test to demonstrate the problem. We created a test that placed 100 simultaneous orders, then ran it under our profiler.

The numbers confirmed my fears: the average transaction took around 3.2 seconds, with a standard deviation too small to be significant. The program spent nearly all that time within a *single* method: verify_order_id(). We started our investigation there.

I was pretty sure a cache was the right answer, but the profiler pointed to another possibility. The method retrieved a list of active order IDs on every invocation, regardless of the validity of the provided ID. Carlann suggested discounting obviously flawed IDs before testing potentially valid ones, so I made the change and we reran the tests. All passed. Unfortunately, that had no effect on the profile. We rolled back the change.

Next, we agreed to implement the cache. Carlann coded a naïve cache. I started to worry about cache coherency, so I added a test to see what happened when a cached order went active. The test failed. Carlann fixed the bug in the cache code, and all tests passed again.

NOTE

Cache coherency requires that the data in the cache change when the data in the underlying data store changes and vice versa. It's easy to get wrong.

Unfortunately, all that effort was a waste. The performance was actually slightly *worse* than before, and the caching code had bloated our previously elegant method into a big mess. We sat in silence for a minute.

What else could it be? Was there a processor bug? Would we have to figure out some way to dump our JIT-compiled code so that we could graph the processor pipelines executing assembly code? Was there a problem with memory pages, or some garbage collector bug? The profiling statistics were clear. As far as we could tell, we had done everything correctly. I reverted all our changes and ran the profiler again: 3.2 seconds per transaction. What were we missing?

Over lunch that day, Carlann and I shared our performance testing woes with the team. "Why don't you let me take a look at it?" offered Nate. "Maybe a fresh pair of eyes will help."

---

[*] This is a fictionalized account inspired by real experiences.

Carlann and I nodded, only too glad to move on to something else. We formed new pairs and worked on nice simple problems for the rest of the day.

The next morning, at the stand-up meeting, Janice told us that she and Nate had found the answer. As it turned out, my initial preconceptions had blinded us to an obvious problem.

There was another method inlined within `verify_order_id()` that didn't show up in the profiler. We didn't look at it because I was sure I understood the code. Janice and Nate, however, stepped through the code. They found a method that was trying to making an unnecessary network connection on each transaction. Fixing it lopped three full seconds off each transaction. They had fixed the problem in less than half an hour.

Oh, and the cache I was sure we would need? We haven't needed it yet.

How to Optimize

Modern computers are complex. Reading a single line of a file from a disk requires the coordination of the CPU, the kernel, a virtual file system, a system bus, the hard drive controller, the hard drive cache, OS buffers, system memory, and scheduling pipelines. Every component exists to solve a problem, and each has certain tricks to squeeze out performance. Is the data in a cache? *Which* cache? How's your memory aligned? Are you reading asynchronously or are you blocking? There are so many variables it's nearly impossible to predict the general performance of any single method.

The days in which a programmer could accurately predict performance by counting instruction clock cycles are long gone, yet some still approach performance with a simplistic, brute-force mindset. They make random guesses about performance based on 20-line test programs, flail around while writing code the first time, leave a twisty mess in the real program, and then take a long lunch.

> The days in which a programmer could predict performance by counting instructions are long gone.

Sometimes that even works. More often, it leaves a complex mess that doesn't benefit overall performance. It can actually make your code slower.

A holistic approach is the only accurate way to optimize such complex systems. Measure the performance of the entire system, make an educated guess about what to change, then remeasure. If the performance gets better, keep the change. If it doesn't, discard it. Once your performance test passes, stop—you're done. Look for any missed refactoring opportunities and run your test suite one more time. Then integrate.

Usually, your performance test will be an end-to-end test. Although I avoid end-to-end tests in other situations (because they're slow and fragile—see "Test-Driven Development" earlier in this chapter), they are often the only accurate way to reproduce real-world performance conditions.

You may be able to use your existing testing tool, such as xUnit, to write your performance tests. Sometimes you get better results from a specialized tool. Either way, encode your performance criteria into the test. Have it return a single, unambiguous pass/fail result as well as performance statistics.

If the test doesn't pass, use the test as input to your profiler. Use the profiler to find the bottlenecks, and focus your efforts on reducing them. Although optimizations often make code more complex, keep your code as clean and simple as possible.

> Use a profiler to guide your optimization efforts.

If you're adding new code, such as a cache, use test-driven development to create that code. If you're removing or refactoring code, you may not need any new tests, but be sure to run your test suite after each change.

Ally
Test-Driven Development (p. 285)

When to Optimize

Optimization has two major drawbacks: it often leads to complex, buggy code, and it takes time away from delivering features. Neither is in your customer's interests. Optimize only when it serves a real, measurable need.

> Performance optimizations must serve the customer's needs.

That doesn't mean you should write stupid code. It means your priority should be code that's clean and elegant. Once a story is done, if you're still concerned about performance, run a test. If performance is a problem, fix it—but let your customer make the business decision about how important that fix is.

XP has an excellent mechanism for prioritizing customer needs: the combination of user stories and release planning. In other words, schedule performance optimization just like any other customer-valued work: with a story.

Allies
Stories (p. 253)
Release Planning (p. 206)

Of course, customers aren't always aware of the need for performance stories, especially not ones with highly technical requirements. If you have a concern about potential performance problems in part of the system, explain your concern in terms of business tradeoffs and risks. They still might not agree. That's OK—they're the experts on business value and priorities. It's their responsibility, and their decision.

Similarly, you have a responsibility to maintain an efficient development environment. If your tests start to take too long, go ahead and optimize until you meet a concrete goal, such as five or ten minutes. Keep in mind that the most common cause of a slow build is too much emphasis on end-to-end tests, not slow code.

TESTERS AND PERFORMANCE

When I work with dedicated testers, they often act as technical investigators for the team. One of the ways they do this is to investigate *nonfunctional requirements* (also called *parafunctional requirements*) such as performance.

Testers should help customers articulate their nonfunctional requirements, then create and maintain test suites that evaluate the software's ability to meet those requirements. These test suites can test stability as well as performance and scalability.

How to Write a Performance Story

Like all stories, performance stories need a concrete, customer-valued goal. A typical story will express that goal in one or more of these terms:

Throughput
    How many operations should complete in a given period of time?

Latency
> How much delay is acceptable between starting and completing a single operation?

Responsiveness
> How much delay is acceptable between starting an operation and receiving feedback about that operation? What kind of feedback is necessary? (Note that latency and responsiveness are related but different. Although good latency leads to good responsiveness, it's possible to have good responsiveness even with poor latency.)

When writing performance stories, think about *acceptable* performance—the minimum necessary for satisfactory results—and *best possible* performance—the point at which further optimization adds little value.

Why have two performance numbers? Performance optimization can consume an infinite amount of time. Sometimes you reach your "best" goal early; this tells you when to stop. Other times you struggle even to meet the "acceptable" goal; this tells you when to keep going.

For example, a story for a server system could be, "Throughput of at least 100 transactions per minute (1,000 is best). Latency of six seconds per transaction (one second is best)." A client system might have the story, "Show progress bar within 1 second of click (0.1 second is best), and complete search within 10 seconds (1 second is best)."

Also consider the conditions under which your story must perform. What kind of workstation or servers will the software run on? What kind of network bandwidth and latency will be available? What other loads will affect the system? How many people will be using it simultaneously? The answers to these questions are likely the same for all stories. Help your customers determine the answers. If you have a standard deployment platform or a minimum platform recommendation, you can base your answers on this standard.

ESTIMATING PERFORMANCE STORIES

You'll often have difficulty estimating performance stories. As with fixing bugs, the cost of optimization stories depends on how long it takes you to find the cause of the performance problem, and you often won't know how long it will take until you actually find it.

To estimate performance stories, timebox your estimate as you do with bug stories (see "Stories" in Chapter 8). If you can't solve the problem within the timeboxed estimate, use that information to create a new optimization story with a more accurate estimate, to schedule for a subsequent iteration.

Questions

Why not optimize as we go? We know a section of code will be slow.

How can you really know until you measure it? If your optimization doesn't affect code maintainability or effort—for example, if you have a choice between sorting libraries and you believe one would be faster for your situation—then it's OK to put it in.

That's not usually the case. Like any other work, the choice to optimize is the choice *not* to do something else. It's a mistake to spend time optimizing code instead of adding a feature the customer wants. Further, optimizing code tends to increase complexity, which is in direct conflict with the goal of producing a simple design. Although we sometimes need to optimize, we shouldn't reduce maintainability when there's no direct customer value.

Ally

Simple Design (p. 314)

If you suspect a performance problem, ask your on-site customers for a ballpark estimate of acceptable performance and run a few tests to see if there's anything to worry about. If there is, talk to your customers about creating and scheduling a story.

How do we write a performance test for situations involving thousands of transactions from many clients?

Good stress-testing tools exist for many network protocols, ranging from ad hoc shell scripts running `telnet` and `netcat` sessions to professional benchmarking applications. Your testers or QA department can recommend specific tools.

Our performance tests take too long to run. How can we maintain a 10-minute build?

Good performance tests often take a long time to run, and they may cause your build to take more time than you like. This is one of the few cases in which a *multistage build* (discussed in "Continuous Integration" in Chapter 7) is appropriate. Run your performance tests asynchronously, as a separate build from your standard 10-minute build (see "Ten-Minute Build" in Chapter 7), when you integrate.

Our customers don't want to write performance stories. They say we should write the software to be fast from the beginning. How can we deal with this?

"Fast" is an abstract idea. Do they mean latency should be low? Should throughput be high? Should the application scale better than linearly with increased activity? Is there a point at which performance can plateau, or suffer, or regress? Is UI responsiveness more important than backend processing speed?

These goals need quantification and require programming time to meet. You can include them as part of existing stories, but separating them into their own stories gives your on-site customers more flexibility in scheduling and achieving business value.

Results

When you optimize code as necessary, you invest in activities that customers have identified as valuable over perceived benefit. You quantify necessary performance improvements and can capture that information in executable tests. You measure, test, and gather feedback to lead you to acceptable solutions for reasonable investments of time and effort. Your code is more maintainable, and you favor simple and straightforward code over highly optimized code.

Contraindications

Software is a complex system based on the interrelationship of many interacting parts. It's easy to guess wrong when it comes to performance.

It's easy to guess wrong when it comes to performance.

Therefore, don't optimize code without specific performance criteria and objective proof, such as a performance test, that you're not yet meeting that criteria. Throw away optimizations that don't objectively improve performance.

Be cautious of optimizing without tests; optimization often adds complexity and increases the risk of defects.

Alternatives

There are no good alternatives to measurement-based optimization.

Many programmers attempt to optimize all code as they write it, often basing their optimizations on programmer folklore about what's "fast." Sometimes these beliefs come from trivial programs that execute an algorithm 1,000 times. A common example of this is a program that compares the speed of StringBuffer to string concatenation in Java or .NET.

Unfortunately, this approach to optimization focuses on trivial algorithmic tricks. Network and hard drive latency are much bigger bottlenecks than CPU performance in modern computing. In other words, if your program talks over a network or writes data to a hard drive—most database updates do both— it probably doesn't matter how fast your string concatenations are.

On the other hand, some programs *are* CPU-bound. Some database queries are easy to cache and don't substantially affect performance. The only way to be sure about a bottleneck is to measure performance under real-world conditions.

Further Reading

"Yet Another Optimization Article" [Fowler 2002b] also discusses the importance of measurement-based optimization. It's available online at *http://www.martinfowler.com/ieeeSoftware/yetOptimization.pdf*.

Exploratory Testing

By Elisabeth Hendrickson

We discover surprises and untested conditions.

Audience

Testers

XP teams have no separate QA department. There's no independent group of people responsible for assessing and ensuring the quality of the final release. Instead, the whole team—customers, programmers, and testers—is responsible for the outcome. On traditional teams, the QA group is often rewarded for finding bugs. On XP teams, there's no incentive program for finding or removing bugs. The goal in XP isn't to find and remove bugs; the goal is *not to write bugs* in the first place. In a well-functioning team, bugs are a rarity—only a handful per month.

Allies

No Bugs (p. 160)
The Whole Team (p. 28)

Does that mean testers have no place on an XP team? No! Good testers have the ability to look at software from a new perspective, to find surprises, gaps, and holes. It takes time for the team to learn which mistakes to avoid. By providing essential information about what the team overlooks, testers enable the team to improve their work habits and achieve their goal of producing zero bugs.

> **NOTE**
> Beware of misinterpreting the testers' role as one of process improvement and enforcement. Don't set up quality gates or monitor adherence to the process. The *whole team* is responsible for process improvement. Testers are respected peers in this process, providing information that allows the whole team to benefit.

One particularly effective way of finding surprises, gaps, and holes is *exploratory testing*: a style of testing in which you learn about the software while simultaneously designing and executing tests, using feedback from the previous test to inform the next. Exploratory testing enables you to discover emergent behavior, unexpected side effects, holes in the implementation (and thus in the automated test coverage), and risks related to quality attributes that cross story boundaries such as security, performance, and reliability. It's the perfect complement to XP's raft of automated testing techniques.

Exploratory testing predates XP. [Kaner] coined the term in the book *Testing Computer Software*, although the practice of exploratory testing certainly preceded the book, probably by decades. Since the book came out, people such as Cem Kaner, James and Jonathan Bach, James Lyndsay, Jonathan Kohl, and Elisabeth Hendrickson have extended the concept of exploratory testing into a discipline.

About Exploratory Testing

Philosophically, exploratory testing is similar to test-driven development and incremental design: rather than designing a huge suite of tests up-front, you design a single test in your head, execute it against the software, and see what happens. The result of each test leads you to design the next, allowing you to pursue directions that you wouldn't have anticipated if you had attempted to design all the tests up-front. Each test is a little experiment that investigates the capabilities and limitations of the emerging software.

Exploratory testing can be done manually or with the assistance of automation. Its defining characteristic is not how we drive the software but rather the tight feedback loop between test design, test execution, and results interpretation.

Exploratory testing works best when the software is ready to be explored—that is, when stories are "done done." You don't have to test stories that were finished in the current iteration. It's nice to have that sort of rapid feedback, but some stories won't be "done done" until the last day of the iteration. That's OK—remember, you're not using exploratory testing to guarantee quality; you're using it provide information about how the team's *process* guarantees quality.

Ally

"Done Done" (p. 156)

NOTE

This switch in mindset takes a little while to get used to. Your exploratory testing is not a means of evaluating the software through exhaustive testing. Instead, you're acting as a technical investigator—checking weak points to help the team discover ways to prevent bugs. You can also use exploratory testing to provide the team with other useful data, such as information about the software's performance characteristics.

Exploratory testers use the following four tools to explore the software.

Tool #1: Charters

Some people claim that exploratory testing is simply haphazard poking at the software under test. This isn't true, any more than the idea that American explorers Lewis and Clark mapped the Northwest by haphazardly tromping about in the woods. Before they headed into the wilderness, Lewis and Clark knew where they were headed and why they were going. President Thomas Jefferson had given them a charter:[*]

> The Object of your mission is to explore the Missouri river & such principal stream of it as by [its] course and communication with the waters of the Pacific ocean, whether the Columbia, Oregon, Colorado or any other river may offer the most direct & practicable water communication across this continent for the purpose of commerce.

Similarly, before beginning an exploratory session, a tester should have some idea of what to explore in the system and what kinds of things to look for. This *charter* helps keep the session focused.

NOTE

An exploratory session typically lasts one to two hours.

The charter for a given exploratory session might come from a just-completed story (e.g., "Explore the Coupon feature"). It might relate to the interaction among a collection of stories (e.g., "Explore interactions between the Coupon feature and the Bulk Discount feature"). It might involve a quality attribute, such as stability, reliability, or performance ("Look for evidence that the Coupon feature impacts performance"). Generate charters by working with the team to understand what information would be the most useful to move the project forward.

Charters are the testing equivalent of a story. Like stories, they work best when written down. They may be as informal as a line on a whiteboard or a card, but a written charter provides a touchstone the tester can refer to in order to ensure she's still on track.

---

[*] *http://www.lewis-clark.org/content/content-article.asp?ArticleID=1047.*

Tool #2: Observation

Automated tests only verify the behavior that programmers write them to verify, but humans are capable of noticing subtle clues that suggest all is not right. Exploratory testers are continuously alert for anything out of the ordinary. This may be an editable form field that should be read-only, a hard drive that spun up when the software should not be doing any disk access, or a value in a report that looks out of place.

Such observations lead exploratory testers to ask more questions, run more tests, and explore in new directions. For example, a tester may notice that a web-based system uses parameters in the URL. "Aha!" thinks the tester. "I can easily edit the URL." Where the URL says *http://stage.example.com/edit?id=42*, the tester substitutes *http://stage.example.com/edit?id=9999999*.

Tool #3: Notetaking

While exploring, it's all too easy to forget where you've been and where you're going. Exploratory testers keep a notepad beside them as they explore and periodically take notes on the actions they take. You can also use screen recorders such as Camtasia to keep track of what you do. After all, it's quite frustrating to discover a bug only to find that you have no idea what you did to cause the software to react that way. Notes and recordings tell you what you were doing not just at the time you encountered surprising behavior but also in the minutes or hours before.

Be especially careful to keep notes about anything that deserves further investigation. If you cannot follow a path of testing in the current session, you want to remember to explore that area in more detail later. These are opportunities for further exploratory testing.

Tool #4: Heuristics

Remember that exploratory testing involves simultaneously designing and executing tests. Some test design techniques are well known, such as *boundary testing*. If you have a field that's supposed to accept numbers from 0–100, you'll probably try valid values like 0, 100, and something in the middle, and invalid values like –1 and 101. Even if you had never heard the term boundary testing, you'd probably consider trying such tests.

A *heuristic* is a guide: a technique that aids in your explorations. Boundary testing is an example of a test heuristic. Experienced testers use a variety of heuristics, gleaned from an understanding of how software systems work as well as from experience and intuition about what causes software to break. You can improve your exploratory efforts by creating and maintaining a catalog of heuristics that are worth remembering when exploring your software. Of course, that same catalog can also be a welcome reference for the programmers as they implement the software.

Some of your heuristics will be specific to your domain. For example, if you work with networking software, you must inevitably work with IP addresses. You probably test your software to see how it handles invalid IP addresses ("999.999.999.999"), special IP addresses ("127.0.0.1"), and IPv6 style addresses ("::1/128"). Others are applicable to nearly any software project. The following are a few to get you started.

None, Some, All

For example, if your users can have permissions, try creating users with no permissions, some permissions, and all permissions. In one system I tested, the system treated users with no permissions as administrators. Granting a user no permissions resulted in the user having root access.

Goldilocks: too big, too small, just right

Boundary tests on a numeric field are one example of Golidlocks tests. Another example might be uploading an image file: try uploading a 3 MB picture (too big), a file with nothing in it (too small), and a file of comfortable size (50 KB).

Position: beginning, middle, end

Position can apply to an edit control: edit at the beginning of a line, middle of a line, end of a line. It can apply to the location of data in a file being parsed. It can apply to an item selected from a list, or where you're inserting an item into a list.

Count: zero, one, many

For example, you could create invoices with zero line items, one line item, and many line items. Or you might perform a search for zero items, one item, or many pages of items. Many systems have a small typographical error related to plurals—that is, they report "1 items found" instead of "1 item found."

Similarly, count can apply in numerous situations: a count of dependent data records (a customer with zero addresses, one address, many addresses, or a group with zero members, one member, many members), a count of events (zero transactions, one transaction, many simultaneous transactions), or anything else that can be counted.

CRUD: create, read, update, delete

For each type of entity, and each data field, try to create it, read it, update it, and delete it. Now try CRUD it while violating system constraints such as permissions. Try to CRUD in combination with Goldilocks, Position, Count, and Select heuristics. For example, delete the last line item on an invoice, then read it; update the first line item; delete a customer with zero, one, or many invoices, etc.

Command Injection

Wherever your software supports text coming from an external source (such as a UI or a Web Services interface), ensure it doesn't ever interpret incoming text as a command—whether an SQL, a JavaScript, or a shell/command-line command. For example, a single quote in a text field will sometimes raise SQL exceptions; entering the word tester's will cause some applications to respond with an SQL error.

Data Type Attacks

For each type of input, try values that push common boundaries or that violate integrity constraints. Some examples: in date fields, try February 29 and 30. Also try dates more than 100 years ago. Try invalid times, like 13:75. For numbers, try the huge ($4,294,967,297 = 2^{32} + 1$) and the tiny (0.0000000000000001). Try scientific notation (1E-16). Try negative numbers, particularly where negative numbers should not be allowed, as with purchase price. For strings, try entering long strings (more than 5,000 characters), leaving fields blank, and entering a single space. Try various characters including common field delimiters (` | / \ , ; : & < > ^ * ? Tab). The list could go on, but you get the idea.

An Example

"Let's decide on a charter for this session," Jill said, settling into the seat next to Michael. Jill was one of the team's testers; Michael was a programmer. "What should we focus on?"

"You know us," Michael replied. "Our code doesn't have any bugs!" He grinned, knowing what was coming.

"Oooh, you'll pay for that one." Jill smiled. "Although I have to say our quality is better than any other team I've worked with. How many bugs did we have last month?"

"It's been a bit high, actually." Michael counted on his fingers. "There was that installer issue... and the networking problem...." He paused. "Four."

"Let's see how that holds up. What's new in the code?"

"Some fairly routine stuff," Michael said. "One thing that's brand-new is our support for multilingual input. But there's nothing to find there—we tested it thoroughly."

"I love a challenge!" Jill said with a wicked grin. "Besides, character-set issues are a rich source of bugs. Let's take a look at that."

"Sure." Michael wrote a card for the session: Explore Internationalization. He clipped the card to the monitor so it would remind them to keep on track.

Jill took the keyboard first. "Let's start with the basics. That will help us know what's going wrong if we see anything strange later on." As she navigated to a data entry screen, Michael wrote the date and time at the top of a new page in his notepad and prepared to take notes.

Jill opened up a character viewer and pasted together a string of gibberish: German, Hebrew, Greek, Japanese, and Arabic characters. "Let's use the CRUD heuristic to make sure this stuff gets into the database and comes back properly." Moving quickly, she saved the text, opened up a database viewer to make sure it was present in the database, then closed the application and reloaded it. Everything was intact. Next, she edited the string, saved it again, and repeated her check. Finally, she deleted the entry. "Looks good."

"Wait a minute," Michael said. "I just had an idea. We're not supposed to allow the user to save blank strings. What if we use a Unicode space rather than a regular space?"

"I'll try it." Jill went back to work. Everything she tried was successfully blocked. "It all looks good so far, but I have a special trick." She grinned as she typed #FEFF into her character viewer. "This character used to mean 'zero-width no-break space.' Now it's just a byte-order mark. Either way, it's the nastiest character I can throw at your input routines." She pressed Save.

Nothing happened. "Score one for the good guys," Jill murmured. "The data input widgets look fairly solid. I know from past experience that you've abstracted those widgets so that if one is working, they're probably all working." Michael nodded, and she added, "I might want to double-check a few of those later, but I think our time is better spent elsewhere."

"OK, what should we look at next?" Michael asked.

"A few things come to mind for us to check: data comparison, sorting, and translation to other formats. Unicode diacritical marks can be encoded in several ways, so two strings that are technically identical might not be encoded using the same bytes. Sorting is problematic because Unicode characters aren't sorted in the same order that they're represented in binary..."

"...and format translation is nasty because of all the different code page and character-set issues out there," Michael finished. He wrote the three ideas—data comparison, sorting, and translation—on his notepad.

"You said it," Jill agreed. "How about starting with the nasty one?"

"Sounds good." Michael reached for the keyboard. "My turn to type," he said, smiling. He handed Jill the notepad so she could continue the notetaking. "Now, where could the code page issues be lurking...?"

When You Find Bugs

Exploratory testing provides feedback about the software and also about the effectiveness of the team's process. When it reveals a bug, it indicates that the team may not be working as effectively as it could. To remedy, fix your software *and* your process as described in "No Bugs" in Chapter 7.

Ally
No Bugs (p. 160)

If you've already used the feedback from exploratory testing to improve both the software and the process, but you're consistently finding a lot of bugs, it means the process is still broken. Don't give up: look for root causes and keep plugging away. It's often a simple case of trying to do too much in too little time.

When the bugs are rampant, you may be tempted to add a QA department to catch the bugs. This may provide a temporary fix, but it's the first step down a slippery slope. Here is an example:

Imagine a team that has been struggling with velocity because stories just never seem to be "done done," as is often the case when customers finds bugs in "done" stories. The programmers are frustrated that they can't seem to prevent or detect the problems that result in their customers rejecting stories.

"I give up," says Wilma to her partner, Betty. "This story is taking too long, and there are too many other stories in the queue. Let's ask Jeff to test this and tell us where all the problems are. He's good at finding bugs."

In fact, Jeff is great at finding bugs. The next morning he delivers a stack of sticky notes to Wilma and Betty that detail a bunch of bugs. They fix the bugs and deliver the story. The customer accepts it, smiling for the first time in weeks. "That was *great*!" says Wilma. "We finally *finished* something!"

On the next story, Betty turns to Wilma and says, "You know, Jeff was so good at finding bugs in the last story...."

"Yeah," Wilma agrees. "Even though there are some more error conditions we could think through, let's see what Jeff has to say."

The pattern continues. The more that programmers rely on testers to find bugs *for* them, the fewer bugs they find themselves. Testers find more and more bugs, but in the end, quality gets worse.[*] The key to having no bugs is not to get better testers, but for the team to take responsibility for producing bug-free software—*before* testers try it. Instead of relying on testers to get the bugs out, use the information that exploratory testing provides to improve your process.

Ally
No Bugs (p. 160)

---

[*] I wrote about this effect in "Better Testing, Worse Quality," at *http://testobsessed.com/wordpress/wp-content/uploads/2006/12/btwq.pdf*. Page past the end of the slideshow to find it.

Questions

Should testers pair with other members of the team?

This is up to your team. Pairing with programmers and customers helps break down some of the natural barriers between testers and other team members, and it helps information flow better throughout the team. On the other hand, programmers may not always have time to pair with testers. Find a good balance.

Won't the burden of exploratory testing keep getting bigger over the course of the project?

It shouldn't. Sometimes teams use exploratory testing as a form of manual regression testing; with each iteration, they explore the new features, and the existing features, and the interactions, and so on. They put so much on the list of things to explore that the time needed for exploratory testing during the iteration becomes unmanageable.

The flaw in this approach is using exploratory testing as a means of regression testing. Use test-driven development to create a comprehensive, automated regression test suite. Focus your exploratory testing on new features (and their interactions with existing features), particularly those features that do things differently from previous features.

> **Ally**
> Test-Driven Development
> (p. 285)

Just as you timebox your releases and work on just the most important features, you can timebox your explorations and test just the most important charters.

How can we get better at exploratory testing?

Exploratory testing involves a set of skills that can be learned. To improve, you should:

Practice
> You can test more than the software your team is developing. Whenever you use software for your own purposes, like word processing or email, try testing it. Also consider applying your testing skills to open source projects.

Get feedback
> Find out what surprises other people discovered, and ask yourself why you didn't see them. Sometimes it's because there were more test conditions you might have tried, so you can add new tricks to your heuristics toolbox. Other times it's because you didn't understand the significance of what you were seeing; you saw the same behavior but didn't recognize it as a bug.

Share tips and techniques
> You can share ideas within your team, and you can reach out to the broader community. Online discussion forums are a good place to start. Other options include round table–style meetings. For example, James Bach hosts WHET, the Workshop on Heuristics and Exploratory Techniques, and James Lyndsay hosts LEWT, the London Exploratory Workshop in Testing. Both are gathering places where testers share stories and experiences.

Results

When you use exploratory testing, you discover information about both the software and the process used to create that software. You sometimes discover missing test cases, incomplete or incorrect understanding of the story, and conversations that should have happened but didn't. Each surprise gives you an opportunity to improve both the software and your development practices. As a team, you use this information to improve your process and reduce the number of bugs found in the future.

Contraindications

Don't attempt to use exploratory testing as a regression testing strategy. Regression tests should be automated.

Only do exploratory testing when it is likely to uncover new information and you are in a position to act on that information. If, for example, there is already a list of known bugs for a given story, additional exploratory testing will waste time rediscovering known issues. Fix the bugs first.

Alternatives

You can use exploratory testing as a mechanism for bug hunting when working with software, particularly legacy software, that you suspect to be buggy. However, beware of relying on exploratory testing or any other testing approach to ensure all the bugs are caught. They won't be.

Some teams don't do any manual or end-to-end testing with XP. These teams are using another mechanism to confirm that they don't produce bugs—presumably, they're relying on user feedback. This is OK if you actually don't produce bugs, which is certainly possible, but it's better to confirm that *before* giving software to users. Still, you might get away with it if the software isn't mission-critical and you have forgiving users.

Other teams use testers in a more traditional role, relying on them to find bugs rather than committing to deliver bug-free code. In my experience, these teams have lower quality and higher bug rates, probably as a result of the "Better Testing, Worse Quality" dynamic.

Further Reading

"General Functionality and Stability Test Procedure for Microsoft Windows Logo, Desktop Applications Edition" [Bach 1999] is the first widely published reference on how to do exploratory testing. The WinLogo certification assures customers that the software behaves itself on Windows. But how do you create a systematic process for assessing the capabilities and limitations of an arbitrary desktop application in a consistent way? Microsoft turned to James Bach, already well known for his work on exploratory testing. The resulting test procedure was made available to independent software vendors (ISVs) and used by certifiers like Veritest. It's online at *http://www.testingcraft.com/bach-exploratory-procedure.pdf*.

"Session-Based Test Management" [Bach 2000] is the first published article that explains in detail how to use session-based test management, which James Bach and his brother Jonathan devised, and which I discussed as Charters and Sessions earlier in this chapter. One of the challenges of exploratory testing is how to manage the process: stay focused, track progress, and ensure the effort continues to yield value. This is the solution. The article is online at *http://www.satisfice.com/articles/sbtm.pdf*.

"Did I Remember To" [Hunter] is a great list of heuristics, framed as things to remember to test. The list is particularly great for Windows applications, but it includes ideas that are applicable to other technologies as well. It's online at *http://blogs.msdn.com/micahel/articles/175571.aspx*.

"Rigorous Exploratory Testing" [Hendrickson] sets out to debunk the myth that exploratory testing is just banging on keyboards, and discusses how exploratory testing can be rigorous without being formal. The article is online at *http://www.testobsessed.com/2006/04/19/rigorous-exploratory-testing/*.

"User Profiles and Exploratory Testing" [Kohl 2005a] is a nice reminder that different users experience software in different ways, and it provides guidance on characterizing user behavior to support exploratory testing. It's online at *http://www.kohl.ca/blog/archives/000104.html*.

"Exploratory Testing on Agile Teams" [Kohl 2005b] presents a case study of using automation-assisted exploratory testing to isolate a defect on an Agile project—which flouts the belief that exploratory testing is a purely manual activity. It complements this chapter nicely. Read it online at *http://www.informit.com/articles/article.asp?p=405514&rl=1*.

"A Survey of Exploratory Testing" [Marick] provides a nice collection of published work related to exploratory testing, including [Bach 1999]'s "General Functionality and Stability Test Procedure for Microsoft Windows Logo." Online at *http://www.testingcraft.com/exploratory.html*.

"Exploring Exploratory Testing" [Tinkham & Kaner] is an in-depth discussion of how exploratory testers do what they do, including strategies such as questioning and using heuristics. Based on work funded in part by an NSF grant, this paper elaborates on exploratory testing practices missing from the then-current draft of the IEEE's *Software Engineering Body of Knowledge* (SWEBOK). Available online at *http://www.testingeducation.org/a/explore.pdf*.

PART III

Mastering Agility

CHAPTER 10

Values and Principles

Until now, I've talked about a very specific approach to agility: one style of applying XP's practices. That's only the beginning.

No process is perfect. Every approach to development has some potential for improvement. Ultimately, your goal is to remove every barrier between your team and the success of your project, and fluidly adapt your approach as conditions change. *That* is agility.

To master the art of agile development, you need experience and mindfulness. *Experience* helps you see how agile methods work. *Mindfulness* helps you understand your experiences. Experience again allows you to experiment with changes. Mindfulness again allows you to reflect on why your experiments worked—or didn't work—in practice. Experience and mindfulness, endlessly joined, are the path to mastery.

So far, this book has focused on experience. Before you can reflect on how agile methods work, you need to experience an agile method working. With its emphasis on practicing XP, this book has given you the tools to do so.

Yet practicing XP isn't enough—you need mindfulness, too. You must pay attention to what happens around you. You must think about what's happening and, more importantly, *why* it's happening. Ask questions. Make small changes. Observe the results. I can't teach you mindfulness; only you have the power to do it.

I can, however, give you some things to think about as you learn. The XP practices are a manifestation of deeper agile values and principles. Think about these as you use XP. When your situation changes, use the values and principles to guide you in changing your practices.

Commonalities

Can any set of principles really represent agile development? After all, agility is just an umbrella term for a variety of methods, most of which came about long before the term "agile" was coined.

The answer is yes: agile methods do share common values and principles. In researching this part of the book, I collected over a hundred different values and principles from several agile sources.* They formed five themes: Improve the Process, Rely on People, Eliminate Waste, Deliver Value, and Seek Technical Excellence. Each is compatible with any of the specific agile methods.

The following chapters explain these themes in terms of principles and practices. Each chapter includes anecdotes about applying the principles to situations beyond standard XP. Where possible, I've borrowed existing names for specific principles.

About Values, Principles, and Practices

Values are ideals. They're abstract, yet identifiable and distinct. For example, XP's values are:

Courage
> To make the right decisions, even when they're difficult, and to tell stakeholders the truth when they need to hear it

Communication
> To give the right people the right information when they can use it to its maximum advantage

Simplicity
> To discard the things we want but don't actually need

Feedback
> To learn the appropriate lessons at every possible opportunity

Respect
> To treat ourselves and others with dignity, and to acknowledge expertise and our mutual desire for success

Principles are applications of those ideals to an industry. For example, the value of simplicity leads us to focus on the essentials of development. As [Beck 2004] puts it, this principle is to "travel light." [Cockburn] says, "Excess methodology weight is costly," and "Discipline, skills, and understanding counter process, formality, and documentation."

Practices are principles applied to a specific type of project. XP's practices, for example, call for colocated teams of up to 20 people. "Sit Together" in Chapter 6 and "The Whole Team" in Chapter 3 embody the principles of simplicity because face-to-face communication reduces the need for formal requirements documentation.

Further Reading

The following books are excellent resources that go into far more detail than I have room for here. Each has a different focus, so they complement each other nicely.

Agile Software Development [Cockburn] focuses on the "individuals and interactions" aspect of agile development. Most of his thoughts correspond to the principles I outline in Chapter 12.

---

* [Beck et al.], [Beck 1999], [Beck 2004], [Cockburn], [Highsmith], [Poppendieck & Poppendieck], [Schwaber & Beedle], [Subramaniam & Hunt], [Shore 2005b], and [Stapleton].

Lean Software Development: An Agile Toolkit for Software Development Managers [Poppendieck & Poppendieck] applies concepts from Lean Manufacturing to agile development, with emphasis on the principles that I describe in Chapter 13 and Chapter 14.

Agile Management for Software Engineering [Anderson 2003] is a bit dense, but it has detailed coverage of the Theory of Constraints, which I discuss in "Pursue Throughput" in Chapter 13.

Practices of an Agile Developer [Subramaniam & Hunt] is an easy-to-read collection of guidelines and advice for agile developers, similar to what I discuss in Chapter 15.

Agile Software Development Ecosystems [Highsmith] looks at several agile methods through the lens of people and principles. Read this if you want to understand agile development in depth.

Extreme Programming Explained [Beck 1999, Beck 2004] discusses the thought process behind XP. It will give you more insight into how agile principles relate to the XP practices. Try to get both editions, if you can; they describe the same basic process from very different perspectives. Studying both books and looking for the underlying commonalities will teach you a lot about agile values and principles.

CHAPTER 11

Improve the Process

Agile methods are more than a list of practices to follow. When your team has learned how to perform them effectively, you can become a great team by using the practices to modify your process.

Throughout this book, I've drawn attention to places where the way you perform XP may vary from how I explain it. No two teams are exactly alike. You'll do some things differently because you have different people and different needs. As you master the art of agile development, you'll learn how and when to modify your process to take advantage of your specific situation and opportunities.

Understand Your Project

To improve your process, you must understand how it affects your project. You need to take advantage of feedback—from the code, from the team, from customers and stakeholders—so you can understand what works well and what doesn't. Always pay attention to what's happening around you. Ask "why": why do we follow this practice? Why is this practice working? Why *isn't* this practice working?

Ask team members for their thoughts. There's an element of truth in every complaint, so encourage open discussion. As a team, reflect on what you've learned. When you discover something new, be a mentor; when you have questions, ask a mentor. Help each other understand what you're doing and why.

In Practice

XP is full of feedback loops—giant conduits of information that you should use to improve your work. Root-cause analysis and retrospectives clearly improve the team's understanding, and other practices reinforce the principles in more subtle ways.

For example, sitting and working together as a whole team gives team members opportunities to observe and absorb information. This is tactical feedback, and it can reveal strategic issues when something unexpected happens. Stand-up meetings and the informative workspace contribute to an information-rich environment.

Perhaps counterintuitively, the practices of energized work, slack, and pair programming also spread useful information. When team members are under pressure, they have trouble thinking about ways they can improve their work. Energized work and slack reduce that pressure. Pair programming gives one person in each pair time to think about strategy.

Test-driven development, exploratory testing, real customer involvement, iteration demos, and frequent releases all provide information about the project, from code to user response.

Beyond Practices

Large and successful free and open source software projects often see a lot of turnover. In the five years I've worked on one of these projects, dozens of people have come and gone. That's normal, especially for volunteers. It can take some time and effort to manage that change in personnel.

Recently, the project lead and our most prolific contributor had to reduce their time commitments. It took us a few months to realize we had lost ground, especially because no one had taken over the project lead's job of producing timely releases. With everyone else reviewing changes and implementing features, our process assumed the lead was still making releases.

This experience helped us see that tying such an important task to a single person was a mistake. To fix it, we all agreed to divide the work. Every month, one of us takes final responsibility for creating the release; this person produces the final tested bundle, makes the appropriate announcements, and uploads the bundle to the master distribution site. With six people available and a release schedule planned to the day, we've found a much healthier rhythm for making regular releases. If one or more developers are unavailable, several other people can perform the same function. It's worked—we've regained our velocity and started to attract new developers again.

Tune and Adapt

When you see the need for a change, modify your process. Make the change for your team alone; though your team may be one of many, it's OK to do things differently. Every team's needs are different.

These changes require tuning. Think of them as experiments; make small, isolated changes that allow you to understand the results. Be specific about your expectations and about the measurements for judging success. These changes are sources of feedback and learning. Use the results of your experiments to make further changes. Iterate until you're satisfied with the results.

Some experiments will fail, and others may actually make the process worse. Team members need to be flexible and adaptive. Your team needs to have the courage to experiment and occasionally fail.

Changing your process requires you to have a holistic view of what you do and why. New agile teams should be cautious about changing their process, as they don't yet have the experience necessary to give them that holistic understanding. Once you have the experience, use the feedback from your changes to improve your process and your understanding of agility.

In Practice

Tuning and adapting is implicit in XP; teams are supposed to make changes whenever they have a reason to do so. Many XP teams use retrospectives to give themselves a more explicit venue for considering changes. I've made retrospectives an explicit practice in this book as well.

The courage to adapt is an important principle, but it's not explicit in any single XP practice. Rather, it's a facet of XP's *Courage* value. Similarly, the need for a holistic view has been an ongoing theme in this book, but no specific practice reflects that principle. Instead, it's part of XP's *Feedback* value.

Beyond Practices

My anecdote about changing our team's release process made it sound like it went more smoothly than it really did. When the project lead left, he took with him much of the knowledge needed to produce a release, knowledge that existed only in his head and not in permanent documents anywhere. We knew this, but decided to take over the release process anyway.

Why? First, we had no choice if we wanted to return to monthly releases, even if there were problems with the process. More importantly, this was the best way we could think of to *identify* problems with our written process. If someone could follow the instructions to produce a full release, even if he had never made a release before, the instructions were good. If not, he could make a list of problems and we'd address them as a group.

That's what happened. We discovered several problems—our distribution system wouldn't distribute our release to the global mirrors, it didn't index our files correctly, and our automatic installer completely failed to configure the source code for custom builds. Fixing each problem required us to improve our overall process.

We made some mistakes, but it was worth it. We've conducted several monthly releases so far. Though the first few were rocky, they've improved over time. It's painless to release our software again.

Break the Rules

Rules are important—they exist for a reason. Yet rules can't anticipate all situations. When established conventions thwart your attempts to succeed, it's time to break the rules.

How do you know when to break the rules? First, you need to understand them and their reasons for existing. That comes with experience. Once you understand the rules, exercise *pragmatic idealism*: establish an underlying set of ideals—such as the agile principles—based on practical results. Embrace your ideals, but ground them in pragmatism. For example, "We want to avoid integration hell" is a pragmatic result that leads to the ideal of "We will *never* check in code that doesn't build or pass its tests."

With the guidance of your principles, question existing conventions. Ask yourself, "Why do we follow this rule? Do we really need it?" Modify, work around, or break the rules that prevent you from achieving success.

Remember, though, that organizational support is central to success. If you break a rule, you might step on someone's toes. Be prepared to explain your experiment. You'll find it's easier to get away with breaking rules when you've demonstrated that you're trustworthy and effective.

In Practice

Rule-breaking exists more in XP folklore than in XP practices. For example, early XP teams told stories of coming in to work on a weekend to dismantle cubicle walls, assuming that it would be easier to ask forgiveness than permission. Ron Jeffries, one of XP's earliest proponents, is famous for saying, "They're just rules"[*] in regard to the XP practices. He later clarified his statement:

> They're not rules, OK? They're techniques. They're tools we apply. They're habits. They're practices—things we practice.... They are, however, darn good things to know how to do, and do well.[†]

Beyond Practices

One of the seemingly inviolate rules of XP is that you always keep code quality high. It's even an agile principle (see "Eliminate Technical Debt" in Chapter 15). Yet even this rule is just a rule.

As cofounder of a brand-new startup, I had an opportunity to show our software at an industry conference. We had a spike solution (see "Spike Solutions" in Chapter 9) that demonstrated some concepts of our software, but it had no tests. We had four weeks to produce a compelling demo.

The right thing to do would have been to redevelop the spike using proper test-driven development. In another situation, I would have done so. Yet in this case, my partner wasn't as familiar with TDD as I was. I had other time commitments and couldn't do much development work. Our choices were for me to forgo my other commitments and use TDD, introduce technical debt by developing the spike, or have no demo for the conference.

We chose to develop the spike. Breaking the rules didn't bother us as much as the fact that developing the spike would incur large amounts of technical debt, but the trade-off seemed worthwhile. We created a great demo to show, and the product was a big hit at the conference. Then we came home and felt the pain of our decision. Four weeks of accumulated technical debt stalled our little startup for almost three *months*. That's a long time.

Still, breaking the rules was the right decision for us under the circumstances. The buzz we generated around our product made the cost of technical debt worthwhile. The key to our success was that we *carefully and knowledgeably* broke a rule to achieve a specific purpose. We were also lucky. None of our competitors introduced a similar feature in the several months that we spent paying down our debt.

[*] "They're just rules!", *http://www.xprogramming.com/Practices/justrule.htm*.

[†] "I was wrong. They're not rules!", *http://www.xprogramming.com/xpmag/jatNotRules.htm*.

CHAPTER 12

Rely on People

Alistair Cockburn's 1999 paper, "Characterizing people as non-linear, first-order components in software development," argues that the people involved in making software affect the project as much as any method or practice. Although Cockburn calls this "stupendously obvious," he rightly describes it as often overlooked.

Almost every challenge in building great software is, in some way, a people problem. That challenge may be communicating effectively, dealing with the unpredictability of moods and motives, or figuring out how to harness people's desire to do the right thing for the team and the project. Few problems are solely technical.

Agile methods put people and their interactions at the center of all decisions. How can we best work together? How can we communicate effectively? Successful software projects must address these questions.

Build Effective Relationships

Unless you're writing software by and for yourself, you will have to deal with at least one other person somewhere during the process. A grudging détente is not enough; you need to work together *effectively*. This means forming solid working relationships that are built on honesty, trust, cooperation, openness, and mutual respect.

You can't force people to do this. The best your agile method can do is *support* these sorts of relationships. For example, one way to engender healthy interaction is to have people sit together and collaborate in pursuit of common goals.

It's far easier, unfortunately, to craft your method in a way that discourages healthy relationships. An extreme example (sadly, one that actually happens) is forcing all developer communication with stakeholders to go through business analysts. As another example, a sure way to damage programmer/tester relationships is to require them to communicate solely through the bug-tracking system.

Blame-oriented cultures also sabotage relationships. Get rid of blame by introducing collaboration and avoiding practices that indicate a lack of trust. Rather than forcing stakeholders to sign a requirements document, work together to identify and clarify requirements and review progress iteratively. Rather than telling developers that they can't produce any bugs and testers that they must find all the bugs, ask developers and testers to work together to ensure that *customers* don't find any bugs.

It's easy—especially for technical people—to get caught up in the details of a particular solution. Encourage cooperation and experimentation while respecting the distinction between ideas and people. Credit isn't important. Being right isn't important. Treating your team members with respect and cooperating to produce great software *is* important.

In Practice

Although no process can enforce effective relationships, XP does a good job of *enabling* them. The most obvious example is the use of a cross-functional team in a common workspace. With the weekly iteration demo, teams reach out to stakeholders as well. XP also emphasizes the importance of including real customers in the process.

Everyday practices such as stand-up meetings, collective code ownership, ubiquitous language, the planning game, and pair programming help reinforce the idea that team members work together to achieve common goals.

Beyond Practices

XP recommends colocated teams for a reason: it's much easier to communicate and form solid working relationships when you're all in the same room. Yet some teams can't or won't sit together. How do you deal with this challenge?

One of my hobbies is working on a long-term free software project, which consists of a core team of developers located around the globe. We communicate virtually, and this has led to some challenges.

For example, one developer—I'll call him "Bob"—has an abrupt communication style. This occasionally leads to friction with people who don't know Bob well and think he's being rude. In fact, he's just not a native English speaker and is laconic by nature. This sort of problem seems to occur in all distributed teams; it's easy to assume the worst about someone's motivation when you can't talk face-to-face.

To prevent the problems from escalating, our team decided to meet in person as often as possible—typically three or four times a year. Bob attended a recent gathering, and afterward, team members commented that they understood his communication style much better. They realized it wasn't personal, but rather an artifact of his culture.

Our team also instituted weekly meetings. They're virtual meetings, but they help us understand what everyone is working on. The meetings contribute to our cohesiveness and shared direction, and they help curtail unhelpful tangents.

A distributed team—particularly one that's staffed with part-time volunteers, as ours is—always faces communication challenges, so it's important to address them and make changes that enable you to work and communicate better.

Let the Right People Do the Right Things

A functioning team is not enough. You need to have the *right* people working well together. You need a diverse range of expertise. Once you find the right people, trust them to do their jobs. Instead of creating a process that protects your organization from its employees, create a process that enables team members to excel.

Give the team control over its own work. They're the experts—that's why they're on the team. Trust them, and back up that trust by giving them authority over the project's success. If you can't trust your team, you don't have the right people. No one is perfect, but you need a team that, *as a whole*, you can trust.

NOTE

Authority over day-to-day decisions extends to your agile process as well. Use the agile principles to change *your own* process rather than allowing someone to impose process changes.

Within the team, anyone can be a leader. Encourage team members to turn to the person or people most qualified to make a necessary decision. For example, when you need design decisions, ask your senior programmers for help. When you need business decisions, ask your most experienced businessperson to make the right choice.

Leadership doesn't mean pounding on the table or shouting, "I'm most senior, so we'll do it my way!" Leadership comes by leading. If the team thinks you're most qualified to make a decision, they'll follow your guidance. If not, don't act as if you have authority over them, even if you think you do. Managers, rather than telling the team what to do, let the team tell you what they need *you* to do to help them succeed.

In Practice

This principle has two parts: first, get the right people, then give them the power do their work right. XP supports the first part by including customers and testers on the team and involving real customers when appropriate.

XP supports the second part—giving team members the power to do their work right—with many of its practices. XP has a coach, not a team lead, who helps, not directs, team members. The planning game helps the team share leadership by acknowledging the expertise of both developers and business experts. As XP teams mature, they practice *self-organization*; they leave behind rules about who is in charge of what, and instead turn to the natural leader for the current task.

Beyond Practices

Adrian Howard tells the story of a team taking responsibility for its success, which helped the organization give it the authority it needed:[*]

> I worked on a (nonagile) project a few years ago where we had a big cork board that had cards for the tasks each of us was doing divided into three areas:

---

[*] Originally posted to the XP mailing list, *http://tech.groups.yahoo.com/group/extremeprogramming/message/88438*. Used with permission.

1. Todo
2. In progress (subdivided by developer)
3. Done

Cards migrated from 1->2->3 over time. Big open plan office so everybody could see the board.

We were initially cursed by interruptions... we drew management's attention to the deadline slippage they caused with very little effect. The development team was regularly shouted at for missing deadlines. Much sadness, overtime and crying into pints.

After some discussion the dev team created a new policy with the cards. As soon as somebody was asked to do something not related to an in-progress task they would get up and, taking the interrupter to the board, move their current in-progress card back to the todo area of the cork board. Only then would they go and solve the new problem.

After a couple of weeks an area below the "todo" section evolved into a[n] "on hold" section —and we asked the interrupter to initial the card when we moved it.

This pretty much stopped trivial interruptions stone cold dead. It also killed the previous blame-the-team culture for deadline slippage. People actually started apologising to *us* when the deadline slipped!

No new information was being gathered. We had always kept comprehensive time sheets and could always point to what we had been doing. What had changed was that the big public display of progress was visibly going backwards when we were interrupted—and the whole company could see it every time it happened, as it happened (and who was causing it).

Build the Process for the People

Agile methods recognize the humanity at the core of software development. Agile methods are built around people, not machines. Working effectively requires an understanding deeper than the surface mechanics of how people interact or who makes decisions.

One aspect of humanity is that we're fallible. We make mistakes, forget important practices, and obstinately refuse to do things that are good for us—especially when we're tired or under stress.

We have strengths, too. We are creative, playful, and—under the right circumstances—passionate and driven to succeed. No machine can match these characteristics.

As you modify your agile method, work with these essential strengths and weaknesses. Don't require perfection; instead, build your process to identify and fix mistakes quickly. *Do* take advantage of your team's creativity. If a task is boring and repetitive, automate it.

Have fun, too. Software development may be big business, but the best developers I know love their jobs. They're passionate about their projects, and they also joke and play. The great teams I know socialize outside of work. There's no way for your agile method to enforce this, but you can create the conditions for it to happen by identifying and eliminating the barriers to natural social interaction.

In Practice

XP's demand for self-discipline seems to violate this principle of understanding human weakness. People aren't good at being self-disciplined all the time, so how can XP succeed?

XP handles the challenge of self-discipline in several ways. First, software developers love to produce high-quality work; once they see the quality of code that XP provides, they tend to love it. They may not always stay disciplined about the practices, but they generally *want* to follow the practices. Allowing people to take responsibility for their own quality encourages them to work to their full potential.

Second, energized work and pair programming give developers the support they need to be disciplined. Developers that want to follow the practices are most likely to break them when they feel tired or frustrated. Energized work reduces the likelihood of this happening. Pair programming provides positive peer pressure and additional support; if one member of the pair feels like taking an ill-advised shortcut, the other often reins him in.

Finally, while XP requires that the team be generally disciplined, it doesn't require perfection. If a pair makes a poor decision, collective code ownership means that another pair is likely to see it and fix it later. Ultimately, XP assumes that the design is fluid—refactoring and incremental design make it much easier to fix mistakes, while iterative design and adaptive planning put the most valuable features of the code under continual review.

XP works with the team's essential humanity in other ways, too. Among them are the automated build, which replaces tedious tasks with automated scripts, and test-driven development, which uses baby steps and constant feedback to help programmers spot and fix mistakes as soon as they occur.

Beyond Practices

A friend—"Mel"—used to work for a small consulting company. The shop had three to five developers and twice that many clients at any time, so it was common for them to work on several projects during the week. To simplify billing, the company used a custom time-tracking application that ran constantly in Windows, requiring developers to enter different billing codes whenever they changed tasks.

That single application was the only reason the developers needed to use Windows, as they deployed almost exclusively to Linux-based platforms. The lack of access to native tools occasionally caused problems. Regular task-switching—the reason for the time-tracking application—was often a more serious problem among the developers than minute-by-minute statistics.

Mel's solution had two parts. First, he dedicated his mornings to small tasks such as addressing bug reports or minor enhancements or customer requests. The minimum billable unit was 15 minutes, which was just about enough time to get into a flow state for any particular project. This left his afternoons (his most productive time) for longer tasks of two to four hours. Very few customer requests needed immediate solutions, and most of the customers were on the East Coast with a three-hour time difference; when he returned from lunch at 1 p.m., his customers were preparing to leave for the day.

The second part of the solution was using index cards to record task times. This was often faster than finding the right billing codes in the application. It also meant that Mel could boot his computer into Linux and stay there, then enter his stats into the application on another machine just before leaving for the day. The other developers noticed Mel's productivity increase, and he was only too happy to share his ideas. When their manager realized that everyone had switched to a new system, the results were inarguable. The developers were happier *and* more productive.

CHAPTER 13

Eliminate Waste

It's difficult to change the course of a heavy cruise ship, whereas a river kayak dances through rapids with the slightest touch of the paddle. Although a cruise ship has its place, the kayak is much more agile.

Agility requires flexibility and a lean process, stripped to its essentials. Anything more is wasteful. Eliminate it! The less you have to do, the less time your work will take, the less it will cost, and the more quickly you will deliver.

You can't just cut out practices, though. What's really necessary? How can you tell if something helps or hinders you? What actually gets good software to the people who need it? Answering these questions helps you eliminate waste from your process and increase your agility.

Work in Small, Reversible Steps

The easiest way to reduce waste is to reduce the amount of work you may have to throw away. This means breaking your work down into its smallest possible units and verifying them separately.

Sometimes while debugging, I see multiple problems and their solutions at once. *Shotgun debugging* is tempting, but if I try several different solutions simultaneously and fix the bug, I may not know which solution actually worked. This also usually leaves a mess behind. *Incremental change* is a better approach. I make one well-reasoned change, observe and verify its effects, and decide whether to commit to the change or revert it. I learn more and come up with better—and cleaner—solutions.

This may sound like taking *baby steps*, and it is. Though I can work for 10 or 15 minutes on a feature and get it mostly right, the quality of my code improves immensely when I focus on a very small part and spend time perfecting that one tiny piece before continuing. These short, quick steps build on each other; I rarely have to revert any changes.

If the step doesn't work, I've spent a minute or two learning something and can backtrack a few moments to position myself to make further progress. These frequent course corrections help me get where I really want to go. Baby steps reduce the scope of possible errors to only the most recent changes, which are small and fresh in my mind.

In Practice

The desire to solve big, hairy problems is common in developers. Pair programming helps us encourage each other to take small steps to avoid unnecessary embellishments. Further, the navigator concentrates on the big picture so that both developers can maintain perspective of the system as a whole.

Test-driven development tprovides a natural rhythm with its think-test-design-code-refactor cycle. The successful end of every cycle produces a stable checkpoint at which the entire system works as designed; it's a solid foothold from which to continue. If you go wrong, you can quickly revert to the prior known-good state.

At a higher level, stories limit the total amount of work required for any one pairing session. The maximum size of a step cannot exceed a few days. As well, continuous integration spreads working code throughout the whole team. The project makes continual, always-releasable progress at a reliable pace.

Finally, refactoring enables incremental design. The design of the system proceeds in small steps as needed. As developers add features, their understanding of the sufficient and necessary design will evolve; refactoring allows them to refine the system to meet its optimal current design.

Beyond Practices

Last summer, I introduced a friend to pair programming. She wanted to automate a family history project, and we agreed to write a parser for some sample genealogical data. The file format was complex, with some interesting rules and fields neither of us understood, but she knew which data we needed to process and which data we could safely ignore.

We started by writing a simple skeleton driven by tests. Could we load a file by name effectively? Would we get reasonable errors for exceptional conditions?

Then the fun began. I copied the first few records out of the sample file for test data and wrote a single test: could our parser identify the first record type? Then I pushed the keyboard to her and said, "Make it pass."

"What good is being able to read one record, and just the type?" she wondered, but she added two lines of code and the test passed. I asked her to write the next test. She wrote one line to check if we could identify the person's name from that record and pushed the keyboard back my way.

I wrote three lines of code. The test passed. Then I wrote a test to identify the next record type. Of course it failed. As I passed back the keyboard, we discussed ways to make it pass. I suggested hardcoding the second type in the parsing method. She looked doubtful but did it anyway, and the tests all passed.

"It's time to refactor," I said, and we generalized the method by reducing its code. With her next test, I had to parse another piece of data from both record types. This took one line.

We continued that way for two hours, adding more and more of the sample file to our test data as we passed more tests. Each time we encountered a new feature of the file format, we nibbled away at it with tiny tests. By the end of that time, we hadn't finished, but we had a small amount of code and a comprehensive test suite that would serve her well for further development.

Fail Fast

It may seem obvious, but failure is another source of waste. Unfortunately, the only way to avoid failure entirely is to avoid doing anything worthwhile. That's no way to excel. As [DeMarco & Lister 2003] said, "Projects with no real risks are losers. They are almost always devoid of benefit; that's why they weren't done years ago."

Instead of trying to avoid failure, embrace it. Think, "If this project is sure to fail, I want to know that as soon as possible." Look for ways to gather information that will tell you about the project's likelihood of failure. Conduct experiments on risk-prone areas to see if they fail in practice. The sooner you can cancel a doomed project, the less time, effort, and money you'll waste on it.

Failing fast applies to all aspects of your work, to examples as small as buying a bag of a new type of coffee bean rather than a crate. It frees you from worrying excessively about whether a decision is good or bad. If you're not sure, structure your work so that you expose errors as soon as they occur. If it fails, let it fail quickly, rather than lingering in limbo. Either way, invest only as much time and as many resources as you need to be sure of your results.

With these principles guiding your decisions, you'll fear failure less. If failure doesn't hurt, then it's OK to fail. You'll be free to experiment and take risks. Capitalize on this freedom: if you have an idea, don't speculate about whether it's a good idea—try it! Create an experiment that will fail fast, and see what happens.

In Practice

One of the challenges of adopting XP is that it tends to expose problems. For example, iterations, velocity, and the planning game shine the harsh light of fact on your schedule aspirations.

This is intentional: it's one of the ways XP helps projects fail fast. If your desired schedule is unachievable, you should know that. If the project is still worthwhile, either reduce scope or change your schedule. Otherwise, cancel the project. This may seem harsh, but it's really just a reflection of the "fail fast" philosophy.

This mindset can be foreign for organizations new to XP. It's particularly troubling to organizations that habitually create unrealistic schedules. When XP fails fast in this sort of organization, blame—not credit—often falls on XP. Yet cancelling a project early isn't a sign of failure in XP teams; it's a success. The team prevented a doomed project from wasting hundreds of thousands of dollars! That's worth celebrating.

Beyond Practices

I once led a development team on a project with an "aggressive schedule." Seasoned developers recognize this phrase as a code for impending disaster. The schedule implicitly required the team to sacrifice their lives in a misguided attempt to achieve the unachievable.

I knew before I started that we had little chance of success. I accepted the job anyway, knowing that we could at least fail fast. This was a mistake. I shouldn't have assumed.

Because there were clear danger signs for the project, our first task was to gather more information. We conducted three two-week iterations and created a release plan. Six weeks after starting the project, we had a reliable release date. It showed us coming in very late.

I thought this was good news—a textbook example of failing fast. We had performed an experiment that confirmed our fears, so now it was time to take action: change the scope of the project, change the date, or cancel the project. We had a golden opportunity to take a potential failure and turn it into a success, either by adjusting our plan or cutting our losses.

Unfortunately, I hadn't done my homework. The organization wasn't ready to accept the possibility of failure. Rather than address the problem, management tried to force the team to meet the original schedule. After realizing that management wouldn't give us the support we needed to succeed, I eventually resigned.

Management pressured the remaining team members to work late nights and weekends—a typical death-march project—to no avail. The project delivered very late, within a few weeks of our velocity-based prediction, and the company lost the client. Because the organizational culture made it impossible to fail fast, the project was doomed to fail slowly.

How could the team have succeeded? In a sense, we couldn't. There was no way for this project to achieve its original schedule, scope, and budget. (Unsurprisingly, that plan had no connection to the programmers' estimates.) The best we could have done was to fail fast, then change the plan.

What could I have done differently? My mistake was taking on the project in the first place. I knew the existing schedule was unrealistic, and I assumed that objective proof of this would be enough to change everyone's mind. I should have checked this assumption and—when it proved incorrect—declined the project.

What could the organization have done differently? Several things. It could have adopted an incremental delivery strategy, where we'd release the software after every iteration in the hope of delivering value more quickly. It could have cut the scope of the first milestone to a manageable set of features. Finally, it could have increased the available resources (up to a point) to allow us to increase our velocity.

Unfortunately, this organization couldn't face failure, which prevented them from changing their plan. Organizations that *can* face failure are capable of embracing change in their projects. Paradoxically, facing failure gives them the ability to turn potential failures into successes.

Maximize Work Not Done

The agile community has a saying: "Simplicity is the art of maximizing the work not done." This idea is central to eliminating waste. To make your process more agile, do less.

However, you can't take so much out of your process that it no longer works. As Albert Einstein said, "Everything should be made as simple as possible, but not one bit simpler." Often, this means approaching your work in a new way.

Simplifying your process sometimes means sacrificing formal structures while increasing rigor. For example, an elegant mathematical proof sketched on the back of a napkin may be rigorous, but it's informal. Similarly, sitting with customers decreases the amount of formal requirements documentation you create, but it substantially increases your ability to understand requirements.

Solutions come from feedback, communication, self-discipline, and trust. Feedback and direct communication reduce the need for intermediate deliverables. Self-discipline allows team members to work without the binding overhead of formal structures. Trust can replace the need to wait days—or longer—for formal signoffs.

Paring down your practices to the responsible essentials and removing bottlenecks lets you travel light. You can maximize the time you spend producing releasable software and improve the team's ability to focus on what's really important.

In Practice

XP aggressively eliminates waste, more so than any method I know. It's what makes XP *extreme*.

By having teams sit together and communicate directly, XP eliminates the need for intermediate requirements documents. By using close programmer collaboration and incremental design, XP eschews written design documents.

XP also eliminates waste by reusing practices in multiple roles. The obvious benefit of pair programming, for example, is continuous code review, but it also spreads knowledge throughout the team, promotes self-discipline, and reduces distractions. Collective code ownership not only enables incremental design and architecture, it removes the time wasted while you wait for someone else to make a necessary API change.

Beyond Practices

ISO 9001 certification is an essential competitive requirement for some organizations. I helped one such organization develop control software for their high-end equipment. This was the organization's first XP project, so we had to figure out how to make ISO 9001 certification work with XP. Our challenge was to do so without the waste of unnecessary documentation procedures.

Nobody on the team was an expert in ISO 9001, so we started by asking one of the organization's internal ISO 9001 auditors for help. (This was an example of the "Let the Right People Do the Right Things" principle, covered in Chapter 12.) From the auditor, we learned that ISO 9001 didn't mandate any particular process; it just required that we had a process that achieved certain goals, that we could prove we had such a process, and that we proved we were following the process.

This gave us the flexibility we needed. To keep our process simple, we reused our existing practices to meet our ISO 9001 rules. Rather than creating thick requirements documents and test plans to demonstrate that we tested our product adequately, we structured our existing customer testing practice to fill the need. In addition to demonstrating conclusively that our software fulfilled its necessary functions, the customer tests showed that we followed our own internal processes.

Pursue Throughput

A final source of waste isn't immediately obvious. The manufacturing industry calls it *inventory*. In software development, it's *unreleased software*. Either way, it's partially done work—work that has cost money but has yet to deliver any value.

Partially done work represents unrealized investment. It's waste in the form of *opportunity cost*, where the investment hasn't yet produced value but you can't use the resources it cost for anything else.

Partially done work also hurts *throughput*, which is the amount of time it takes for a new idea to become useful software. Low throughput introduces more waste. The longer it takes to develop an idea, the greater the likelihood that some change of plans will invalidate some of the partially done work.

To minimize partially done work and wasted effort, maximize your throughput. Find the step in your process that has the most work waiting to be done. That's your *constraint*: the one part of your process that determines your overall throughput. In my experience, the constraint in software projects is often the developers. The rate at which they implement stories governs the amount of work everyone else can do.

To maximize throughput, the constraint needs to work at maximum productivity, whereas the other elements of your process don't. To minimize partially finished work, nonconstraints should produce only enough work to keep the constraint busy, but not so much that there's a big pile of outstanding work. Outstanding work means greater opportunity costs and more potential for lost productivity due to changes.

Minimizing partially done work means that everyone but the constraint will be working at less than maximum efficiency. That's OK. Efficiency is expendable in other activities. In fact, it's important that nonconstraints have extra time available so they can respond to any needs that the constraint might have, thus keeping the constraint maximally productive.

> **NOTE**
> These ideas come from *The Theory of Constraints*. For more information, see [Goldratt 1997], an excellent and readable introduction. For discussion specific to software development, see [Anderson 2003].

In Practice

XP planning focuses on throughput and minimizing work in progress. It's central to the iteration structure. Every iteration takes an idea—a story—from concept to completion. Each story must be "done done" by the end of the iteration.

XP's emphasis on programmer productivity—often at the cost of other team members' productivity—is another example of this principle. Although having customers sit with the team full-time may not be the most efficient use of the customers' time, it increases programmer productivity. If programmers are the constraint, as XP assumes, this increases the team's overall throughput and productivity.

Beyond Practices

Our project faced a tight schedule, so we tried to speed things up by adding more people to the project. In the span of a month, we increased the team size from 7 programmers to 14 programmers, then to 18 programmers. Most of the new programmers were junior-level.

This is a mistake as old as software itself. Fred Brooks stated it as *Brooks' Law* in 1975: "Adding manpower to a late software project makes it later" [Brooks, p.25].

In this particular project, management ignored our protestations about adding people, so we decided to give it our best effort. Rather than having everyone work at maximum efficiency, we focused on maximizing throughput.

We started by increasing the size of the initial development team—the Core Team—only slightly, adding just one person. The remaining six developers formed the SWAT Team. Their job was not to work on production software, but to remove roadblocks that hindered the core development team. Every few weeks, we swapped one or two people between the two teams to share knowledge.

This structure worked well for us. It was a legacy project, so there were a lot of hindrances blocking development. One of the first problems the SWAT Team handled was fixing the build script, which would often fail due to Windows registry or DLL locking issues. By fixing this, the SWAT Team enabled the Core Team to work more smoothly.

Later, we had to add four more inexperienced programmers. We had run out of space by this time. Lacking a better option, we put the new programmers in a vacant area two flights of stairs away. We continued to focus our efforts on maintaining throughput. Not wanting to spread our experienced developers thin, we kept them concentrated in the Core Team, and since the SWAT Team was working well, we decided to leave the new team out of the loop. We deliberately gave them noncritical assignments to keep them out of our hair.

Overall, this approach was a modest success. By focusing on throughput rather than individual efficiency, we were able to withstand the change. We more than doubled our team size, with mostly junior developers, without harming our productivity. Although our productivity didn't go up, such a deluge of people would normally cause a team to come to a complete standstill. As it was, pursuing throughput allowed us to maintain our forward momentum. In better circumstances—fewer new developers, or developers with more experience—we could have actually increased our productivity.

CHAPTER 14

Deliver Value

Your software only begins to have real value when it reaches users. Only at that point do you start to generate trust, to get the most important kinds of feedback, and to demonstrate a useful return on investment. That's why successful agile projects deliver value early, often, and repeatedly.

Exploit Your Agility

Simplicity of code and process are aesthetically pleasing. Yet there's a more important reason why agility helps you create great software: it improves your ability to recognize and take advantage of new opportunities.

If you could predict to the hour how long your project would take, know what risks would and wouldn't happen, and completely eliminate all surprises, you wouldn't need agility—you would succeed with any development method.

However, what you don't know is exciting. A new crisis or happy discovery next week could completely change the rules of the game. You may discover a brilliant new technique that simplifies your code, or your customer may develop a new business practice that saves time and money.

Want to deliver real value? Take advantage of what you've learned and change your direction appropriately. Adapting your point of view to welcome changing requirements gives you great opportunities. Delivering value to your customer is your most important job. Aggressively pursuing feedback from your customer, from real users, from other team members, and from your code itself as early and as often as possible allows you to continue to learn and improve your understanding of the project. It also reveals new opportunities as they appear.

Agility requires you to work in small steps, not giant leaps. A small initial investment of time and resources, properly applied, begins producing quantifiable value immediately. As well, committing to small amounts of change makes change itself more possible. This is most evident when customer requirements outline their needs at a very high level, through stories that promise further clarification during development.

Aggressively seeking feedback and working in small steps allows you to defer your investment of resources until the last responsible moment. You can start to see the value from a piece of work as you need it, rather than hoping to benefit from it someday in the future.

In Practice

XP exploits agility by removing the time between taking an action and observing its results, which improves your ability to learn from this feedback. This is especially apparent when the whole team sits together. Developing features closely with the on-site customer allows you to identify potential misunderstandings and provides nearly instant responses to questions. Including real customers in the process with frequent deliveries of the actual software demonstrates its current value to them.

XP allows changes in focus through short work cycles. Using simultaneous phases enables you to put a lesson into practice almost immediately, without having to wait for the next requirements gathering or testing or development phase to roll back around in the schedule. The short work unit of iterations and frequent demos and releases create a reliable rhythm to make measured process adjustments. Slack provides spare time to make small but necessary changes within an iteration without having to make difficult choices about cutting essential activities.

Beyond Practices

I worked for a small startup whose major product was an inventory management system targeted at a specific retail industry. We had the top retailers and manufacturers lined up to buy our project. We were months away from delivery when our biggest customer ran into a problem: the license for their existing point-of-sale system suddenly expired. The software included a call-home system that checked with the vendor before starting.

Our plans included developing our own POS system, but that was at least several months away. Our current system managed inventory, but we hadn't done specific research on supporting various terminal types, credit card scanners, and receipt printers.

This was our largest customer, and without its business, we'd never succeed.

After discussing our options and the project's requirements with the customer, we decided that we could build just enough of the POS system within six weeks that they could switch to our software and avoid a $30,000 payment to the other vendor.

We were very fortunate that our existing customers needed very little work from us in that period. We shifted two-thirds of our development team to the POS project. Though we started from an open source project we'd found earlier, we ended up customizing it heavily.

After two weeks of development, we delivered the first iteration on a new machine we had built for the customer to test. We delivered weekly after that. Though it was hard work, we gradually added new features based on the way our customer did business. Finally, the only remaining task was to change a few lines in the GUI configuration to match the customer's store colors. We saved our customer plenty of money, and we saved our account.

Only Releasable Code Has Value

Having the best, most beautiful code in the world matters very little unless it does what the customer wants. It's also true that having code that meets customer needs perfectly has little value unless the customer can actually use it. Until your software reaches the people who need it, it has only potential value.

Delivering actual value means delivering real software. Unreleasable code has no value. Working software is the primary measure of your progress. At every point, it should be possible to stop the project and have actual value proportional to your investment in producing the software.

Any functional team can change its focus in a week or a month, but can they do so while maximizing their investment of time and resources to deliver software regularly? Do they really finish code—does "done" mean "done done"—or do they leave an expanding wake of half-finished code? Do they keep their project releasable at any time?

Agility and flexibility are wonderful things, especially when combined with iterative incremental development. Throughput is important! Besides reducing thrashing and waste, it provides much better feedback, and not just in terms of the code's quality. Only code that you can actually release to customers can provide real feedback on how well you're providing value to your customers.

That feedback is invaluable.

In Practice

The most important practice is that of "done done," where work is either complete or incomplete. This unambiguous measure of progress immediately lets you know where you stand.

Test-driven development produces a safety net that catches regressions and deviations from customer requirements. A well-written test suite can quickly identify any failures that may reduce the value of the software. Similarly, continuous integration ensures that the project works as a whole multiple times per day. It forces any mistakes or accidents to appear soon after their introduction, when they're easiest to fix. The 10-minute build reduces the bottlenecks in this process to support its frequency.

Practicing "no bugs" is a good reminder that deferring important and specific decisions decreases the project's value—especially if those decisions come directly from real customer feedback.

Beyond Practices

I was once on a project that had been running for four months and was only a few weeks away from its deadline when it was abruptly halted. "We're way over budget and didn't realize it," the manager told me. "Everybody has to go home tomorrow."

We were all contractors, but the suddeness of the project's cancellation surprised us. I stayed on for one more week to train one of the organization's employees—"Joe"—just in case they had the opportunity to pick up the code again in the future.

Although this wasn't an XP project, we had been working in iterations. We hadn't deployed any of the iteration releases (I now know that would have been a good idea), but the last iteration's result *was* ready to deploy. Joe and I did so, then spent the rest of the week fixing some known bugs.

This might have been a textbook example of good project management, except for one problem: our release wasn't usable. We had worked on features in priority order, but our customers gave us the wrong priorities! A feature they had described as least important for the first release was in fact vitally important: security. That feature was last on our list, so we hadn't implemented it. If we had deployed our interim releases, we would have discovered the problem. Instead, it blindsided us and left the company without anything of value.

Fortunately, the company brought us back a few months later and we finished the application.

Deliver Business Results

What if you could best meet your customer's need without writing any software? Would you do it? Could you do it?

Someday that may happen to you. It may not be as dramatic as telling a recurring customer that he'll get better results if you *don't* write software, but you may have to choose between delivering code and delivering business results.

Value isn't really about software, after all. Your goal is to deliver something useful for the customer. The software is merely how you do that. The single most essential criterion for your success is the fitness of the project for its business purposes. Everything else is secondary—not useless by any means, but of lesser importance.

For example, agile teams value working software over comprehensive documentation. Documentation is valuable—communicating what the software must do and how it works is important—but your first priority is to meet your customer's needs. Sometimes that means producing good documentation. Usually it means delivering good software, but not always. The primary goal is always to provide the most valuable business results possible.

In Practice

XP encourages close involvement with actual customers by bringing them into the team, so they can measure progress and make decisions based on business value every day. Real customer involvement allows the on-site customer to review these values with end-users and keep the plan on track. Their vision provides answers to the questions most important to the project.

XP approaches its schedule in terms of customer value. The team works on stories phrased from the customer's point of view and verifiable by customer testing. After each iteration, the iteration demo shows the team's current progress to stakeholders, allowing them to verify that the results are valuable and to decide whether to continue development.

Beyond Practices

A friend—"Aaron"—recently spent a man-month writing 1,500 lines of prototype code that generated $7.8 million in revenue during its first demo.

As a graduate student, he interned with a technology company doing research on handwriting recognition with digital pens containing sensors and recording equipment. A customer made an off-hand remark about how useful it might be to use those special pens with printed maps. Suddenly, Aaron had a research assignment.

The largest potential customer used an existing software package to send map data to field agents to plan routes and identify waypoints. Aaron modified the pen software to send coordinate information on printed pages. Then he found a way to encode the pen's necessary calibration data on color laser printouts. The final step was to use the API of the customer's software to enter special pen events—mark waypoint, identify route, etc. In effect, all of his code merely replaced the clunky mouse-based UI with the act of drawing on a custom-printed map, then docking the pen.

A few minutes into the first demo, the customer led the sales rep to the control room for a field exercise. After installing the software and connecting the pen's dock, the rep handed the pen and a printed map to one of the techs. The tech had never seen the product before and had no training, but he immediately circled an objective on the map and docked the pen. In seconds, the objective appeared on the vehicle displays as well as on the PDAs of the field agents.

The customer placed an order for a license and hardware for everyone at the location. That's business results.

Deliver Frequently

If you have a business problem, a solution to that problem today is much more valuable than a solution to that problem in six months—especially if the solution will be the same then as it is now. Value is more than just doing what the customer needs. It's doing what the customer needs *when* the customer needs it.

Delivering working, valuable software *frequently* makes your software more valuable. This is especially true when a real customer promotes the most valuable stories to the start of the project. Delivering working software as fast as possible enables two important feedback loops. One is from actual customers to the developers, where the customers use the software and communicate how well it meets their needs. The other is from the team to the customers, where the team communicates by demonstrating how trustworthy and capable it is.

Frequent delivery tightens those loops. Customers see that their involvement in the process makes a real difference to their work. Developers see that they're helping real people solve real problems. The highest priority of any software project is to deliver value, frequently and continuously, and by doing so, to satisfy the customer. Success follows.

In Practice

Once you've identified what the customer really needs and what makes the software valuable, XP's technical practices help you achieve fast and frequent releases. Short iterations keep the schedule light and manageable by dividing the whole project into week-long cycles, culminating in a deliverable project demonstrated in the iteration demo. This allows you to deliver once a week, if not sooner.

Practicing the art of "done done" with discipline keeps you on track, helping you identify how much work you have finished and can do while reminding you to pursue throughput. Keeping a ten-minute build reminds you to reduce or remove any unnecessary technical bottlenecks to producing a release. The less work and frustration, and the more automation, the easier it is to deliver a freshly tested, working new build.

Beyond Practices

According to founder Cal Henderson,[*] the photo-sharing web site Flickr has practiced frequent delivery from its earliest days. There was no single decision to do so; it was just an extension of how its founders worked. Rather than batching up new features, they released them to users as soon as possible. This helped simplify their development and reduced the cost of fixing bugs.

---

[*] Via personal communication.

The early days of Flickr were somewhat informal. When there were only three committers on the project, asking if the trunk was ready to deploy required asking only two other people. Now the team assumes that the trunk is always ready to deploy to the live site. The most important component of this process is a group of strong and responsible developers who appreciate the chance to manage, code, test, stage, and deploy features. The rest of the work is standard agility—working in small cycles, rigorous testing, fixing bugs immediately, and taking many small risks.

The results are powerful. When a user posts a bug to the forum, the team can often fix the problem and deploy the new code to the live site within minutes. There's no need to wait for other people to finish a new feature. It's surprisingly low-risk, too. According to Henderson, "The number of nontrivial rollbacks on the Flickr code base is still zero."

CHAPTER 15

Seek Technical Excellence

I like logical frameworks and structures. When I think about technical excellence, I can't help but wonder: "What's the intellectual basis for design? What does it mean to have a good design?"

Unfortunately, many discussions of "good" design focus on specific techniques. These discussions often involve assumptions that one particular technology is better than another, or that rich object-oriented domain models or stored procedures or service-oriented architectures are *obviously* good.

With so many conflicting points of view about what's obviously good, only one thing is clear: good isn't obvious.

Some folks describe good design as elegant or pretty. They say that it has the *Quality Without a Name* (*QWAN*)—an ineffable sense of *rightness* in the design. The term comes from Christopher Alexander, a building architect whose thoughts on patterns inspired software's patterns movement.

I have a lot of sympathy for QWAN. Good design *is* Truth and Beauty. There's just one problem. My QWAN is not your QWAN. My Truth and Beauty is your Falsehood and Defilement. My beautiful domain models are uglier than your stored procedures, and vice versa.

QWAN is just too vague. I want a better definition of good design.

Software Doesn't Exist

Let me digress for a moment: software doesn't exist. OK, I exaggerate—but only slightly.

When you run a program, your computer loads a long series of magnetic fields from your hard drive and translates them into capacitances in RAM. Transistors in the CPU interpret those charges, sending the results out to peripherals such as your video card. More transistors in your monitor selectively allow light to shine through colored dots onto your screen.

Yet none of that is software. Software isn't even ones and zeros; it's magnets, electricity, and light. The only way to *create* software is to toggle electrical switches up and down—or to use existing software to create it for you.

You write software, though, don't you?

Actually, you write a very detailed specification for a program that writes the software *for* you. This special program translates your specification into machine instructions, then directs the computer's operating system to save those instructions as magnetic fields on the hard drive. Once they're there, you can run your program, copy it, share it, or whatever.

You probably see the punchline coming. *The specification is the source code.* The program that translates the specification into software is the compiler. Jack Reeves explores the implications in his famous essay, "What is Software Design?"*

Design Is for Understanding

If source code is design, then what *is* design? Why do we bother with all these UML diagrams and CRC cards and discussions around a whiteboard?

All these things are abstractions—even source code. The reality of software's billions of evanescent electrical charges is inconceivably complex, so we create simplified models that we can understand. Some of these models, like source code, are machine-translatable. Others, like UML, are not—at least not yet.

Early source code was assembly language: a very thin abstraction over the hardware. Programs were much simpler back then, but assembly language was hard to understand. Programmers drew flow charts to visualize the design.

Why don't we use flow charts anymore? Our programming languages are so much more expressive that we don't need them! You can read a method and see the flow of control.

Before structured programming:

```
1000 NS% = (80 - LEN(T$)) / 2
1010 S$ = ""
1020 IF NS% = 0 GOTO 1060
1030 S$ = S$ + " "
1040 NS% = NS% - 1
1050 GOTO 1020
1060 PRINT S$ + T$
1070 RETURN
```

After structured programming:

```
public void PrintCenteredString(string text) {
    int center = (LINE_LENGTH - text.Length) / 2;
    string spaces = "";

    for (int i = 0; i < center; i++) {
        spaces += " ";
    }

    Print(spaces + text);
}
```

OK, it's not entirely true that modern languages make the flow of control obvious. We still run across huge 1,000-line methods that are so convoluted we can't understand them without the help of a design sketch. But that's bad design, isn't it?

---

* *http://www.bleading-edge.com/Publications/C++Journal/Cpjour2.htm.*

Design Trade-offs

When the engineers at Boeing design a passenger airplane, they constantly have to trade off safety, fuel efficiency, passenger capacity, and production cost. Programmers rarely have to make those kinds of decisions these days. The assembly programmers of yesteryear had tough decisions between using lots of memory (space) or making the software fast (speed). Now, we almost never face such speed/space trade-offs. Our machines are so fast and have so much RAM that once-beloved hand optimizations rarely matter.

In fact, our computers are so fast that modern languages actually *waste* computing resources. With an optimizing compiler, C is just as good as assembly language. C++ adds virtual method lookups—four bytes per method and an extra level of indirection. Java and C# add a complete intermediate language that runs in a virtual machine atop the normal machine. Ruby[*] *interprets* the entire program on every invocation!

How wasteful. So why is Ruby on Rails so popular? How is it possible that Java and C# succeed? What do they provide that makes their waste worthwhile? Why aren't we all programming in C?

Quality with a Name

A good airplane design balances the trade-offs of safety, carrying capacity, fuel consumption, and manufacturing costs. A *great* airplane design gives you better safety, and more people, for less fuel, at a cheaper price than the competition.

What about software? If we're not balancing speed/space trade-offs, what are we doing?

Actually, there is one trade-off that we make over and over again. Java, C#, and Ruby demonstrate that we are often willing to sacrifice computer time in order to save programmer time and effort.

Some programmers flinch at the thought of wasting computer time and making "slow" programs. However, wasting cheap computer time to save programmer resources is a wise design decision. Programmers are often the most expensive component in software development.

If good design is the art of maximizing the benefits of our trade-offs—and if software design's only real trade-off is between machine performance and programmer time—then the definition of "good software design" becomes crystal clear:

A good software design minimizes the time required to create, modify, and maintain the software while achieving acceptable runtime performance.

Oh, and it has to work. That's nonnegotiable. If a Boeing jet can't fly, its fuel efficiency doesn't matter. Similarly, a software design must work.

Great Design

Equating good design with the ease of maintenance is not a new idea, but stating it this way leads to some interesting conclusions:

1. *Design quality is people-sensitive.* Programmers, even those of equivalent competence, have varying levels of expertise. A design that assumes Java idioms may be incomprehensible to a programmer

---

[*] Prior to Ruby 2, that is.

who's only familiar with Perl, and vice versa. Because design quality relies so heavily on programmer time, it's very sensitive to which programmers are doing the work. A good design takes this into account.

2. *Design quality is change-specific.* Software is often designed to be easy to change in specific ways. This can make other changes difficult. A design that's good for some changes may be bad in others. A genuinely good design correctly anticipates the changes that actually occur.

3. *Modification and maintenance time are more important than creation time.* It bears repeating that most software spends far more time in maintenance than in initial development. When you consider that even unreleased software often requires modifications to its design, the importance of creation time shrinks even further. A good design focuses on minimizing modification and maintenance time over minimizing creation time.

4. *Design quality is unpredictable.* If a good design minimizes programmer time, and it varies depending on the people doing the work and the changes required, then there's no way to predict the quality of a design. You can have an informed opinion, but ultimately the proof of a good design is in how it deals with change.

Furthermore, great designs:

- Are easy to modify by the people who most frequently work within them
- Easily support unexpected changes
- Are easy to maintain
- Prove their value by becoming steadily easier to modify over years of changes and upgrades

Universal Design Principles

In the absence of design quality measurements, there is no objective way to prove that one design approach is better than another. Still, there are a few universal principles—which seem to apply to any programming language or platform—that point the way.

None of these ideas are my invention. How could they be? They're all old, worn, well-loved principles. They're so old you may have lost track of them amidst the incessant drum-beating over new fads. Here's a reminder.

The Source Code Is the (Final) Design

Continue to sketch UML diagrams. Discuss design over CRC cards. Produce pretty wall charts on giant printers if you want. Abstractions like these are indispensible tools for clarifying a design. Just don't confuse these artifacts with a *completed* design. Remember, your design has to *work*. That's nonnegotiable. Any design that you can't turn into software automatically is incomplete.

If you're an architect or designer and you don't produce code, it's programmers who *finish* your design for you. They'll fill in the inevitable gaps, and they'll encounter and solve problems you didn't anticipate. If you slough this detail work off onto junior staff, the final design could be lower quality than you expected. Get your hands dirty. Follow your design down to the code.

Don't Repeat Yourself (DRY)

This clever name for a well-known principle comes from Dave Thomas and Andy Hunt. Don't Repeat Yourself is more than just avoiding cut-and-paste coding. It's having one cohesive location and canonical representation for every concept in the final design—anything from "the way we interface with a database" to "the business rule for dealing with weekends and holidays."

Eliminating duplication decreases the time required to make changes. You need only change one part of the code. It also decreases the risk of introducing a defect by making a necessary change in one place but not in another.

Be Cohesive

This old chestnut is no less essential for its age.[*]

A cohesive design places closely related concepts closer together. A classic example is the concept of a date and an operation to determine the next business day. This is a well-known benefit of object-oriented programming: in OOP, you can group data and related operations into the same class. Cohesion extends beyond a single class, though. You can improve cohesion by grouping related files into a single directory, or by putting documentation closer to the parts of the design it documents.

Cohesion improves design quality because it makes designs easier to understand. Related concepts cluster together, which allows the reader to see how they fit together into the big picture. Cohesion reduces error by improving the reader's ability to see how changes to one concept affect others. Cohesion also makes duplication more apparent.

Decouple

Different parts of a design are *coupled* when a change to one part of the design necessitates a change to another part. Coupling isn't necessarily bad—for example, if you change the date format, you may have to change the routine to calculate the next business day.

Problems occur when a change to one part of the design requires a change to an *unrelated* part of the design. Either programmers spend extra time ferreting out these changes, or they miss them entirely and introduce defects. The more tenuous the relationship between two concepts, the more loosely coupled they should be. Conversely, the more closely related two concepts are, the more tightly coupled they may be.

Eliminating duplication, making designs cohesive, and decoupling all attack the same problem from different angles. They tie together to improve the quality of a design by reducing the impact of changes. They allow programmers to focus their efforts on a specific section of the design and give programmers confidence that they don't need to search through the entire design for possible changes. They reduce defects by eliminating the possibility that unrelated parts of the design also need to change.

---

[*] Coupling and cohesion come from [Constantine]'s 1968 work on structured programming, "Segmentation and Design Strategies for Modular Programming." In that article, he presents ways to analyze coupling and cohesion based on static code analysis. I've phrased his ideas more generally.

Clarify, Simplify, and Refine

If good designs are easy for other people to modify and maintain, then one way to create a good design is to create one that's easy to read.

When I write code, I write it for the future. I assume that people I'll never meet will read and judge my design. As a result, I spend a lot of time making my code very easy to understand. Alistair Cockburn describes it as writing *screechingly obvious code:*[*]

> Times used to be when people who were really conscientious wrote Squeaky Clean Code. Others, watching them, thought they were wasting their time. I got a shock one day when I realized that Squeaky Clean Code isn't good enough.
>
> ...
>
> It occurred to me that where they went down a dead end was because the method's contents did not match its name. These people were basically looking for a sign in the browser that would say, "Type in here, buddy!"
>
> That's when I recognized that they needed ScreechinglyObviousCode.
>
> At the time [1995], it was considered an OK thing to do to have an event method, doubleClicked or similar, and inside that method to do whatever needed to be done. That would be allowed under Squeaky Clean Code. However, in ScreechinglyObviousCode, it wouldn't, because the method doubleClicked only says that something was double clicked, and not what would happen. So let's say that it should refresh the pane or something. There should therefore be a method called refreshPane, and doubleClick would only contain the one line: self refreshPane.
>
> The people fixing the bug knew there was a problem refreshing the pane, but had to dig to learn that refreshing the pane was being done inside doubleClick. It would have saved them much effort if the method refreshPane was clearly marked in the method list in the [Smalltalk] browser, so they could go straight there.... The reading of the code is then, simply: "When a doubleClicked event occurs, refresh the pane" rather than "When a doubleClicked event occurs, do all this stuff, which, by the way, if you read carefully, you will notice refreshes the pane."

Screechingly obvious code is easier to produce through iterative simplification and refinement. Bob Martin has a great example of this in "Clean Code: Args—A Command-Line Argument Parser."[†]

Fail Fast

A design that fails fast (see Chapter 13) reveals its flaws quickly. One way to do this is to have a sophisticated test suite as part of the design, as with test-driven development. Another approach is use a tool such as assertions to check for inappropriate results and fail if they occur. Design by Contract [Meyer] makes designs fail fast with runtime checks of class invariants and method pre- and post-conditions.

Failing fast improves design by making errors visible more quickly, when it's cheaper to fix them.

---

[*] *http://c2.com/cgi/wiki?ScreechinglyObviousCode*

[†] *http://www.objectmentor.com/resources/articles/Clean_Code_Args.pdf*

Optimize from Measurements

Everyone can quote Tony Hoare about premature optimization,[*] at least until they reach *their* pet optimizations. Optimized code is often unreadable; it's usually tricky and prone to defects. If good design means reducing programmer time, then optimization is the *exact opposite* of good design.

Of course, good design does more than just reduce programmer time. According to my definition, it "minimizes the time required to create, modify, and maintain the software *while achieving acceptable runtime performance.*"

Although well-designed code is often fast code, it isn't *always* fast. Optimization (see "Performance Optimization" in Chapter 9) is sometimes necessary. Optimizing later allows you to do it in the smartest way possible: when you've refined the code, when it's cheapest to modify, and when performance profiling can help direct your optimization effort to the most effective improvements.

Delaying optimization can be scary. It feels unprofessional to let obviously slow designs slide by. Still, it's usually the right choice.

Eliminate Technical Debt

You probably aren't lucky enough to work on a project that follows these principles all the time. (I rarely am.) Even if you are, you're likely to make mistakes from time to time. (I certainly do.)

Despite our best intentions, technical debt creeps into our systems. A lot of it—perhaps most of it—is in our designs. This *bit rot* slowly saps the quality of even the best designs.

Eliminating technical debt through continuous code maintenance and refactoring has only recently been recognized as a design principle, and some people still question it. It's no less essential for the controversy. In fact, it may be the *most important* of all the design principles. By focusing on removing technical debt, a team can overcome any number of poor design decisions.

Principles in Practice

These universal design principles provide good guidance, but they don't help with specific languages or platforms. That's why you need design principles for specific languages, such as [Martin]'s list of the principles of object-oriented class design.[†] Unfortunately, when you take universal design principles and turn them into specific design advice, you lose something important: context. Every design decision occurs in the context of the whole design—the problem domain, other design decisions, the time schedule, other team members' capabilities, etc.

Context makes every piece of specific design advice suspect. Yes, you should listen to it—there's a lot of wisdom out there—but exercise healthy skepticism. Ask yourself, "When is this *not* true?" and "What is the author assuming?"

Consider the simple and popular "instance variables must be private" design rule. As one of the most widely repeated design rules, it often gets applied without real thought. That's a shame because without context, the rule is meaningless and easily misused.

---

[*] "Premature optimization is the root of all evil."

[†] The Single Responsibility Principle, Open-Closed Principle, Liskov Substitution Principle, Dependency-Inversion Principle, and Interface Segregation Principle.

It's true that instance variables should often be private, but if you want to *understand* the rule and when to break it, ask *why*. Why make instance variables private? One reason is that private variables enforce encapsulation. But why should anyone care about encapsulation?

The real reason private variables (and encapsulation) are good is that they help enforce decoupling. Decoupled code is good, right? Not always. *Appropriately* decoupled code is good, but it's OK for closely related concepts to be tightly coupled.

However, closely related concepts should also be *cohesive*. They should be close together in the code. In object-oriented programming languages, closely related concepts often belong in the same class.

This is where the "instance variables must be private" rule comes from. When you have an urge to make an instance variable public, it's a sign that you have both a cohesion problem *and* a coupling problem. You have a cohesion problem because closely related concepts aren't in the same class. You have a coupling problem because concepts that the code structure says are unrelated must change together.

The *real* problem is that programmers follow the letter of the rule without stopping to consider the context. Rather than taking the time to think about coupling and cohesion, many programmers just slap a public accessor and mutator (getter and setter) on a private variable.

Now what good does that do?

```
public class MySillyClass {
    private string _myFakeEncapsulatedVariable;

    public string getMyFakeEncapsulatedVariable() {
        return _myFakeEncapsulatedVariable;
    }

    public void setMyFakeEncapsulatedVariable(string var) {
        _myFakeEncapsulatedVariable = var;
    }
}
```

From a coupling standpoint, there's very little difference between this code and code that uses a public variable. The code follows the letter of the rule, but ignores its spirit: don't let other classes have access to your implementation details! From a design perspective, a public variable is equivalent to this code, and it would certainly make a poor design decision more obvious.

Pursue Mastery

A good software design minimizes the time required to create, modify, and maintain the software while achieving acceptable runtime performance.

This definition, and the conclusions it leads to, are the most important things I keep in mind when considering a design. I follow some core design principles, and I have some techniques that are useful for the languages I work with. However, I'm willing to throw away even the design principles if they get in the way of reducing programmer time and, most importantly, solving real customer problems.

The same is true of agile software development. Ultimately, what matters is success, however you define it. The practices, principles, and values are merely guides along the way. Start by following the practices rigorously. Learn what the principles mean. Break the rules, experiment, see what works, and learn some more. Share your insights and passion, and learn even more.

Over time, with discipline and success, even the principles will seem less important. When doing the right thing is instinct and intuition, finely honed by experience, it's time to leave rules and principles behind. When you produce great software for a valuable purpose and pass your wisdom on to the next generation of projects, you will have mastered the art of successful software development.

References

[Ambler & Sadalage] Ambler, Scott, and Pramodkumar Sadalage. 2006. *Refactoring Databases: Evolutionary Database Design*. Boston: Addison-Wesley Professional.

[Anderson 2003] Anderson, David. 2003. *Agile Management for Software Engineering: Applying the Theory of Constraints for Business Results*. Upper Saddle River, NJ: Prentice Hall.

[Anderson 2006] Anderson, David. 2006. "HP gets 3.4x productivity gain from Agile Management techniques" (posted March 15). Agile Management blog. *http://www.agilemanagement.net/Articles/Weblog/HPgets3.4xproductivitygai.html*

[Astels] Astels, David. 2003. *Test Driven Development: A Practical Guide*. Upper Saddle River, NJ: Prentice Hall.

[Bach 1999] Bach, James. 1999. "General Functionality and Stability Test Procedure for Microsoft Windows Logo, Desktop Applications Edition." *http://www.testingcraft.com/bach-exploratory-procedure.pdf*

[Bach 2000] Bach, Jonathan. 2000. "Session-Based Test Management." *http://www.satisfice.com/articles/sbtm.pdf*

[Beck 1999] Beck, Kent. 1999. *Extreme Programming Explained, First edition*. Boston: Addison-Wesley Professional.

[Beck 2002] Beck, Kent. 2002. *Test Driven Development: By Example*. Boston: Addison-Wesley Professional.

[Beck 2004] Beck, Kent. 2004. *Extreme Programming Explained, Second edition*. Boston: Addison-Wesley Professional.

[Beck & Fowler] Beck, Kent, and Martin Fowler. 2000. *Planning Extreme Programming*. Boston: Addison-Wesley Professional.

[Beck et al.] Beck, Kent et al. 2001. Manifesto for Agile Software Development. *http://agilemanifesto.org/*

[Belshee] Belshee, Arlo. 2005. "Promiscuous Pairing and Beginner's Mind: Embrace Inexperience." *Proceedings of the Agile Development Conference (July 24-29)*. Washington, DC: IEEE Computer Society, 125-131. *http://dx.doi.org/10.1109/ADC.2005.37*

[Berczuk & Appleton] Berczuk, Stephen P., and Brad Appleton. 2002. *Software Configuration Management Patterns: Effective Teamwork, Practical Integration*. Boston: Addison-Wesley Professional.

[Boehm] Boehm, Barry. 1987. "Industrial Software Metrics Top 10 List." *IEEE Software*. 4(9): 84-85.

[Brooks] Brooks, Frederick P. 1995. *The Mythical Man-Month: Essays on Software Engineering, 20th Anniversary Edition*. Boston: Addison-Wesley Professional.

[Cockburn] Cockburn, Alistair. 2001. *Agile Software Development*. Boston: Addison-Wesley Professional.

[Cockburn & Williams] Cockburn, Alistair, and Laurie Williams. 2001. "The Costs and Benefits of Pair Programming." *Extreme Programming Examined*. Eds Succi, G., Marchesi, M., 223-247. Boston: Addison-Wesley. *http://www.cs.utah.edu/~lwilliam/Papers/XPSardinia.PDF*

[Coffin] Coffin, Rod. 2006. "A Tale of Two Projects." *The Conference on AGILE 2006 (July 23-28)*. Washington, DC: IEEE Computer Society, 155-164. *http://dx.doi.org/10.1109/AGILE.2006.3*

[Cohn] Cohn, Mike. 2005. *Agile Estimating and Planning*. Upper Saddle River, NJ: Prentice Hall.

[Constantine] Constantine, Larry. 1968. "Segmentation and Design Strategies for Modular Programming." Eds. T. O. Barnett and L. L. Constantine. *Modular Programming: Proceedings of a National Symposium*. Cambridge, MA: Information & Systems Press.

[Cunningham] Cunningham, Ward. 1994. "The CHECKS Pattern Language of Information Integrity." *http://c2.com/ppr/checks.html*

[DeMarco 1995] DeMarco, Tom. 1995. *Why Does Software Cost So Much?: And Other Puzzles of the Information Age*. New York: Dorset House Publishing Co.

[DeMarco 2002] DeMarco, Tom. 2002. *Slack: Getting Past Burnout, Busywork, and the Myth of Total Efficiency*. New York: Broadway Books.

[DeMarco & Lister 1999] DeMarco, Tom, and Timothy Lister. 1999. *Peopleware: Productive Projects and Teams*. New York: Dorset House Publishing Co.

[DeMarco & Lister 2003] DeMarco, Tom, and Timothy Lister. 2003. *Waltzing With Bears: Managing Risk on Software Projects*. New York: Dorset House Publishing Co.

[Denne & Cleland-Huang] Denne, Mark, and Jane Cleland-Huang. 2003. *Software by Numbers: Low-Risk, High-Return Development*. Upper Saddle River, NJ: Prentice Hall.

[Derby & Larsen] Derby, Esther, and Diana Larsen. 2006. *Agile Retrospectives: Making Good Teams Great*. Raleigh and Dallas: Pragmatic Bookshelf.

[Evans] Evans, Eric. 2003. *Domain-Driven Design: Tackling Complexity in the Heart of Software*. Boston: Addison-Wesley Professional.

[Feathers] Feathers, Michael. 2004. *Working Effectively with Legacy Code*. Upper Saddle River, NJ: Prentice Hall.

[Fowler 1999] Fowler, Martin. 1999. *Refactoring: Improving the Design of Existing Code//citetitle>. Boston: Addison-Wesley Professional.*.

[Fowler 2000] Fowler, Martin. 2000. "Is Design Dead?" *http://www.martinfowler.com/articles/designDead.html*

[Fowler 2002a] Fowler, Martin. 2002. Patterns of Enterprise Application Architecture. Boston: Addison-Wesley Professional.

[Fowler 2002b] Fowler, Martin. 2002. "Yet Another Optimization Article." *http://www.martinfowler.com/ieeeSoftware/yetOptimization.pdf*

[Fowler 2003] Fowler, Martin. 2003. "Cannot Measure Productivity." *http://www.martinfowler.com/bliki/CannotMeasureProductivity.html*

[Fowler & Scott] Fowler, Martin, and Kendall Scott. 1999. *UML Distilled: A Brief Guide to the Standard Object Modeling Language, Second Edition*. Boston: Addison-Wesley Professional.

[Gamma et al.] Gamma, Erich, Richard Helm, Ralph Johnson, and John Vlissides ["Gang of Four"]. 1995. *Design Patterns: Elements of Reusable Object-Oriented Software*. Boston: Addison-Wesley Professional.

[Goldratt 1992] Goldratt, Eliyahu M. 1992. *The Goal: A Process of Ongoing Improvement*. Great Barrington, MA: North River Press.

[Goldratt 1997] Goldratt, Eliyahu M. 1997. *Critical Chain: A Business Novel*. Great Barrington, MA: North River Press.

[Hendrickson] Hendrickson, Elisabeth. 2006. "Rigorous Exploratory Testing" (posted April 19). *http://www.testobsessed.com/2006/04/19/rigorous-exploratory-testing/*

[Highsmith] Highsmith, Jim. 2002. *Agile Software Development Ecosystems*. Boston: Addison-Wesley Professional.

[Hunt & Thomas] Hunt, Andrew, and David Thomas. 1999. *The Pragmatic Programmer: From Journeyman to Master*. Boston: Addison-Wesley Professional.

[Hunter] Hunter, Michael ["The Braidy Tester"] 2004. "Did I Remember To" (posted July 7). *http://blogs.msdn.com/micaheVarticles/175571.aspx*

[Janzen & Saiedian] Janzen, David, and Hossein Saiedian. 2005. "Test-Driven Development: Concepts, Taxonomy, and Future Direction." *IEEE Computer Society*. 38(9): 43-50.

[Jeffries et al.] Jeffries, Ron, Ann Anderson, and Chet Hendrickson. 2000. *Extreme Programming Installed*. Boston: Addison-Wesley Professional.

[Kaner] Kaner, Cem. 1987. *Testing Computer Software*. Blue Ridge Summit, PA: TAB Books.

[Katzenbach & Smith] Katzenbach, Jon R., and Douglas K. Smith. 1994. *The Wisdom of Teams: Creating the High-Performance Organization*. New York: HarperBusiness.

[Kerievsky] Kerievsky, Joshua. 2004. *Refactoring to Patterns*. Boston: Addison-Wesley Professional.

[Kerth] Kerth, Norman. 2001. *Project Retrospectives: A Handbook for Team Reviews*. New York: Dorset House Publishing Co.

[Kohl 2005a] Kohl, Jonathan. 2005. "User Profiles and Exploratory Testing" (posted June 12). *http://www.kohl.ca/blog/archives/000104.html*

[Kohl 2005b] Kohl, Jonathan. 2005. "Exploratory Testing on Agile Teams." InformIT, Nov 18. *http://www.informit.com/articles/article.aspx?p=405514*

[Kohn] Kohn, Alfie. 1999. *Punished By Rewards: The Trouble with Gold Stars, Incentive Plans, A's, Praise, and Other Bribes*. Boston: Mariner Books.

[Lacey] Lacey, Mitch. 2006. "Adventures in Promiscuous Pairing: Seeking Beginner's Mind." *Proceedings of the Conference on AGILE 2006 (July 23-28)*. Washington, DC: IEEE Computer Society, 263-269. *http://dx.doi.org/10.1109/AGILE.2006.7*

[Little] Little, Todd. 2006. "Schedule Estimation and Uncertainty Surrounding the Cone of Uncertainty." *IEEE Software*. 23(3): 48-54. *http://www.toddlittleweb.com/Papers/Little%20Cone%20of%20Uncertainty.pdf*

[Mah] Mah, Michael. 2006. "Agile Productivity Metrics" Keynote Address, Better Software Conference & EXPO, Las Vegas, June 2006. *http://www.sqe.com/Events/Archive/bsc2006/keynotes.html*

[Maister et al] Maister, David, Charles Green, Robert Galford. 2000. *The Trusted Advisor*. New York: Free Press.

[Manns & Rising] Manns, Mary Lynn, and Linda Rising. 2004. *Fearless Change: Patterns for Introducing New Ideas*. Boston: Addison-Wesley.

[Marick] Marick, Brian. A Survey of Exploratory Testing. *http://www.testingcraft.com/exploratory.html*

[Martin 2002] Martin, Robert C. 2002. *Agile Software Development, Principles, Patterns, and Practices*. Upper Saddle River, NJ: Prentice Hall.

[Martin 2005] Martin, Robert C. 2005. "Clean Code: Args A Command-line Argument Parser." Published on the Object Mentor, Inc web site (Nov 26). *http://www.objectmentor.com/resources/articles/ Clean_Code_Args.pdf*

[Mason] Mason, Mike. 2006. *Pragmatic Version Control: Using Subversion (The Pragmatic Starter Kit Series), Second Edition*. Raleigh and Dallas: Pragmatic Bookshelf.

[McConnell 1996] McConnell, Steve. 1996. *Rapid Development: Taming Wild Software Schedules*. Redmond, WA: Microsoft Press.

[McConnell 2005] McConnell, Steve. 2006. *Software Estimation: Demystifying the Black Art*. Redmond, WA: Microsoft Press.

[Meyer] Meyer, Bertrand. 2000. *Object-Oriented Software Construction, Second Edition*. Upper Saddle River, NJ: Prentice Hall.

[Miller] Miller, Charles. 2003. "Stand-Up Meeting Antipatterns" (posted November 19). The Fishbowl blog. *http://fishbowl.pastiche.org/2003/11/19/standup_meeting_antipatterns*

[Montagna] Montagna, Frank C. 1996. "The Effective Postfire Critique." Fire Engineering magazine, July 1. *http://www.chiefmontagna.com/Articles/pdf/*critique.pdf

[Mugridge & Cunningham] Mugridge, Rick, and Ward Cunningham. 2005. *Fit for Developing Software: Framework for Integrated Tests*. Upper Saddle River, NJ: Prentice Hall.

[Nielsen] Nielsen, Jakob. 1999. *Designing Web Usability: The Practice of Simplicity*. Berkeley, CA: Peachpit Press.

[Overby] Overby, Stephanie. 2003. "The Hidden Costs of Offshore Outsourcing Offshore Outsourcing the Money." *CIO*. magazine, Sept 1. *http://www.cio.com/archive/090103/money.html*

[Poppendieck & Poppendieck] Poppendieck, Mary, and Tom Poppendieck. 2003. *Lean Software Development: An Agile Toolkit for Software Development Managers*. Boston: Addison-Wesley Professional.

[Pugh] Pugh, Ken. 2005. *Prefactoring*. Sebastopol, CA: O'Reilly Media, Inc.

[Rainsberger] Rainsberger, J. B. 2004. *Junit Recipes: Practical Methods for Programmer Testing*. Greenwich, CT: Manning Publications, Co.

[Rooney] Rooney, Dave. 2006. "The Disengaged Customer" (posted Jan 20). The Agile Artisan blog. *http://agileartisan.blogspot.com/2006/01/disengaged-customer-introduction.html*

[Schwaber & Beedle] Schwaber, Ken, and Mike Beedle. 2001. *Agile Software Development with SCRUM*. Upper Saddle River, NJ: Prentice Hall.

[Shore 2004a] Shore, Jim. 2004. "Continuous Design." IEEE Software 21(1):20-22. *http:// www.martinfowler.com/ieeeSoftware/continuousDesign.pdf*

[Shore 2004b] Shore, Jim. 2004. "Fail Fast." IEEE Software 21(5):21-25. *http://www.martinfowler.com/ ieeeSoftware/failFast.pdf*

[Shore 2005a] Shore, Jim. 2005. "Agile Requirements" (posted Nov 30). *http://www.jamesshore.com/Blog/ Agile-Requirements.html*

[Shore 2005b] Shore, Jim. 2005. Agile development resources. *http://c2.com/cgi/wiki?JimShore*

[Sink] Sink, Eric. 2004. "Source Control HOWTO" (posted Aug 27). Eric Weblog. *http:// www.ericsink.com/scm/source_control.html*

[Smith] Smith, Steven M. 1997. "The Satir Change Model" (posted Oct 4). Steven M. Smith & Associates, LLC. *http://www.stevenmsmith.com/my-articles/article/the-satir-change-model.html*

[Standish] Standish Group. 1994. "The CHAOS Report." The Standish Group International, Inc. *http:// www.standishgroup.com/sample_research/chaos_1994_1.php*

[Stapleton] Stapleton, Jennifer. 1997. *DSDM: A Framework for Business Centered Development*. Boston: Addison-Wesley Professional.

[Subramaniam & Hunt] Subramaniam, Venkat, and Andy Hunt. 2006. *Practices of an Agile Developer: Working in the Real World*. Raleigh and Dallas: Pragmatic Bookshelf.

[Teasley et al.] Teasley, Stephanie, Lisa Covi, M. S. Krishnan, Judith Olson. 2002. "Rapid Software Development Through Team Collocation." *IEEE Trans. Softw. Eng.* 28(7):671-83. *http://dx.doi.org/ 10.1109/TSE.2002.1019481*

[Tinkham & Kaner] Tinkham, Andy, and Cem Kaner. 2003. "Exploring Exploratory Testing." Presented at SQE's Software Testing, Analysis & Review Conference, Orlando, FL, July 2003. *http:// www.testingeducation.org/a/explore.pdf*

[Tuckman] Tuckman, B. W. 1965. "Developmental sequences in small groups." Psychological Bulletin 63:384-99. *http://dennislearningcenter.osu.edu/references/GROUP%20DEV%20ARTICLE.doc*

[Ury] Ury, William. 2007. *The Power of a Positive No: How to Say No and Still Get to Yes*. New York: Bantam Books.

[Van Schooenderwoert] Van Schooenderwoert, Nancy. 2006. "Embedded Agile Project by the Numbers with Newbies." *The Conference on AGILE 2006 (July 23-28)*. Washington, DC: IEEE Computer Society, 351-366. *http://dx.doi.org/10.1109/AGILE.2006.24*

[Wiegers 1999] Wiegers, Karl E. 1999. *Software Requirements*. Redmond, WA: Microsoft Press.

[Wiegers 2001] Wiegers, Karl E. 2001. *Peer Reviews in Software: A Practical Guide*. Boston: Addison-Wesley Professional.

[Williams] Williams, Laurie. 2002. *Pair Programming Illuminated*. Boston: Addison-Wesley Professional.

[Wirfs-Brock & McKean] Wirfs-Brock, Rebecca, and Alan McKean. 2002. *Object Design: Roles, Responsibilities, and Collaborations*. Boston: Addison-Wesley Professional.

[Yap] Yap, Monica. 2005. "Follow the Sun: Distributed Extreme Programming Development." *The Conference on AGILE 2006 (July 23-28)*. Washington, DC: IEEE Computer Society, 218-224. *http:// dx.doi.org/10.1109/ADC.2005.26*

[Yip] Yip, Jason. 2006. "It's Not Just Standing Up: Patterns of Daily Stand-up Meetings." *http://www.martinfowler.com/articles/itsNotJustStandingUp.html*

[Yourdon] Yourdon, Edward. 1999. *Death March: The Complete Software Developer's Guide to Surviving 'Mission Impossible' Projects.* Upper Saddle River, NJ: Prentice Hall.

Index

We'd like to hear your suggestions for improving our indexes. Send email to *index@oreilly.com*.

example, 345–346
heuristics, 343–345
legacy code and, 59, 348
pair programming and, 76
producing high-quality code, 20
test-driven development (TDD) and, 300
testers and, 34
XP lifecycle and, 20
exposure (risk), 227
Extreme Programming (see XP)

test-driven development and, 300
Theory of Constraints and, 42
lifecycles, 18–27
local builds, 178–182
locking model (version control), 170
lost iterations, 240

M

maintainability of software projects, 4
management
bugs and, 166
change and, 54, 95
coaches and, 34
commitments to, 54, 228–230
pledge to, 54
pressure from, 229–230
reporting to, 144–148
retrospectives and, 94
success and, 5, 7
support, importance of, 44
trust and, 104–109
manifesto for Agile software development, 9
mastery, pursuing, xiii, 11, 353, 388
matrix-managed organizations, 39
mentors, 12
coaches, contrasted with, 12
colocated teams and, 45
merciless refactoring, 328
(see also refactoring)
merging (version control), 170
methods (process), 6, 9
customizing (refining), 11, 353, 357
incrementally designing, 323
mindfulness, 42
études and, xv, 70
mastering agility and, xiii, 353
practicing, 70
XP, required for, 69
mini-études, xv, 154
minimum marketable feature (MMF), 209
miracle of collaboration, 221
mitigation (risk management), 226
MMF (minimum marketable feature), 209
mock objects, 298
mock-ups, 28, 32, 274
modeling (domain), 126
Montagna, Frank, 92
multipliers (risk), 224, 230
multistage integration builds, 187

mute mapping, 93

N

n-tier architecture, 324
navigating, 71, 75
bugs and, 163
first iteration, 56
incremental design and, 323, 328
root-cause analysis and, 89
slack and, 246
network architect, 33
no bugs, 25, 160–169
adopting XP and, 167
agile principles and, 362
communication and, 124, 163, 362
customer reviews and, 277
customer tests and, 162, 278
"done done", 158
expectations, 166
exploratory testing and, 24, 164, 167, 341–342,
346, 347, 348
legacy code and, 59, 167
novices, 166
novices and, 161
pair programming and, 162
planning and, 242, 256
programmers and, 33, 161–163
reproducing, 171
risk and, 225
security and, 166
stories, 256
technical debt and, 40
ten-minute build and, 182
test-driven development and, 62, 162, 285
testers, 164
testers and, 34, 162
time dependencies and, 304
ubiquitous language and, 125, 126, 127
XP lifecycle and, 20
no silver bullets, 3
noncolocated teams, 45, 86, 119, 258, 362
(see also sit together)
none, some, all heuristic, 344
nonfunctional/parafunctional requirements, 20, 256,
337
nulls, coddling, 304
NUnit, 296
NUnitAsp, 305

asynchronous integration, contrasted with, 186, 188

About the Authors

James Shore, signatory number 10 to the Agile Manifesto, has been coaching agile teams large and small before they were called agile. He brings both breadth and depth to his discussion of agile development. In 2005, the Agile Alliance recognized James with their most significant award, the Gordon Pask Award for Contributions to Agile Practice. James is an internationally recognized speaker who consults for companies interested in agile development. He writes about agile development on his top-ranked blog, jamesshore.com.

Shane Warden is the technical editor of the O'Reilly Network, specializing in programming, Linux, and open source development. Among other books for O'Reilly, he is the author of the *Extreme Programming Pocket Guide*, which distilled Extreme Programming into a concise explanation and reference. Many readers have commented that they buy copies for all of their customers to explain how they work. Ward Cunningham (cocreator of Extreme Programming) considers it the best explanation of the practice.

Colophon

The cover image is from *www.veer.com*. The cover fonts are Berthold Akzidenz Grotesk and Orator. The text font is Adobe's Meridien; the heading font is ITC Bailey.